From Loyalist to Founding Father

From Loyalist to Founding Father

The Political Odyssey
of William Samuel Johnson

ELIZABETH P. McCAUGHEY

1980
Columbia University Press
New York

As a dissertation this book was awarded
the Bancroft Dissertation Award by a
committee of the faculty of the Graduate
School of the Arts and Sciences of
Columbia University

Map of Connecticut on pp. vi–vii reprinted from *From
Puritan to Yankee*, by Richard L. Bushman (Cambridge,
Mass.: Harvard University Press), p. i. Copyright © 1967
by the President and Fellows of Harvard College. Used by
permission of the publisher. Drawn by Samuel H. Bryant
from a Map by Bernard Romans, "Connecticut and Adja-
cent Parts," Amsterdam, 1777 and by Cóvens, Mortier and
Cóvens, Jr.

Columbia University Press
New York   Guildford, Surrey

Library of Congress Cataloging in Publication Data

McCaughey, Elizabeth P.   1948–
  From Loyalist to Founding Father.

  Bibliography: p.
  Includes index.
  1. Johnson, William Samuel, 1727–1819.
2. Connecticut—Politics and government—Colonial
period, ca. 1600–1775.   3. United States—Politics
and government—1783–1789.   4. Legislators—United
States—Biography.   5. United States. Congress.
Senate—Biography.   6. College presidents—United
States—Biography.   7. Columbia University—Presidents—
Biography.   I. Title.

E302.6.J7M3   973.3'092'4 [B]   79-17042
ISBN 0-231-04506-9

For my parents
Albert and Ramona Peterken

Colebrook
Canaan
Norfolk
Hartland
Suff
Winchester
Salisbury
Simsbury
LITCHFIELD
HAR
Goshen
Cornwall
Torrington
New Hartford
Wind
Sharon
Harwinton
Kent
Litchfield
Farmington
CO
HOUSATONIC
COUNTY
Waterbury
New Milford
Woodbury
RIVER
New Fairfield
STRATFORD
WATERBURY
NAUGATUCK
Wallingford
Wallingford
Danbury
Newtown
NEW HAVEN
Dur
FAIRFIELD
COUNTY
Ridgefield
Reading
Derby
New Haven
Guilfo
New
York
COUNTY
Branfor
Bedford
Milford
Stratford
Norwalk
Fairfield
Stamford
Greenwich
New York
LONG ISLAND

Sam. H. Bryant · 1967

Somers
Stafford
Union
Woodstock
Killingly
nfield
W I N D H A M
Ashford
Willington
R D
Tolland
Mansfield
Pomfret
Coventry
C O U N T Y
ford
Bolton
Windham
Canterbury
thersfield
Glastonbury
Hebron
Plainfield
T Y
Lebanon
Voluntown
dletown
Colchester
Norwich
Preston
Haddam
East
Haddam
N E W   L O N D O N
C O U N T Y
New
London
Groton
Stonington
Saybrook
illingworth
Lyme
FISHERS
ISLAND

Part

of

Providence

R h o d e

Island

CONNECTICUT

QUINEBAUG

RIVER

THAMES   RIVER

RIVER

S O U N D

Connecticut in 1765

A Scale of Miles

0   10   20   30

Contents

Acknowledgments

I am indebted to Elizabeth Abbe Harlow, who guided me through the immense collection of Johnson papers at the Connecticut Historical Society; to Fred Byrne, who made my years in the Columbia University library so enjoyable; to Davida Scharf, who carefully (and cheerfully) typed the manuscript; and to Leslie Bialler of Columbia University Press, whose wit and enthusiasm made the publication ordeal such fun.

For his valuable ideas and gentle criticisms, I am especially grateful to Eric McKitrick, who will always be my teacher. Finally I thank my husband, Thomas K. McCaughey. His patience, encouragement, and generosity made this book possible.

E.P.McC.

From Loyalist to Founding Father

Samuel Johnson, by John Smibert (Ca. 1730-1740)
Columbiana, Columbia University

Chapter One

Fathers and Sons

"*T*rain up the child in the way he should go, and when he is old he will not depart from it."[1] On this maxim, Samuel Johnson raised up his oldest son, William Samuel, whom he lovingly dubbed Sammy. Samuel Johnson was an intent and serious father, who with sternness but affection instilled in his son the lessons and loyalties he had formulated early in his own life.

In 1696 Samuel Johnson was born into a prominent and respected Connecticut family. His great-grandfather Robert Johnson had joined the exodus from England to the New World in 1638. With a group of fellow Yorkshiremen, the emigré Johnson planted the New Haven colony as an ideal Puritan community, free from persecution by the Church of England and its tyrannical Archbishop Laud, and committed to the communal religious life prescribed by John Calvin. When Robert Johnson died at New Haven in 1691, he bequeathed four sons to the New England experiment. One son attended Harvard College and settled in the Bay Colony, two remained in New Haven, and the fourth son William ventured out to the neighboring town of Guilford.[2]

William Johnson earned recognition for the second generation of Johnsons in New England. When he testified to the Guilford congregation that he had experienced a "conversion" and was in direct communion with God, the congregation admitted him as an active communicant in the town's church. For many years thereafter he was elected a deacon. Everyone in Guilford attended the Congregational church and paid taxes for its support, but only the converted, Guilford's "visible saints," enjoyed the privileges of full church members, holding church offices and participating in the Lord's Supper.[3]

William Johnson also took an active part in town government. He served as a militia officer, as Guilford's town clerk, and later as a deputy to the Connecticut General Assembly.[4] It was to be expected that as an eminent figure in the church, William Johnson would also be considered an appropriate leader in civic affairs. Ministers and magistrates in every Puritan community worked in close partnership to ensure that their town would be safe from spiritual heresies and social disorder. The town magistrates stood ready to punish anyone who failed to attend the Congregational Church, neglected to pay taxes for the livelihood of the minister, or challenged the clergy's strict dogma of predestination. In turn, ministers vigorously preached obedience to local and colonial leaders.[5]

Into William Johnson's esteemed family were born his son Samuel (1670–1727) and his grandson Samuel (1696–1772), who was the fourth generation of Johnsons in the colony and the father of William Samuel Johnson. The elder Samuel, like his father William, became a pillar of the Guilford church.[6] The younger Samuel was tutored in his early years by his grandfather William, who lived until 1702, and afterwards by local pastors. Even as a boy, Samuel Johnson "could think of nothing but books." He had an "impatient curiosity to know everything that could be known." In the autumn of 1710, he went on to the Collegiate School of Connecticut, which would be renamed in honor of its benefactor Elihu Yale eight years later. The college was envisioned by its founders to be the bulwark of religious orthodoxy in Connecticut and the training school for the colony's Puritan clergy. Young Johnson's keen interest in learning and his easy mastery of the ancient languages made him well suited for a ministerial career. This was the customary calling for New England's most talented and industrious scholars, and from Samuel Johnson's boyhood, he was "both by himself and his friends designed for the pulpit."[7] In 1710 no one suspected that Samuel Johnson would cast off his Puritan heritage and openly challenge the New England church. He seemed an unlikely rebel.

Nine boys gathered at the Collegiate School that fall to enter the class of 1714. For three years they labored under a curriculum that was plainly medieval. The books available to Samuel Johnson's tutors were at least a century old. But in Johnson's senior year, the ideas that had reshaped European thought finally reached the tiny college. Connecticut's agent in London, Jeremiah Dummer, had collected for the college library an impressive array of books that included the scientific writings of

Newton, the philosophy of Bacon and Locke, the literary works of Milton and Shakespeare, and the theology of England's leading Anglican divines.[8] Had anyone foreseen the impact of these new books on the colony's prized young scholars, the Dummer collection would surely have been banned from the library. Of the nine students who graduated in 1714, three would forsake the Puritan church.

Samuel Johnson embarked on an intense and unrelenting study of the new European learning. The empiricism of Locke, the cosmology of Newton, Copernicus and Kepler, and the inductive method of Bacon made the curriculum of his undergraduate years seem to Johnson "nothing but the scholastic cobwebs of a few little English and Dutch systems that would hardly now be taken in the streets."[9] Yet the new science was wholly compatible with Puritan theology. Natural causes could be reconciled with the ultimate sovereignty of God, and regularity in the universe seemed to attest to God's wisdom.[10] It was the philosophical and theological works in the Dummer collection that directly attacked the Puritan doctrines of original sin, predestination, and the helplessness of man. For Johnson and for all of New England, a crisis was nearing.

The deistic philosophy of the Enlightenment proclaimed that each man could rely on his unaided reason to understand not only the physical world, but also God, and to conduct himself in a moral way through which he could ultimately achieve salvation. To the Puritans, this exaltation of man's reason and man's capacity to earn salvation was Arminianism, a sinful demeaning of God's sovereignty. The Anglican theologians were also guilty of Arminianism. They too rejected the notion of man's total depravity, but unlike the Deists, they did not remove all the mystery and spirituality from religion. Reason alone, said the Anglicans, could never guide men to a moral life and salvation. Every man was imbued with an element of God's spirit, and it was this spirituality, not simply reason, that promised redemption. It was the church's task to cultivate this spirit through worship and instruction. Reason, once directed to holy purposes, could be trusted to verify what faith first revealed.

The rationalism of Locke was too radical for young Samuel Johnson, who saw that it pointed to infidelity and the abandonment of God. Anglicanism retained the spirituality that was an essential aspect of his church upbringing. For Samuel Johnson, the Episcopal doctrine was an appealing compromise between Puritanism's faith in the unseen and the Enlightenment's surrender to reason, between the Puritans' dark vision of a helpless, depraved humanity and the Deists' sovereign, rational man.[11]

As Johnson tirelessly probed the Anglican writings, he also became convinced that the Episcopal clergy, not the clergy of Puritan New England, were the true ministers of Christ. In the Church of England, a minister was ordained by a bishop whose office originated with the primitive Christian church. But in New England it was the congregation, or at times clergyman from nearby towns, who ordained the parish minister. The authority of the Episcopal clergy resided in the unbroken succession of ordinations that began with Christ's apostles. The lay-ordained clergy of New England lacked the historic and divine authority of the apostolic succession. They were, Johnson came to lament, "usurper[s] in the House of God."[12]

What made the Anglican claim so appealing to Johnson were "the great animosities and often virulent separations" that he saw disrupting his native church.[13] The order and harmony of the Congregational Church in grandfather William Johnson's youth was giving way to disorder and contention, as ministers and laymen alike argued noisily over the proper means to recapture the zealous piety and carry on the orthodox church of New England's founding generation. Questions of church membership, clerical authority, preaching and praying styles excited heated controversies and divided congregations long united in worship. Discontented parishioners boldly questioned the spiritual gifts of their minister and denounced his cold, uninspiring preaching. At times, they refused to provide his livelihood and even abandoned his church in unlawful separation.[14] Samuel Johnson deplored the "dark and melancholy and even spiteful and malicious spirit" that surrounded the turmoil. To blame, he suspected, was the principle of congregational church government "in which every brother has a hand" and the Puritan practice of extempore prayer, which "tended too much to conceit and self-sufficiency and to endless feuds, censoriousness and uncharitableness."[15] For Johnson, the strict hierarchial government and formal liturgy of the Church of England seemed a promising remedy to the divisions and disaffections that were troubling the New England churches.[16]

In the autumn of 1719, Samuel Johnson answered a call to preach at the Congregational meetinghouse in West Haven, and the following May he was ordained. Johnson accepted the office with grave doubts and a heavy heart. Already he was convinced that episcopacy was the proper form of church government, that predestination was wrong and even blasphemous, and that the Book of Common Prayer was superior to extempore praying. He was deeply troubled that his own ordination lacked divine authority. But he also knew that an outright declaration for the Episcopal Church would bring painful censure on his family and damage his own promising career.[17] In 1708 the Connecticut General Assembly had reluctantly amended the colony's laws to permit dissenting Protestants to worship under the care of a minister of their own persuasion. The concession was made in an unfriendly spirit, and the colony's few Anglicans, Baptists, and Quakers were still taxed to support the Congregational Church. The Episcopal parish at Stratford was the only one in the colony, and the Anglicans there suffered harassment and persecution.[18]

Mary Johnson appealed to her son to forbear for peace's sake, but "the passionate entreaties of a tender mother" were more than balanced by the curiosity and courage of six young Congregational pastors who met often with Johnson to discuss the Anglican alternative. Each had probed the Dummer collection. Four of the six were sons of Yale, including James Wetmore and Daniel Browne, who graduated with Johnson in 1714. In company with the Yale men were two Harvard graduates, Jared Eliot, who was at one time Johnson's grammar school teacher, and Timothy Cutler, whose apostasy would arouse the greatest uproar. Cutler was rector of Yale College.[19]

By 1722 mutual encouragement and, no doubt, a certain youthful arrogance had helped the seven to forget their fears and hesitations. On September 13, they confronted the Yale trustees. They confessed their doubts regarding the sanctity of their ordinations and announced their intentions to embrace the Church of England. The trustees were shocked and angered, and before long all New England shook with rage over the devilish offense.[20] The Massachusetts pastor Cotton Mather, who followed closely the events at New Haven, told the trustees that the seven apostates

have cast a vile indignity upon those burning and shining lights, the excellent servants of God, who were the leaders of the flocks that followed our Lord Jesus into this wilderness, and upon the ministry of them and their successors. . . . A degenerate offspring have declared these men of God . . . to be not true ministers, but usurpers of the ministry and invaders of the sacred office, robbers that have not entered in by the door.

One Connecticut minister resolved that "it is now a time with us that we must put on our armour and fight, or else let the good old cause, for which our fathers came into this land, sink and be deserted."[21]

The trustees reacted defensively. In October they dismissed Rector Cutler and Tutor Browne from the college and enacted measures to ensure that no one tainted with Arminianism would receive an appointment to the college again.[22] So strong was the reaction that even three decades later, when Samuel Johnson's oldest son William Samuel entered Yale, the scientific and theological ideas represented in the Dummer collection would still be excluded from the curriculum.

For three of the apostates, the scorn and grief of their neighbors and fellow clergymen was too much to bear. They relented in order to remain, at least publicly if not in their private thoughts, within the native church. Cutler, Browne, Johnson, and Wetmore held fast. Their minds were set on Episcopal ordination.

After a long ocean passage, Johnson, Cutler and Browne reached England on December 15, 1722. Wetmore followed several months later. News of the Yale confrontation had preceded them to London, and they were greeted with warm interest by their adopted church. Toward the end of March, after many interviews and considerable instruction, Samuel Johnson and his two companions were ordained by the Bishop of Norwich. Soon afterward, Edmund Gibson, Bishop of London, approved their appointments as missionaries of the Society for the Propagation of the Gospel in Foreign Parts (SPG), which was the patron organization for all the Episcopal clergymen and parishes in the British colonies. The Society's purpose, as expressed in the charter granted to it by Queen Anne, was to promote religion in those regions of the empire that were destitute of any Christian church. In practice, the Society's activities ranged beyond the battle against heathenism, and it relied on gifts from its benefactors to supply colonial Anglicans with clergymen of their own persuasion. Johnson was appointed to preach at the Stratford, Connecticut mission, Cutler to preside over Christ's Church at Boston, and Browne to serve at Bristol, Rhode Island.[23]

The ordination of the Yale apostates signified the beginning of a native American clergy for the Episcopal Church in New England. But already there were signs promising misunderstanding and resentment between the New England-born missionaries and their English patrons. Johnson worried greatly that without a resident bishop, colonial Anglicans would be deprived of the full benefits of Episcopal government and promising candidates for the Episcopal ministry would be discouraged by the long and dangerous pilgrimage to London. The disaster that befell Daniel Browne confirmed Johnson's fears. On Easter Eve, Browne died of smallpox contracted during his lengthy stay in the disease-ridden city.[24] Johnson urged Gibson to appoint a colonial bishop,[25] but the request, as we shall see shortly, was one that neither Gibson nor any other churchman could indulge. During Samuel Johnson's six months in England, he did not begin to comprehend how few of the powers and privileges of a securely established national church remained to the Church of England. Over the next four decades, nine of the fifty-one candidates who journeyed to England for Episcopal orders would die before returning.[26] From Stratford, Johnson would plead urgently for an American bishop. His passionate appeals and the disappointing responses from the mother church would create ill will on both sides.

On November 5, 1723, after nearly seven weeks at sea and many more weeks traveling over land, Samuel Johnson rode into Stratford to begin his pastoral work.[27] Here, four years later, his first son William Samuel would be born. The Anglicans of Stratford and the neighboring towns, about seventy families in all, were busy raising an Episcopal meetinghouse, the first one in the colony.[28] They were a hardy and determined people who had already labored for nearly two decades to organize their own church and secure an Episcopal minister. The story of their struggle to break away from the town's Congregational church forms an important prologue to Samuel Johnson's experiences at Stratford, and in turn, to William Samuel Johnson's boyhood there. For out of this early struggle emerged an accommodation between the Stratford Anglicans and the town's Puritan majority which, although begrudging and strained at first, became friendlier as time passed. It meant that William Samuel Johnson would grow up knowing the peacefulness and good will of his Puritan neighbors.

The effort was begun in 1702, when the ten or fifteen Anglican families then residing in Stratford petitioned the SPG for a resident missionary. Their requests went unanswered until 1706, when Rev. George Muirson, the Society's missionary at Rye, New York, began visiting and administering the sacraments. Muirson organized the tiny group into a parish with wardens and vestrymen, in bold defiance of Connecticut law, which until 1708 prohibited any separation from the Congregational Church. His efforts alarmed the Stratford magistrates, who threatened him and his followers with imprisonment.[29] Yet the Anglican exodus into Muirson's fold also brought peace to the Congregational meetinghouse. That meetinghouse had been divided since 1702 over the selection of John Reed as minister. It appears that Reed's flirtation with Episcopal doctrine aroused this controversy and that Reed counted the Stratford Anglicans as his supporters. In 1706, Reed resigned his Congregational ministry to join Muirson's church. The departure of Reed and his supporters allowed the town's orthodox worshippers to settle a minister of irreproachable Calvinist convictions, concluding a long and noisy dispute.[30]

Muirson died two years later, and the Anglicans were forced to return to the Congregational church. Once again that church began the difficult search for a minister agreeable to everyone. In 1709 Timothy Cutler was chosen, and the quiet that prevailed in Stratford under his care suggests that he managed to gratify both the orthodox majority and the Anglican minority. (Indeed, ten years later Cutler even won the confidence of the Yale trustees, who made him rector of the college until his notorious apostasy.) With Cutler's removal to Yale in 1719 the turmoil over the selection of a minister resumed.[31] Peace was not restored until 1722, when the SPG finally acceded to the Stratford Anglicans' repeated petitions for a missionary and dispatched Rev. George Pigot. His arrival enabled the Anglican dissidents to once again withdraw from the Congregational church and allowed the Puritan townsmen to call a suitably orthodox preacher, Hezekiah Gold, whose ministry was to go unchallenged for the next twenty years.[32] Pigot labored hard that year, organizing the Episcopal mission, overseeing the construction of a meetinghouse, and inviting the Anglicans from nearby towns to join his church. But he longed for an appointment in Rhode Island, which he considered his home, and in 1723 his wish was granted. Johnson came to Stratford as his replacement.[33]

The Stratford Anglicans, so long without a minister and uncertain of Pigot's tenure, were gladdened by Johnson's arrival. How the town's Puritan majority would receive him was less certain. The signs were mixed, some promising harmony, others portending ill will. The townsmen had already sanctioned the raising of an Episcopal meetinghouse on Stratford's common lands. They were even willing to exempt the Anglicans from ecclesiastical taxes, although Connecticut law required that everyone contribute to the livelihood of the Congregational minister.[34] Neighboring towns, where the Anglicans were fewer in number and less troublesome, made no tax concession.[35] The long awaited harmony within Stratford's orthodox church after the exodus of the Anglican dissidents probably inspired the town's gestures of accommodation.

Despite these changes, the Puritan majority must have regarded the planting of the rival church as, at best, a mixed blessing. They were undoubtedly as upset by the appearance of the Episcopal meetinghouse as the New England clergy had been in 1722 by the apostasy at Yale. Orthodox New Englanders had always preached the necessary unity of town and church, a unity that was more jealously guarded as it became increasingly fragile. Especially distressing was the loss of prominent parishioners such as Daniel Shelton. The earliest Stratford Anglicans were an unimpressive group, mostly poor tradesmen and farmers recently arrived from England.[36] Later a number of wealthy farmers from Stratford's interior section, among them Daniel Shelton, grew sympathetic to the cause and joined Muirson's church. Upon Muirson's death, Shelton returned to the Congregational meetinghouse and became an esteemed parish leader. His departure to the new Episcopal mission fifteen years later could not be taken lightly.[37]

Although in the long run the establishment of the Episcopal mission would reduce tensions between Stratford's Anglicans and Puritans, time was needed to heal the wounds of schism. The first signs of conciliation were visible in the raising of a meetinghouse and the tax relief accorded the Anglicans. Yet much animosity remained. During Samuel Johnson's first year at Stratford, he felt "alone surrounded with bitter enemies."[38] How differently his son William Samuel would feel, born after the initial discord had subsided, and growing up in a community where Puritans and Episcopalians lived peacefully together.

Samuel Johnson's earliest reports to the Society were mixed with praises for his flock at Stratford and complaints against the Connecticut lawmakers. The completion of the Episcopal meetinghouse on Christmas Day, 1724, warmed him deeply. Even more pleasing was the erection in 1728 of a second church, this one at Fairfield.[39] But the legal burdens that the Anglican minority endured troubled him fiercely, and he repeatedly warned his English patrons that the Episcopal Church could never flourish under such hardships. Anglican families were scattered up and down the Connecticut coastline. Those within twenty or thirty miles came to the Stratford mission as often as travelling conditions permitted, and Johnson would frequently ride as far as New London, seventy miles eastward, to preach. These remote families, lacking the regular services of an Episcopal minister, were compelled by law to worship within the Congregational Church.[40] At nearby Fairfield, Anglican worshippers suffered harassment and imprisonment for refusing to pay taxes to support the Congregational establishment.[41] The root of the trouble, Johnson told Bishop Gibson, was the Connecticut charter, which the colony's magistrates flaunted as their license to make any law they pleased, even one repugnant to the Church of England. Johnson urged that the charter be revoked and replaced with a system of laws favorable to an Episcopal establishment.[42]

Johnson also admonished Gibson and the SPG that the appointment of a colonial bishop was vital to the survival of the church in New England. It was impossible, said Johnson, for one lone missionary to minister to every Anglican in the colony. Already Johnson had transformed his Stratford home into a miniature divinity school, where several young Yale graduates resided and prepared themselves for ordination. But how many of these candidates would meet the tragic fate of Daniel Browne, and how many others would be dissuaded by the prospect of the perilous journey?[43]

Johnson's English patrons were helpless to answer his appeals. No one in England was more receptive than Gibson to arguments for a colonial episcopate, and Gibson carefully drafted a proposal to that end.[44] But the power to legislate on ecclesiastical matters resided not with the Bishop of London or the SPG but with Parliament. It was Sir Robert Walpole, the leader of the Whig majority, who would decide the issue. Walpole was determined to maintain a strong Parliamentary alliance in support of the Hanoverian monarchy, and he perceived that it required the cooperation of the nation's Nonconformists and, most important, the united support of the Church of England. Sending a bishop to the colonies, he realized, would raise fear among the Nonconformists that the Whig party was initiating intolerant policies reminiscent of Archbishop Laud, whose oppression of non-Anglicans had driven many to New England a century before. Walpole also apprehended that Gibson's proposal would divide the Church of England. On the one side were the Jacobite clergy who resented the church's waning political power and the Hanoverian monarchy's toleration of dissenters. Raising the proposal in Parliament and then rejecting it would provoke the wrath of the Jacobite clergy. On the other side were the majority of Episcopal clergymen who favored toleration. They, like the Nonconformists, would regard Gibson's proposal as a subtle step toward a complete Episcopal hierarchy in America. Walpole would not entertain a proposal that threatened to disturb his fragile political equilibrium.[45]

Finally Walpole recognized that the dispatch of an American bishop would greatly alarm the colonists, and he would not hazard a negative reaction from the American dominions.[46] Gibson's proposal anticipated many of the colonists' objections. American bishops would enjoy neither civil powers nor ecclesiastical authority over non-Anglicans. But Gibson failed to persuade Walpole, and the Bishop of London dared not introduce into Parliament a measure that lacked the chief minister's support.[47]

Gibson also felt compelled to act cautiously on the Stratford missionary's complaints against the Connecticut tax laws. Gibson opened a correspondence with Connecticut's Governor Talcott, but to Johnson's mind, the Bishop's stance was shamefully timid. The persecution of the Anglicans at Fairfield continued, Johnson told Gibson, because the Connecticut lawmakers "say [that] your Lordship begs pardon if you have desired anything inconsistent with the law of the government."[48] Gibson's wary approach to the conflicts that pitted Anglicans against Puritans continued a policy to which the SPG had adhered for many years. Samuel Johnson's predecessors at Stratford, George Muirson and George Pigot, had pleaded with the Society for relief from the hostile actions of the Congregational majority, but their complaints had met a stony silence.[49] No one in London would venture to challenge the Connecticut government.

Thus, Samuel Johnson's earliest years in the service of the church brought many disappointments, but his personal life took a happy turn. In the autumn of 1725 he married Charity Floyd Nicholl of Brookhaven, Long Island. Brookhaven lay directly across the Sound from Stratford, and Johnson sometimes sailed the twenty miles to preach there. The Episcopal congregation was building a "handsome Church" and waited for the appointment of a permanent missionary. On one of his journeys, Samuel Johnson met Mrs. Nicholl, the widow of a prominent Episcopal lawyer and judge. Charity brought to the Johnson household the conviviality of her two sons and daughter, and the wealth of her prosperous late husband.[50] After two years of marriage to Samuel Johnson, she gave birth to his first child, William Samuel. Four years later, a second son, "Billy," was born.[51] Samuel Johnson joyfully embarked upon the care and education of his two sons. He had a tender affection for young children and marvelled that "those little creatures from the beginning, do consider and reflect a prodigious deal more than we are commonly apt to imagine; . . . we ought to think little children to be persons of much more importance than we usually apprehend them to be; and [consider] how indulgent we should be to their inquisitive curiosity . . . ; [and] with how much candor, patience and care we ought to bear with them and instruct them."[52]

From the year of William Samuel's birth, Samuel Johnson saw the burden of his pastoral duties lighten. In 1727, Henry Caner took over Johnson's ministry at Fairfield. Caner had studied theology with Johnson while teaching school in Fairfield, and in 1726 he had journeyed to England for Episcopal orders and a commission from the SPG.[53] In the early 1730s, four more Connecticut men were ordained in England and returned to the colony as missionaries of the Society: Samuel Seabury, John Beach, Ebenezer Punderson and Jonathan Arnold. All four were likenesses of Johnson himself: sons of Yale who had been ordained originally into the Congregational ministry.[54] This expansion was the handiwork of Samuel Johnson, not of any aggressive tactics by the SPG. Johnson preached at New Haven, encouraged the Yale students' inquiries about the church, and prepared them for ordination. When they returned from England, he comforted them in times of loneliness and hardship and gave them the leadership and discipline that a colonial bishop might have provided.[55]

The new missionaries assumed many of the burdens that had formerly taken Samuel Johnson on tiring journeys far from Stratford. Time was made for the care of his two young sons. "O my God," he prayed, ". . . let me live to see them well educated and engaged in thy service!"[56] William Samuel and Billy learned their lessons not at the nearby Congregational school but in their father's home. Yet the Johnson household must have seemed to the young boys just like a schoolhouse. Yale graduates preparing for ordination were almost always in residence, and Samuel Johnson also took in the sons of several New York families for more elementary education. Under his tutelage, William Samuel, Billy, and the New York boys learned the Episcopal catechism, as well as the traditional lessons in grammar, mathematics, and the ancient languages, which were a necessary preparation for college.[57] Most likely, Rev. Johnson took William Samuel and Billy on his missionary rounds to Stratford and the neighboring towns,[58] for he cherished the hope that one day his sons would follow him into the ministry.[59] But the future lay ahead, unknown, and for Samuel Johnson full of forlorn hopes.

Parental cares did not deter Johnson from his campaign against the colony's ecclesiastical laws. In 1727, the Episcopalians of Fairfield sent a memorial to the Connecticut General Assembly asking to be relieved from paying rates for the support of the town's Congregational minister. The Assembly granted their request. The legislators did not realize the timid policy to which the SPG and Bishop Gibson were committed. What the lawmakers did know was that Samuel Johnson had sent complaints to London attacking the colony's charter. The relief granted to the Fairfield Anglicans was a desperate measure of conciliation by the Assembly, which feared a wholesale attack on the colony's privileges of self-government.[60] The lawmakers' exaggerated notion of the Church of England's intentions and political power seemed to work for the benefit of the Connecticut Anglicans in 1727, but in the long run this notion would impede the acceptance of the Episcopal Church in the colony. New England's century-old fear of Episcopal tyranny would bring failure to Samuel Johnson's appeals for a colonial bishop and imperil the fortunes of his son William Samuel, who would one day aspire to a political career in the Puritan colony.

The relief measures enacted by the Assembly only heightened Samuel Johnson's impatience with the Connecticut government and his disillusionment with the SPG and the Bishop of London. The 1727 law provided that the money paid by Anglican taxpayers could be awarded to an Episcopal minister, but only when the Anglicans lived conveniently close to an Episcopal mission and attended services regularly. The law was open to a very narrow interpretation, because few Connecticut towns were supplied with resident missionaries. Repeated complaints against the illiberal law were received in London with sympathy but no action.[61]

In the 1730s, Samuel Johnson assumed the task of organizing the Connecticut missionaries into a united front against the colony's lawmakers. It is uncertain how often the missionaries met,[62] but the 1738 convention made its proceedings known to both the Connecticut General Assembly and churchmen in London. In the previous year, the General Assembly had voted to sell a large section of the colony's public lands and appropriated the revenue to the individual towns, which would use it to support their schools and orthodox churches. When the missionaries met in 1738, they drafted a memorial to the Assembly and a letter to the SPG protesting that the Church of England was deprived of an equitable share of the revenue. Neither their memorial nor their appeals to England met with any success.[63]

Throughout William Samuel Johnson's childhood, his father waged a tireless battle against the Connecticut government. In the early 1730s, the elder Johnson also engaged the Congregational clergy in a noisy pamphlet dispute. Samuel Johnson issued three public letters in defense of the Episcopal Church.[64] The letters, working at cross purposes with the conciliatory policy of the SPG, hindered rather than advanced the acceptance of Anglicanism in New England. Of greater significance for young William Samuel Johnson's future, the letters revealed his father's insensitivity to the religious and political anxieties that troubled New England. It was an unenviable burden that young Johnson would shoulder when he set out to earn a political following in the Puritan colony: how to manage the fiery will of his father and win the affection and esteem of the Connecticut voters.

The letters gave new life to old hatreds. Samuel Johnson outspokenly challenged the Puritan way of ordaining ministers, reiterating the arguments that had shocked and angered the Yale trustees and all New England a decade earlier.[65] He also unwisely accused the Puritan church of lacking a sound ecclesiastical government and of failing to preserve community order.[66] Johnson's accusation regarding the disorders in the New England churches was not unfounded. The community disturbances and clerical contentions that had influenced his apostasy continued in the 1730s. A sizeable minority of the orthodox church at Guilford, where Samuel Johnson was born, accused their pastor of lacking piety and broke off from his church in 1731.[67] Indeed it was the accuracy of Johnson's accusation that made it so impolitic. If the Congregationalists were failing to sustain the ideal of a unified church community, the most extreme and distressing manifestation of that failure was the emergence of a wholly native Anglican church. Finally, Johnson insisted that the Church of England was the established religion of the entire British Empire, including the North American colonies.[68] Johnson's argument served only to nourish New England's mistaken fear that British churchmen and politicians aimed to Episcopize the provinces and destroy the colonial charters. This was the very fear that Walpole, Gibson, and the SPG sought to dispel.

In 1734, the Congregational clergy of Hampshire County, Massachusetts, laid before Bishop Gibson their grievances against the Episcopal missionaries. The missionaries were guilty of "insinuating that [our] ministry is no Ministry, not having had Episcopal Ordination," of provoking "disorder and confusion in our churches," and of endeavouring to "wrest from us" the religious liberty for which "our Fathers left their Native Land ... that they might in a place of their own serve God according to their own Consciences in peace, without giving offense to the then Governing powers."[69] The orthodox clergy's letter to Gibson summed up New England's prejudices against the Church of England. To the Puritans, that church still symbolized persecution, popery and political oppression. Samuel Johnson's public letters revealed how swiftly and completely his own passionate churchmanship had isolated him from the main currents of New England thought.

The sustained hostility of the 1730s between the Anglican missionaries and Puritan pamphleteers and lawmakers con-

trasted starkly to the accommodating spirit in which the Stratford Congregationalists accepted Samuel Johnson's church.
The townspeople did not take their cues from the New England
polemicists or the Assembly. Had it been otherwise, William
Samuel Johnson's childhood would have been a sorry one indeed.
The town's willingness in the early years to offer tax relief to
Rev. Johnson's communicants had promised that his church
would gain more and more welcome once the initial bitterness
had faded. Community harmony did not hinge on religious
consensus, at least not after the wounds suffered by the dismem-
berment of the orthodox church had had time to heal. Many
of the Anglican parishioners had ties of kinship and neighborly
cooperation with the Congregational majority, and these ties
helped the town to forget the pain of religious schism.[70] In the
winter of 1735–1736, the proprietors of Stratford's common lands
showed their good will by granting the Episcopal Church a share
of this land equal in proportion to what had been given to the
orthodox church. In 1734, the town answered "yes" when
Samuel Johnson requested permission to erect an Episcopal
school, although Stratford already had two Congregational
schoolhouses. Just seven years earlier, Johnson's request had
incurred opposition.[71]

Samuel Johnson's appeals to the SPG to provide a salary
for an Episcopal schoolmaster went unanswered for many years,
and the first evidence we have of the school's existence is in
1738.[72] By that year William Samuel had nearly completed his
preparation for college. But the town's willingness to allow the
Episcopal school, like the other gestures of accommodation,
must have made an impression on young Johnson nevertheless.
Born too late to experience the hardships and fears that his
father had endured when the mission first opened, William
Samuel grew up expecting only friendship and respect from
his Puritan neighbors. At Yale, his expectations would be
strengthened and confirmed.

Chapter Two

From Pulpit to Bar

~~~ ❧❧ ~~~

*I*n September 1740, one month before his thirteenth birthday, William Samuel Johnson entered Yale College.[1] Yale
imparted to him a thorough understanding of the New England
way and cast his character in a design very different from the
zealous and partisan churchmanship of his father.

To Connecticut citizens, Yale was the citadel of education,
but to any stranger who passed through New Haven, the college
must have seemed nothing more than a tiny, impoverished, and
provincial academy. It was housed entirely in the one wooden
structure that had been dedicated to Elihu Yale in 1718; now it
was in disrepair and too small to accommodate more than half
the students.[2] Yale, in contrast to Harvard, enjoyed only local
fame. Of the thirteen freshmen who arrived with William
Samuel Johnson in September, ten were from Connecticut and
three came from nearby New York.[3] Yale also stood behind
Harvard in the teaching of mathematics and the natural sciences.
Until 1722, there had been promising signs that Yale would
abandon the medieval folklore of natural philosophy and enter
the world of modern Newtonian science. In 1719, Samuel Johnson, who was then a tutor at the college, had used the new
ideas contained in the Dummer collection to educate his students
in up-to-date mathematics and scientific methods, and after his
departure to the parish at West Haven, his progressive approach
had been carried on by Rector Cutler and Tutor Browne. But
with the dramatic confrontation between the Yale trustees and
the Anglican apostates in 1722, the scientific as well as the theological ideas represented in the Dummer collection were put
aside. Between 1722 and 1740, while Harvard developed an increasingly secular curriculum, Yale steadily emphasized religion
and allowed science to languish.[4]

William Samuel Johnson entered Yale at a momentous time,

17

for in 1740 the college came under the direction of a new rector, Thomas Clap. Previous Yale rectors had shared the administration of the college with the trustees, but from Clap's first days in New Haven, he ruled alone. He gave new life to mathematics and science at Yale, while jealously guarding the college's role as the stronghold of orthodox Puritanism. The new rector was an enthusiastic and learned follower of the Enlightenment. He corresponded and collaborated with a host of inventors and experimentalists, disregarding how radically their religious views might differ from his own.[5] Clap shared a warm intellectual friendship with Samuel Johnson, and the new rector worked in close partnership with the Anglican missionary to reshape the Yale curriculum.[6] Mathematics, heretofore taught only to seniors, was introduced to William Samuel Johnson and his classmates in their freshman year. Astronomy and physics, which were Clap's own loves, were modernized. Equipment was solicited from benefactors throughout the colonies and Europe, and tutors with scientific talents were recruited.[7] William Samuel Johnson displayed more interest and ability in the traditional studies of Latin and Greek than in the new science, but the import of the revised curriculum could be seen in the accomplishments of Johnson's fellow students, who became the first generation of Yale-trained Newtonian scholars.[8]

Mathematics and science may have acquired new importance at Yale, but religion continued to dominate the curriculum. Young Johnson and his classmates attended regular exercises in moral philosophy and ethics that focused largely on Puritan doctrine, departing very little from the lessons taught at the college in 1710, when Samuel Johnson first enrolled. Saturday classes were devoted expressly to New England theology. On six days of the week, the students also assembled for morning and evening prayers with Rector Clap.[9] Clap agreed with the founders of the college that Yale's first duty was to uphold religious orthodoxy. He apprehended that if the Englightenment's emphasis on reason were allowed to invade the realm of ethics and moral philosophy at Yale, Puritanism would falter. Clap closely scrutinized the religious beliefs of the two or three tutors who taught the lower classes and reserved for himself the education of the seniors.[10] At Yale, William Samuel Johnson received a thorough introduction to New England church life.

To Clap, Arminianism of any color menaced Puritan

orthodoxy, and he was just as troubled by the spread of Anglicanism in Connecticut as by the rationalist theology that was making notable headway in neighboring Massachusetts. Before coming to Yale, Clap had presided over the First Church of Windham, where he had earned his reputation as an outspoken defender of the Congregational establishment and "a terror to evil-doers." In 1735, he had excommunicated Israel and Goody Folsom for sympathizing with Episcopal doctrine and inviting the Anglican missionary from nearby New London to preach privately in their parish.[11] Despite Clap's hostility toward the Episcopal Church, William Samuel Johnson and his Anglican classmates enjoyed the evenhanded treatment accorded other Yale students and even a measure of religious toleration that clearly violated the college laws. For example, Clap drew up the student rankings for each entering class. Yale was a tiny model of the Connecticut social hierarchy, and each freshman was assigned a rank that corresponded to his social standing among his peers. A student's rank remained fixed throughout his college career, and the tradition was not taken lightly. The rector assigned William Samuel Johnson third place among the fourteen members of his entering class, just below Benjamin Woolsey, whose father was a wealthy Long Island gentleman farmer, and Hezekiah Huntington, whose position at the top of the class reflected his father's membership in the Connecticut legislature's upper house.[12] College law required that every student attend the Sunday services of Rev. Joseph Noyes, who was pastor of New Haven's orthodox First Church. But Clap often allowed Johnson and the other Anglicans to attend Episcopal services in West Haven, where a mission had opened earlier in 1740, and to hear the sermons of travelling Episcopal divines who stopped in New Haven from time to time. About once a month, Johnson returned to Stratford to hear his father preach, and on other occasions remained in his chamber to avoid the Congregational worship. "The Rector and tutors," reported his father, "indulge him as much as they dare, being friendly disposed to serve me as much as they are able without hazarding the resentment of the government that supports them"[13] Clap recognized that Yale could either buttress or destroy orthodoxy in Connecticut, and he had no qualms about purging the library of heretical works. On more than one occasion, he pulled from the shelves deistic sermons and Baptist tracts, but apparently he allowed the Anglican students to pore over the same works that had inspired the apostasy

of Cutler and Johnson in 1722. Samuel Johnson carefully guided
his son's studies in this direction, sending William Samuel an
outline of the books to be examined and signing his letters "your
affectionate father and best friend."[14]

The contrast between Clap's vehement anti-Anglicanism
and his permissiveness toward Episcopal students at Yale is
intriguing, but several reasons underlay this seeming paradox.
First, Clap undoubtedly was inspired by the same fear that had
moved the General Assembly to legalize Anglican worship in
1708 and provide tax relief for the Fairfield Anglicans in
1727—the fear that any blatant persecution of Episcopalians
could endanger the college's charter and even the constitution
of the colony.[15] Secondly, the Church of England seemed to
pose no real threat to orthodoxy at Yale in the 1740s. There was
no Church of England in New Haven to challenge the religious
leadership of Rev. Noyes. Samuel Johnson continued to prose-
lytize at the college, but these efforts, and the presence of an
Anglican mission at West Haven, failed to produce a surge in
the number of Yale graduates who declared for the Episcopal
Church. From the defection of Cutler and Johnson in 1722, the
proportion of Anglican to orthodox graduates had remained
about one in ten.[16] (Clap's toleration of the Anglican minority
ceased suddenly in 1753, when the SPG established a mission
within view of the college itself.) Finally, while William Samuel
Johnson was at Yale, the rector was vexed with a disciplinary
problem of much graver proportions than either the unorthodox
views of the Anglican minority or the typical student pranks that
would always pique college presidents. In Johnson's freshman
year, his Puritan classmates became infected with a religious enthusiasm that threw the college into a tumult, imperilled Clap's
command of the students, and even threatened to overturn Connecticut's church establishment.

It began on a Friday late in October, when George Whitefield, a travelling preacher from England, captivated the Yale
students and, in fact, nearly everyone in New Haven with his
fiery Calvinist sermons on the depravity of man and the glory
of an all-powerful God. Whitefield had arrived in New England
a month before, and had travelled down the Connecticut Valley
from Springfield and through Hartford before reaching New
Haven. On his route he left a trail of emotionally shattered
crowds. His method was to depict the horrors of damnation and
the humiliation of man's sinfulness in such terrifying, vivid terms

that crowds of listeners experienced immediate conversions. They behaved in bizarre ways, fainting, crying, and writhing in mental and bodily torment. Wherever Whitefield preached, the townspeople displayed an exceptional concern for their spiritual lives and flocked to church in great numbers.[17] To many people in Connecticut who had long lamented the decline of piety, Whitefield's effectiveness seemed to promise that the thriving church of their forefathers could be reborn.[18]

New Haven, like the other towns on Whitefield's route, fell under the evangelist's sway. Other itinerants followed Whitefield to New Haven, imitating his frenetic style and echoing his terrifying Calvinist message. The winter of 1740–1741 was intensely cold and uncommonly long, but equally extreme was the heat of religious fervor at the college. The Yale boys deemed the regular morning and evening prayers insufficient, and held private prayer meetings in their rooms. They hurried to the revival meetings in town, and sometimes even followed the itinerants to neighboring villages.[19] Everyone at the college, including William Samuel Johnson, was inspired by curiosity if not unbounded enthusiasm for the revival. Stratford was also visited by the evangelical exhorters, and Samuel Johnson felt only disdain for the "convulsions and involuntary agitations" of the Puritan congregations and for the "foolish and vicious conduct" and "hideous outcries" of the itinerants. He even suspected the roaming preachers of "very odd familiarities with women."[20] No doubt Samuel Johnson warned his son in the strongest terms against the revival enthusiasm, but William Samuel Johnson was among the many students who purchased copies of the sermon preached by Ebenezer Pemberton at the college hall in April.[21] The elder Johnson may have been vexed by his son's curious interest in the revival, but Clap was gladdened by the first signs of enthusiasm among the Yale students. In fact, nearly all the New England clergy were pleased by the increase in church membership and the new spiritual zeal of their parishioners. To the Congregational ministers, the first wave of the revival seemed to promise a great awakening.[22]

In the summer of 1741, however, Clap grew alarmed by the bold demeanor of many of the students. The boys who were swept up in the revival interrogated their classmates on spiritual matters and even dared to challenge the religious fitness of their tutors. What probably triggered these excesses were the exhortations of Gilbert Tennent, a Presbyterian preacher from New York who visited the college in April, and James Davenport, the arch-fanatic of the Great Awakening, who sailed into New Haven from his parish on Long Island sometime that summer. Tennent denounced the established clergy of New England for preaching in a cold, unaffecting manner and for neglecting the cardinal doctrines of original sin and predestination. His most famous sermon expounded the "Dangers of an Unconverted Ministry." Davenport viciously attacked Noyes for lacking the gift of grace that could inspire and convert his congregation.[23]

Even more alarming than the renegade behavior of the Yale students was the fact that the evangelists' message excited Puritans all over Connecticut to rebel against their ministers and the colony's ecclesiastical laws. The itinerants provoked a violent eruption of the pietistic sentiment that had threatened disorder within Connecticut churches for the last twenty years. Connecticut's pious revivalists, dubbed New Lights, denied that their unawakened neighbors had a rightful place in the church. In defiance of the clergy's county associations, which licensed and disciplined the local pastor, the New Lights also insisted that anyone who displayed the gift of grace could come into a town and call the people to worship. The most radical New Lights were ready to abandon their minister and split off from his church if he refused to heed the evangelists' message and adopt a fervent preaching style. Across Connecticut, in numerous towns, New Lights repeated the unlawful separation that had been rehearsed at Guilford ten years earlier.[24]

As New Light fervency swelled, the established clergy grew hostile to the Awakening. What the evangelists termed a "harvest" of converted souls, about two-thirds of the New England ministers condemned as an epidemic, a contagious madness. The deplored itinerant preaching, criticism and abuse of the clergy, schisms in the churches and the breaking up of the parishes, disobedience to the county associations and the colony's ecclesiastical laws.[25] The opponents of the revival, called Old Lights, warned that "Separate meetings are subversive of Peace Discipline and Government; Lay open the Sluices and make a Gap to let in a Flood of Confusion and Disorder; and very awfully portend the Ruin of these Churches unless a Stop be Put to them."[26] Clap launched the Old Light counter-offensive against the destruction of the ecclesiastical order. In September 1741 he addressed the Yale students, warning them against excessive enthusiasm, banning itinerants from the college, and forbidding the students to attend the exhorters' prayer meetings. At Clap's instigation, the Yale trustees "Voted, that if any students of this College shall directly or indirectly say, that the Rector, either of the Trustees or Tutors are hypocrites, carnal or unconverted men, he shall for the first offense be expelled." The trustees' resolution was no mere threat, and in November Clap expelled the best student in the junior class for disparaging Tutor Whittelsey as a teacher who lacked saving grace.[27] That same month the established clergy of Connecticut came together at Guilford and resolved that no pastor could be censured, dismissed from office, or abandoned by his parishioners without the sanction of the clergy's county associations.[28] The Connecticut General Assembly, quick to give the ministers' resolves all the force of colonial law, met the following spring and passed a series of statutes that were designed to smother the Awakening. Itineracy was banned. Anyone who separated from his legally established parish or refused to pay taxes for its support was to be fined and imprisoned.[29] For the next quarter century Connecticut New Lights would wage a bitter political campaign against the restrictive legislation and its Old Light supporters.

The Connecticut laws were more successful in restricting itineracy than in preventing church schism. In May 1742, just as the new laws went into effect, the enthusiasts of New Haven split off from Rev. Noyes's church, destroying the peace and homogeneity of the college town. Disorder was also rampant at Yale, despite Clap's forceful discipline. Ezra Stiles, who was a freshman that year, later recounted that "multitudes were seriously, soberly and solemnly out of their wits." In desperation, the rector suspended classes in the spring and sent all the students home.[30]

William Samuel Johnson's return to Stratford in the summer of 1742 was not a happy retreat from the contentions wrought by the revival, for none of the Connecticut towns escaped the controversy that surrounded the Great Awakening. In 1740 Whitefield had stirred up enthusiasm in Stratford, and in the years thereafter, a horde of itinerants followed him through the town, arousing welcome from some townspeople and opposition from others. Stratford township embraced five Congregational parishes, each with its own orthodox minister. These included Stratford Old Society, where Rev. Hezekiah Gold ministered in competition with Johnson's Episcopal mission, and the newer inland parishes of Ripton, Unity, Stratfield, and Long Hill.

Gold and the Congregationalist pastors at Ripton and Stratfield welcomed the itinerants and greeted the Awakening ardently, but the townspeople were by no means unanimous on
the virtues of wandering exhorters or the New Light enthusiasm
of their own preachers. By the summer of 1742 a movement was
underway to unseat Hezekiah Gold.[31]

To Samuel Johnson, the turmoil surrounding the Awakening at Stratford was satisfactory proof that Puritanism was
breathing its last gasp.[32] He spared no energy in recruiting
troubled Old Lights to the Episcopal Church. In 1739, he had
reported to London that of the four hundred families residing
in Gold's parish, sixty-seven belonged to the Church of England.
Three years later, Johnson boasted eighty-seven. In 1742 the tiny
and humble mission at Old Stratford was replaced by a new
edifice, architecturally ornate and topped with a stately gold
weathercock that towered six feet above the church spire. The
following year, a second Episcopal church would be raised, this
one at Ripton parish, where a number of discontented Old Lights
joined together with earlier Anglican converts. "The distrac-
tions of the times," Samuel Johnson proudly told his SPG
superiors, "have in many instances been improved to open
people's eyes and awaken their attention towards the Church
as their only refuge."[33]

Yet trouble within the Congregational establishment would
mean trouble, as always, for the Episcopal cause as well. Samuel
Johnson's zealous churchmanship blinded him to this all-too-
dependable rule. The apostasy of several Old Lights to the
Church of England embittered Gold and his entire congregation
against the Stratford mission after more than a decade of harmony. In the summer of 1741, one year before William Samuel
Johnson's return home, Gold warned the elder Johnson, "You
are guilty of fishing in troubled waters, . . . for many that are
now communicants with you, were members of our church,
who left us in a very unrulable and disorderly manner (and have
justly the heavy charge of convenant-breakers lying upon
them)."[34] Although a few Stratford Old Lights fled the frenzy
in their own church to join the Church of England, most of the
town's antirevivalists were intent upon treading the narrow path
of Puritan orthodoxy and orderly worship. They shunned the
intemperate emotionalism of the Awakening but cleaved to the
hard doctrines of original sin and a merciless God. They chose
to endure the acrimonious divisions within their church and

search tirelessly for an Old Light minister to replace Gold, rather than submit to Episcopacy. Nothing more aptly symbolizes their dual aversion to evangelical excesses and Arminian heresy than the reasons the Old Lights gave for their dismissal of Hezekiah Gold: his New Light sympathies *and* the heretical beliefs of his wife, who was by birth and steady conviction an Anglican.[35] The turmoil and schisms that emerged from the Great Awakening begot hostility between Anglicans and Puritans, as well as between Old Lights and New Lights, but Samuel Johnson did not heed the ominous signs of trouble to come. Six years later, this contention between the churches would destroy his greatest hope. William Samuel Johnson would flee the religious discord at Stratford and renounce the missionary career for which his father had nurtured and educated him.

In the autumn of 1742 Clap recalled the students, and education at Yale took on a quiet and orderly spirit that had been unknown to William Samuel Johnson in his freshman and sophomore years. The unruliest New Light dissidents declined to return. Instead, they set up at New London an experimental seminary for evangelical religion, the so-called Shepherd's Tent, which the Connecticut General Assembly promptly legislated out of existence.[36] Johnson's junior and senior years were happy and successful. He formed a warm friendship with Rector Clap, and at graduation in September 1744 he received the Berkeley scholarship for excellence in the ancient tongues.[37] After taking their degrees, most of his classmates left the college to become tradesmen, doctors, or schoolmasters, or to read for the bar.[38] William Samuel Johnson, with scholarship in hand, embarked upon a fifth year of theological studies, in company with the other Yale graduates who aspired to the ministry. However, it was at Stratford, not at Yale, that most Connecticut Anglicans received their final preparation for Episcopal orders, and in 1746 Johnson returned to the home and tutelage of his father.

Preparation meant poring over ecclesiastical histories, Latin, Hebrew, and Greek writings, and reading prayers and lessons at Ripton parish, where the Episcopal congregation had erected St. Paul's Church in 1743 and still awaited an ordained missionary of their own.[39] For Johnson, the next two years were filled with discontent and anxious self-examination. "I can never be useful to mankind in any sedentary course of life," he despaired.[40] He longed for a career that promised excitement and public esteem. At that time, all New England was alarmed by the threat of a French invasion, and the glamour and glory of the French and Indian War excited his imagination. "Where Men Fight for Liberty, for the Support of Virtue and in Defense of the Rights of Mankind," Johnson told a former Yale classmate, "They Deserve all the Eulogies that the Brightest Imagination & the most Sublime history can bestow upon them. . . ."

And suppose Arms is what I am calculated for, when was there a fitter time to sacrifice to Man, when a nobler Opportunity to Sacrifice my life in Defence of Liberty than now when our Exorbitant Enemies would [prey] upon the Liberties of Europe and make Slaves of all Mankind, as if there was no Government more Eligible than that of French Dragoons, nor any Happiness for Man but in Wooden Shoes.[41]

To another friend from Yale, Johnson confided, "I Love a Soldier ere I love my Life & had been one but that my Mother's Will & Father's Uncontrolled Desire have made me what I am."[42]

Johnson began a frequent and intimate correspondence with one of his college friends, William Smith, Jr., to whom he confessed the longings and doubts that he dared not reveal to his father. Smith hailed from a family of New York attorneys, and upon graduation from Yale began his preparation for the law. The young New Yorker often complained of the hectic schedule, the harassments and banalities of a legal career, and urged Johnson to appreciate his contemplative life in the church. "How calm, how easy, how refined may be your thoughts," he told Johnson, "without the least interruption, Voluntarily Banished from noise you emphatically possess yourself in peace. Oh sweet retreat how greatly longed for."[43]

Johnson must have read with bitter irony his friend's idealization of the missionary life, for Johnson's pastoral duties at Ripton had thrust him to the front lines in the battle between Stratford's churches. Ever since St. Paul's Episcopal Church was raised at Ripton, the parish's Puritan worshippers had waged open war against their Anglican neighbors. In fact, on the very day the church was opened, Ripton's New Light pastor, who was vexed by discontented Old Lights and angered by the departure of some antirevivalists to Episcopacy, so aroused his parishioners against the new church that they attacked it with fistfuls of dung.[44] As at Old Stratford parish twenty years before, the acceptance of the Anglican church in Ripton would be a slow process, and the contention between Old Lights and New Lights promised to make that process long and tumultuous.[45]

William Samuel Johnson dreamed of a military career, but he did not envision himself as an ecclesiastical soldier like his father in a lifetime of church feuds. He was born too late to feel the stinging hatred and distrust that Samuel Johnson had endured in the first years at the Stratford mission. In the 1730s, Anglicans and Congregationalists had lived peacefully together at Stratford, and young Johnson's childhood was untroubled by religious rivalries and intolerance. At Yale he was schooled in the orthodoxies and traditions of the New England way and befriended by Rector Clap, the Puritan tutors, and students. At Ripton, when the full force of anti-Anglican sentiment first threatened his rapport with the New England establishment, Johnson's immediate impulse was to escape the conflict.

The bitter religious contentions of the 1740s made a deep impression upon many of Connecticut's younger generation, including Ezra Stiles, who was a freshman at Yale when Clap surrendered to the revival tumult and sent the boys home. Ezra, far more than William Samuel, possessed the contemplative spirit, intellectual temperament, and religious zeal that would make him an exemplary minister. But the revival controversy, in which Ezra's Old Light father Reverend Isaac Stiles was assaulted mercilessly by New Light malcontents, alienated the younger Stiles from a church calling. Thus, when the parishioners of Stockbridge called Ezra Stiles to be their pastor in 1750, he refused the invitation and embarked on a career in law.[46]

By the summer of 1746 Johnson too was eyeing a career at the bar. For him, the law was an escape from church feuds and the monotony of his ecclesiastical studies into the bustling world of business that filled his friend Smith's letters. "For what Study is there more Useful more Advantageous than the Study of Mankind," Johnson told Smith, "this Difficult Sense is to be Obtained by Reading them in the Original & Observing them While in Life & Action & not as I am obliged to do in the Writings of those who have been long dead."[47] It was not inappropriate that young men like Johnson and Stiles, successful Yale graduates from respected families, should aspire to a career at the bar. Traditionally, a knowledge of the law was considered by Connecticut men as an essential qualification for public service. Men who were destined by family connections and education for a life of political leadership customarily schooled themselves in judicial procedure, though they seldom practiced law as their primary occupation.[48] Even more important, by mid-century, business and commerce were expanding rapidly, and with these, litigation. For the first time professional attorneys were in great demand, and the practice of law promised higher social status and more lucrative rewards than ever before.[49] "I know no more honourable Profession than that of the Divine nor at the Same time one less honoured," Johnson explained to Smith. "The Reasons you Suggest are very Strong why Divines Should be honoured but it is because men generally have a greater Regard to their Temporal than their Spiritual Interests that the Gentlemen of your Profession have the Greatest Share of Respect & Applause."[50]

To Ezra Stiles, abandoning the pulpit for the bar was a heartrending decision, and the youthful Yale graduate would return to the ministry within a few years.[51] But to William Samuel Johnson, the more painful task was confessing his decision to his father. For a year, Johnson confided his new ambition only to his friend Smith. Then, in June 1747, Johnson set out for Harvard to procure a master's degree. In colonial times this was a common practice that required only the ample recommendation of an esteemed educator, in Johnson's case the generous praises of Rector Clap, and the eight pounds or so that the college demanded from the candidate.[52] Samuel Johnson worried over the distance that separated him from his son. He cautioned William Samuel to avoid that "free thinking" rationalist religion that was so rampant in Boston and to shun the charms of the female world that might ensnare him in "youthful lusts." But William Samuel Johnson was comforted by the distance between Stratford and Cambridge, and took the occasion to declare to his father that he felt suited for the bar, not the pulpit. To his son's disturbing confession, Samuel Johnson replied, "if a man is not pleased with the business he follows it cannot be expected he will succeed in it." But consider the "superior intrinsic excellency and usefulness of the ministry," the elder Johnson urged, and remember that while human "nature cannot be eradicated yet it may be corrected." In his next letter, Samuel Johnson cautioned his son against the temptations of profit and glory to which youthful passions often succumb. Age has a great advantage over youth, he wrote, "having had larger opportunities of trial, both of the treachery of a tempting world, and of the instability and deceitfulness of the heart of man." The elder Johnson, gladdened that a military career was "now at least in great measure out of the question" and probably fearful of losing his son's affection entirely, searched for a reconciliation. "Perhaps it is only the knowledge of yourself as you now are, in the heat of youth, that makes you apprehensive that you are not well calculated for divinity. . . . I doubt not but with careful management of yourself, you will in a few years grow more sedate, and your taste may much alter. However, as you profess that you have no notion of hurrying into life, you will do well to study law industriously two or three years."[53]

For both father and son, the truce that summer was uncomfortable and indecisive. Samuel Johnson still clung to his dearest hope that his son would one day follow him to the pulpit. And the younger Johnson harbored grave doubts about his own abilities and his father's expectations. After returning to Stratford in July, William Samuel Johnson recorded the new path on which he was embarking. "[I] have been so hardy as to venture upon the rough arduous & Intricate Study of the Law which I am determined to pursue this Winter & perhaps for Life provided I find I can make proficiency therein & it is agreeable to my father."[54]

Once again Johnson turned to his confidant William Smith, Jr. for guidance. Smith's father was one of the few college-educated lawyers in New York, and his knowledge of the law had earned him wide acclaim throughout the colony. The elder Smith was drafting the first digest of New York laws and legal precedents, which his son and William Livingston, another young Yale graduate, would publish in 1752.[55] William Smith, Jr. sent Johnson a copy of the rough draft as a guideline for his studies, and extracted a promise to guard the copy from public disclosure. Johnson marvelled at the sophistication of the New York system, against which Connecticut legal knowledge seemed rude and unsystematic. He wrote to Smith that before receiving the text, the "Law appeared like a confused heap of Unintelligible & Unpleasant Reading without beginning or End & I was half Discouraged before I began. . . . I must henceforth Consider Mr. Smith as the Conductor of my Studies & the founder and Conductor of all that knowledge which I may attain in the Law."[56]

Despite Smith's expert guidance and Johnson's diligent application to his studies, the young law student remained apprehensive. In May 1748, he despaired to his New York friend, "My head is so full of the Jargon of the Bar and the Din of Contention that I fear I shall Scarcely be able to write Common

Law." That same month he notified the SPG of his intention
to quite his pastoral duties at Ripton, but he added in his letter
to the Society, "It is not impossible that I may alter my Views &
hereafter enter the Service of the Ch[urc]h which If I Should I
shall be extremely obliged to the Society for any future Notice
they shall be pleased to take of me."[57]

Johnson severed his ties to the ministry with some hesitancy,
but his parishioners at Ripton relinquished his pastoral care
without any misgivings. For a year the SPG had provided the
young lay reader with a stipend for presiding at Ripton, but the
Episcopalians there had found Johnson's half-hearted churchmanship plainly embarrassing. In September 1748 they complained to the Society that "we were laughed at by the Dissenters
for having a lawyer for our priest, which discouraged many of
our people so that they would not go to hear him" The Ripton
churchwardens pleaded with the Society to send "a true son of
the established church, . . . if not, we fear that many of our young
people will turn to the Dissenters as many have done already."[58]

Johnson's stepbrother, Benjamin Nicoll, who was already a
successful attorney in New York, and William Smith, Jr., who
was impressed with his Stratford friend's "great capacities" for
the law, prodded Johnson to come to New York. Smith, who was
a Presbyterian and enjoyed teasing Johnson for his Anglican
allegiances, promised "the practice in this province will keep
you from poverty, that great evil, and enable you to spend the
latter days Bishop-like in an easy abundance."[59] Johnson was by
no means immune to the enticements of profit and success, but
his ambitions were fixed on a career in Connecticut, where the
future seemed even more promising. He judged that his temperament was more suited to legal practice in Connecticut than in
New York. "There Industry Application & a good collection of
Books in general does the Business," he told Smith, "here a
teeming fruitful Imagination will make the best figure."[60] Smith
agreed. "The practice of the Laws of your Country," Smith
told his Connecticut friend, "will not discourage your boldest
attempts, for you are not shackled by a slavish regard to Old
Entries & Precedents, insipid Reports & unpolished Commen-
taries and Annals, and an endless String of Acts of Parliament
. . . with you a man must go farther and do that which lies beyond
the reach thought and study of 9/10ths of the Practisers among
us, to shew the Reason of a Resolution, to Demonstrate its exact
agreements with the Case before him to prove that the Same
Reason holds in your colony and extends there."[61]

Johnson realized that his vigorous course of study under Smith's direction and his determination to focus all his energies on the mastery of the law would give him a greater advantage in Connecticut, where the older generation of attorneys relied on an amateur knowledge of the law, than in New York, where "there are so many great men already in the business & more young men of excellent parts & Genius coming on that I fear . . . I should never be able to accomplish myself."[62] In fact, Johnson's professional training would soon distinguish him from the older generation of Connecticut lawyers. Even Roger Wolcott, at that time Chief Justice of the Superior Court in Connecticut, Deputy Governor of the colony and soon to be Governor, was a clothier by trade. Wolcott had begun his political career as a town selectman, and when he advanced to the Connecticut legislature in 1709, he was admitted to the Connecticut bar as a matter of course. Although Wolcott presided over the colony's highest court, the prestige of his military exploits and even his local fame as a poet surpassed his scant acquaintance with the law.[63]

In 1749, when Johnson opened his practice, men of Wolcott's stamp still dominated the bar, but this was a period of transformation, and the future of attorneyship lay with a corps of professionally trained, full-time lawyers. When, in 1756, the Connecticut legislature devised a system to tax the profits of the colony's most thriving attorneys, it would list Johnson and his friend Jared Ingersoll among the twelve most successful. Most of the twelve still earned their livelihoods in farming and small commercial enterprises, but for Ingersoll and Johnson the law was their exclusive vocation and their knowledge of it was extensive. Among all Connecticut lawyers before the Revolution, only Ingersoll and Johnson would earn professional recognition outside the colony, and within Connecticut their expertise would be in constant demand.[64]

Undoubtedly political ambition, too, influenced Johnson to establish his practice in Connecticut. Smith's polemical talents would soon win for the New Yorker a wide political following, and it was to Smith that Johnson turned not only for legal training but also for lessons in oratory. "I am all in a flame and burn to be what you so well describe," Johnson confessed to his friend.[65] Johnson possessed all the credentials that could one day carry him to the Connecticut General Assembly: a respected family background, a Yale degree, and now a superior legal education. Connecticut's legislators, armed almost to the man with at least a rudimentary knowledge of the law and untroubled by any theories regarding the separation of powers, appointed themselves to the highest judicial and executive posts in the colony.[66] Johnson had only to look to the career of his Stratford neighbor Robert Walker to anticipate the wealth and honor he might one day capture for himself. Walker, the son of an old Stratford family, a graduate of Yale in 1730, and an attorney by trade, had represented Stratford in the General Assembly since 1745. By 1760 he would rise to become a judge on the Superior Court, and by 1768 an assistant on the Governor's Council.[67] William Samuel Johnson, unlike his father, considered himself a full-fledged member of the Connecticut elite, not an estranged rebel from the Congregational establishment. His tranquil childhood at Stratford and his happy and successful years at Yale had prepared him to expect esteem and friendship from his social and intellectual peers. At one time, the elder Johnson would caution his son, "you could not indeed be faithful to your government as to their views so far as religion is concerned, . . . as they have such a perpetual secret venom against the Church."[68] To the younger Johnson, his father's hostile and fearful attitude seemed unwarranted as he began his practice in 1749.

Not only ambition and a rapport with the Connecticut establishment but also the lures of romance kept Johnson in Connecticut. Some time after his journey to Harvard in the summer of 1747, Johnson began courting Ann Beach, who was the daughter of William Beach, a wealthy Stratford Anglican and generous contributor to Samuel Johnson's church.[69] "She has no Beauty to recommend her being rather homely than handsome," young Johnson told Smith, "yet her Deportment to me has been so Benevolent kind Generous intermin^d with a certain [warmth] & affability tempered with reserve & caution that I cannot but have a particular regard for her and I confess to you as a Friend I take a vast Deal of pleasure in her acquaintance & Conversation." Johnson was quick to protest that he was no slave to Miss Beach's charms. "You may laugh at *me*," he wrote to Smith, "but I assure you I am not yet fallen into the Dutch you mention nor so near approach'd it that I cannot easily return whenever motives of Interest & Prudence shall Induce me . . . let me tell you that I think I have been too much acquainted with the female World to be romantically in love . . . I have too much levity in my Constitution to Doat too long upon one Object. Change is my Dear Delight."[70]

No one was better acquainted than Smith with the young lawyer's cavalier attitude toward women. Smith shared Johnson's hearty appreciation for the attractions of the female sex, and the two friends often swapped stories of their romantic adventures. But even Smith had chided Johnson on at least one occasion for encouraging the affection of a Connecticut maiden without intending to marry her.[71] Then at Harvard, Johnson had pledged his hand to a Massachusetts woman, whose identity is now buried in the secrecy of the past. When he returned to Stratford and met Ann Beach, he broke the Massachusetts engagement without delay, ceremony, or apparent regret, explaining to a friend that "there is a Fascination in Women that even Wisdom cannot resist."[72]

Miss Beach's charms were even more alluring than her suitor was willing to confess. In 1748 Johnson was at that midway point between indifference and love, at the stage called "having a fancy for," when a lover's will is the weakest and his passions confound all self-knowledge and reason. "The Chains, if they will bear that name which I now sustain I am indeed not displeased with, for they afford me a great deal of pleasure which I should otherwise be deprived of. But they are neither Chains of Brass nor Steel," he told Smith, "they are but Silken Cords broken at pleasure." Smith was not to be fooled by his friend's protestations. "Who but a man wretchedly in Love and fond of it too," Smith replied, "can talk so feelingly . . . of Tender passions . . . a man so far gone in Love is to be humored."[73]

In November 1749, Johnson took Ann Beach for his bride. It was a marriage founded on love, dangerously unmindful of all practical considerations. Before long, the fiery-tempered Mrs. Johnson would resent her husband's long absences from Stratford on legal and political business.[74] Gradually it would be Samuel Johnson who provided Ann with emotional support and her children with the paternal affection, education, and discipline for which their father found little time.[75]

An even greater vexation to the ambitious young Johnson than his wife's demanding temperament was the aggressive Anglicanism of the Beach family, which threatened to destroy Johnson's political opportunities even before they began to materialize. Had Johnson remained committed to a church career, his marriage to Ann Beach would have been a fortuitous and happy match. Ann's uncle, John Beach, was the most popu-

lar Episcopal preacher in Connecticut, with thriving congregations at Newtown and Redding. Except for Samuel Johnson,
John Beach was also the most energetic and outspoken defender
of New England Episcopacy. Beach had attended Yale College
and entered the Congregational ministry before falling under
Samuel Johnson's sway. In 1732 the young preacher renounced
his Congregational orders and journeyed to England for Episcopal ordination and a commission from the SPG. A decade later,
when the Massachusetts pastor Noah Hobart attacked the propriety of the SPG's missionary activities in New England, Beach
issued a series of sharp-witted public letters in defense of the
New England missionaries.[76] By 1749, John Beach's name was
synonymous with the Anglican campaign.

William Samuel Johnson fled the ecclesiastical contention
at Ripton and renounced the missionary career for which his
father had prepared him. But with his marriage to Ann Beach,
he found himself once again in the camp of New England's
most aggressive churchmen. Over the next twenty years, as
Samuel Johnson and John Beach engaged in open warfare
against their sectarian rivals, the ambitious Stratford lawyer
would wage his own difficult campaign—to win the esteem of the
Connecticut establishment without forsaking his church and
his family.

Chapter Three

Ecclesiastical Warfare on Every Front

*I*n 1753, the war against Episcopacy erupted with new passion and fury. The battleground was New York. For the past several years, the New York Assembly had raised funds by public lotteries to erect a college in the colony. In March 1752, Trinity Church offered a handsome site for the college, with the intention that the president of the college would always be an Episcopalian, and that worship and religious instruction would conform to the Church of England. The Trinity gift was tempting, for the land was worth more than the Assembly's entire college fund. Later that year, Samuel Johnson was nominated for the presidency, and the Johnson family became embroiled in a noisy public controversy over the sinister dangers of an Episcopal college.[1]

The men who sounded the alarm were William Livingston, a Presbyterian lawyer and legislator, and his two law partners, John Morin Scott and William Smith, Jr. In the spring of 1753, this so-called Triumvirate opened fire against the Trinity proposal in a series of weekly broadsides that carried the title *The Independent Reflector*.[2] Livingston railed against the intemperate, intolerant religious zeal of the New England clergy and their archrivals, the Anglicans. The Trinity vestrymen, Livingston charged, design to make the New York college a counterforce to the Puritan regimes at Yale and Harvard. Reminding his readers of the "inhuman persecutions" that had been conducted in New England in the name of religion, he queried, "shall . . . all denominations among us, feel the weight of crimes they have never committed; and shall the sins of their brethren in New England be visited upon them!"[3]

Despite the outcry from the Triumvirate, the plans for an

Anglican college made headway. In November 1753, the Assembly-appointed board of trustees confirmed Samuel Johnson's nomination as president, and the following spring he took up residence in New York. Then, in October, the Anglicans secured another victory when New York's acting governor, James Delancey, bypassed the Assembly and granted the college a royal charter on the terms of the Trinity donation.[4] Delancey's action signalled a second round of fire between the Anglican penmen and the Triumvirate, with both sides doing battle in competing columns of the *New-York Mercury*.[5] Livingston accused the Anglicans and the Delancey politicians of subverting legislative government, and used every polemical tactic to equate the college's royal charter with a malign crown-church conspiracy aimed at the destruction of New York's civil and religious liberties.[6] But the controversy, which would rage on for the next two years, was no mere epilogue to the granting of the charter. Should the Livingston faction prevail, the lottery funds and public support for the college would be lost.

William Samuel Johnson was greatly annoyed by his father's hasty removal to New York. Samuel Johnson soon summoned his wife and his younger son Billy to his side, heaping all the problems of the Stratford mission on William Samuel. The mission was left without a minister, which incited the town authorities to clamor for the Episcopal church's share of the ecclesiastical taxes.[7] But the churchmen squabbled endlessly over the selection of a suitable new preacher. William Samuel Johnson, never sympathetic to ecclesiastical quarreling, did not hide his impatience with "this waspish feeble foolish wayward People, whom it is evident no man can please because they cannot even please themselves."[8] Even more vexing than the petty disputes at Stratford were the bitter hostilities at New York. Although Samuel Johnson would not confess to taking part in the newspaper war, his son discerned the Anglican pieces "to have passed through [his father's] hands if not to have originated there."[9] In fact, Samuel Johnson was busy collaborating with the Anglican penmen from behind the scenes, intending to avoid any public prominence in the pamphlet war. But William Samuel warned his father that such efforts could not escape notice.[10] Young Johnson's stepbrother, Benjamin Nicoll, a New York attorney and ardent supporter of Trinity Church, was also writing a vindication of the Anglican college, drawing the family farther into the center of the controversy.[11] By June 1754

Rev. Johnson was beseeching William Samuel to compose a legal rebuttal to Livingston's pieces, but the cautious Stratford lawyer refused. "You know I am generally averse to disputes of this kind," he admonished his father,

as tending more to irritate the passions than to convince the under-standing of people. What is wrote in this way, is most generally read only by those persons who are before prepossessed on one side or other of the question. But especially averse am I towards engaging myself in any controversial writings . . . [and] of all persons, you nor I nor any of the family should be in the least concerned in any disputes with respect to the college. For those in the opposition to have it in their power once to suggest that you are at the head of a party, or promoting any particular scheme, must be highly prejudicial, and will give them great strength in their endeavors to bias the Assembly.[12]

To Samuel Johnson, his son's caveats seemed almost cowardly. "Even caution," the elder Johnson retorted, "may be carried too far. . . . We must have resolution to do good in spite of opposition."[13]

William Samuel Johnson knew that his father's conspicu-ous churchmanship could only hurt the Trinity campaign. Undoubtedly he also worried over his own legal career, which was thriving on New York business brought to him by his family connections and by his old friend William Smith, Jr. Johnson despised "the envenomed and malicious [triumvirate] faction," and when the New York controversy erupted, his intimate corre-spondence with Smith broke off abruptly.[14] But to appear per-sonally in the controversy would risk more than friendship. It would imperil his flourishing practice as an attorney. Johnson knew that his political future, too, must be carefully guarded. In 1753, the Assembly had appointed him an ensign in the militia. The next year he was elevated to captain.[15] Traditionally such militia appointments were the first steps to town leadership and then colony-wide political eminence. Johnson was not the first Anglican to be so honored. Since the initial years of concord between Stratford's Episcopalians and Puritans in the 1730s, several Episcopalians had commanded the militia, served as town selectmen, and eventually represented Stratford at the General Assembly.[16] But any sharp dispute between Anglicans and non-Anglicans threatened to shatter Johnson's political expectations. To be sure, Livingston's propaganda alone could

hardly arouse Connecticut voters against their Anglican neighbors. The *Reflector's* tirades against Puritan bigotry, sectarian
education, and "The Absurdity of Civil Magistrates Interfering
in Matters of Religion" sorely offended New England sensibilities.[17] But beginning in 1753, Connecticut became embroiled
in a controversy that dangerously resembled the New York college battle. For Johnson, caution was imperative. If the New
York and Connecticut issues exploded into one intercolonial
panic over the menacing power of the Episcopal Church, his
political ambitions would be blasted.

The Connecticut controversy was ignited single-handedly
by Rector Clap, whose stubborn determination to preserve Calvinist orthodoxy at Yale had not abated since Johnson's own
college years. What had changed was Clap's allegiance to the
Old Light cause and his fierce opposition to revivalism. Clap
grew alarmed that, in their quest to rid Connecticut churches of
irrational zeal and unlawful separations, the Old Light clergy
were permitting piety to languish. He worried that the antirevivalists were growing cool to the terrifying message of original sin and predestination and neglecting the importance of
the conversion experience.[18] The vigilant Yale rector suspected that his students were imbibing dangerously Arminian
notions from Rev. Noyes, the Old Light pastor of New Haven's
First Church. Noyes's influence over the Yale boys had to be
stopped. Then in 1753 another threat to Puritan orthodoxy at
Yale inspired Clap to drastic action. That year Trinity Church
was erected within eye's view of the college, and an SPG missionary, Reverend Ebenezer Punderson, arrived in New Haven
to preside over the new Episcopal mission. Reverend Samuel
Johnson, who had long pressed his London superiors to supply
a mission at New Haven, was overjoyed by the event,[19] but Clap
saw it as a fearful encroachment upon the college town's Congregational solidarity. Reacting against swelling Old Light
Arminianism and the Anglican invasion, Clap suddenly withdrew the Congregational students from Noyes's church in October and forbade the Episcopal students to attend the Church of
England. He commanded all the students, including the Anglicans, to worship only at the college under the supervision of a
professor of divinity whom Clap and the trustees intended to
select.[20]

The attack on Noyes and the implied affront to all the colony's Old Light ministers provoked a torrent of criticism. For
the next decade the Old Light clergy and their political allies

would brand Clap as a power-hungry clerical dictator and struggle to break his hold over the college.[21] In contrast, only a few voices were raised against the infringed privileges of the Anglican students. Yet within six months, the Anglicans were free to attend services at the new mission. This remarkably speedy victory was the handiwork of the president of King's College, Samuel Johnson. Even at King's College, where the Church of England was recognized by the college charter, Johnson informed Clap, the boys were allowed to attend the Sabbath service of their choice. But Samuel Johnson's notions of sectarian education were too liberal for the Puritan Rector. The elder Johnson, never one to yield in the war between the churches, finally brandished his most powerful weapon. The Yale College charter, he warned Clap, rested on a tenuous legal foundation, for it was granted only by the colony of Connecticut, not, as was the usual fashion, by the crown. Should neither Clap nor the General Assembly release the Anglican students to worship freely, Johnson continued, the crown authorities surely would hear of this deplorable condition and render the college charter void. Clap surrendered.[22]

It was a victory for Samuel Johnson and a double victory for his son. Early in the conflict, William Samuel Johnson had acceded to his father's urging and had penned a private admonition to Clap, but when the elder Johnson prodded his son to publish the letter, the cautious attorney refused.[23] William Samuel Johnson undoubtedly worried that his own stand in the dispute would be confused with his father's attacks on the college charter, a fear that Samuel Johnson found incomprehensible and irksome. "Who would think you had so much fire and impetuousity as I have, that should compare your letter to Mr. Clap with mine? You needed not on that account to be cautious," his father argued.[24] Young Johnson's prudent demeanor, which so vexed his hot-tempered and zealous father, soon brought its own rewards. The King's College dispute was quieted in December 1756, when the Assembly awarded the college one-half the lottery fund and assured the Livingston faction that no further public money would be expended for the Anglican school.[25] The Episcopalians at Yale were happily restored in their rights, and William Samuel Johnson had managed to avoid any public notice in either dispute. With his reputation unscathed and his law practice flourishing, he was a certain candidate for public office.

In December 1760, the Stratford inhabitants elected Johnson one of their seven selectmen, in whose hands all the affairs of the community would reside for the ensuing year.[26] This honor was a mere prelude to the momentous event of April 1761, when the Stratford voters bestowed on Johnson the town's highest responsibility. Each April and September, every Connecticut town elected two deputies to the General Assembly, which convened in May and October to make the colony's laws and settle its disputes. Johnson's election reflected his high social and economic standing. A thriving legal practice, gifts of land from his father and father-in-law, and successful investments in shipping and mining and a host of commercial ventures already had made young Johnson a wealthy figure in the community.[27]

The election of an Anglican deputy to the Assembly was not likely to cause a stir. Episcopalians were plentiful in Fairfield County, but even in the western counties, where the Church of England had scant support, towns had been know to elect an Anglican deputy. The time-honored equation between wealth and civil authority was seldom violated, even to slight a prosperous churchman.[28] Stratford voters were remarkably prone to electing Anglican deputies, although the Episcopalians had only a small share of the town's wealth and population. The Stratfordites rotated the Assembly posts among the town's several distinguished personalities, never allowing leadership to rest too long with one man. But with notable frequency at least one, and on rare occasion both, posts went to Anglicans. A curious rivalry was at work. The community was officially divided into five Congregational parishes, some sympathetically New Light and others adamantly antirevival, and the parishes feuded relentlessly. An Old Light from Stratford parish, for example, would cast his vote for an Anglican rather than yield to a New Light from Ripton parish.[29] The pattern held true in May 1761, when Johnson and a Congregationalist, Capt. Samuel Adams, were called to office.

The year 1761 brought family joy as well as political triumph. In his first eleven years of marriage, William Samuel Johnson fathered five daughters, and he longed for a son. In 1757, Ann had given birth to a boy, but he had died almost instantly. Four years later, on October 23, Johnson rejoiced over the birth of a son, Samuel William.[30] It was a happy conclusion to a decade that Johnson would recall with pride. He had won esteem as a lawyer and recognition as a civic leader. Yet his father's memories of that decade were filled with sadness. Despite the victory over Clap, the last ten years had brought a succession of grave disappointments and personal tragedies for Samuel Johnson.

The college at New York languished, contrary to all Rev. Johnson's expectations and efforts. In the first decade, only about five boys graduated each year.[31] Even more disheartening to the aging Episcopal leader were the dismal reports from England on the possibility of an American episcopate. Samuel Johnson's hopes soared in 1748, when Thomas Sherlock succeeded Edmund Gibson as Bishop of London and embarked upon a vigorous campaign for an American episcopate. But after four years, the wearied Sherlock confessed to Johnson that "others who have more power and influence, do not see the thing in the light that we do, and I have but little hopes of succeeding at present."[32] To the King and his ministers, the preservation of political stability took precedence over church matters. British statesmen still perceived that sending a bishop to the colonies would arouse a storm of colonial protest, antagonize English Nonconformists, and provoke a fierce battle between Jacobite and tolerationist churchmen.[33] In 1758, Thomas Secker, Archbishop of Canterbury, warned Samuel Johnson that pressing for an American bishop "at present would certainly prove both fruitless and detrimental. They alone are judges of opportunities, who know the disposition and influences of persons and parties; which cannot always be explained to others."[34]

Secker's veiled references to reasons of state and political pragmatism were painfully difficult for Samuel Johnson to accept, because by 1758 the campaign for an American bishop had become a tragically personal quest. Two years earlier Samuel Johnson's younger son Billy was struck fatally with smallpox as he journeyed home from England after receiving Episcopal orders. An American bishop would have made the pilgrimage to England unnecessary. Even as Billy prepared for the journey in the autumn of 1755, his father had apprehended the perils. "I tremble at the thoughts of the difficulties and danger to which he must be exposed," the elder Johnson had written to William Samuel.[35] The news of Billy's fatal illness, which was carried in the London newspapers, reached New York in September 1756.[36] "There was nothing in the world I was so ambitious of," the Episcopal missionary despaired, "as to have a son of mine employed in the service of God and that venerable Society to whom I have myself been under so many and great obligations."[37] Twice Samuel Johnson's dearest ambition had been denied. After hearing of Billy's death, he reminded his only surviving child: "Dear son, you are now my all."[38] For William Samuel Johnson, it was an uncomfortable psychological burden. Too often the rising young lawyer had been forced to choose between his own amibitions and the demands of his father—at Ripton parish, in the King's College controversy, and during the dispute with Clap. The elder Johnson had never masked his disapproval or denied his disappointment, and again in 1756 he expressed his distress: "Some of our friends seem to fear that the love of this world is gaining too great an ascendant in you . . . we cannot be too much upon our guard against its allurements, especially one that has it so much in his power as those of your profession."[39]

The decade, so successful and full of promise for William Samuel Johnson, held yet another tragedy for his father. Two years after Billy's fatal illness, Charity Johnson died. Samuel Johnson was overcome by loneliness. "Indeed it seems very ridiculous, and I am really ashamed of the thoughts of matrimony at this time of day," he confessed to his son, "but in truth it seems so doleful in old age to be destitute of a contemporary companion."[40] Whatever embarrassments the aged Johnson entertained were soon banished from his mind, and in 1761 he married Sarah Beach, Ann Johnson's mother.

This double union between the Johnsons and the Beaches was strangely portentous, for within the year the two families were wed in battle against the furious forces of the Puritan clergy, who had declared war on the SPG in New England. In 1762, a Connecticut Congregational clergyman, Noah Welles, publicly denounced the SPG's presence in New England as a betrayal of the Society's original purpose. "They supplied the most opulent towns in *New England*, yea and all the *discontented corners* of dissenting parishes with missionaries," Welles charged, "while they left *sundry thousands* in *Carolina* (who had no minister of any sort, and who upon this account applied to the Society) to remain almost wholly destitute of the gospel. Yea they neglected the Indians almost altogether, tho' twas one great design for which they were incorporated by charter, to convert them to Christianity."[41]

The issue Welles raised was not new. The same grievances had been voiced by the Hampshire County ministers in 1734 and by Noah Hobart in the pamphlet war of the 1740s. No one felt the sting of anger more than the Congregational clergy of eastern Massachusetts, where the SPG had boldly opened a mission at Cambridge in 1759, practically on the doorstep of Harvard College.[42] Soon after Welles's accusations came to print, a Boston pastor, Jonathan Mayhew, accused the SPG of a deliberate and diabolical scheme. "The Society," he charged, "have long had a formal design to dissolve and root out all our New England churches; or, in other words, to reduce them all to the episcopal form." What better evidence have we, he asked, than the churchmen's clamor for American bishops and the "superb edifice" at Cambridge, which "it was supposed by many . . . was even from the foundation designed for the *Palace* of one of the *humble successors* of the apostles?"

Will they never let us rest in peace, except where all the weary are at rest? Is it not enough that they persecuted us out of the old world? Will they pursue us into the new to convert us here? compassing sea and land to make us proselytes, while they neglect the heathen and heathenish plantations! What other new world remains as a sanctuary from their oppressions in case of need?[43]

The attacks by Welles and Mayhew provoked a barrage of rebuttals from New England churchmen, including John Beach and Samuel Johnson. British church leaders witnessed the growing clamor with alarm. Archbishop Secker had repeatedly warned the American missionaries to put aside their public appeals for a bishop and trust him to pursue the issue privately, lest they arouse a protest from the "dissenters."[44] Now Secker cautioned Samuel Johnson that the accusations be answered only with "very mild and friendly remonstrances." "Other ways of answering," Secker added, ". . . would do us little good, but perhaps much harm."[45] Secker himself assumed the task of responding to Mayhew's alarming prediction. The Archbishop explained that if ever bishops were sent to America, they would not wield any civil authority, reside in New England, or rely on ecclesiastical taxation for their livelihood. Secker's assurances echoed the restrictive proposals advanced by Gibson forty years earlier and by Sherlock just five years earlier.[46]

Even Mayhew openly praised Secker's "cool temper," "candor," and "excellent sense." But the Boston pastor's mind was not set at ease by the Archbishop's temperate assurances, and he responded with a second warning to his fellow colonists. "In arbitrary reigns and foolish and wicked administrations,"

Mayhew wrote, "the bishops have commonly been the most useful members or instruments, that the crown or court had, in establishing a tyranny over the bodies and souls of men." Granted that the present administration has a wise regard for "the *liberties and privileges* of the subject" and "*a tender concern for the interest and prosperity of his Majesty's American colonies*," he reasoned, "yet may not times alter, and administrations change? Who knows what the next reign or administration may bring. . . . Bishops being once fixed in America, pretexts might easily be found, both for increasing their number and enlarging their power."[47]

To the New Englanders, the threat seemed real. Their apprehensions of ecclesiastical tyranny were based on a century-old understanding of church-state relations, and on memories of the persecuting Archbishop Laud and his conspiratorial partner on the throne, King Charles I. The England of Archbishop Secker and King George III bore little resemblance to the kingdom of Laud and Charles I. The Church of England no longer wielded awesome political power. Even Secker's vision of a restricted American episcopate was unduly optimistic in 1763. In December of that year, Thomas Hollis, a leading English Nonconformist and ardent friend to the New England Congregationalists, assured Mayhew that there was no reason to fear the creation of a colonial episcopate.[48]

Although New Englanders were reacting to an unreal danger, the colonial clamor over the SPG's missionary activities brought very real problems for Rev. Johnson and his lawyer son. To the elder Johnson came the discouraging news that the Society would not appoint any more missions in New England and New York. We must avoid all appearances, Secker wrote, "of making it our business to episcopize New England, as Dr. Mayhew expresses himself."[49] Most disturbing to William Samuel Johnson were the New England pamphleteers' direct attacks on Anglican politicians. Mayhew preached that "it would be little short of infatuation" for Congregationalists to vote for a churchman. "This would be to put a sword into the hand of their enemies." Connecticut's Noah Welles accused the colony's Anglicans of plotting to "overthrow" the Congregational establishment. "And as this cannot be better done than by getting into their general assemblies," Welles warned, "hence it is that they are all firmly united in voting for some popular churchmen for assemblymen."[50] Welles's accusation enraged the usually

cool-tempered Stratford lawyer. Johnson immediately enlisted
John Beach to prepare a rebuttal. "I will not conceal from you,"
he wrote to Beach,

that I have been solicitous that you should undertake an answer to the
vile, ill-natured pamphlet which has been lately published. . . . I am
not indeed proud of these kinds of controversies. . . . I do not wish any-
body to answer this fool according to his folly. . . . But a principal
object I apprehend should be . . . to show the fatal tendency of writings
of this kind to inflame party, create and maintain animosities, bitterness and ill-nature amongst mankind and render them devoid not
only of all Christian but even of all human and social virtues.[51]

Despite Johnson's alarm, the angry attacks on Anglicans
in politics presented no immediate peril to his advancement.
Stratford continued to elect an Anglican to one of the town's
two Assembly seats in each election,[52] and Johnson himself
had pinpointed the reason in his letter to John Beach:

How ridiculous then is it to talk of churchmen's aspiring to power. . . .
Let them compare us with the other sects, the New Light, Separatists,
Anabaptists, how much do they out do us in pursuing and acquiring
public influence. The N.L. within my short memory were a small
party, merely a religious one . . . and in this short period of their con-
tinual struggles they have acquired such an influence as to be nearly
the ruling part of the government owing to their superior attention
to civil affairs and close union among themselves in politics.[53]

In fact, the political struggle between the Old Lights and
the New Lights had kept the colony in near chaos for the last
decade. Much of the turmoil stemmed from Clap's maneuvers
against New Haven's Old Light preacher, Joseph Noyes, in
1753. Two years later, the colony's boldest antirevivalists unleashed a torrent of criticism against Clap and persuaded the
Assembly to revoke its annual financial subsidy for the college.[54]
The Old Light triumph of 1755 did not end the feud. In 1759
the New Lights of New Haven tried without success to withhold their share of the parish's ecclesiastical taxes from Noyes.[55]
In nearby Wallingford, the New Lights also took an aggressive
stand. There the conservative majority had chosen to settle and
ordain an Old Light pastor. But the revivalists protested and
urged the clergy's county association, which was predominantly
New Light, to intervene and prevent the ordination. The Wallingford dispute came before the General Assembly in May.

The New Lights were confident of victory. Their numbers dominated the lower house of the legislature, and already they had
managed to overturn many of the antirevival laws, including
the ban on itinerant preaching. But when the case was heard,
numbers gave way to the conservative authority of Governor
Fitch and his twelve-member Council, who vetoed the New
Lights' petition at the October session.[56]

To William Samuel Johnson, the dispute hardly deserved
to be called "religion." At bottom, he judged, it was "a Question
of Power which is ever eagerly pursued by ambitious Men."
Long aloof from the doctrinal issues that pitted pietists against
Old Lights, he deemed the controversy "not of that Importance
which the Zeal of Parties would put upon it." Johnson felt
special disdain for the Wallingford New Lights who, he believed, grasped unfairly for consociation power to suppress
the town's Old Light majority.[57] Yet when the issue came before
the Assembly that October, Johnson found himself attorney for
the New Light party, just as he had argued for the Clap faction
against Rev. Noyes in New Haven's Superior Court. "I, a poor
hackney lawyer for bread," he explained to his friend Jared
Ingersoll, "am compelled to espouse the cause of parties whose
spirit I cannot enter into. . . . In all these affairs," he added, "I endeavor to follow our friend Pope's advice, to retain native moderation and only go as the storm drives."[58]

The New Lights' defeat provoked a flurry of political activ-
ity. Rumors abounded that the revivalists were plotting to oust
Governor Fitch and his Old Light councillors in the general
election. The anticipated coup came to nothing, but many men
in Connecticut lamented the demise of political order and social
harmony.[59] The storm did not abate after the rumored political
plot of 1759. Talk circulated wildly of Clap's secret involvement in the New Lights' political maneuvers, and consequently
the clamor against his leadership of Yale College grew louder
and louder. Finally, in 1763, the very year in which Mayhew was
sounding his anti-Episcopal alarm, the demands for an investi-
gation of Clap's leadership were too strong to be ignored, and
the Assembly agreed to hear a complaint against the rector. On
this occasion the Old Lights enlisted the aid of William Samuel
Johnson and Jared Ingersoll, who presented the case for a formal
inquiry into the college situation.[60] Ingersoll, who was a member of Noyes's Old Light congregation, had been in England
during the 1759 contest, but in 1763 he made himself a conspic-

uous partisan for the Old Light cause.[61] Johnson's demeanor was again aloof. This time the Assembly's New Light majority prevailed, and the two lawyers lost the case.

In 1763 the battle between Old Lights and New Lights overshadowed all concern over Anglican intrigues. One Pennsylvania man told his Connecticut friend, "I am heartily grieved for the contention & divisions that are like to prevail in Connecticut; I highly esteem that church & people, & had almost determin'd to make it the retreat of my old age; but am vexed that they bite & devour one another. Nothing can be more fatal to their piety, morals, or liberty; they will be swallowed by the Episcopal church, who envy their prosperity & will avail themselves of these divisions."[62] But before two years had passed, the Anglican peril would excite great fear in the hearts of Connecticut men. Mayhew had warned that although the "present administration" has "*a tender concern for the interest and prosperity of his Majesty's American colonies* . . . who knows what the next reign or administration may bring?" In 1764, the colonists learned that the King's new chief minister, George Grenville, was plotting a dangerous subversion of American rights, taxation without representation. What else could be intended but ecclesiastical oppression as well? Had not Mayhew observed that "in arbitrary reigns and foolish and wicked administrations, the bishops have commonly been the most useful members or instruments, that the crown or court had, in establishing a tryanny over the bodies and souls of men."[63] For years William Samuel Johnson had prudently avoided any public prominence in the Episcopal cause. The events of the coming year would measure the worth of Johnson's cautious demeanor. Could the ambitious Connecticut politician safely escape the anti-Episcopal rancor of his patriot countrymen?

William Samuel Johnson, by Thomas McIlworth (Ca. 1761)
Courtesy Hirschl and Adler Galleries

Rise to Prominence

On March 9, 1764, George Grenville presented his American revenue program to the House of Commons. Colonial taxation was Grenville's remedy to pay the enormous debt that confronted Great Britain after the French and Indian War and to meet the heavy cost of defending the North American territory acquired during that war. After the Peace of Paris in 1763, the British Empire included a vast expanse of western American land that was in constant peril from Indian uprising and repossession by the French. A steady supply of British troops was necessary to defend the American frontier, and Grenville resolved that the colonists would share the military expense.[1]

Most of Grenville's nineteen proposals were designed to enforce strictly the existing laws that regulated American commerce and to expand the list of foreign goods on which the colonists would pay import duties. The duty on foreign molasses, first imposed in 1733 and about to expire, would be extended. New duties would be laid on foreign-produced indigo, European fabrics, coffee, and a host of other goods that the provinces imported from outside the empire. Several proposals aimed to curb the colonists' widespread and flagrant violation of the trade laws. All ships were to be bonded and carry cargo certificates. Colonial offenders, who had previously sought their hearings in the common law courts, where a jury of their peers was likely to vote for acquittal, would henceforth be tried at the new Court of Vice Admiralty at Halifax, where a single judge presided. Finally Grenville resolved that "toward further defraying the said Expenses, it may be proper to charge certain Stamp Duties in the said Colonies and Plantations."[2]

Events moved rapidly. After two weeks, the House of Commons overwhelmingly approved Grenville's program. The so-called Sugar Act was drafted, approved by the House of Lords and the House of Commons, and on April 15 it received the King's signature. The Sugar Act renewed the tax on molasses, expanded the list of dutied foreign goods, and instituted the enforcement measures Grenville had proposed.[3] Only the stamp tax, which the Commons had also endorsed, awaited enactment.

The dreadful news of the burdensome duties reached Connecticut early in May, and the colony's General Assembly reacted without delay. The Assembly appointed a committee, headed by Governor Fitch, to draft arguments against the Sugar Act and the proposed stamp tax. Jared Ingersoll, the best constitutional lawyer in Connecticut, was invited to assist the committee.[4] No one doubted what the committee's response to the Sugar Act would be. Johnson, who observed the Assembly session, warned that the new duties would destroy the province's livelihood in trade.[5] Even more certain was that the committee would challenge the constitutionality of a stamp tax, for the colonists sent no representatives to Parliament, and taxation without representation was an unprecedented and, in American eyes, unjustifiable extension of Parliament's authority. To Thomas Whately, Joint Secretary of the Treasury and the man responsible for drafting the Stamp Act, Ingersoll sent a warning that parliamentary taxation "would go down with ye people like Chopt hay." He told Whately, "the people think if the precedent is once established, Larger Sums may be Exacted and that at a time when the Same shall be less needed, & that in short you will have it in your power to keep us just as poor as you please."[6]

Connecticut's case against the Sugar Act and the stamp proposal was read and approved at the Assembly's October session. The pamphlet, penned by Fitch, deplored the new duties as an intolerable weight on the colony's depressed economy. Connecticut dared not question the legality of the import duties. Although the express purpose of the Sugar Act was to raise a revenue in the colonies, laying duties had long been considered a necessary tool for regulating the trade of the empire. The argument's main thrust was that the proposed stamp tax "or other internal taxes [imposed] on the Colonies in America, by parliamentary Authority, will be an Infringement of . . . Rights and Privileges and deprive the Colonists of their Freedom and Inheritance." The Assembly instructed the Governor to prepare "an humble and earnest Address to the Parliament of Great Britain . . . against said bill for a stamp duty or any other bill for

an internal tax on this Colony" and authorized Ingersoll to assist
Connecticut's regular agent, Richard Jackson, in presenting the
colony's arguments before Parliament.[7]

The other colonies were also quick to act. Conspicuously
present in all their petitions to Parliament and in the flurry
of pamphlets and broadsides that appeared that winter were
professions of humility, obedience, and affection for British
authority. Connecticut's official instructions to Jackson conceded
that if Parliament "in their Superior Wisdom Shall Judge it
Expedient to and do pass an Act for laying those Burdens upon us
we must Submit. We never pretend in the least to Question
whether Acts of Parliament . . . are binding but always Submit to
them as binding."[8] Governor Stephen Hopkins, popular leader of
the Rhode Island Assembly, admitted that if Parliament enacted
the unjust stamp tax, it would be the colonists' "indispensable
duty cheerfully to obey and patiently to submit thereto."[9] The
Massachusetts House of Representatives adopted as its semi-
official statement the pamphlet of James Otis, who argued that as
soon as Parliament recognized the injustice of its ways, it would
renounce the odious tax. Otis counseled patience and peaceful
petitions.[10] No one advocated outright resistance.

America's confidence in the benign intentions of Parliament
and the effectiveness of its own petitions proved unrealistic. On
February 2, 1765, Ingersoll, Jackson, and the agents for South
Carolina and Pennsylvania met privately with Grenville, but
their arguments against American taxation failed to move the
British minister.[11] Five days later, Grenville appeared before the
House of Commons with fifty resolutions to lay a colonial stamp
tax on a vast array of items from newspapers and pamphlets to
legal documents, mortgages, almanacs, playing cards, tavern
licenses, and advertisements. Ingersoll wrote despairingly to
Governor Fitch that Parliament refused to hear colonial arguments against taxation without representation. "The Point of
Authority of Parliament to impose such a Tax I found on my
arrival here was so fully and Universally yielded that there was not
the least hopes of making any impression that way. . . . the House
would not suffer to be brought in, nor would any one Member
Undertake to Offer to the House, any Petition from the Colonies
that held forth the Contrary of that Doctrine." Ingersoll's report
was brutally accurate. The petitions from Connecticut, Virginia,
and South Carolina were rejected without a hearing, and no

Member even dared offer the remonstrances from Massachusetts and New York. On March 22, the Stamp Act became law, and was scheduled to go into effect on November 1.[12]

Ingersoll felt helpless. "No man sees in a stronger light than I do the dangerous tendency of admitting for a principle that the Parliament of Great Britain may tax us ad libitum. I view it as a gulph ready to devour but when I look all around I am at a loss for a plan." He was resigned to accepting Grenville's assurances and passing them on to his countrymen. "Let us then, instead of predicting the worst," Grenville had urged, "hope that Mutual Interest as well as duty will keep us on both Sides within the bounds of Justice. We trust we shall never intentionally burden you unreasonably: if at any time we shall happen to do it by Mistake, Let us know it & I trust it will be remedied."[13] In fact, all the colonial agents saw the futility of further argument, and acceded to testing the good faith of the Grenville administration. Three Americans in London, George Meserve of New Hampshire, George Mercer of Virginia, and Jared Ingersoll, willingly accepted posts as stamp distributors in their colonies. Benjamin Franklin, who urged Ingersoll to take the Connecticut appointment, nominated his confidant and political colleague John Hughes for the Pennsylvania spot. "The offer," Ingersoll explained, "was made generally to those who had appeared as the Agents or friends of the colonies to take it themselves or nominate their friends, & none of them all refused that I know of. . . ."[14] But the colonists' spokesmen in London grossly miscalculated how their countrymen would receive the news of the Stamp Act. The error was politically fatal for Ingersoll, nearly so for his friend William Samuel Johnson.

Word of the Stamp Act reached America early in May, two months before Ingersoll's ship touched shore. Americans everywhere condemned the act unequivocally. "This single stroke has lost Great Britain the Affection of all her Colonies," the Triumvirate penman William Smith declared.[15] Despite universal indignation, there was no talk of open resistance that spring. In fact, a host of eminent Connecticut men, among them William Samuel Johnson, wrote to Ingersoll volunteering to assist in the distribution of stamps for their own towns. "Since we are doomed to Stamps and Slavery & must submit," Johnson assured Ingersoll in June, "we hear with pleasure that your gentle hand will fit on our Chains and Shackles who I know will make them as easie as possible. . . . If you propose to have a Subaltern in every town, I shall be at your service for Stratford if it be agreeable."[16] But hostility toward the stamp tax and stamp distributors quickly mounted. By late summer angry words were giving way to violent deeds. Ingersoll's very life was in peril, and even his volunteer assistants would be lucky to escape the colonists' wrath.

On August 9, a hateful attack on Ingersoll appeared in the *Connecticut Gazette*. Ingersoll's assailant charged "that same rapacious and base spirit which prompted you to undertake the ignominious task will urge you on to every Cruel and oppressive Measure."[17] Five days later, an angry mob of Boston patriots strung up an effigy of stamp distributor Andrew Oliver, and burned and buried the image in mock execution. On the right arm of the flaming effigy were appended these lines: "What greater joy did ever New England see / than a stampman hanging on a tree." To add to their joy, the mob swept down on Oliver's home, which they plundered and left in shambles.[18] The terrified stampmaster resigned the next morning. Ingersoll's would-be assistants grew apprehensive. Nathaniel Wales, who had offered to distribute stamps for Windham, penned his resignation on August 19.[19] The other volunteers, including Johnson, let silence speak for their change of heart. On August 21 and 22, Ingersoll's effigy was hanged from the gallows at Norwich and burned upon a bonfire at New London. The crowds cried, "There Hangs a Traitor, There's an Enemy of His Country." The ceremony was repeated at Windham, Lebanon, Lyme, and West Haven.[20]

Violence, or the mere threat of violence, forced the resignations of the stamp distributors in nearly every colony.[21] Yet Ingersoll held fast to his post until the Connecticut Assembly could meet and decide whether or not to enforce the Stamp Act. The Assembly was scheduled to convene on September 19 for an emergency session. In June, the Massachusetts House of Representatives had urged every colonial legislature to select delegates for a convention to be held in October at New York. There a united colonial response to the Stamp Act would be devised. Johnson and his fellow lawmakers hurried to Hartford in September to consider the Massachusetts proposal and select delegates to the Stamp Act Congress. But Connecticut's most aggressive patriots would not let the stampmaster's fate rest with the Assembly. A band of men in military array captured Ingersoll as he travelled to Hartford and compelled him to resign.[22] The Connecticut Assembly's first order of business was to repudiate the terroristic methods of the mob. Fitch issued a proclamation calling upon all civil and military officers to suppress such unlawful proceedings. Next, the legislators endorsed the Massachusetts proposal for a Stamp Act Congress, and appointed Eliphalet Dyer, William Samuel Johnson, and David Rowland to the Connecticut delegation.[23] For Johnson and Rowland, it was a narrow escape to victory. Both men had volunteered to assist Ingersoll in the odious task of enforcing the Stamp Act, but their offers had gone unnoticed.[24] Johnson's appointment to the Stamp Act Congress would elevate him rapidly to prominence among Connecticut's patriots.

Johnson, Dyer, and Rowland hastened to New York for the opening of the Congress on Monday, October 7. There delegates from nine colonies were assembled. The first day they chose a chairman, examined one another's credentials, and established a voting procedure, giving each delegation one voice in the crucial issues to be decided. On Tuesday, deliberation began on "the rights and privileges of the British American colonists," a question that would occupy the Congress for the next eleven days. A few delegates, notably the chairman, Timothy Ruggles, wanted to discuss only the stamp tax's grievous effects on the colonial economy, but the majority was determined to argue the constitutionality of taxation without representation.[25] The Massachusetts delegation was bound by the instructions of its legislature: "If it should be said, that we are in any manner represented in Parliament, you must by no means concede to it."[26] The instructions to the Connecticut delegates were less explicit. Yet Johnson was convinced that parliamentary taxation and trial without jury signalled the first steps in a deliberate malevolent plot by the British government to destroy American liberty. He apprehended that "the Ministry have had a formed design . . . to reduce the Colonies to the State & Condition of the Roman Provinces in the Times of the Caesars, to bring them immediately under the Government of the King & his Council & eventually that the will of the Prince sho'd be their Law." Johnson's mind fixed upon "the late Acts divesting us the Privilege of taxing ourselves & the trial by our Peers, which must Soon have us in the Situation they seem to wish us in, of absolute Slaves." Fortunately, he told Christopher Gadsden of the South Carolina delegation,

they have of late precipitated their measures, and by that means opened our Eyes. Had they proceeded by slow and insensible degrees . . . perhaps in a couple of years they might have effected their baneful purpose. But by pressing it too much and making more haste than good speed they have defeated the whole design and given such an Alarm as will forever keep America upon her guard.[27]

The Connecticut delegates knew well that their constituents would insist upon a full statement of American rights. The colony's newspapers were filled with warnings that should the power to tax and to judge without jury be admitted once, no liberty or property would be safe in the future.[28]

On October 19, after twelve days of intense and unrelenting debate, the Congress agreed to fourteen resolutions setting forth "the most essential rights and liberties of the colonists" as Englishmen and "the grievances under which they labor by reason of several late acts of parliament." The Congress resolved that among the invaluable and "undoubted rights of Englishmen" were trial by jury and taxation only by consent. The Stamp Act, "by imposing taxes on the inhabitants of these colonies, and the said act, and several other acts, by extending the jurisdiction of the courts of vice admiralty beyond the ancient limits, have a manifest tendency to subvert the rights and liberties of the colonists."[29]

The resolutions began with a declaration that "his majesty's subjects in these colonies, owe the same allegiance to the crown of Great Britain, that is owing from his subjects born within the realm, and all due subordination to that august body, the parliament of Great Britain."[30] The statement was vague, and contrasted starkly to the confident and precise statements against parliamentary taxation and admiralty trials. The Congress was groping for a distinction between those parliamentary powers that were necessary to secure the dependence of the colonies and the general welfare of the empire and those parliamentary actions that encroached unnecessarily upon American freedom. It was, admitted the weary Delaware delegate, "one of the most difficult tasks I ever yet saw undertaken, as we had carefully to avoid any infringement of the prerogative of the crown and the power of parliament—and yet in duty bound to fully assert the rights and privileges of the colonies."[31] The crux of the problem was the Sugar Act.[32]

The intent of the Sugar Act was plain, "that a revenue be raised," the preamble read.[33] But the import duties could also be justified as a regulation of trade, and virtually no one in America questioned Parliament's authority to regulate the commerce of the empire. How could the authority of Parliament be recognized without inviting higher and higher levies on the goods that the colonists consumed? In 1764, most Americans had ignored the dilemma. Their fears had focused on the unprecedented proposal for a stamp tax. When the colonial assemblies hurriedly convened that year to protest the Sugar Act and the impending Stamp Act, only New York and North Carolina had challenged the constitutionality of the new import duties as revenue measures, arguing that "all Impositions, whether they be internal Taxes, or Duties paid, for what we consume" equally impoverish a people. The other colonies, including Connecticut, had merely complained against the duties as onerous, albeit legitimate, commercial regulations.[34] But by 1765, the dilemma could no longer be ignored. Parliament's refusal to hear American arguments against the proposed Stamp Act or to offer relief from the burdensome import duties made the threat of ever-increasing British taxation seem suddenly and perilously real. No wonder the delegates at the Congress settled on the nebulous phrase "due subordination." An outright acknowledgement of Parliament's sovereignty in matters of trade threatened to reduce the colonies to poverty.

   Johnson was dissatisfied with the indeterminate wording of the resolves. He had worked long and hard on his own eleven-page statement of colonial rights: "Although the due subordination of the Colonies to the Crown and Parliament . . . are what every Intelligent American [wishes]," Johnson wrote, . . .

Yet it is most humbly conceived that this subordination and dependency is sufficiently secured . . . by the general superintending power and authority of the whole Empire indisputably lodged in that August Body the Parliament of Great Britain which Authority is clearly admitted here so far as in our Circumstances is Consistent with the Enjoyment of our Essential Rights as Freemen and British Subjects, and we further humbly Conceive that by the Constitution it is no further admissible in Great Britain itself. Is is also submitted whether there is not a vast difference between the Exercise of Parliamentary Jurisdiction in general Acts for the Amendment of the Common Law, or even in general Regulations of Trade and Commerce for the Empire and the Actual Exercise of that Jurisdiction in levying External and Internal Duties and Taxes on the Colonists while they neither are nor can be represented in Parliament. The former may well consist with a reasonable Measure of Civil Liberty in the Colonies but we must beg leave to say that how the latter is consistent with any degree of Freedom we are wholly at a loss to Comprehend.[35]

Johnson's draft openly acknowledged Parliament's authority to govern colonial commerce, but it also explicitly denied that such authority included the power to tax. Why a majority at the Congress preferred to borrow only the phrase "due subordination" from Johnson's draft is open to conjecture. The Congress's resolves contained no outright denial of Parliament's authority to impose "external" taxes on trade, and for that reason, no explicit recognition of the powers that remained to Parliament. Although the resolves stated that "all supplies to the crown" were "free gifts of the people," only the Stamp Act and the extension of the Vice Admiralty jurisdiction were singled out as having "a manifest tendency to subvert the rights and liberties of the colonists." Regarding the new import duties, the Congress resolved that the duties "will be extremely burthensome and grievous, and from the scarcity of specie, the payment of them absolutely impracticable." The newness and difficulty of the task, it seems, impeded a precise and confident statement of the limits to parliamentary power.[36]

William Livingston's recollection of the debate lends a clue to the Congress's hesitancy. Livingston, one of the New York delegation, recalled:

What gave us most trouble was whether we should insist on a Repeal of all acts laying Duties on Trade as well as the Stamp Act all agreed that we ought to obey all acts of trade and that they should regulate our Trade but many were not for making an explicite declaration of an acknowledgement of such a Power. I thought and many with me that if we did not do it there was not the least hope of success, for except Britain could regulate our Trade her colonies would be of no more use to her than to France or any other power, and that it is impossible to suppose that she would ever give up the point of internal taxes except the other were fully secured and acknowledged.[37]

Livingston apparently regarded the taxation and regulation of trade as one, inseparable power, and he was willing to concede that power to Parliament in order to win "the point of internal taxes." But a majority of the Congress, including William Samuel Johnson, were unwilling. Johnson, however, probably shared Livingston's concern that unless the Americans offered an explicit acknowledgement of Parliament's authority to regulate

trade, their petitions would be rejected in England without a
hearing. To Johnson, the phrase "due subordination" was
inadequate. He confessed to the New Jersey delegate, Robert
Ogden, that he wished "the Congress had adopted the other Plan
[his own] of admitting the general superintendence of Parliament
& limiting their Power by the Principles & Spirit of the
Constitution . . ." The plan, explained Johnson, "sufficiently
excludes all Constitutional Right to tax us, & effectually Secures
the fundamental privilege of trial by jury as well as every other
Right Essential to British Liberty." Johnson's Connecticut
colleague Eliphalet Dyer was also uneasy with the wording of the
resolves, but both men believed "union so necessary disunion
so fatal" that they lent their full support to the Congress's
declarations.[38]

The delegates completed their work with greater confidence
and dispatch once the resolves were approved. On Saturday,
October 19, committees were formed to draft petitions to George
III and the two houses of Parliament. By Wednesday, all three
petitions were ready, and they displayed a precision and
assertiveness that were lacking in the Congress's earlier efforts.
The long and tiresome debate had not been in vain. Although the
delegates once again began by offering "all due subordination to
the parliament of Great Britain," they also

humbly submitted whether there not be a material distinction, in
reason and sound policy at least, between the necessary exercise of
parliamentary jurisdiction in general acts, and the common law, and the
regulations of trade and commerce, through the whole empire, and the
exercise of that jurisdiction by imposing taxes on the colonies.[39]

The statement echoed Johnson's draft and openly questioned the
justice of taxes on trade as well as on other property. To Johnson's
disappointment, the Congress had not discarded the phrase "due
subordination" for a fuller acknowledgement of the powers that
remained to Parliament, an omission that would be repeated
many times in the coming decade and exacerbate Anglo-
American misunderstandings.[40] But the Congress had succeeded
in framing a clear statement of the American position: that "acts
of parliament imposing duties and taxes on these colonies"
violate "those invaluable rights and liberties" belonging to all
Englishmen.[41]

Only six of the delegations affixed their names to the finished
documents. The representatives from Connecticut, New York,

and Maryland were bound to consult their assemblies before ratifying the work of the Congress.[42] The most timid spirits at the Congress were troubled that they might be "engaged in a traitorous conspiracy." The chairman, Timothy Ruggles, and the New Jersey delegate, Robert Ogden, although authorized to ratify the proceedings, refused to sign.[43] But the same quest for unanimity that shaped the Congress's deliberations greeted the delegates upon their return home. Ogden was branded as a traitor and hanged in effigy up and down New Jersey.[44] Johnson, Rowland, and Dyer hastened to New Haven, where the General Assembly immediately approved the Congress's work and authorized the delegates to sign. The Connecticut legislators commanded their agent in London, Richard Jackson, "to prefer those petitions and support them with your utmost influence, skill, and ability, and leave no probable means unattended" to secure repeal of the odious acts.[45] On the Congress's petitions rested Johnson's hopes for a peaceful settlement with the mother country. "May God give us success in this most important affair," he prayed. "I am Convinced our People will never submit to these fatal acts, but rather Sacrifice their lives in resistance to them. Sho'd the Ministry therefore be so infatuated as to insist upon them . . . I see nothing but ruin, destruction, & desolation before us."[46]

Connecticut patriots were quick to reward Johnson's conspicuous opposition to the Stamp Act. Every autumn, when Connecticut voters elected deputies to the General Assembly, they also cast their nominations for the Governor's Council, which was elected each spring from among the leading twenty names. In the fall of 1765, Johnson's name appeared among the twenty,[47] an unusual honor for one who had served only three terms in the Assembly.

Rumors abounded that Johnson would even be chosen to replace Connecticut's agent, Richard Jackson, whose timid defense of colonial rights was eyed suspiciously by his constituents.[48] Jackson was convinced that Parliament would never yield the power to tax its American provinces. He called the colonists' doctrine of no taxation without representation "chimerical" and outspokenly insisted that Connecticut submit to the Stamp Act until repeal was won by more prudent arguments.[49] After much consideration, the Assembly decided merely to warn Jackson in the strongest language that "we can by no means be content that you should give up the matter of right."

The "Right of the Colonists to tax themselves, & the Privilege of Trial by Jury" must be insisted upon "as what we can never recede from."[50] Johnson's mission to England was averted, but only temporarily.

The Stamp Act crises elevated new men to political prominence in Connecticut, but it also occasioned the sudden political demise of figures long esteemed in the province. Fervent patriots made frantic appeals in the press and from the pulpit that only the most ardent anti-stamp men be elected to high office.[51] Of the 132 delegates who sat in the May session of the Assembly, nearly half were turned out in the autumn election of 1765,[52] a disquieting event in a colony that so revered its magistrates. And this was a mere prelude to the political tumult that would erupt on November 1 and climax in the spring election of 1766.

Connecticut patriots warred bitterly among themselves over how to thwart the odious stamp taxes. Men of cautious demeanor counselled patience until Parliament could redress America's grievances, but bolder men were ready to nullify the Stamp Act by illegal means. Parliament commanded that the act be enforced beginning November 1, and that every colonial governor take an oath, before that date, to uphold it. Governor Fitch worried that to refuse would endanger the Connecticut charter, an easy prey for an angry Parliament. Fitch knew that enforcing the act was impossible. No man dared perform the duties of stampmaster, and the stamps were being kept under tight military guard at New York. Swearing the oath, Fitch reasoned, would safeguard the colony without actually submitting to parliamentary taxation. On October 31, he assembled the Council to witness the ceremony, but only four assistants lent their approval. A majority of the Council walked out in protest.[53] More than one Connecticut man knew that taking the oath spelled "political death" for the Governor and his four faithful assistants. At Hartford, an angry multitude ceremoniously buried a copy of the Stamp Act and with it an effigy of the Governor.[54]

After November 1, the advocates of resistance, who claimed the name Sons of Liberty, carried on their noisy campaign against submission to the Stamp Act. Throughout the eastern half of the colony, they called public meetings to stir up popular resistance, while local magistrates looked on helplessly or joined the proceedings.[55] At the General Assembly's October session, the colony's lawmakers had voted that no business requiring stamps should be transacted after November 1. The lawmakers were intent on respecting the laws of Parliament without relenting to the Stamp Act. Such quiescence enraged the liberty men. They angrily warned the lawmakers against "inculcat[ing] the Doctrine of passive Obedience, or any other Doctrine tending to quiet the Minds of the People, into a tame Submission to any unjust Propositions."[56] On December 14, the radical patriots forced the port collector, Duncan Stewart, to clear ships from New London without the required stamps. Before long, the courts in eastern Connecticut had opened to conduct civil proceedings without the necessary stamps. Judges and lawyers in other parts of the colony stayed home, afraid to violate a law of Parliament.[57] William Samuel Johnson was troubled with indecision. Whether the courts should open, he could not answer. "The times are in every Sense difficult," he reflected, and require "an uncommon degree of wisdom." From Massachusetts came a sobering message penned by James Otis, who had sat with Johnson at the Congress. "T'is much to be feared," Otis wrote, that "the Parliament will charge the colonies with presenting a petition in one hand and a dagger in the other." Johnson too worried that the entire American cause might be branded "notorious and seditious." Patience and circumspection must not be abandoned, he warned Eliphalet Dyer, one of the assistants who had walked out on Fitch. It was rumored that Dyer inspired the eastern agitators from behind the scenes. "While the meetings of the People are regular, decent & modest," Johnson told Dyer, ". . . . they may be of some help."[58]

By spring 1766, the turbulence and unlawful proceedings had spread to the west, and everywhere men suspected of faint-heartedness to the cause were hanged in effigy and tarred and feathered.[59] The inquisition had begun. Ingersoll, who was fated for another ordeal at the hands of the vigilantes, despaired that "all the Springs of Government are broken, and nothing but Anarchy and Confusion appear in prospect."[60] These words were more than the bitter lamentations of a political outcast. Respected citizens, men of unbendable Whig convictions, feared that the illegal and terroristic tactics of the liberty men encouraged "lax notions of civil authority" among the people and invited harsh reprisals against the Connecticut charter.[61]

Many stalwart patriots resented the inquisitorial tactics of the Sons of Liberty. "A fine country of Liberty we live in," exclaimed Joseph Chew, who vehemently opposed the stamp tax. "I am now become the attention of the Sons of Liberty," he told Ingersoll, "for that I Carry on a very traterous & wicked Correspondance with you."[62] Even Connecticut's spokesman at the Stamp Act Congress, William Samuel Johnson, was assailed for consorting with Ingersoll. In early November, Ingersoll had written to Thomas Whately, urging that at least the most burdensome stamp taxes be repealed. The ex-stampmaster's continued correspondence with British statesmen provoked anger and suspicion. A committee of liberty men visited Ingersoll, demanded the letters, and published them in a distorted form in the *New London Gazette*. Ingersoll was accused of writing "home to England to Encourage the Continuation of ye Stamp Act with some few Alterations . . . & [of stating] that if there was an Omission on these points the Act might go down with the people." Johnson knew that the accusations against his friend were false, but when he took "some pains to set the affair in its true light," he too was accused of consorting with the enemy. Johnson immediately resolved to intervene no further. "Such are the delicacy of the times," the ambitious young lawyer reflected, "that no man can expect to escape Censure, the first point is not to have deserved it, & the next to Conduct with the best Prudence we can after the Event. . . ."[63]

In 1765 hardly anyone seriously contemplated a revolt against the mother country, but the leaders of violent resistance were working toward another kind of revolution—against the colony's conservative lawmakers. It was no coincidence that the most aggressive spokesmen for resistance hailed from the counties eastward of the Connecticut River, or that the liberty men were so unmerciful to Fitch and Ingersoll. The colony's eastern politicans had two long-standing scores to settle with their political rivals from the west. One dispute was over religion. The easterners had welcomed the Great Awakening warmly, and they had not forgotten the oppressive antirevival laws enacted by the colony's Old Light western politicians. Just months before the Stamp Act crisis, Fitch had issued a pamphlet criticizing New Light church government.[64] Fitch's decision to swear the stamp oath made him an easy target for the New Lights' wrath. The easterners had another grievance against the western lawmakers, the refusal of Fitch, Ingersoll, and other cautious men to sanction a dangerous land scheme called Susquehannah.

Throughout the eighteenth century, Connecticut's population had grown rapidly, and land shortage, especially to the east of the Connecticut River, became a vexing problem.[65] In 1753,

easterners from Windham County devised a daring solution to the
shortage. They claimed that Connecticut's territory did not stop
at the New York border, but extended westward all the way to the
Pacific, from "sea-to-sea," as stated in the original Connecticut
charter. Their claim ignored the territorial rights of New York
and Pennsylvania. The claimants established the Susquehannah
Company, and laid plans to erect settlements along the Susquehannah River in Pennsylvania's Wyoming Valley. First they
would purchase titles to the land from the Iroquois Indians
who resided there. No measures were considered to compensate or
negotiate with the Pennsylvania government.[66] The plan was
quickly put into action. In 1754 the company in a roundabout
way enlisted the aid of an Indian trader of disreputable character,
John Henry Lydius, to negotiate a land purchase from the
Iroquois. Lydius produced a document of dubious legal standing,
especially when compared with the properly negotiated treaty
between Pennsylvania and the Indians. Next the company
resolved to obtain a formal recognition of the sea-to-sea claim
from the crown.[67]

In ordinary times, the company's claim would have seemed
ridiculous, for Connecticut had never challenged the crown's
grants to the colony of New York and to the Penn family as the
proprietors of Pennsylvania. The eastern men were raising the
sea-to-sea claim after nearly a century of acquiescence in the
territorial boundaries of these two colonies.[68] But during the
economic tensions of the 1750s, Connecticut men were eager to
believe the company's arguments and join the venture. The
number of stockholders soared.[69] By 1762, however, many men
began to see the folly and dangers of the scheme. That year, Fitch
publicly exhorted the company to abandon its plans. Fitch knew
that the Penn family was appealing to the crown to obstruct the
Susquehannah invasion, and he feared that the "wild scheme"
would bring royal disfavor on Connecticut and even endanger its
ancient charter. He also warned against hostile reprisals from the
Iroquois and the Pennsylvanians.[70] The General Assembly too
urged caution, and exculpated the colony from any official
involvement in the venture.[71] Ingersoll also spoke out against the
company's plan. Four years earlier, the Susquehannah leaders
had engaged Ingersoll to defend the sea-to-sea claim before the
crown, but Ingersoll returned from England convinced that the
plan could not succeed. He was well acquainted with the Penn
family's powerful connections in England, and he undoubtedly

knew that the British government was more concerned with
maintaining peaceful Indian relations in Pennsylvania than with
gratifying the Susquehannah adventurers.[72]

The company's aggressive promoters refused to heed Fitch,
Ingersoll, or the Assembly. Defiantly, they voted to double the size
of their Pennsylvania expedition.[73] A year later, in 1763, Fitch
received orders from the crown that the Connecticut settlers were
to abandon the Pennsylvania lands, and that the two colonial
governments were to resolve the dispute peacefully.[74] The company was loath to comply, and before long the dire predictions
of the British government and Connecticut's conservatives were
realized. In October, the angry Indians massacred the invaders
and wiped out the Susquehannah settlement.[75] Yet the Susquehannah issue was not dead. Eliphalet Dyer, who had promoted
the venture from its inception, stepped up his efforts to win
the crown's approval.[76] Meanwhile, although the settlers halted
their activities, political agitation for the company continued,
and eastern hostility toward the company's opponents mounted.
By 1765, the easterners were determined to discredit the colony's
western lawmakers, especially stampmaster Ingersoll and Governor Fitch, whom they blamed for many of the Susquehannah
Company's misfortunes, as well as for the colony's laws against
New Light evangelism.[77]

The eastern faction's efforts to vilify their rivals as traitors
to American liberty provoked angry reactions from many Connecticut patriots. One New Haven man, a true enemy of the
stamp tax, complained, "all that dont run the extravagant Length
of a giddy and distracted Mob are looked upon as Enemies to their
Country and Betrayers of its Liberties. Among other fine Devices
to set People together by the ears," he told Ezra Stiles, "a Man's
religious Principles are made the Test or shall I say the badge of
his political creed. An Arminian [Old Light] and a Favourer of
the Stamp Act signify the same Man: think then in what a
situation some of your friends are."[78]

Nevertheless, the easterners' tactics were fast swaying public
opinion. Months before the spring election of 1766, rumors filled
the air that Fitch and his four loyal assistants would be ousted. In
the east, the Sons of Liberty lauded their favorites and denounced
their rivals at county-wide meetings,[79] an unprecedented practice
in the quiet colony. Early in December, Johnson reported that
even his own western region was sure to reject the Fitchites in the

coming election, but he worried that popular sentiment lacked any positive direction. The westerners, he told Eliphalet Dyer, have no set ideas on who their new leaders should be. If the easterners have "an Eligible plan we may cooperate with you."[80] Dyer quickly took up the proposal. "As to any New Scheme about the Stamp Act or in Answer to your request therein," the eastern leader wrote, "it may be depended upon that one Mr. Wm. Samuel Johnson of Stratford who arrived at the honor of being one of the 20 last October will be one of the Council next May." By year's end, the two Stamp Congress delegates had forged a pact of mutual support. Dyer assured Johnson that the violent and unruly assemblies in the east would be carried no further, and Johnson suggested privately that Dyer would make a suitable governor.[81]

It was a curious partnership between the Susquehannah ringleader and the cautious Stratford lawyer who had long kept aloof from the colony's factional quarrels. Dyer had no guarantee that, should Johnson enter the Council, he would support eastern interests. Before the Stamp Act crisis erupted, Johnson had privately told Dyer that he considered the sea-to-sea claim "clear and equitable,"[82] but he had never taken a public stance on the issue. Regarding the colony's religious dispute, Johnson's record held even less promise for the easterners. Johnson had avoided any conspicuous role in the Old Lights' battle against the revival, but he had presented the Old Lights' petition against Thomas Clap to the General Assembly in 1763, and Samuel Johnson's dispute with Clap over the treatment of Episcopal students at Yale had no doubt created a certain coolness between the rector and the Johnson family. Moreover, William Samuel Johnson's friendship with the outspoken antirevivalist Jared Ingersoll was no secret to Dyer.[83] Apparently Dyer was not letting partisan considerations blind him to the exigencies of political battle. Until 1765, the advocates of New Light worship and Susquehannah had met only failure in their attempts to discredit their conservative rivals. Most Connecticut voters would play no part in the factional contest and refused to oust their long-esteemed leaders. Only the Anglo-American crisis could rouse the freemen from their deferential ways. And many voters, especially in the west, still resented the erosion of political stability and the violent excesses of the liberty men. The eastern politicos cound not expect to execute a political revolution that excluded moderate western voices. Men like Johnson, acclaimed as patriots and unassociated with the notorious agitation in the east, were essential to overthrow the Fitchites.

On January 13, New London County's Sons of Liberty called a county-wide convention at Lyme, where they laid plans for the spring election.[84] Benjamin Gale, an outspoken critic of New Light religion and Susquehannah politics, called the assemblage the "Babel Convention." Gale's haughty disdain for the liberty men did not restrain him from sending "spies" to the meeting. According to Gale, the eastern schemers chose Abraham Davenport of Stamford, along with Robert Walker and William Samuel Johnson of Stratford as the colony's next assistants from the west.[85]

The future seemed promising for Johnson, yet victory was not yet in hand. During the Stamp Act crisis, New England's fear of Episcopal tyranny exploded with new intensity, and until the ballots were counted in April, Johnson could not be sure that his years of caution and quiet demeanor had shielded him effectively from the anti-Episcopal rancor. In 1763, Mayhew had warned of a diabolical conspiracy between church and crown. The Stamp Act made that partnership suddenly seem dangerously real. John Adams sounded the alarm in the Boston newspapers in August, 1765. Ecclesiastical despotism and the destruction of American property rights, he wrote, constituted the "first step" in a "direct and formal design to enslave America."[86]

The imprudent actions of the Connecticut missionaries magnified these fears. Although the Episcopal clergymen abhorred the Stamp Act, they exploited the anti-Stamp Act clamor of their dissenting neighbors to advance the cause of an American bishop. In letter after letter, they reminded their British superiors that only an Episcopal establishment could promote obedience and loyalty to the crown.[87] At their annual convocation in the autumn of 1765, the Connecticut missionaries publicly denounced the "unreasonableness and wickedness" of the Stamp Act resistance, which they deemed "nothing short of rebellion."[88] These outspoken professions of loyalty did not elude the vigilant patriots. The efforts of Reverend Samuel Peters to quell the spirit of resistance in his town were rewarded with particular harshness. On December 19, the angry mob that had just executed effigies of Ingersoll and Grenville marched on to Peters's home and thoroughly intimidated the notorious Anglican.[89] Hate and suspicion filled the air, casting the political fortunes of William Samuel Johnson into suspense.

In April, Connecticut's freemen flocked to the polls and turned out their conservative leaders. The easterners' favorite, William Pitkin, unseated Thomas Fitch; the governor's four loyal assistants gave up their posts to men who had won popular acclaim in the Stamp Act crisis.[90] It was a dramatic victory for the political agitators from the east and a personal triumph for William Samuel Johnson, who became the first and only Anglican ever to sit on the colony's Council.

How revolutionary was the election of 1766? Fitch's defeat signalled the birth of a new style of Connecticut politics. The high passions aroused by the Stamp Act quickly became the tools of the easterners, who captured the political arena to defeat their long-time rivals. Factionalism was out in the open. The politics of deference gave way to electioneering, party slates, and open challenges to the wisdom and loyalty of the colony's long-esteemed lawmakers. There is no better symbol of this revolutionary change than the fate of Thomas Fitch, cautious guardian of the Connecticut charter and prudent spokesman for American rights. Anticipating neither the high emotions evoked by the Stamp Act nor the powerful new weapons wielded by his partisan enemies, he quickly fell victim to the politics of faction.

Patriot agitators depicted the electoral contest of that year as a decisive struggle between the true friends and the betrayers of American liberty. In fact, however, the stamp crisis made few loyalists and even fewer revolutionaries. More Americans agreed on the injustice of the Stamp Act than on any other question in the decade preceding the War of Independence. In all the colonies, only a very few men believed the old Tory doctrine that British authority was unlimited, sacred, and unquestionable.[91] In 1765, and throughout the prerevolutionary decade, Americans were universally committed to the Whig ideals: personal liberty and government by consent. Men like Fitch and Ingersoll were branded as traitors to their country because of the responsibilities of their offices, the prudence of their temperaments, and the jealousies of their factional rivals. The dreadful events that would push the colonists to independence and civil war lay hidden in the future. In 1765, virtually no one talked of war and separation. Among the patriots and political victors of that year were many future loyalists, including William Samuel Johnson. Independence, war, and the destruction of the British Empire, not the issue of parliamentary taxation, would break the unanimity of the Whig cause.[92] The stamp crisis of 1765 and the electoral contests of the following year were no rehearsal for the civil war that would confront Americans ten years later.

The crucial test of loyalty, to the British Empire or the American cause, lay far ahead. But William Samuel Johnson faced a more immediate challenge. In 1766, fidelity to the Congregational establishment or to the Church of England was the potent issue that imperilled his political fortunes, and even the repeal of the Stamp Act could not remove that peril. Johnson's elevation to the Council disquieted more than a few of the colony's leaders. For decades, Connecticut towns had sent Anglican deputies to the General Assembly. Even in the spring of 1766, when Anglo-American tensions swelled anti-Episcopal sentiment to floodmark levels, Stratford, Newtown, and Derby returned churchmen to the Assembly.[93] The selection of deputies was a local matter. In towns like Stratford, the years of communal reconciliation, the kinship ties between Anglicans and Puritans, and the enduring equation between wealth and authority all counterbalanced the rising tide of suspicion against the Episcopal Church. But the election of the governor's assistants was a colony-wide affair, in which familial ties and neighborly understanding counted for little. The outcome of the 1766 election meant clearly that Johnson's opposition to the Stamp Act and his participation in the Stamp Congress had overshadowed his Anglican identity, at least in the minds of most Connecticut freemen. Ezra Stiles, who abhorred the Church of England as the single greatest threat to American liberty, regarded Johnson's victory with alarm. To the Old Light minister, it signalled the Episcopal Church's quest to become politically "important," and Stiles despaired that the New Lights from the east should agree to such a hazardous partnership with a churchman.[94] The fears expressed in Stiles's diary suggest a touch of paranoia,[95] but many Connecticut men of more moderate emotions were also loath to accord Johnson the full responsibilities and honors of a governor's assistant.

Every May and October, the Assembly made appointments to the colony's military and judicial posts, and customarily the lawmakers reserved the highest appointments for themselves. Tradition dictated that the governor's assistants be named to the colony's highest tribunal, the Superior Court, or to one of the county courts. Yet that spring, the Assembly passed over Johnson for men of conspicuously fewer qualifications. Among the new judges of the Superior Court was Roger Sherman, a self-made lawyer who had neither a Yale education nor a distinguished Connecticut ancestry. Of the six men chosen to preside over the county courts for the coming year, only two had been elected governor's assistants.[96] Johnson undoubtedly felt slighted, but the Assembly's distrust of churchmen was not new. Long before the Stamp Act raised anti-Episcopal feelings to new heights, Anglican townsmen had won seats in the Assembly, only to be excluded from the appointive offices that their fellow deputies confidently expected and received.[97] In 1766, Johnson's political victory was far from complete.

In mid-May, soon after Johnson took his seat on the Council, news reached Connecticut that Parliament had repealed the Stamp Act. The word spread quickly, and Connecticut and all the colonies began celebrating rather than cursing their British connection. Bells were rung, glasses were raised, and sermons heard in praise of Parliament and George III.[98] The cause for celebration was illusory, but the spirit was joyously, triumphantly real.

Accompanying the official announcement of the Repeal Act was a second statute, the Declaratory Act, which explicitly confirmed the authority of Parliament to make laws binding on the colonies "in all cases whatsoever" but omitted any specific reference to taxation.[99] Johnson studied the acts and with his colleagues in the legislature drafted an address of gratitude to the King. Like nearly every patriot, he eagerly interpreted the repeal as an unequivocal victory over taxation without representation and as proof that Parliament would hear and redress the grievances of its American subjects. The ambiguity of the Declaratory Act hardly aroused concern among the colonists, who regarded the act as a mere formality.[100] But the act was not empty words, as anyone close to the British political scene well knew.

Colonial resistance to the Stamp Act had presented the British ministry with a formidable problem. Even before the Stamp Act became law on November 1, the colonists had begun boycotting British imports. By the spring of 1766 British trade to the provinces was at a standstill, and unpaid debts to British merchants were mounting quickly. Of even graver concern to the Rockingham ministry, which had succeeded that of George Grenville in the summer of 1765, was the prospect of an Anglo-American war. War would be an open invitation for Great

Britain's European enemies to resume the contest for empire, from which England had emerged victorious in 1763.[101] Although desperate for an Anglo-American settlement, the ministry knew it could not yield to colonial arguments and renounce Parliament's authority to tax the colonies. In 1766, as in 1764, Parliament was convinced of its constitutional right to extract an American revenue. The Rockingham ministry could not surrender to the American claim without dealing a fatal blow to its own leadership in Parliament.[102] In mid-March the ministry fixed upon a strategy that would quiet colonial discontent without conceding an iota of British supremacy. In the repeal of the Stamp Act, which passed both houses of Parliament and received the King's signature on March 18, was this statement: "And whereas the Continuance of said Act would be attended with many Inconveniences, and may be productive of Consequences greatly detrimental to the Commercial Interests of these Kingdoms. . . ." No recognition was accorded to the colonists' arguments against the constitutionality of American taxation.[103]

Even so, Parliament demanded that the Repeal Act be accompanied by a firm declaration that parliamentary power remained undiminished. The Declaratory Act was deliberately ambiguous, to avert any adverse American reaction, but its meaning was clear to everyone present at the debates.[104] The Rockingham strategy thus laid the foundation for a decade of Anglo-American misunderstanding. Before long, Parliament, confident of its unlimited supremacy over America even in matters of taxation, would again take up the dual problems of a debt-ridden British treasury and the expense of defending the American territories. New attempts would be made to secure an American revenue. Just one month after the joyous celebrations of repeal, Johnson's mind filled with apprehension. He watched with alarm the events in nearby New York. There British commanders, under orders from Parliament, were demanding that their troops be quartered and supplied at the colonists' expense. "Such a step," he warned his friend Christopher Gadsden of South Carolina, will "awaken the suspicion of the People & endanger that Harmony which I hope to be established between the Mother Country & the Colonies."[105] Johnson's fears were not unfounded.

Chapter Five

A Connecticut Yankee
in London

⤛⤜⤛⤜

"You ask my opinion of this country. . . . The wealth, magnificence and splendor of the nobility, gentry and rich Commoners and the extreme misery and distress of the poor, are extremely amazing on the one hand and disgusting on the other." With these words, Johnson described to his Connecticut friends his first impressions of London. "The majesty, dignity and power of the kingdom," Johnson continued,

fill me with affection, wonder and reverence, while its factions and follies excite disrespect and contempt. Their luxury, dissipation and splendid vices of the age confound all ideas of simplicity, modesty and economy while a certain nobleness and generosity of soul . . . challenges your respect and esteem. In a word, everything is too much in extremes.[1]

In 1767 Johnson embarked upon a mission that took him to the seat of the British Empire and the largest city in the western world. London in that year was a sprawling metropolis of over half a million people, the vortex of imperial trade and government and the center of British culture.[2] From this pulsating capital, new wares and entertainments, new laws and theories, constantly radiated to the outlying corners of England and the provincial towns of America. It was an exciting and unfamiliar setting into which Johnson ventured on the evening of February 8, 1767. But the explanation behind this change of scene is by no means mysterious.

Johnson came to London as Connecticut's special agent to represent the colony before the Privy Council in a dispute with the Mason family. He was to assist Connecticut's regular agent, Richard Jackson. The Masons, also of Connecticut, claimed an enormous piece of Connecticut land which the Mohegan Indians, the original owners, had deeded to them. For nearly a century, the colony had been troubled with conflicts arising over the settlers' deeds to Indian lands. To allay this trouble, the General Assembly had long maintained that without its sanction no land title from the Indians was valid. When the Assembly refused to ratify the Mason deed, the family retorted that the Assembly had no right to judge ownership of the land, which only the Indians could bestow. After investigating committees in 1721, 1738, and 1745 had failed to uphold the Mason family claim, the Masons exercised their right to a final adjudication in the mother country before the Privy Council.[3]

In February 1766, the Privy Council instructed Connecticut to appear for the final trial of the case. In October 1766 the General Assembly took measures to send a delegate on behalf of the colony. Eliphalet Dyer was chosen first, but declined the long mission; Johnson was then chosen.[4] Among the colony's many lawyers, few besides Johnson could rival Dyer's reputation for legal acumen.

Having collected the necessary documents and conferred with many on the case, Johnson rode to New York and boarded a packet. On Christmas Day, he set sail for England. The winter passage of thirty days was "tempestuous" and longer than he had anticipated, but he suffered only one day of seasickness. His small cabin seemed quite adequate and his shipboard companions pleasing enough.[5] The packet touched shore at Falmouth on January 30, 1767. Johnson was eager to leave that dirty Cornish port town, and he set out immediately for London, reaching his destination on Sunday evening, February 8.[6]

The advice of his Connecticut friends proved useful right away, and he found his lodging at the same house in Lancaster Court, Westminster, where Dyer had boarded four years before on the Susquehannah Company mission. Soon after, Johnson hired the services of Ingersoll's former servant, Sally.[7] Lancaster Court was a sensible choice, for Westminster was the hub of the nation's politics. There he found the Court of St. James, the two houses of Parliament, the law courts and government offices, and the archbishop's palace at Lambeth. Westminster and London were still two politically separate cities, but that distinction now eluded the eye. The two cities had locked into one as London outgrew its boundaries, sprawling out to fill in the gaps between other towns and suburbs in a haphazard answer to its own commercial needs.[8]

With the necessities of his stay secured, Johnson paid his first visit to Richard Jackson. Like many agents of this decade, Jackson was a native Englishman, a lawyer, and a Member of Parliament. He had served Connecticut since 1760, while also representing Massachusetts (1765-1766) and Pennsylvania (1763-1769). It was Jackson who first guided Johnson through the political departments and machinery of state and introduced him to the amusements of the city.[9]

The theatre was the most popular entertainment for the fashionable classes, and increasingly with the middle sort of people as well. Johnson quickly became a devotee, passing countless evenings in Covent Garden, the center of the city's night life. Plays by Shakespeare were presented alternately with the newest sentimental dramas of Sheridan, Richardson, and Goldsmith. Johnson had sampled Shakespeare in New York, but the sentimental dramas were a new experience which often pleased him but occasionally offended his New England sensibilities.[10] Another favorite pastime was to promenade in the Mall in St. James's Park, where Londoners of every rank flaunted their finery, new or second-hand. For North Americans, London had always defined the vogue in manners, dress, art, and literature. Johnson appeared often at the Mall to observe the spectacle and report the latest in fashion to his wife. It was an amusing sight. Although stylish men had shortened their wigs from shoulder length to the conservative pigtail peruke, women's headgear had abandoned simplicity for outlandish display. They paraded with not-so-miniature gardens and architectural replicas atop their heads. "In a word," Johnson wrote home, "their fashions are very ridiculous & deserve not Imitation."[11]

Taverns, called coffee houses by the British, housed the day-to-day social life of the city, and drunkenness was not considered an exceptional condition, nor gambling a vice. Indeed, the British had managed to advance into the recesses of debauchery while appearing to still stand on the threshold of conventionality. Various coffee houses were the chosen meeting places of bankers, merchants, politicians, and colonial agents. Almost nightly, Johnson visited the Mitre Crown & Anchor or one of the other houses favored by American agents and colonial travelers. Here he read the latest news of America, swapped conjectures on British politics, and received his mail from the latest ship. But drunkenness and gambling impressed him unfavorably.[12]

In the affluent western part of the capital stood the homes of nobles, wealthy politicians, and merchants. Paris, not London, was the pinnacle of European grandeur, and London notables lived in a comparative simplicity that disappointed visitors from the Continent. But the lavishness of London shocked Johnson's New England sense of virtue. He felt obliged to assure his father;

Do not however imagine that by indulging my curiosity, and being conversant with the grandeur of Europe, I shall be tempted to disregard or look down upon America, or that my home will appear mean or despicable to me. My attachments there are too strong to be relaxed. . . . I like to look behind the gay curtain, but when I do I find little to admire and less to be attached to. . . . Riches, state magnificence, etc. cast a deceitful glare around all objects, both persons and things, which at a distance wonderfully magnifies them, and makes one imagine them to be very desirable; as we approach nearer, the deception vanishes, and we too often find them mean, contemptible, and exceedingly deficient in all intrinsic worth.

London was a city of contrasts, and none greater than that between wealth and poverty, which disappointed Johnson's Yankee notions of political economy. "Indeed to say [the] Truth," Johnson told his father,

E[ngland] do's by no means strike me as I expected it would. My Ideas of it were too much heighten'd & I Imagine this is very generally the case with us in Am[eric]a. It is true here is Prodig[ious] magnificence & splendour but on the other hand there is also great Meanness. You see surpris[ing] Grandeur, Wealth & Luxury, but you also behold abject Poverty & Wretchedness. There is no equality, all is extremes, and a bad Oeconomy discovers itself in everything.[13]

Samuel Johnson had felt a similar displeasure some forty years earlier, when he arrived in England as a candidate for Episcopal orders.[14] The same New England sense of virtue that inspired William Samuel Johnson's commentary informed his father's character as well. In 1767 the elder Johnson told his son, "Your account of the drawing room and Sir John Cust's family are also very entertaining, in all which I feel with you. You have after all a just sense of the vanity of grandeur without domestic satisfaction, and I trust you will in a little time be weary of show, and I hope e'er long return wiser and better, with a strong sense of the infinitely solid worth and pleasure of true piety."[15]

Nothing disappointed William Samuel Johnson more that the impiety and irreverence of the mother church. Episcopacy in England lacked the zeal and seriousness of purpose that characterized worship in New England, both Anglican and Puritan. In England, only the Nonconformists treated religion enthusiastically. The Episcopal clergymen read their prayers hastily, without feeling. English bishops, lured by the attractions of London, spent long months at the capital every year, leaving their country dioceses unattended. "Too many of the superior clergy of England," Johnson told his father,

have little virtue and less religion, who obtain their preferments without merit, merely by court favor or family connexions, and are a reproach to their profession, which they consider solely as a means of procuring wealth to be avariciously hoarded for a provision for a family, or vilely squandered in vice and dissipation, or at best, consumed in luxury, indolence, and ease, while they care no more about religion or the Church, or anything that is virtuous or praiseworthy, than they do for the miracles or mosques of Mahommet, and I fear believe just as much of the one as of the other. . . . Upon this sad subject I could a Tale unfold which (in the expressive phrases of Shakespeare) would harrow your soul, but I cannot bear to give you pain, and decline a subject which makes my own heart ache whenever it occurs.[16]

Johnson was surprised to discover how little he had known of the mother country before his arrival, but he soon learned that Englishmen were even less enlightened about his native land. He wrote in his diary, "I heard a respectable Counsellor at Law ask Mr. Jackson gravely in the Hall [Westminster] whether Philadelphia was in the E or West Indies & said he had a Notion it was upon the coast of Sumatra. Such is their knowledge of America."[17] The hardest obstacle impeding any agent's success was the mistaken ideas of America on which the British relied to conduct colonial affairs. Shortly after Johnson's arrival, England and America would fall into another dispute over colonial taxation, and Johnson would watch despairingly as the British government exacerbated the dispute with one blunder after another, owing to their absurd impressions and unreliable reports of colonial conditions.

Jackson and Johnson shared a common interest in the law, and on their first meeting the two agents toured the great judicial tribunals at Westminster. Jackson was a barrister, the highest rank within the English legal profession. As a member of this elite, he was able to introduce his new colleague to prominent figures on the bench and at the bar. In England, attorneys or solicitors were lesser figures who completed the preliminary work on a case, after which the barristers determined the principles and fine issues involved and argued the case before the bench. In Connecticut, where both legal theory and professional training were just developing, this distinction was unknown. In England, Johnson could not be a lawyer; in Connecticut, he was both attorney and barrister. When the courts were in session, Johnson, like his friends Ingersoll and Dyer several years before, attended the hearings almost daily and recorded consequential decisions in his diary to bring home to his own practice.[18]

Of course, the court to which Johnson's attention was turned most intently was the Privy Council. To Connecticut, historically subject to so little interference from the mother country, the Privy Council was known only as a court of appeal. But to most of the colonies, this large ceremonial body was the voice of authority for colonial government. It reviewed legislation passed in the colonial assemblies and settled disputes between royal officials and the assemblies.

The Privy Council occupied an intermediate position in the hierarchy of executive decision-making for the empire. Above it stood the ministry, also called the cabinet or the administration, a body of the King's advisers that consisted of the three great officers of state and a number of departmental ministers. For those problems of government on which Parliament legislated, the ministry's role was to formulate a policy on behalf of the crown for Parliament's consideration. But through most of the century Parliament had left the management of the colonies to the ministry, and the responsibility had resided chiefly with the Secretary of State for the Southern Department and the First Lord of the Admiralty. Few of the statesmen who held these two posts had any knowledge or interest in the colonies, and so the ministers had relied on subordinate boards and councils staffed by colonial experts. Customarily the Secretary of State for the Southern Department had turned to the Privy Council. The Privy Council traditionally made the final decisions in all colonial matters for which the Southern Department was ultimately responsible, as in the Mohegan dispute. The Privy Council in turn relied on a larger, more capable body, the Board of Trade, for information and advice. So, too, did the First Lord of the Admiralty, who was responsible for the enforcement of the navigation acts. The Board of Trade conducted a regular correspondence with colonial governors, drafted instructions to royal governors for the approval of the Privy Council, and was the repository of available information on colonial affairs. Johnson was to appear many times before the Board of Trade, which would initially review the Mohegan case and recommend a decision to the Privy Council.

After a few days spent touring Westminster and the amusements of the city, Jackson took Johnson to the Board of Trade to meet its secretary, John Pownall, and to set in motion the hearing of the case. In view of Jackson's very cordial relationship with the Board of Trade and with Lord Shelburne, who was the Secretary of State for the Southern Department, it seemed reasonable to expect that every effort would be made to assist Connecticut in a speedy conclusion of the Mohegan dispute. But a closer look at the British political scene in 1767 made that expectation appear unduly optimistic.[19]

Two changes had already occurred in the 1760s that drastically altered the system of colonial management just described. First, members of the King's ministry had adopted a curious new interest in colonial policymaking. No longer complacent to relegate their authority to the traditional councils and boards, ministers had begun to formulate their own plans for America and to lay them before Parliament for approval. It began in 1764 when George Grenville, then Chancellor of the Exchequer, won parliamentary sanction to tax the colonies. And the trend continued. The Secretary of State for the Southern Department, upon receiving colonial petitions, now sent many to Parliament rather than to the Privy Council and the Board of Trade for consideration.[20]

That colonial policy had become a subject of frequent parliamentary debate reflected a still larger change in the structure of British politics: the emergence of a contentious, unremitting factionalism in Parliament. With the accession of George III, England had embarked on a period of chronic political turmoil that contrasted sharply to the stability of the century's first sixty years. From George III's first day on the throne until Johnson's arrival in England, four ministries had been dissolved and the fifth was then struggling to hold office. This instability stemmed from George III's inability to select a cabinet that held his confidence and also commanded the support of a majority of Parliament. To some degree, the King's excessive distrust of politicians was to blame. But a more powerful factor was also at work: the fragmentation of the once cohesive Whig party into several factions that ceaselessly contended for control of the ministry. Personal ambition, rather than differences of policy or principle, for the most part inspired this contest. It was the prospect of gaining a place in the cabinet that largely determined the size of Grenville's, or Pitt's, or Rockingham's following in Parliament, for upon entering the ministry these parliamentary leaders had at their disposal patronage and other favors to handsomely reward their supporters. To govern, the King and his cabinet required the consent of Parliament, but could expect only opposition and obstruction from party leaders unattached to the ministry. None of the ministries of the 1760s was composed of a single party. In order to minimize the criticism raised by excluded factions, coalition cabinets were chosen. Yet with so many hungry factions vying for a place in the government, even this strategy was insufficient. Neglected factional leaders, intent upon winning power, seized upon any issue, including colonial policy, to discredit the administration. The dilemma was visible in the parade of ministries that came and went from 1760 to 1767 and their imprudent, hastily conceived, and frequently changing conduct of American affairs.[21]

On coming to power, George III, who distrusted the powerful Pitt-Newcastle coalition that had governed for several years, replaced the Duke of Newcastle as First Lord of the Treasury with the Earl of Bute; dismissed William Pitt as Secretary of State for the Southern Department, appointing the Earl of Egremont in his place; and named the Duke of Bedford as Lord Privy Seal, displacing the Earl of Temple. The new so-called Bute ministry was pleasing to the King but failed to win the support of Parliament, where Pitt enjoyed a large following. George III was forced to reshape his ministry in 1762–1763.[22] The outcome was the Grenville administration, in which George Grenville became First Lord of the Treasury. Grenville, unlike most parliamentary leaders, came into the ministry with a definite policy in mind, to tighten colonial regulation and secure an American revenue.[23] Soon colonial resistance to his Stamp Act and domestic clamor over the use of general warrants provided all-too-powerful issues around which parliamentary factions could rally to embarrass the Grenville administration. The followers of Pitt and the supporters of the Marquis of Rockingham and the Duke of Bedford, all excluded in the transition from the Bute to the Grenville cabinets, succeeded in turning Parliament against Grenville. In the summer of 1765, the ministry was reshaped. The Marquis of Rockingham advanced to the post of First Lord of the Treasury and brought together a ministry of his own followers.

Rockingham came to power without an American program. He had raised a protest against the Stamp Act solely with the hope of displacing Grenville and winning the support of William Pitt, who opposed taxation of the colonies on principle. But Rockingham knew that an unqualified repeal of the Stamp Act would alienate the many Members of Parliament who disagreed with Pitt. The solution Rockingham devised was the Declaratory Act. With this pragmatic course, which left the issue of an American revenue open to conflicting interpretations and invited future Anglo-American misunderstanding, the new chief minister managed to quiet most parliamentary contention.[24] Nevertheless, the ministry was doomed to fall shortly after the Stamp Act repeal. Rockingham resented sharing the ministry with the King's personal friends, who wielded patronage he would have enjoyed and who failed to support his legislative program in Parliament. As a result of this personal conflict between Rockingham and the King's followers, the administration was dissolved.[25]

In July 1766, the King negotiated the formation of a new Cabinet with William Pitt at its head. Pitt's large following in the House of Commons made him a logical choice. Moreover, the King was confident that Pitt would be willing to share power and patronage with the King's small circle of followers. Pitt promised to create a coalition ministry of all factions, a ministry without party. In return, George III awarded him a peerage, with the title Earl of Chatham. Chatham accepted the Cabinent post of Lord Privy Seal for himself and appointed the Duke of Grafton as First Lord of the Treasury in place of Rockingham. Chatham chose the Earl of Shelburne, who agreed with his views on American taxation, for the Southern Department. To Charles Townshend, who sympathized with the Grenvillian policy of taxing America, he awarded the chancellorship of the Exchequer, and he allowed Rockingham's ally, General Conway, to manage the Northern Department. The result was an administration beset by internal divisions. Townshend was intent upon embarrassing the Chathamites, seizing control of the ministry for himself, and securing a program pleasing to Grenville. The new administration was also assaulted from without by parliamentary leaders such as Grenville, Rockingham, and Bedford. None of these opposition spokesmen was content to see patronage so sparsely distributed among the competing factions. By the new year 1767, the Chatham ministry was tottering toward dissolution, and Chatham's chronic gout, which forced him into seclusion, robbed the ministry of its only capable, disinterested manager.[26]

For Johnson, arriving in England at this time, the scene was almost incredible. Reflecting in a letter to Ingersoll on Connecticut's own bout with factional turmoil, he wrote, "But to one observ[ing] the violence of Faction & Party here what has happen'd with you scarcely seems an object & is like the light ruffle of the Fish Pond compared with the rough raging of the Tempestuous Ocean."[27] To predict the outcome, he said, would require "more skill in the doctrine of chances than was professed by Newton and all the mathematicians of the last age."[28]

But two consequences of this near-anarchy in politics soon became clear to the Connecticut agent. First, American affairs, now thrown into the parliamentary arena as a subject of partisan debate, would surely suffer.[29] Secondly, the Mohegan dispute was too inconsequential to be seized upon as a partisan issue and would remain outside Parliament under the care of the Privy Council and the Board of Trade. But the frequent turnover of ministers, and the reshuffling of lesser government officials that always followed this turnover, made a speedy settlement of the Mohegan dispute unlikely. The president of the Privy Council, Johnson reported, was too engrossed in the constant shuffle of ministers to attend to business.[30] Within a year of Johnson's arrival, when his patience with the situation was nearly exhausted, he would write: "It is a humiliating sensation to be dangling after the great & dancing from office to office, watching, peeping, prying, induring Insolence & cringing to power. You would not like it."[31]

Chapter Six

Townshend Lays His Taxes

ohnson had been in London only a few days when his attention to the Mohegan case and the amusements of the
city was diverted by the drama in Parliament. There American
affairs occasioned an intense debate. Within ten days of his
arrival, Johnson wrote home despairingly that the raging between parliamentary parties might produce grave consequences
for the colonists: "In a word the Question seems not to be
what is best but what is at present expedient and will most effectually subserve the Interests & Views of Party."[1] The occasion
for his observation was Charles Townshend's recently announced plan to impose new taxes on the Americans and George
Grenville's inflammatory accusations before Parliament that
the colonists no longer intended obedience to the mother country.[2] These attacks, which were aimed as much at chief minister
Chatham for his conciliatory views about America as at the
colonies, had begun just before Johnson reached England.

Parliament had reconvened on January 26, 1767, after its
traditional holiday recess, to debate two issues: the territorial
acquisitions of the East India Company, a subject of little concern to our story as yet, and the need for an increased American
revenue, a problem ministries since 1763 had broached unsuccessfully. The Chatham administration was beset with the
herculean task of financing the defense of the vast North American territory acquired in 1763 and leading Great Britain out of
a huge wartime debt while preserving Anglo-American harmony.
The ministry was unequal to the task.[3]

Chatham, whose illness kept him in seclusion, had abdi-
cated all leadership of his "ministry without party." The administration had become a set of independent departments with no
leader and no agreement on policy. As First Lord of the Treasury,
Grafton was responsible for formulating a budget, but he lacked

any initiative.[4] The problem of defense thus devolved upon the Earl of Shelburne, head of the Southern Department. Shelburne's plan was to retrench military expenses, withdraw troops from the interior of America, and return the management of Indian–settler relations on the frontier to the individual colonies.[5] But Townshend, Chancellor of the Exchequer, was eager to secure the leadership of the ministry and of Parliament, and to push through a different plan: taxation of the colonies, increased authority for royal officials over the Americans, and a Board of Commissioners of Customs to be stationed in America. All these measures were designed to secure an American revenue and pay for British troops in the colonies. Shelburne, like Chatham, was apprehensive of reviving an Anglo-American dispute over the issue of taxation and was willing to risk a frontier Indian war as the lesser of two evils. Townshend had been committed for a long time to procuring an American revenue. As early as 1754 he had proposed it to the ministry and in 1765 had strongly supported Grenville's stamp tax.[6] In January 1767 Townshend opened the debate on the British military in America with a mocking denunciation of Chatham's refusal to tax the colonists.[7] All spring, Townshend would contend for control of the ministry and for parliamentary backing on his American program.

Unwittingly the colonists had provided Townshend with his strongest weapon against the Chatham wing of the ministry: colonial disobedience to Parliament. As Parliament opened its debate on colonial expenses, news arrived that New York had refused to comply fully with the Quartering Act, which had been passed by Parliament in May 1765. The act required that British troops stationed in each colony be quartered in barracks, stables, inns, or other unoccupied dwellings and supplied with candles, firewood, rum, and other provisions at the colony's expense. Few colonists believed before 1768 that the presence of the British troops itself violated American liberties. But the New Yorkers apparently felt that for Parliament to dictate the exact manner in which they quartered and supplied the troops was tantamount to a direct tax.[8] The colony's disobedience to the Quartering Act was exacerbated by a petition from New York City's merchants to Parliament, which came before the House of Commons on February 16, 1767. In the petition, the merchants attacked virtually every aspect of the navigation acts, and added fuel to the fire that Townshend and Grenville sought to ignite in Parliament.[9]

The opposition to the Quartering Act and the challenge to the navigation laws created a sudden and drastic reversal in Parliament's sentiment toward the colonies in the spring of 1767. Throughout February and March, when American affairs intermittently occupied Parliament's attention, Johnson sent home letter after letter despairing of the change. "Some of the Lords treated us with the most opprobrious Lang[uage] which tried all my Patience to endure & was really shocking to an Am[erican's] Ears."[10] Johnson blamed the uproar in Parliament on Grenville and his followers: "Mr. G[renville] . . . loses no opportunity to attack us, and reproach the late Ministry as having given up the honor of the nation; . . . I fear everything from him, and would deprecate his advancement to the conduct of affairs as the worst of evils that could happen to my country."[11] Johnson also reported that America had lost many friends in Parliament since the winter.[12] The anger of the Rockingham faction was to be expected. New York's refusal to obey Parliament challenged the Declaratory Act. This act was Rockingham's own, and to stand by it in every situation was a political exigency. Moreover, while still in the ministry, the Rockinghamites had modified the navigation acts in several ways to quiet the complaints of the colonial merchants.[13] Having boasted of the reconciliation of colonial traders to British trade regulation, the Rockinghamites were particularly embarrassed by the New York merchants' petition.[14]

Johnson was confident during February and March that the Chatham administration was firm in its friendship for the colonies and would not be bullied into abandoning its conciliatory course.[15] Americans remembered Chatham's opposition to the stamp tax, and Johnson, like his fellow countrymen, still trusted the chief minister. Johnson was mistaken in several respects. First, Chatham did not perceive the Quartering Act as an attempt to tax the colonists, and he was angered by New York's disobedience to Parliament. Although he had opposed the Declaratory Act for its implied assertion of the taxing power, he was a staunch supporter of parliamentary sovereignty in all other cases. Moreover, from a political viewpoint Chatham could not defend New York and still retain the confidence of an angry Parliament. Even when he briefly emerged from seclusion in March, Chatham made no defense of the colony.[16] Secondly, Johnson underestimated the growing popularity of Townshend in Parliament. On the struggles within the ministry, Johnson wrote home: "One comfort we Americans may derive from all the Contentions and confusions here: that while they are thus immersed in cabals, and so busy about their own affairs, they will not probably have leisure to contrive anything very mischievous to America, towards which many are however enough disposed."[17] In fact, by the middle of March, Townshend had already scored a major victory against Chatham on the regulation of the East India Company's finances.[18] Within two months, Townshend's dominance of the ministry on the American question would be complete.

Finally, Johnson placed too much confidence in the ability and willingness of Secretary of State Shelburne to obstruct any harsh measures against the colonies. Johnson procured an audience with Shelburne in mid-March, no doubt due to the influence of Jackson, who was on friendly terms with the minister.[19] Shelburne greeted Johnson with kind assurances that he was in control of the ministry's colonial policy and entertained no harsh feelings against America. Johnson conceded in his report home that Shelburne's guarantees "might perhaps be only the Lang[uage] of the Courtier," but he trusted Shelburne's testimony over the more candid and sage advice of another British politician, Thomas Whately. Jackson's close relationship with the Grenville faction, as well as the Chatham ministry and the Rockinghamites, enabled his coagent Johnson to confer with politicians of every persuasion. Jackson had worked with Whately in the Grenville administration, where Whately had served as secretary to Grenville in 1765. Afterwards Whately continued to play an important role in determining the Grenville party's strategy on the colonial question. Johnson and Whately became warm friends and chatted often on many topics, but on Whately's political views, especially his high praise for Grenville, Johnson once exclaimed "Credat Judaeus!"[20] Whately vigorously warned the Americans and their agents that every faction in Parliament was committed to the Declaratory Act and determined to reestablish civil authority in the colonies.[21] Johnson was too affronted by Whately's "mistaken Princip[les] & Ill Opinions" of the colonies to weigh his advice realistically.[22] Instead Johnson clung to Shelburne's assurances. Actually Shelburne neither controlled the ministry nor sympathized with New York's protests. Shelburne was crippled politically because he was a member of the House of Lords instead of the House of Commons, which was the center of the colonial debate, and he was no match for the oratory of Townshend and Grenville.[23] Shelburne was also severely antagonized by the action of New York. In fact, in a meeting of the ministers in April, Shelburne would propose even harsher measures[24] against that colony than its outspoken adversary, Charles Townshend.

Despite Johnson's overly sanguine view in February and March, he, like the other colonial agents, warned the Americans to conduct themselves quietly and prudently lest any additional provocation inflame Parliament and arm Townshend and Grenville still more. Johnson was greatly relieved that the Connecticut General Assembly had willingly complied with the Quartering Act, and he urged his colony to continue in its cautious course.[25]

But within a few days of Johnson's warning, news of the actions of Connecticut's neighbor, Massachusetts, dispelled any hope that the British-American disagreements would subside before Parliament retaliated with severe measures. By early April, Parliament's anger was heightened by reports that the Massachusetts General Court had tried to circumvent an order issued by the Secretary of State for the Southern Department in 1766. The Secretary had instructed the Massachusetts legislature to compensate loyal crown servants whose persons or property had been assaulted in the Stamp Act riots. The order had been sent at the behest of Commons, which had resolved in February 1766 that such compensation be made by all the colonies. The Secretary's instructions angered many in Massachusetts, who believed that Parliament could not compel the colonists to pass laws that in effect taxed themselves. Dennys De Berdt warned the colony later in 1766 that Shelburne, the new Secretary of State for the Southern Department, was determined to enforce his predecessor's order and was embarrassed by Massachusetts' intransigence. Finally, in December 1766, the Massachusetts General Court agreed to provide compensation, but it appended to its money bill an indemnity clause that granted full pardon for anyone involved in the riots. The Board of Trade reviewed the indemnity clause in March and April 1767, and concluded that the colony was obligated by the Declaratory Act to provide for compensation, as Parliament had dictated, without any restrictive clauses.[26] Johnson, who was present in Parliament when the Duke of Bedford opened the discussion on the Massachusetts bill, grew impatient with British politicking. He felt sure that the dispute would have remained between the Southern

Department and the colony had Chatham's rivals in Parliament not seized upon this example of colonial disobedience to discredit the administration.[27] Johnson lamented that Chatham's stature had declined greatly and that an abatement of tensions was unlikely: "Very unhappy . . . it is for us, that maltreating us should subserve the purposes of opposition and that we should become the object of party, since, if it produces no other ill effect . . . tends to alienate affection and instil principles most pernicious to both countries."[28] By the middle of April 1767, it was apparent to Johnson that the imprudence of New York and Massachusetts had unleashed angry reactions in Parliament. But Parliament took no immediate action. All awaited a proposal from the administration, which had promised to present its program for the regulation of the colonies by the second week in May.[29]

On May 13, Commons met as a committee of the whole to hear the ministry's plan. Townshend began by denouncing New York's resistance to the Quartering Act and calling for the suspension of the colony's legislature until the New Yorkers showed a due obedience to the laws of Parliament. Then he presented his plan for the more effectual regulation of all the colonies. Salaries for royal governors and judges were to be provided by an independent revenue, instead of by the colonial assemblies, whenever and wherever crown authority seemed threatened. To secure this revenue, an American Board of Commissioners of Customs would be established in the colonies to compel the effective collection of duties, and new import duties would be laid on British manufacturers and on tea that was shipped to Great Britain and then reexported to the colonies.[30]

With the exception of Jackson and Charles Garth, agent for South Carolina, who were Members of Parliament, the colonial agents were excluded from the galleries on May 13. The next day, Johnson sought out various accounts of the debate, breakfasting with Whately, then on to Jackson, and afterwards to Trecothick, a Member of Parliament from London, who was an ally of Rockingham and a close friend to Jackson. On the fifteenth and seventeenth, when the debates on Townshend's proposals were renewed, the agents again were barred from attendance, but Johnson clandestinely took his seat in the galleries. Townshend had swayed a large majority in Commons. By the seventeenth, when Townshend's resolutions were adopted by the House of Commons, Johnson could see that Parliament was unanimous in its determination to secure its authority over the colonies. None of the principles involved in the Chancellor's proposals was seriously questioned, not even by those Members of Parliament who had taken the lead in repealing the Stamp Act.[31] It was simply a matter of time until the acts embodying the proposals were drafted, passed, and approved by the King. Johnson abandoned the capital on June 13 for a month-long tour of the country, passing through Oxford, Stratford-on-Avon, and into Wales, and returning to London in the middle of July.

By July 2, George III had signed three bills to provide for an American revenue. These bills established an American Board of Customs Commissioners; imposed import duties on glass, painters' colors, lead, paper, and tea; commanded the colonial courts to grant customs officers general writs of assistance for unlimited search and seizure; and provided that the funds so raised were to support civil government. The same day, the King signed into law the New York Restraining Act, although the suspension of that colony's legislature was immediately seen to be unnecessary because New York by then had acceded to the Quartering Act.[32]

Johnson considered the act against New York unwisely severe, tending only to widen the breach between Great Britain and her colonies. As to the revenue acts, it was the proposed use of the revenue, to make governors and judges independent of the colonial assemblies and dependent on the crown, that Johnson instantly deemed the most dangerous. He warned that in the royal colonies

the Governors will be rendered independent of the people, and, wanting no support from them, will have very little inducement to call the Assemblies together; nay in time, and it may be feared very soon, the King's governments will all become sinecures for the support of the friends of the administration here, and an American governor need not know whether his government is in that country or in Indostan, in Bengal, or at the Cape of Good Hope, nor have any concern with it, other than to receive the salary appointed for him, which will enable him to buy a borough and qualify him to prostitute his vote in the service of that Minister who shall give him his government.

The Judges, too, while they are made independent of the people, by the establishment of their salaries, are left perfectly dependent upon the Crown.

Johnson assured his Connecticut constituents that the charter
colonies would continue to select and support their own governors and judges. "This great inconvenience, however, they will
be subjected to," he warned, "that while they pay their full proportion of those duties by which civil establishments of the other
Colonies will be supported, they must maintain theirs at their
own expense; which in event amounts to the payment of a tax
to the other Colonies."[33]

Neither the agents nor the colonists could fail to see the
tragic irony in the Chatham government's sponsoring of the
Townshend proposals, which violated Chatham's principle
against taxing the colonies and imposed upon New York the
harshest law against colonial self-government before 1774.[34] To
Johnson and to Benjamin Franklin, with whom Johnson conferred almost daily at times, the blame lay on Grenville, who had
convinced Parliament that the colonists aimed at immediate
independence and had embarrassed the Chatham ministry into
proposing the severe program.[35] Witnessing the success of Grenville's tactics only increased Johnson's disillusionment with
British government: "People in power who ought to proceed
only upon the most sure grounds are I find very apt to take up
the most Idle Reports, and incredible prejudicial representations & make them the basis for their Opinions & Conduct."[36]
But Johnson, like Franklin, admitted that the provocations
from New York and Massachusetts had provided the Grenville
faction with its vital weapon, and neither agent spared the colonies in his reports home. Johnson wrote with a tinge of
bitterness:

The friends of the Ministry say they wished to have done nothing with
regard to America; but that the imprudences of that country since the
repeal of the Stamp Act had given their enemies so much advantage
against them, that they found it absolutely necessary to do something
in order to secure themselves and keep peace here, . . . and that, whatever seems disagreeable to the Colonies, they must now blame themselves for, as being the necessary consequence of their own indelicacy
with respect to the dignity of this country and the authority of Parliament, which they are indispensably obliged to vindicate.[37]

With Parliament steadfast in its determination to tax the
colonies, Johnson advised his constituents that redress now lay
with themselves. Home industry and frugality must replace the
consumption of British tea and manufactures. At the same time,

a cautious, quiet demeanor must disarm the colonists' critics in Parliament.[38] For the rest of the summer, while Parliament recessed and its members abandoned the city for the pleasures of their country seats, Johnson attended to the Mohegan case. Little progress could be made on the case with so few government officials in town, so in the autumn Johnson toured the majestic cathedral towns, visited the great country seats of Parliament, among them Jackson's and Townshend's, and succumbed like most American visitors to a fanciful search for traces of his British ancestors. All the while he awaited news of America's reaction to the Townshend duties.[39]

In November, Members of Parliament returned to their city residences to begin another legislative session and to launch a new social season. On the twenty-fourth, Johnson attended the opening of Parliament by the King in the House of Lords. On that day the chamber was crowded with members of both houses, who had discarded their everyday wear for colorful fur-trimmed robes and had convoked to view the ceremonial procession of His Majesty's servants and the arrival of the King in a gilded coach. Although the dignity of this ceremony impressed even the Yankee-tempered Johnson, who usually disdained lavishness and pomp, the opening of Parliament left Johnson more troubled than awed. From the first day of the session, the opposition parties seized upon the news of Boston's resistance to the Townshend acts to hammer away at the Chatham ministry's inability to discipline the colonies.[40] Boston had received word of the Townshend Acts by late August, and in October a town meeting had adopted resolutions that forbade the importation of British goods, encouraged domestic manufacture, and called upon other towns and colonies to join the resistance.[41]

Boston's economic boycott accorded with Johnson's earlier advice, but the public clamor surrounding the colonial resistance provided a new weapon for the advocates of stern colonial regulation. Johnson wrote home in December that the boycott must be carried on with as little noise as possible, lest all the colonies suffer repressive measures like those meted out to New York the previous summer. Let each individual, he said, practice frugality and industry in his own private life, without parade, public associations, votes, and subscriptions, which can only give umbrage in England and strengthen the colonists' enemies. Johnson's advice, though repeated by the other agents, was hardly practicable.[42] Could a unified colony-wide boycott have come about without aggressive public organization and inflammatory outcries against the new taxes? Probably not.

The unfriendly declarations against the colonies in the November and December meetings of Parliament were just the first sobering sign to the agents that they could expect no gestures of conciliation from Great Britain. In the fifteen months to follow, Johnson would see parliamentary sentiment against the colonists harden and their friends in the ministry forced to resign. In this same period, Johnson would gradually formulate his own strategy for his countrymen, a steadfast denial of parliamentary taxing power and a demand for full repeal of the Townshend acts on this principle. His strategy would meet resistance not only from British officialdom but also from the other colonial agents.

When Parliament reconvened in January 1768 after its customary holiday and adjournment, an essentially new ministry was at the helm. Since the passage of the Townshend Acts, Johnson had reported home frequently that the divided and weak Chatham ministry would have to resign or reorganize itself to quell Parliamentary opposition. With the death of Charles Townshend in September, the necessity had become irresistible.[43] Although the old ministry had been nominally led by Chatham, the Duke of Grafton had shouldered the responsibility for holding the administration together, and all fall he had negotiated with the opposition parties—the Grenvillites, the Bedfordites, and the Rockinghamites—to secure sufficient support in Parliament. In January the negotiations came to a climax with the alliance of the Bedfordites and the ministry, and with the creation of a new office, the Secretary of State for the American Department, to be manned by Lord Hillsborough. Bedford offered his party's support for the ministry in exchange for two cabinet posts which were awarded to his followers, Lord Gower and Viscount Weymouth. As advocates of a stringent colonial policy, the Bedfordites also demanded that Shelburne relinquish all control of colonial affairs. Consequently, the new American Department was created to assume complete direction of American affairs, heretofore divided among several ministers, including Shelburne.[44]

The transferral of all American business to this new department presented one more obstacle impeding a speedy resolution of the Mohegan case. In response to Ann Johnson's impatient pleas that her husband return home, Johnson grieved that "All

American affairs will now be thrown into an entire new channel, all is to begin anew with Lord Hillsborough; new negotiations are to be commenced, new connections formed & c. which is an unhappy delay to all who have any affairs of that country to solicit." As to the effects of this ministerial reorganization on the Anglo-American crisis, Johnson was optimistic. He predicted that the alliance of the Bedfordites with the ministry would fatally weaken the opposition parties, especially the anti-American Grenvillites. Grenville, reported Johnson, had relied on Bedford's support in Parliament, and with the other opposition party, the Rockinghamites, disinclined to cooperate with Grenville on colonial issues, Americans would now be safe from Grenville's assaults.[45]

Johnson's prediction was ill-founded. First, the reorganized ministry no longer reflected Chatham's conciliatory views toward America. The stature of Shelburne had been drastically reduced, and Grafton's leadership would soon yield to the aggressive policies of the Bedfordites.[46] Secondly, the cooperation between Grenville and Bedford had been no unnatural alliance. The Bedfordites' accession to the ministry threatened greater, not diminished, support for Grenville's anti-American stance. Thirdly, the refusal of the Rockinghamites to negotiate an alliance with Grafton boded ill for the colonies. The Rockinghamites preferred to battle the Grafton ministry in Parliament, aiming for its complete overthrow, rather than to share power in the Cabinet. With this choice, Rockingham sacrificed the opportunity to shape the administration's colonial policy. For Rockingham and his followers, total political victory took precedence over a friendly settlement with the Americans.[47]

Johnson greeted the elevation of Hillsborough to the new American Department more sanguinely than the other colonial agents. Benjamin Franklin and Dennys De Berdt, for example, reported home that Hillsborough was no friend to colonial liberty. Johnson, by contrast, related that "Lord Hillsborough is esteemed a nobleman of good nature, abilities, and integrity. . . . As a native of Ireland, and possessed of vast property there, it may be hoped he has formed reasonable notions of the rights and liberties of the distant branches of this empire, and would not be disposed to confine all power and all political felicity to the shores of this island."[48] The appraisals of Johnson's fellow agents were more astute. Hillsborough had worked long on the Board of Trade, serving as its president under the

Grenville administration. He was committed to a tighter regulation of colonial affairs, and in his new post at the head of the American Department, his views would eclipse the more flexible ideas of Shelburne and Grafton.[49]

The events of the new year, 1768, soon taught Johnson to discard his mistaken confidence in the reorganized Grafton ministry. Johnson hastened to greet the new minister who would direct all American affairs and to recommend the interests of Connecticut to his favor. His first interview with Hillsborough early in February filled the agent with alarm. Connecticut's charter had always permitted the colony to legislate with no interference from the Privy Council, which reviewed all laws passed by the assemblies of the royal colonies. But Hillsborough was ready to challenge Connecticut's legislative independence. The argument between Hillsborough and Johnson on the colony's charter privileges made a deep impression on the agent, who told the Governor of Connecticut that the colony had much to fear from this new minister.[50]

It soon became apparent to Johnson that the rest of the new ministry was just as eager as Hillsborough to tighten colonial regulation. On February 24, Lord North, successor to Charles Townshend, introduced into Parliament a bill to establish four additional Vice-Admiralty courts in North America, at New York, Boston, Philadelphia, and Charleston. The bill was the final link in the Townshend system for a tighter colonial administration, the one proposal that had not been enacted before the late chancellor died. It passed in Parliament with no significant debate and became law on March 8, 1768. Johnson wrote home that, "notwithstanding all the flattering things [said] by the present ministry," he expected only unfriendly schemes from them.[51]

In March, Parliament reached its statutory seven-year limit. It was the last Parliament of the century to survive a full term. All winter, its members had been distracted by the demands of the approaching election. Johnson was appalled by the corrupt campaign practices, which made every man's vote a thing to be bought with money and drink.[52] But what most horrified him was the way in which the friends of the ministry vilified any candidate who espoused affection for the colonies. "Strange objections these, you will say!" he told Connecticut's Governor Pitkin,

especially in the mouths of those who, at the same time insist that the members of Parliament which they elect are also the representatives of America. It has, I know, been long the labor of our enemies to render the cause of the Colonies unpopular, and they would now, it seems have a friendship for America constitute an odious character in the city of London, and render enmity to that country a necessary qualification for a member of Parliament in this . . . what could the Colonies then have to expect or rather what might they not fear from a legislature thus constituted.[53]

In April, Hillsborough took his first major disciplinary step against the colonies, a step that carried Johnson still farther from his initially favorable assessment of the Grafton-Bedford ministry. In an effort to arouse a unified American resistance against the Townshend Acts, the Massachusetts House of Representatives had dispatched a letter on February 11 to every other colonial assembly, setting forth Massachusetts' opposition to the acts and soliciting proposals for united action. On April 2, Hillsborough notified Governor Francis Bernard that the circular letter must be rescinded or the legislature dissolved. On June 30, 1768, the Massachusetts House voted not to obey Hillsborough's command, and the legislature was summarily dissolved. To Johnson, this attack on the Massachusetts legislature was, in one word, "despotic." His report home expressed disbelief at so severe a measure.[54]

The determination of the new ministers, especially Hillsborough, to meet every incident of colonial resistance with more forceful measures was made clear again in July, when they ordered British troops to Boston. On June 10, a mob of Boston citizens, angered by the seizure of John Hancock's sloop for a customs violation, had forced customs officials to seek safety at the fortress of Castle William in Boston harbor. When news of the incident reached England, the Bedfordites in the ministry, together with Hillsborough, insisted that this threat to civil authority be challenged with force. Over the objections of Shelburne, who dreaded alienating the colonists still further, the ministry dispatched two regiments to Boston and awaited news of their arrival.[55] Johnson condemned the administration's decision as "arbitrary and injudicious." To the ministry's contention that the Boston mob threatened anarchy in the colonies, Johnson countered that no colony had ever rivalled England for popular tumults and riots. Commenting on Parliament's general election just three months earlier, Johnson had written to a friend in Massachusetts, "I see by the Papers you fav[ored] us with & others since arrived that you are not quite calm in America, but all the Stamp Act riots & confusion there were not to be compar'd with those which have been seen within this Month past in this City & several Parts of the Kingdom.''[56]

When Johnson heard of the ministry's decision to send troops, he grew alarmed for the safety of his own colony. He worried that violent and noisy protests would provoke harsh reprisals, and he warned his constituents that the ministry would not hesitate to attack even the ancient Connecticut charter. Despite Johnson's appeals for moderate and orderly resistance, he placed the ultimate blame for colonial unruliness not on his countrymen but on the ineptitude and injustice of British rule. The ministers, he judged, "need to be reminded that all free states are subject to these inconveniences, and that the only effectual way to prevent them is to govern with wisdom, justice, and moderation.''[57]

The imposition of military rule over the Boston citizenry in the summer of 1768 dispelled Johnson's last hopes that the present administration, and particularly Lord Hillsborough, would treat colonial grievances in a spirit of reconciliation.[58] The impetus to repeal the Townshend Acts had to come from America. One year earlier, when the acts were passed, Johnson had urged his countrymen to try economic coercion. It now seemed more necessary than ever. But to Johnson it was also becoming more and more a reality and not just a hope, for news flooded into England that summer that a nonimportation movement was steadily gaining in America. Boston had taken the lead in October 1767, when it pledged not to import or consume a long list of British goods. Before the old year ended, Newport and Providence and several eastern Connecticut towns had adopted similar resolutions. As 1768 began, town meetings all over New England forswore the consumption of British imports. The Boston and New York merchants ventured to propose a league of nonimportation among the merchants of the three great ports, but the Philadelphians refused.[59] Yet out of that city came the most popular and influential statement of the American position, John Dickinson's famous *Letters from a Farmer in Pennsylvania to the Inhabitants of the British Colonies.*

Dickinson's *Letters* openly challenged the Declaratory Act. Parliament, he said, could regulate the trade of her colonies, but it could not impose duties solely to raise revenue. Taxation was not a power essential to the supremacy of Parliament or the imperial relationship. He warned that when respectful applications to the mother country proved ineffectual, the colonies must defend their rights with a more persuasive measure, an economic boycott of British goods.[60] News of Dickinson's wide acclaim in the colonies reached England in the spring of 1768, and a London edition of the *Letters* soon appeared. That summer, Johnson studied the *Letters* and praised them in his reports home.[61] The nearly universal popularity of the *Letters* in America undoubtedly bolstered his determination to deny Parliament's taxing authority and his confidence that the colonists were ready to back that denial with a steadfast nonimportation program. By late summer, Johnson was imploring his Connecticut constituents not to concede to right to tax. Although the ministry argued that repeal could not be granted while the colonists challenged this right, Johnson advised that to relent would prove fatal. He urged his countrymen to act concertedly to stifle British trade.[62]

With his own stand on the Townshend dispute firmly defined, Johnson was ready to speak out for his colony, but he could do nothing while Connecticut's government remained silent. Throughout September he waited anxiously for official word that Connecticut intended to oppose the taxes. At last, in October, after an uncommon delay of four months at sea, the Connecticut Assembly's response to the Townshend Acts reached Johnson's hands. At its spring session, the Assembly had authorized petitions to the King and Lord Hillsborough and had drafted instructions to its agents, Jackson and Johnson. The petitions unequivocally denounced the duties as a violation of the British constitution and the Connecticut charter, deplored the intended use of the revenue as a threat to lawful government, and warned that to continue the acts would prove fatal to the imperial connection.[63] The colony's instructions to its agents were just as plain, that they, "in the strongest manner possible, consistent with decency, press the reasons and arguments which in their opinion most clearly entitle 'em to relief."[64] The colony had refrained from petitioning Parliament, reasoning that an address to that body might seem a "faint Confession of Parliament's right to lay these impositions upon us"[65] Although no colony had given the nonimportation movement the force of law, Connecticut had come daringly close by imposing its own tax on goods brought into the colony by noninhabitants. The Connecticut tax was a direct thrust at merchants in neighboring New York, Massachusetts, and Rhode Island who continued to import.[66]

Together with the colony's official statements came a host

of private reports from Connecticut patriots. Roger Sherman testified to Johnson that the colony judged the Townshend duties "as unconstitutional as the Stamp Act, and the Application of the Moneys to be raised as Great a Grievance as the Duty themselves." William Williams reported that "the Colonies are much united & . . . will be more so." He cautioned Johnson not to cringe from a forthright presentation of the colony's position: "We cannot fear that your Resolution shakes, but in your situation hearing & seeing all on one side & the Puissance of [the] Country &c. it would not be strange if you fear for us."[67]

Armed with these new communications, Johnson immediately confronted Hillsborough with the colony's opposition to all parliamentary taxation. Hillsborough retorted that while the question of right was raised, the colony's grievances would go unanswered. And, he added, any refusal to obey the laws of Parliament would be met with "the whole fleet and army of England."[68] Johnson left this heated interview with little expectation that repeal could be won before the full effects of a colonial boycott were felt in England. He now turned his attention to the approaching session of Parliament, faintly hopeful that some attempt to conciliate the colonies would be made. But the hostile temper of Parliament soon quashed this slim hope.[69]

The Parliament that convened in November 1768 was visibly chagrinned and angered by America's widespread nonimportation agreement and the petitions challenging Parliament's unlimited authority.[70] The stage was thus set for a second attack by the colonies' enemies within and without the ministry. Once again, rash and heated statements from Boston provided a ready target. All autumn, Johnson had cautioned his countrymen against "Ill Judged Outrages & Tumults & Acts of violence which forge the weapons of our Enemies." Other colonial agents had been equally unsparing in their admonitions.[71] But in early September, when word reached Boston that the ministry had dispatched troops to restore civil authority in the city, a town meeting had resolved boldly that Parliament's laws could not bind Massachusetts and that the citizens would defend themselves with armed force against the military threat. It was no wonder that Boston tempers had reached this extreme. Its General Court was dissolved, an American Board of Customs Commissioners watched over it, and an unsympathetic governor cried home for military support. The town meeting resolutions proved to be empty threats. On September 28, a flotilla of warships had entered the harbor and the British troops had disembarked with no resistance from the city.[72] Nevertheless the resolutions had aroused a powerful reaction in England. Johnson reported to the Governor of Connecticut that the Massachusetts declarations against parliamentary authority and the

intimations they gave relating to troops and the preparation of their arms, were considered here as steps directly tending to rebellion. It was expected that the troops would be opposed, should they attempt to land, that Massachusetts Bay, if not all the Colonies must henceforward be considered as in a state of actual rebellion; and measures were concerting to proceed against them in that light. . . . During the period nothing but war and desolation were thought of. All hopes of repeal of the late Act, or any reconciliation, seemed to be at an end. Such was the situation of things here when the news arrived that the troops had landed at Boston without opposition. . . . The spirit of resentment subsided. To this succeeded a calm contempt of that people and the Bostonians are now considered as having made a vain bluster and parade to no purpose.[73]

To his friend Ingersoll, Johnson confessed his impatience with the imprudent Bostonians. "Boston had indeed made a most insignificant figure and exposed themselves to infinite ridicule in this country," the Connecticut agent wrote.

They were certainly very unwise to talk of their arms when they did not intend to use them. Indeed they should have known that the weapons of their warfare were not carnal. . . . Their resolution to import no goods and to encourage frugality and industry could they keep them and engage their neighbors to join with them would have infinitely more weight there than any other opposition they can make, but one is apt to suspect now that they have no more firmness in that respect than with regard to arms and mean only to bluster and make believe which will never answer the end.[74]

From the opening day of Parliament, the ministry seized upon this spectacle at Boston to discredit the advocates of conciliation. Johnson soon realized that the ministry was under the sway of the aggressive Bedfordites. Chatham and Shelburne had resigned in October, disgusted with the dispatch of troops to Boston and harassed by pressures from the Bedfordites. Only the voice of Grafton in the ministry and the threat of opposition from Parliament prevented further acts against the colonies.[75]

On December 15, Hillsborough presented to the House of

Lords a series of resolutions that were filled with harsh words
but devoid of any plan for solving the Townshend dispute. The
resolutions condemned the illegal proceedings at Boston and
threatened punishment for all instigators of colonial rebellion.
They were adopted by the Lords after only a perfunctory debate.
After a recess for the holidays, the same resolutions were taken
up in January by the House of Commons, where the debate continued into the next month. Yet the length of the debate was no
indication that the colonies could hope for support from the
ministry's chief opponents, the Rockinghamites. Rockingham
was politically obliged to defend the Declaratory Act, and confined his attacks to challenging the competence of the administration. Johnson observed. "it is surprising how few friends we
have [in Parliament] who are so upon real principle." Even
those who had been the warmest advocates of the colonies at the
time of the Stamp Act repeal, he reported, were governed by "no
conviction[s] but those of the moment, no purpose but to serve
ambition."[76]

Johnson deplored the resolutions laid before Parliament.
Wisdom in England and prudence in America, he felt, could
alone resolve the dispute. Yet the ministry's resolutions were
"aimed at justifying its own previous policy and appearing
bold and firm in England, instead of restoring tranquility and
happiness to the empire. Until this second goal is their aim,
nothing will be done and things will grow worse."[77] It was
obvious to Johnson that the colonies could expect no relief
during the present session. The administration, he wrote, was
"flushed with success . . . in humbling the Bostonians" and
"seem inflexible in this resolution not to repeal the Laws complained of by the Colonies, at least for this session of Parliament nor until the Colonies submit to give up, or at least wave,
the point of Right."[78] Yet Johnson admonished his countrymen
not "to be Intimidated by Ministerial threats," and he urged
them to continue their economic boycott until their point was
won. "Were the prudent spirit of frugality once diffused through
the bulk of the people of America," he told the Governor of
Connecticut, "the whole difficulty would be over."[79]

Johnson's bold advice in the face of ministerial threats
must have been discomfiting to a large minority in Connecticut who sympathized with their fellow colonists' arguments
against taxation but feared antagonizing the British authorities.
Connecticut leaders were more united in the Townshend dis-

pute than they had been in the Stamp Act crisis. Governor
Pitkin and Lieutenant Governor Trumbull were ardent advocates of nonimportation. In 1765 the Connecticut legislature,
like lawmakers in most of the colonies, had refused to condone
any open resistance to parliamentary law, despite the clamor of
the eastern politicians. But by 1768, the spokesmen for resistance had secured a majority in the General Assembly. Nevertheless a sizeable number of Connecticut's respected citizens still
feared that public associations and intemperate publications
against the mother country could prove fatal to the colony's
charter. Until 1765 such caution had never been confused with
disloyalty to the colony. But now the western towns that refused
to join the boycott were embarrassed in the newspapers, and
men of cautious demeanor were branded as "Tories" by their
more zealous neighbors.[80] All winter Johnson received despairing reports from the colony's conservatives. And from Boston
came the woeful letters of Nathanial Rogers, the Massachusetts
merchant most savagely victimized by the enforcement campaign of the Boston boycotters.[81] In answer, Johnson condemned patriotic zeal turned to "licentiousness." But such
excesses did not temper his commitment to the nonimportation
campaign. Johnson preached that where merchants refused to
join the nonimportation effort, citizens must adopt noncon-
sumption to embarrass them into compliance.[82]

The hesitancy of Connecticut conservatives to antagonize
the ministry with bold constitutional claims and economic
retaliation wrought little change in Connecticut's official reaction to the Townshend Acts and influenced Johnson's own
plan of action even less. But his determination to press for a
total concession of Parliament's right to tax the colonies met
the resistance of another group, the other colonial agents,
whose cooperation was vital. In late summer 1768, when the
ministry first showed that it had no intention of redressing
American grievances, several colonial agents had begun to
confer frequently, looking for some common course of action
to win repeal. A decision on strategy was held in abeyance until
the sense of Parliament on colonial matters had been revealed
and the ministry's official policy had been announced.[83] On
December 6, several days before Hillsborough presented his
resolutions to the House of Lords, the minister summoned the
agents and reiterated the unequivocal terms for repeal that
he had advanced to Johnson in October. The Townshend

duties, he told the agents, would not be withdrawn while the colonists challenged Parliament's right to tax.[84] By February 1769 the agents could see that Parliament supported Hillsborough's firm policy. The agents agreed that a joint petition for repeal on behalf of all the colonists should be tried. In February and March 1769 they met three times to determine precisely the demands they would present to Parliament. The main issue was whether to challenge Parliament's right to lay any tax on the colonies or to argue only against the unreasonable burden of the Townshend duties and the unfortunate disaffection these duties had excited in America. Agreement faltered on this issue.[85]

Johnson feared that an outright concession of Parliament's right to tax would open the way to future abuses. He also viewed the ministry's terms of repeal with scepticism. He was convinced that, on the one hand, the ministry's professed devotion to parliamentary sovereignty was mere political rhetoric. On the other hand, the promise to relieve the colonists as soon as the question of right was dropped could not be trusted. Johnson concluded that to petition only against the inconvenience of the duties would risk immeasurable consequences with no guarantee of any success. He no doubt also felt bound by his own colony's bold repudiation of Parliament's taxing power.[86]

The agents all acknowledged that the Townshend duties were unwise, ill-considered, and ought to be repealed. But some of the British-born agents, whose allegiance to parliamentary sovereignty rivaled their sympathy for the colonies, found the Americans' limitations on parliamentary power offensive and unsupportable. Other agents, who privately endorsed the colonists' denial of the taxing power, feared that raising the Townshend dispute to the level of a constitutional debate, in which one side or the other must concede the right and emerge the loser, would devastate their chances to secure a speedy settlement with the present ministry.[87]

Richard Jackson rejected Johnson's position in the agents' debate as constitutionally unsupportable and tactically naive. Jackson was both a colonial agent and a Member of the House of Commons. His dual status offered enormous advantages to Connecticut. He could monitor and exploit the most sensitive changes in parliamentary sentiment. He sat on influential committees and worked closely with the heads of state. But whenever colonial claims broached the issue of parliamentary sovereignty, Jackson's dual roles became irreconcilable. During the Stamp Act crisis, Jackson had advised Connecticut that to deny Parliament's taxing power was to attack its authority to make any laws at all for the colonies. The Americans' notion that sovereignty could be divided was unacceptable to Jackson. At the same time, he had argued in Parliament that although that body's power was undoubtedly universal and unlimited, it was prudent to refrain voluntarily from taxing the colonies while they were unrepresented by colonial members. Throughout the 1760s Jackson adhered to this position, and advocated colonial representation in Parliament, a solution that Johnson and most other Americans rejected as impracticable.[88] Jackson's allegiance to Parliament made him suspect in the eyes of some Connecticut patriots. In 1769 Governor Pitkin assured Johnson that although his original mission on the Mohegan case had met with little success to date, "I am persuaded, the Sum expended for the Maintenance of [an] Agent, an American born, who sees and feels the worth of Liberty, has tasted its Pleasures, and is an Expectant of enjoying its future happy fruits, is well appropriated."[89]

Johnson's interpretation of the limits of parliamentary power was closer to his countrymen's own convictions, but Jackson offered them a more realistic appraisal of the conditions on which repeal might be secured. Johnson had reasoned falsely that because British politicians let their principles subserve their ambitions, the ministry would yield to the constitutional position of the colonists as soon as their boycott brought pressure from British merchants. Jackson knew this to be wrong. He understood that it would be politically devastating to any British party to yield one iota of parliamentary authority. When Jackson served as secretary to Chancellor Grenville earlier in the decade, the agent had found it futile to question the principle of raising an American revenue. In 1764, when Grenville first announced his intention to impose a stamp tax on the colonists, Jackson had perceived that any challenge from North America to Parliament's authority in matters of taxation would only excite the ministry to hasten its proposal and embarrass Parliament into approving it. Jackson's warnings to the Americans to be silent on the issue of right, warnings which were repeated by many of the colonists' friends in government, went unheeded, and the stamp tax had become law.[90] In 1766 Jackson had watched the Rockingham ministry anxiously devise the

Declaratory Act, the only means to quiet the colonies without incurring the wrath of a Parliament that jealously guarded its sovereignty. Jackson must have reasoned in 1769 that the Grafton-Bedford ministry, like its predecessors, could not buckle under to any colonial claims against parliamentary authority.

Although Jackson's acute understanding of British political exigencies failed to sway Johnson, it no doubt greatly impressed the leader of the agency group, Benjamin Franklin. Jackson and Franklin had been confidants for a decade,[91] but by 1768 they had come to disagree over the extent of Parliament's authority. Franklin privately questioned the right of Parliament to tax Americans or even legislate for them on matters other than the regulation of trade.[92] Nevertheless, his public position on the Townshend Acts closely conformed to Jackson's in the spring of 1769. In the February and March meetings of the agents, Franklin pushed for a joint petition that would be silent on the issue of rights. Jackson had promised to present such a petition in Parliament, and Franklin drafted it, but the agents as a group could not agree to endorse it.[93]

Jackson and Franklin were supported by the South Carolina agent, Charles Garth, who proposed that Franklin prepare the draft, and by Dennys De Berdt, who acted on behalf of the Massachusetts House of Representatives. Garth and De Berdt were convinced, with Dickinson, that the Townshend duties were unconstitutional.[94] But they were resolved to win repeal on any terms, so long as the breach between the two countries was healed. They were confident that no ministry would ever again dare incur the colonial clamor and political chaos that the stamp tax and the Townshend duties had evoked. The colonists would be safe from any future taxes, although the issue of right remained unsettled.[95] Unlike Johnson, they felt that the colonists risked nothing by passing over the constitutional issue, but jeopardized any relief by insisting on rights. They heeded seriously the ministry's warnings that no challenge to parliamentary authority would be tolerated.[96]

Another participant in the agents' debate, William Bollan, contested De Berdt's position. Bollan, like Johnson, insisted that the colonists' constitutional arguments be included in the agents' petition.[97] Johnson acted as an ideologue, a role he would abandon after 1770. Bollan spoke as an opportunist, guided solely by popular opinion in Massachusetts. In 1762 the Massachusetts House of Representatives had dismissed Bollan as their agent, one reason for the dismissal being his close connection with the colony's royal officeholders.[98] By the late 1760s Bollan apparently believed that an alliance with the patriot party promised the brightest career, and to win this party's favor, he challenged De Berdt's cautious advice.[99]

Of the major participants in the agents' February and March 1769 conferences, it was Johnson who was sincerely convinced that their common petition must include the colonists' explicit denial of parliamentary taxing power. Bollan's support for Johnson no doubt bespoke personal ambition rather than conviction. The other agents knew that no British politician, within or without the ministry, would risk conceding a portion of Parliament's sovereignty. After only three attempts, the agents abandoned the search for a mutually agreeable petition. Such ready surrender was uncharacteristic of men like Franklin, but by the end of March he and the other agents had reluctantly adopted Johnson's sceptical assessment of the ministry's promise. Parliament was now in session, but the administration was taking no steps to work out with Parliament a practical settlement to the Townshend dispute. The agents began to doubt that the ministry would support a proposal for immediate repeal, regardless of the conciliatory terms on which relief might be requested by the colonies.[100]

The pessimism of the agents was confirmed in April when a Member of Parliament proposed that the duties be repealed, not because they were unconstitutional but because they were detrimental to the nation's trade. The proposal came from Thomas Pownall, who had at one time served as a crown-appointed governor in New Jersey and Massachusetts, and was considered an expert on colonial affairs. Pownall was intent upon restoring imperial harmony, and he allowed the task to consume all his energies. By 1769 he had published four editions of his treatise, *The Administration of the Colonies*, and he continued to search for a workable solution to the imperial problem. He was also to exert a weighty influence on Johnson's understanding of the Anglo-American conflict. Johnson had met Thomas Pownall through the latter's brother, John Pownall, who was secretary to the Board of Trade and under-secretary in the American Department. John Pownall would help make the final recommendation of the Board of Trade to the Privy Council in the Mohegan case, and Johnson conferred

with him frequently. Thomas Pownall was a close friend to
Johnson and to Franklin, and by 1768 he was working with
these two agents on a revision of the Mutiny Act. He realized
that the presence in America of British troops, commanded
only by the British military and unanswerable to local colonial
authorities, was an unnecessary antagonism to the Americans.
He viewed the Townshend duties in the same way.

Pownall's proposal before Parliament to repeal the duties
vigorously upheld the sovereignty of Parliament in all matters,
including taxation. Pownall was too closely connected with the
administration and too familiar with its partisan rivals in Parliament to doubt that any challenge to Parliament's authority
would be summarily rejected. Instead, he argued that colonial
policy could not be conducted in any strictly legalistic way.
The Townshend duties, like many colonial regulations enacted
since 1763, revoked privileges that the colonists had long enjoyed and had come to accept as rights, and disrupted that commercial harmony on which the empire thrived. Pownall urged
Parliament to stop conducting colonial policy as a pawn between warring parties, to lay aside the issue of right, an issue
that no party dared question, and to unite behind a policy that
could restore goodwill and commerce with the Americans. The
ministry quashed Pownall's proposal and insisted that the
withdrawal of the Townshend duties would not be debated in
the present session. Parliament adjourned on May 9, with no
terms of settlement to offer the Americans.[101]

The agents informed the colonists that it was futile to send
any petitions to Parliament. The appeals from New York and
Pennsylvania had been rejected summarily, and the colonists'
friends in Parliament had been silenced.[102] Already the agents
who had disagreed with Johnson in March were coming to
distrust Hillsborough's ultimatum. By fall, their readiness to
compromise on the issue of right dissipated completely. Johnson predicted equally grave reactions from the Americans. He
told Governor Pitkin, "Thus all the applications of the Colonies are rejected, or ineffectual. There seems no farther hope
that anything will be done in their favor this Session. . . . Such
is the attention paid to the united voice of all America and this
their boasted readiness to hear and address all real grievances!
That the Colonies will resent this treatment of them nobody
can doubt."[103]

Chapter Seven

Conspiracy or Confusion?

$\mathcal{T}$he military threats and heated warnings with which the Grafton-Bedford ministry responded to colonial resistance, and the refusal of Parliament to offer any relief from the Townshend duties, led many Americans reluctantly to suspect an odious plot. One Bostonian told Johnson, "I am under greater apprehension from a sullen silence that appears among the Calm Moderate People of property through this Country. . . . They begin Seriously to fear that England desires to Enslave them." From Philadelphia came word that "the colonies see plainly that the Ministry have adopted a settled plan to subjugate America to arbitrary power; that all the late acts respecting them tend to this purpose." To Connecticut's Lieutenant Governor, the late events revealed an "attempt to establish despotism."[1] The evidence, to many Americans, was foreboding: taxes imposed without the consent of the taxed, suspension of the New York and Massachusetts assemblies, trial without jury in the Courts of Vice Admirality, military force imposed upon the citizenry at Boston, colonial petitions rejected as seditious, and an American Board of Commissioners of Customs to spy upon the Americans and live luxuriously off an American revenue.[2]

Nowhere was America's growing fear more clearly expressed than in John Dickinson's *Letters from a Farmer*. The evidence suggests, the Farmer told his countrymen, that the ministry's present plan, if executed, will "sink them into slaves." And what assurances do the colonists have that Parliament will obstruct this pernicious plan? None, said the Farmer, for the Members of Parliament seem to be under the ministry's control and willing to impose any civil, ecclesiastical, or military despotism on America that the ministry might propose. The *Letters* exposed the ultimate conclusion to which this indictment of the

105

King's cabinet and Parliament would carry the colonists in
1776. Should respectful petitions and orderly economic resistance fail to win redress, and "if at length it becomes *undoubted*,
that an inveterate resolution is formed to annihilate the liberties
of the governed, the *English* history affords frequent examples
of resistance by force . . . it can never be justifiable until the
people are *fully* convinced that any further submission will be
destructive to their happiness."[3]

In 1769 the idea of a deliberate ministerial plot to subvert
American liberty was for most colonists still a mere suspicion.
With each British-American conflict, the suspicion would seem
more of a reality, and the time for armed resistance would draw
nearer. As the colonists' belief in this subversive design evolved
over the next seven years, the gap, barely visible in 1769, between
their interpretation of British colonial policy and Johnson's
understanding of it would grow larger. In 1769 Johnson rejected the notion of any malign conspiracy by the British government. In 1775 this decision would set him apart from his
fellow Americans, for whom the evidence of such a conspiracy
had become irresistible and armed force had become the ultimate defense.

No one filled the part of the Puritan in Babylon more than
Johnson. He was horrified that the struggle for control of the
ministry and its attendant offices and pensions overshadowed
the dispatch of public business. Rival factions contend wan-
tonly for place and power, he told his Connecticut constituents,
while "the affairs of the nation are suffered to take their chance
& proceed or stand still as Accident may direct."[4] All policy, he
despaired, begins and ends with the ministry, and Members of
Parliament support or denounce it according to the dictates of
personal ambition. Parliament no longer speaks for the people,
who begin to view it with contempt.[5] For Johnson, the multitude of riots that plagued London in 1768 manifested clearly
the sunken esteem of Parliament and its inability to attend to
the needs of the nation. Sailors, coalheavers, hatters, weavers,
and journeymen assaulted their employers, petitioned, marched,
and demonstrated until Johnson apprehended "the most fatal
consequences" should the government fail to answer their discontents.[6] He was thunderstruck by the sordidness of the parliamentary elections, in which "intrigue, Party, Interest & Money"
determined the victors. "If these things and some others I might
mention do not in the end ruin this Kingdom," he told one Con-

necticut man, "there might be some special Reason in Providence for Preserving it, contrary to what has happened in all other Ages & States."[7]

Although Johnson abhorred the politics of self-interest and party and feared for the future of British government, he discerned within the distracted condition of the nation no deliberate plot to defraud the Americans of their rights. Instead, for him the scene revealed a succession of ministries that were so harassed from without by rival factions and divided from within by ambitious politicians that they were incapable of formulating any colonial policy. Johnson lamented that the war between parties preoccupied the heads of state until they could govern neither the nation nor its American provinces.[8] They relied on exaggerated and misleading reports of colonial rebelliousness. Their policies were hastily conceived to answer the momentary demands of party strategy.[9] In 1767, after only a few days in London, Johnson had warned his countrymen that colonial policy was becoming a pawn in the contest for place and power.[10] Within four months, his worst fears had been confirmed in the Townshend Acts. Johnson had reported that the acts were the work of one ambitious minister eager to embarass the rest of the Chatham administration and win a following for himself in Parliament. Townshend had epitomized the self-serving politician who crippled the ministry from within.[11] Similarly, the resolutions that Hillsborough presented to Parliament in the winter of 1768–1769 were proof enough to Johnson that the Grafton-Bedford ministry was too distracted by parliamentary opposition and convulsed with internal dissension to address American grievances. "Foolish men and unwise!" he wrote. "Too obstinate to retract, too weak and irresolute to advance, they have chosen this insignificant middle measure of resolution,—seeming to do something, yet really doing nothing,—which can produce only contempt."[12]

From his first-hand observation of the British political scene, Johnson concluded that the confusions of party competition, not the sinister designs of a wicked ministry, were to blame for the unwise and unjust measures taken against the colonies. His judgement also reflected the influence of his close companion, Thomas Pownall, with whom Johnson met often to discuss the American question. Pownall's treatise, *The Administration of the Colonies*, attracted the attention of everyone interested in American affairs. The Connecticut agent studied it, discussed it with the other agents, and sent it to his constituents.[13] In it, Pownall argued that "from the moment that American affairs became an object of politics, they became the tools of faction." He warned that as long as colonial interests were so bantered about and abused, "the mother country and her colonies will continue to live in perpetual jealousies, jarrings and disputes" until the empire is brought to its ruin.[14]

Johnson and Pownall were especially troubled that the administration acted upon the most spurious and partisan accounts of the American resistance. Their worries focused on two sets of letters, those written by Governor Bernard of Massachusetts to Lord Hillsborough in the summer of 1768, around the time when John Hancock's sloop was seized by customs officers in Boston harbor, and those sent by a small group of New Englanders to Thomas Whately in 1768 and 1769. Bernard blamed all the clamor in Massachusetts against the Townshend Acts on a small group of fiery partisans who, he argued, were intent upon undermining royal authority in the colony. Protesting that these partisans had aroused the Boston citizenry to the brink of insurrection, Bernard urged Hillsborough to dispatch British troops to the city and to curtail the colony's political privileges. Whately's network of correspondents included Bernard's Lieutenant Governor, the former stamp distributor for Massachusetts, and a few of Bernard's sympathizers in Connecticut and Rhode Island. Their letters to Whately resounded with the same story that Bernard told Hillsborough.[15]

Thomas Pownall could scrutinize the administration's every step toward the colonies. He enjoyed valuable political connections himself, and his brother John Pownall held the important position of secretary to the Board of Trade. Undoubtedly Thomas Pownall knew that Bernard's reports had spurred Hillsborough to send troops to Boston in the summer of 1768. He must have learned also that Bernard's suggestions had become the basis for Hillsborough's plan to revamp the Massachusetts charter along stricter lines, a plan the minister began promoting in January 1769. Finally, as a Member of Parliament, Pownall witnessed the debate in Commons in the winter of 1768–1769 over the so-called Massachusetts Bay Papers. The papers, which included Bernard's letters to Hillsborough, were presented by Hillsborough to win support for his harsh resolutions against the colony. The papers proved most effective for alarming and angering Parliament.[16] Pownall could see that

Bernard's misleading correspondence, which belittled America's real grievances and attrributed the disorders to a small minority of factional firebrands, was stiffening resistance on both sides of the ocean. British statemen failed to interpret colonial protests against the Townshend Acts as a serious grievance that demanded redress. Instead, they put down the protests with force and threatened the Americans with additional unwelcome regulations.[17] The Massachusetts patriots, with whom Pownall kept in close touch, were frantic over the Bernard faction's "partial and false representations."[18] The president of the Massachusetts Council told Pownall that "peace, harmony & confidence can never be restored . . . unless it procures the removal of some persons here from office, particularly Governor Bernard, in whom all confidence is lost." The colony's patience with their governor, and with a ministry that relied on his lies, was nearing its end.[19]

Undoubtedly, in his almost weekly meetings with Johnson, Thomas Pownall confessed his concern over the Bernard and Whately letters. But Johnson was alerted to the content of these letters and their baneful effects from other sources as well. The Connecticut agent's wide circle of correspondents included Massachusetts men from both the patriot and Bernard factions. He often exchanged views with Nathaniel Rogers, who was a strong supporter of the Bernard-Hutchinson party and a frequent correspondent of Whately's. In all likelihood, what Rogers told Johnson was repeated in the Massachusetts merchant's reports to Whately. Rogers wrote to Johnson that the arrival of the British troops was a welcome relief to the Bostonians, who abhorred the "wretched state" to which the popular party had reduced civil authority. Rogers even suggested that Johnson was losing popularity with the colony's royal officials, because they suspected that the Connecticut agent was overly sympathetic to the Bay Colony's patriot party. Johnson replied, "It is objected to me that I favor the Popular party. I do so most certainly. I am obliged to do so by principle and conscience."[20]

On July 27, 1768, Johnson entered in his diary that he had talked that day with Whately on "the late Intelligence from America," and on August 23, he noted that he "spent the evening with . . . Mr. Whately & John Pownall on the Intelligence just arrived from Boston."[21] Most likely, it was on these two occasions that Johnson learned of the letters Whately was receiving and their influence on the administration through

Whately's close friend, John Pownall.[22] It is certain that Johnson was also aware of the Bernard letters before the politically
ambitious William Bollan stole them from their British owner
and sent them to the Massachusetts Council in April 1769. That
March, Johnson wrote home that the Bostonians were suffering
"undue punishment" owing to the false reports of "interested"
American informers.[23] Johnson also observed the debates in
Parliament, when the Massachusetts Bay Papers were read and
Hillsborough's resolutions were adopted. We cannot be sure
that he knew of Hillsborough's plan to alter the Masschusetts
charter as early as that winter, for he makes no reference to the
plan in his correspondence until August. But it is not unlikely
that in one of Johnson's frequent interviews with Hillsborough, the minister revealed his intention. On previous meetings
with the Connecticut agent, Hillsborough had never held back
his views on colonial policy, no matter how they might offend
an American.

Through his valuable political acquaintances and daily
attendance at Westminister, Johnson learned that the Grafton-
Bedford ministry was being misled by the distorted and partisan
reports of the Bernard faction, and that the ministry's unwise
measures, particularly against Boston, were due in great part to
those reports. Bollan's daring theft of the letters gladdened
Johnson. He told Eliphalet Dyer that the exposure of the letters
proved how the administration's "severe reactions" to the disorders at Boston resulted from the "false intelligence received
from the colonies, which exaggerates every circumstance."[24] To
Johnson, the letters exculpated the British from any malign
intent, though not from negligence. The ministry's seeming
malevolence was, in fact, attributable to the spurious reports of
a few malicious men who resided under the Americans' own
noses. But the exposure of the letters only made Johnson's countrymen more anxious. Like Pownall, Johnson received angry
protests from Massachusetts that indicated how the ministry's
reliance on these perfidious reports was creating fear and disaffection in American minds.[25]

Johnson apprehended grave consequences from the rising
tensions and suspicions in England and America. "The truth
perhaps is," he warned one colonist, "that neither side are so
bad or have so mischievous designs as the other imagines . . . and
we are in danger of falling together by the ears in the dark without understanding what we are quarreling about."[26] He believed

that if the grounds for disagreement between the colonies and the mother country were understood and dealt with openly, a speedy settlement could be reached. The burden, he insisted, lay with Parliament and the ministry, who must put aside party considerations and spurious rumors to confront the Townshend dispute with reason, moderation, and adequate information.[27] Yet by the summer of 1769 Johnson retained little hope that the British would meet the task until the colony's nonimportation campaign forced the issue. "Their intestine divisions and party squabbles," he wrote, ". . . have really risen to a most alarming height and not only prevent a just and sober attention to the real interest & happiness of the nation, but actually seem to threaten a dissolution of the whole political system and the ruin of the empire."[28]

In 1769 Johnson agreed with America's most ardent patriots that the Townshend Acts must be resisted until relief was won. The distinction between Johnson's interpretation of the Anglo-American crisis and the colonists' growing suspicion of a well-laid plot against liberty could be seen not in the actions they endorsed but only in the different words they chose to describe the cause of the crisis. Johnson spoke in terms of "neglect," "misguided policy," and a ministry "embarrassed and perplexed with domestic divisions and party rage." His countrymen warned of deliberate designs and conspiracies.[29]

The two decades of British government before the American Revolution were one long storm that rocked the nation year after year and intermittently reached out to convulse the colonies as well. One incident during this stormy period, the reelection of John Wilkes to Parliament on March 28, 1768, proved especially tempestuous. Wilkes's election was also the one issue that already plainly revealed how differently Johnson and his fellow countrymen viewed the British government. The sequence of events that ensued from this momentous election excited the colonists' suspicions of a well-laid ministerial plot to destroy liberty. Johnson construed the same events as a comedy of errors that demonstrated the ministry's incapacity to govern the nation or even to protect its own political fortunes.

The clamor attending John Wilkes's election in 1768 surprised no one. Since early in the decade, Wilkes had been a controversial figure as a Member of Parliament and an outspoken journalist who had filled his newspaper, the *North Briton*, with daring and abusive political editorials. His campaign against

the Treaty of Paris in 1763 had aroused the ire of Georgee III
and the King's chief minister, George Grenville. Grenville,
who was determined to silence the agitator, had had Wilkes
arrested in 1763 on a "general warrant" or unlimited power of
arrest. But as a member of the House of Commons, Wilkes was
protected by parliamentary privilege and immune from prosecution for seditious libel. The following year Grenville had
persuaded Parliament to expel Wilkes, who had immediately
fled to the Continent to avoid prosecution. In 1768 the notorious journalist daringly returned to London to stand for Parliament in the general election. His bold tactics and colorful
personality, the social unrest of that year, and the traditional
hostility of the city toward the powers at Westminster carried
him to victory in the outlying suburb of Middlesex, although
the same factors were insufficient to win his election in London
proper.[30]

Johnson was as dismayed by Wilkes's success as by every
other aspect of that general election. To the Connecticut agent,
Wilkes was nothing more than "an outlaw who has insulted
his Sovereign & . . . Blasphemed his God, of the most abandon'd
Principles & dissolute Manner in private life, without money
& without apparent Friends of any Conseq[uence]."[31] For two
days after the election, Wilkes's supporters invaded the streets
of London and Westminster, throwing the city into anarchy.
The scene, to Johnson, was shocking.[32] But Wilkes was the darling of colonial patriots, and his election was celebrated in all
the provinces with toasts to "Wilkes and Liberty." The Americans cared nothing about Wilkes's personal character. To them,
he was a victim and foe of parliamentary power. In the eyes of
the colonists, the general warrant was an odious cousin to the
writs of assistance with which customs officers searched and
seized American ships.[33] Wilkes was popular for other reasons,
too. He had championed the colonists' hero, William Pitt,
against the accession of Bute. He had been expelled under the
ministry of George Grenville, the notorious instigator of the
Stamp Act. And while he was in exile, his newpaper, the *North
Briton*, had attacked the Townshend acts and had risen to the
defense of American rights.[34] From his election in 1768, every
step of Wilkes's career would be followed with adulation in the
colonial press.[35]

To Johnson, Wilkes was a despicable opportunist, and the
connection between his cause and American freedom was a mere

illusion. "If he and his friends were once in power," Johnson wrote home, "things I doubt would proceed as usual, they would take very good care of themselves, very little of the public and in particular with respect to America. I am told he has lately said he could answer the *Farmer's Letters* in two pages and entirely overset his whole system."[36] Franklin, too, could see no legitimate connection between Wilkes's election and American rights.[37] But the opinions of the two agents went unheeded. The events of the following year would heighten the colonists' conviction that Wilkes and America were falling victim to one and the same conspiracy against liberty.

Although Wilkes won the election, he had yet to secure acquittal for libel. Shortly after his victory at Middlesex, he surrendered and was sentenced to two years' imprisonment. To keep his plight alive in the public mind, in November he formally claimed his new seat in Parliament. All winter the House of Commons deliberated on the seating of Wilkes. On February 3, 1769, Commons declared him expelled from Parliament, as it had done in 1764. Three times in the spring of 1769 the Middlesex voters reelected Wilkes and three times, on February 15, March 16, and May 8, the House of Commons again expelled him. The refusal of Parliament to seat Wilkes enraged the British public. No law prohibited a criminal guilty of seditious libel from membership in Parliament. The expulsion was widely interpreted as an infringement of the voters' right to choose their own representatives.[38] The repeated expulsion of Wilkes was no more alarming than was the massacre of May 10 at St. George's Field. Here a mob, which had assembled that day in support of the imprisoned Wilkes, was fired upon by a regiment of Foot Guards summoned to maintain civil order.[39] The incident served only to cast the government in an odious light. The imposition of military force on the citizenry and the exclusion of the voters' representative from Parliament inspired London's radical political reformers to establish the Society of Supporters of the Bill of Rights. The society aimed to raise financial support for Wilkes and to capture the attention of the entire nation to his plight. Its members organized a country-wide campaign to petition the King for the dismissal of the Grafton-Bedford ministry and the election of a new Parliament.[40]

Many colonists watched the petition campaign with anticipation and sent their money to fill the coffers of the Wilkes fund. In 1768 the question of general warrants had provided the chief

link between America's grievances and Wilkes's cause. But by
1769 the expulsion of Wilkes and the massacre at St. George's
Field had raised colonial anxieties to fever pitch. The massacre
made the presence of troops in Boston seem more threatening,
and the interference with the Middlesex election cast the suspension of the New York and Massachusetts assemblies into a
general pattern of obstructing representative government.[41]
"We yet too sensibly feel the loss of every right, liberty, and
privilege that can distinguish a freeman from a slave," the
Boston Sons of Liberty wrote to Wilkes, "not to sympathize
in the most tender manner with you in the conflict you have
been so long engaged in."[42]

Johnson followed the events of the Wilkes case with rapt
attention. He attended the argument of the case at Westminster,
read the *North Briton* at the New England Coffee House, and
even rode out to St. George's Field to observe the confusion on
the day of the massacre. He saw how the expulsion of Wilkes
had inflamed Englishmen everywhere, and he blamed the ministers for their foolishness. They had blundered into an action
that was contrary to the spirit of the constitution on the provocations of one incendiary outlaw. Johnson concluded that,

The present ministry seem to be admirably skilled in the Arts of fomenting, encreasing & keeping up Strife, Animosity, Contest & to have
little ability in soothing Composing & quieting the Contentions &
disturbances wh[ich] have arisen in almost every part of the Empire.
The tumults here upon the Subject of the Midd[lesex] Election &
Mr. W[ilkes's] affairs might easily have been prevent'd by Prudence
or quieted by Policy, instead of which Adm[inistration] have by their
negligence & Ill conduct not only permitted but provoked their
encrease.[43]

The imprudent expulsion of Wilkes brought down upon
the Grafton-Bedford administration not only the anger of the
London radicals and American patriots but also the calculated
wrath of the opposition parties in Parliament, which were eager
to exploit any issue to discredit and overturn the ministry. In
1768 the Rockingham and Chatham factions had ignored
Wilkes's cause, but in 1769 they threw their support behind the
Wilkes campaign and joined the cry for new elections and the
dismissal of the King's cabinet. The entire spring session of
Parliament was consumed by the Wilkes affair, which helps to
explain why Parliament arose in May without offering any

plan of accommodation on the Townshend dispute. More importantly, many members of Parliament came to associate the Wilkes protest and American resistance to the Townshend Acts as two sides of the same attack on the government's authority, and they resolved to combat domestic and American radicalism alike.[44]

By the summer of 1769, the ministry's inability to subdue the resistance in America and quiet the clamor at home caused nearly everyone to expect a change of administration. Thomas Whately told one of his Boston correspondents that "the crisis in our affairs [and] the discontents of the people [in America] will soon make the establishment of a more able administration necessary." Commenting on America's noisy support of Wilkes, Whately warned his Boston friend that "Your people are poor politicians in exulting as they do in our disorders, & not seeing that from thence results the necessity for a government equal in firmness & stability to the occasion."[45] Johnson too looked for a change of leadership, and he anticipated the event without enthusiasm. Before Parliament adjourned that spring, Johnson had despaired "how few friends we have there who are so upon real principle."[46] He predicted that should the ministry lose the confidence of Parliament, a coalition of the Rockingham, Chatham, and Grenville factions would take the reins of government. The Rockinghamites, he knew, were determined advocates of the Declaratory Act and would brook no challenge to parliamentary sovereignty. Johnson warned his countrymen that Rockingham and Grenville thought alike on matters of taxation and would first "lull" the Americans "to sleep" with "gently guarded declarations" and "the moment they repose in filial confidence . . . it will then become expedient to tax them because it may be done with success."[47] The Connecticut agent reminded his countrymen that during the spring session of Parliament, the Rockingham faction had not pressed for the removal of the Townshend duties and did "not seem this session really to have wished the repeal of the act but rather that it should remain to embarrass the present Ministers, and as a means of their destruction, to whom they hope to succeed. . . . Indeed this must be the case with every party in some degree; the Colonies, therefore, if they are wise, will take care not to become the dupes of any party."[48]

Johnson was just as troubled by the prospect of Chatham's return to power. Chatham, he knew, was no advocate of colonial taxation. But Johnson found Chatham's determination to regulate the colonies strictly in all other matters plainly incompatible with the enjoyment of American liberty. The Connecticut agent alerted his countrymen to Chatham's "dangerous idea of a right to restrain us from absolutely every species of manufacture." Said Johnson: "It is with him but a word and a blow, and the one commonly so soon succeeds the other, that it is sometimes difficult to determine which issued first." Johnson concluded that the colonies were as safe under the Grafton ministry as they would be under a pro-Wilkes coalition:

Whether we of the Colonies have much reason to wish for a speedy change of Administration, I am in doubt. . . . perhaps we shall find no set of men so little able to carry into execution any vigorous measures against the Colonies. . . . They certainly wish to have as little as possible upon their hands, and will interfere no farther than is absolutely necessary for their own security in any distant dissensions, either European or American, that they may, as I have said, with more collected attention and force apply themselves to their domestic disputes and to the security and increase of their own power, the ultimate object of all their conduct & designs. . . .[49]

He told his constituents to depend on no British party for their liberty, and to trust only their own firmness and frugality to restore American rights.[50]

Johnson's apprehensions about a new Chatham ministry reflected his broadening view of the Anglo-American dispute. By 1769, Johnson had come to realize that the dispute between the colonies and the mother country no longer revolved around the single question of Parliament's taxing power. His countrymen complained of a host of grievances, such as trial without jury, military rule in Boston, and the obstruction of the colonial assemblies. To be sure, all of these grievances had grown out of the attempt to raise an American revenue for the support of the British military on the frontier. But a resolution of Anglo-American tensions now demanded some mutual agreement on the extent and limits of parliamentary sovereignty in all affairs.

Johnson was not given to systematic theorizing on a grand scale. He was convinced that the colonists must win from Parliament an unequivocal abdication of the taxing power, but he would offer no specific suggestions on how to limit Parliament's role in other matters. On the other hand, he abhorred the innovations in imperial regulation that had been imposed on the colonists since 1763. When Connecticut's leaders asked his advice on the constitutionality of writs of assistance, Johnson encouraged the colony's Superior Court to withhold the writs from the customs officers.[51] On the other hand, he understood that no one in Great Britain would tolerate the stand taken by the Boston patriots in 1768 to the effect that Parliament had no jurisdiction over the colonies whatsoever.[52] He hoped that some middle point, halfway between unlimited paraliamentary sovereignty and complete colonial autonomy, might be hit upon. The responsibility, he observed pessimistically, lay with the ministry.[53]

It is safe to reason that if the Americans had not been separated from Westminster by three thousand miles of ocean, and all the unfamiliarity that such distance entailed two centuries ago, they might have perceived, as Johnson did, the opportunistic motives underlying Wilkes's return to London and the participation of the ministry's political adversaries in the Wilkes crusade. The colonists might have recognized the dangerous notions of parliamentary sovereignty to which America's supposed allies, the Rockinghamites and the Chathamites, subscribed.[54] They might have understood the relationship between Britain's tumultuous political situation and its disastrous conduct of colonial policy. Most importantly, they might have rejected the myth of a malign, well-laid plan to destroy British and American liberty.

Franklin, like Johnson, was distressed by his countrymen's swelling suspicions of a ministerial conspiracy. He too was convinced that the British government acted not so much "from a malignity of heart" as from an "insanity of head."[55] Even in 1767 Franklin had diagnosed the problem. The Americans were fast losing their fondness for the empire, Franklin had observed, "and yet there remains among that People so much Respect, Veneration and Affection for Britain, that if cultivated prudently, with kind Usage and Tenderness for their Privileges, they might easily be governed still for Ages, without Force or Considerable Expense. But I do not see here a sufficient Quantity of the Wisdom that is necessary to produce such Conduct, and I lament the Want of it."[56] The fuss made over Wilkes dismayed Franklin, who found it "an extraordinary event, to see an outlaw and exile, of bad personal character, not worth a farthing, come over from France, [and] set himself up as a candidate for the capital of the Kingdom."[57] He told the colonists that "it hurts you here with sober and sensible men, when they see you so easily infected with the Madness of English Mobs."[58] Yet few Americans heeded the advice of Franklin and Johnson. Instead, the colonists identified their cause with the fate of Wilkes and followed closely the campaign for a new parliamentary election and the dismissal of the ministry. They were bitterly disillusioned by year's end. Parliament upheld its verdict against Wilkes, and George III stood by his cabinet and refused to call another election. Many colonists grew fearful that the King and Parliament had fallen under the sway of evil ministers and that British liberty was in grave danger.[59]

As the notion of a deliberate conspiracy against liberty swelled larger and larger in colonial minds, so too did the dread of ecclesiastical tyranny. Governor Trumbull alerted Johnson and Jackson that "the Motion for a Bishop in the American colonies, occasions much Noise, & many altercations on this side of the Water. Great part of the opposition arises, from Fear and tender concern for our religious Liberties, much more precious than those of a civil Nature."[60] Trial without jury, British troops in Boston, the expulsion of Wilkes, and taxation without representation made an American episcopacy seem imminent. The Massachusetts General Court alerted its agent, Dennys De Berdt, that "the establishment of a Protestant Episcopate in America is also very zealously contended for. And it is very alarming. . . .

The revenue raised in America for aught we can tell, may be as constitutionally applied toward the support of Prelacy as of Soldiers and Pensioners: If the property of the subject is taken from him without his consent, it is immaterial whether it is done by one man or five hundred; or whether it is applied for the support of ecclesiastick or military power, or both.[61]

The outspoken demands of the American-born missionaries for a bishop were also to blame for the New Englanders' alarm. By 1766, after years of fruitless waiting, the missionaries had determined to take matters into their own hands and press their cause in America when they could not win their point in England. Their campaign was blundering and naive, and their ill-considered, aggressive tactics provoked a furious response. In the forefront of the new campaign was Samuel Johnson, who had recently retired from King's College. Behind Johnson stood four spirited young churchmen: Samuel Seabury, Charles

Inglis, and Myles Cooper of New York, and Thomas Chandler of New Jersey, to whom Johnson was gradually passing the leadership of the Episcopal cause. On Chandler, the aged Johnson bestowed the responsibilities and expectations that other fathers confidently reserved for their own sons. Four times over the next year, churchmen from Pennsylvania, New York, New Jersey, and Connecticut gathered together to lay plans for the campaign. At Samuel Johnson's suggestion, they enlisted Chandler to compose *An Appeal to the Public in Behalf of the Church of England in America*, which reiterated many of the assurances that Secker had offered Mayhew four years earlier. The churchmen's frequent intercolonial gatherings raised curiosity and suspicion in American minds, and the appearance of Chandler's *Appeal* in 1767 set off an explosive controversy.[62]

The Boston Congregationalist Rev. Charles Chauncy hastened to expose Chandler's arguments as mere artifice, and over the next four years the two clergymen battled wits in a long pamphlet war. Chauncy contended that Chandler's proposal for a bishop without political powers had no precedent in the Church of England. Episcopalians aimed at nothing less than a complete ecclesiastical hierarchy with courts, tithes, and penalties for Nonconformists.[63] In 1768, the famous New York Triumvirate carried the controversy out of narrow clerical circles and into the newspapers and the public eye. Days after the Triumvirate's "American Whig" first appeared in the press, the Presbyterian politicians of Philadelphia joined the outcry in a column dubbed the "Centinel." Although the New York and Philadelphia press campaigns resounded a familiar theme— the nefarious partnership between church and state in England—the "Centinel" and the "American Whig" attracted unprecedented attention to the dangers of an Episcopal establishment.[64]

The theme of impending Episcopal tyranny fit neatly into the larger scheme of ministerial despotism that the colonists apprehended, but it bore no resemblance to the reality of church politics in England. The Chatham administration and its successor, the Grafton-Bedford ministry, refused to sponsor an American bishop for the very reasons that had impelled Walpole to oppose it years earlier. British statesmen were loath to alarm the colonial dissenters and their politically powerful brethren in England.[65] No one knew this better and anguished more over the rising clamor in America than William Samuel Johnson.

From his first days in England, Johnson labored unrelentingly on behalf of an American episcopate. His father had urged him to use his opportunity well and had provided letters of introduction to Archbishop Secker and other important figures in the mother church.[66] Even the excited debate in Parliament on Lord Townshend's proposals did not divert him from pressing his father's cause. In the spring of 1767, Johnson met repeatedly with the Archbishop, the Bishop of London, and the Secretary of the SPG. To the Connecticut agent, they reported only failure in their efforts to win approval for a colonial bishop.[67] In July, Johnson presented his case directly to Lord Shelburne, but Shelburne offered no encouragement. Political parties, Johnson told his father, were too consumed by the business of winning and holding power to attend to such a risky affair as an American bishop. The *Appeal*, he added, would sway no minds here.[68] The following year, Johnson again reported home that political considerations posed an insurmountable obstacle to an American episcopate.[69]

William Samuel Johnson's references to reasons of state, like the explanations penned by Secker and other British churchmen, exasperated the colonial missionaries, whose zeal blinded them to the church's precarious political position. Let the Church of England send bishops to America without the ministry's approval, Samuel Johnson and his fellow missionaries, retorted.[70] All the while, they continued their aggressive, noisy pamphlet war against the prejudices of their New England neighbors. Their persistent indiscretions tried the younger Johnson's patience. Repeatedly the Connecticut agent warned his father that the public debate over a colonial bishop could not help the cause in England and could only hurt it in America. "You do not know enough . . . ," Johnson admonished his father, "to judge Properly of this affair."[71]

The raging controversy in the colonies must have troubled William Samuel Johnson for another reason too. As his countrymen's dread of Anglican tyranny swelled, so too did their distrust of Episcopal agents. The troubled career of William Bollan offered a lesson to the Connecticut agent. In 1762, when the Massachusetts clergy raised a frightful alarm against Episcopacy in New England, the colony's House of Representatives had quickly dismissed their Episcopalian agent, William Bollan, and had appointed in his stead a conspicuous spokesman for Nonconformity, Jasper Mauduit.[72] Even before Johnson departed for England, one Connecticut divine had warned him of the frequent suspicion that he might use his new office to distress the Congregational establishment and advance the missionaries' cause. Reverend Chauncey Whittelsey had admonished Johnson that "any such Attempt, as is apprehended, would, at once, render you obnoxious to the Resentments of the People."[73] Johnson took the warning to heart. In April 1767, he told his father that a bishop would not be sent to America, "so that my countrymen (if there are any of them jealous of me) may make themselves easy as to any mischief they may imagine I might do them."[74] Johnson pursued his father's cause with the greatest caution in England and insisted that the colonial churchmen keep his name out of the public controversy at home.[75] There is no evidence that his persistent appeals to British church leaders and statesmen attracted any notice in America. In 1769 Governor Trumbull confidently entrusted Connecticut's religious liberties to Johnson's protection. "If the motion for a Bishop in the American Colonies is pushed," Trumbull wrote, "I trust you will use your influence to prevent his having authority to exercise spiritual jurisdiction over such who are not professors of the Church of England, and secular powers of any nature or kind whatever."[76]

Johnson assured Trumbull that "It is not intended at present to send any Bishops into the American Colonies; had it been, I should certainly have acquainted you with it." Seizing the opportunity to allay his countrymen's exaggered fears, Johnson added that the proposal for a colonial episcopate was "merely a religious, in no respect a political design. . . . More than this would be thought disadvantageous rather than beneficial; and would be opposed, I assure you, by no man with more zeal than myself, even as a Churchman. Nay, I have the best grounds to assure you, that more would not be accepted by those who really understand and wish well to the design were it offered."[77] Reports from the other colonial agents, American travelers, and even the colonists' Nonconformist allies in Great Britain confirmed Johnson's testimony, but these assurances failed to relieve American anxiety.[78] Ecclesiastical tyranny had become an immovable fear, born of a century-old distrust of the Church of England, nurtured by a growing belief in ministerial conspiracy, and open to no reasonable argument. As this fear swelled in the next decade, the impending breach between Johnson and his countrymen would grow wider.

The spectre of American bishops merely intensified the distrust and fear that had taken hold of Americans during the Townshend Acts crisis. By the summer of 1769, colonial patriots were filled with alarm at the events of the past two years. In 1767 new taxes had been thrust upon them without their consent, and a host of placemen had been dispatched to the colonies to man the American Board of Customs. The next year, the powers of the Courts of Vice Admiralty had been extended, imposing trial without jury in all the major ports, and British troops had landed in Boston to subdue the citizenry. In the spring of 1769, Parliament had turned a deaf ear to colonial pleas for redress and had issued harsh threats against the American protestors. With terrified hearts, the Americans witnessed the rising clamor over Wilkes. They associated his arrest under a general warrant with the odious writs of assistance, compared his expulsion with the obstruction of legislative government in Massachusetts and New York, and related the massacre of his followers at St. George's Field to the threat of military force in Boston. It is little wonder that many colonists, so distant from the scene of events, would suspect in the happenings of these two years a deliberate intent to rob the colonists, and indeed all Englishmen, of their liberties. Surely the words of the *Letters from a Farmer* must have resounded in their minds, that "if at length it becomes undoubted that an inveterate resolution is formed to annihilate the liberties of the governed, the *English* history affords frequent examples of resistance by force. . . ."[79]

Before the Stamp Act crisis, hardly an American could have been found who entertained the idea of separating from Great Britain. But with mounting apprehension, the colonists now began talking of independence. Connecticut's Governor Pitkin asked Johnson, "Is it not to be feared that these hard measures will prevent the continuance of that good agreement, harmony and confidence that ought to subsist between us and our mother country? Is not mistrust and disaffection the natural result of restraint and oppression?"[80] Pitkin's successor expressed the dreadful prediction even more plainly: "It is hard to break connections with our mother country; but when she strives to enslave us, and turn all our labors barely to her own emoluments, without considering us as her sons and free-born fellow subjects, the strictest union must be dissolved."[81]

Even those colonists who understood the frenzied state of British politics and dismissed any deliberate plot against the

Americans predicted that the dispute would rage on until only the most dire alternative remained. One American wrote Johnson, "How unhappy for a state are party differences, when the zealous must justify the conduct of their party, right or wrong, beneficial or injurious to the state; in these circumstances I must join with those who think the danger great, which will prevail."[82] Johnson was unsurprised to hear his fellow colonists contemplating the once inconceivable notion of independence. When Parliament ended its spring session in 1769 without offering the colonists a conciliatory plan to settle the Townshend dispute, he complained to his friend Benjamin Gale that "we shall go on contending and fretting [with] each other till our prophecy shall, as it certainly will be, fulfilled and we become separated states."[83]

To most colonists, the prospect of separation presented insurmountable obstacles. Governor Pitkin queried anxiously, "Where should we go? Don't we idolise the British Constitution, government and nation and despise all other states in comparison thereof? Shall we set up a kingdom by ourselves? Every Colony has such peculiarities of their own that they are so fond of, that if we had number and wealth sufficient, the Colonies would never unite into one state." Pitkin urged the Connecticut agent to press for some means of compromise "before it is too late."[84] John Dickinson, whose *Letters* raised the prospect of armed rebellion for all to contemplate, also eyed such a course with great misgivings: "A multitude of Commonwealths, Crimes and Calamities—Centuries of mutual jealousies, Hatreds, Wars of Desolation; till at last the exhausted Provinces shall sink into Slavery under the Yoke of some unfortunate Conqueror." The result, he said, is that "we must bleed at every vein."[85]

Johnson, like Dickinson, worried over the political instability of the colonies. The factional controversies that had rocked Connecticut's political order in 1766 were still fresh in his mind as he wrote three years later:

If we were wise and could form some system of free government upon just principles, we might be very happy without any connection with this country. But should we ever agree upon anything of that nature, should we not more probably fall into factions and parties amongst ourselves, destroy one another and become at length the easy prey [and] property of the first invaders?[86]

The perils of independence that Johnson envisioned made him all the more insistent that an Anglo-American settlement could be reached. "The rights of the people are not inconsistent with those of the Crown," he said, "nor the interests of that country with those of Great Britain. Those who separate them are enemies and traitors to both."[87] In Connecticut, the hazards of separation evoked a similar response. Governor Pitkin assured the Connecticut agent that "a Perfect Harmony with Great Britain is our Desire."[88]

By 1769, imprudent and rash British measures had pushed many colonists to suspect the worst of the mother country and to ponder a final separation. But the idea was a new and frightening one. Colonial distrust toward Great Britain had not reached that critical point where a majority of Americans would undertake this unknown and perilous course. As the *Letters from a Farmer* warned, rebellion "can never be justified until the people are *fully* convinced that any further submission will be destructive to their happiness."[89] Johnson's understanding of the reasons underlying Britain's unwise colonial conduct had already diverged from his countrymen's mounting belief in a deliberate subversion of American rights. But neither Johnson nor his fellow colonists could predict that this divergence would one day make him their enemy in war. The drastic consequences of colonial suspicions were yet to be realized. Only timorous whispers of independence and armed resistance signalled the extreme course to which these suspicions would one day propel the patriots. In 1769 most Americans were still eager to believe that reconciliation was possible. Their eyes, like Johnson's, were turned toward Parliament, which was to meet again in the fall of that year. They believed, as Johnson did, that their proper weapon was economic retaliation.

Chapter Eight

Defeat and Disillusionment

During the summer and fall of 1769 all attention was on Westminster, where Parliament would begin a new session after Christmas. Wilkes's friends waited to see whether their petition campaign would bring about the collapse of the Grafton ministry. Americans hoped that their boycott against British goods would force the repeal of the Townshend duties. Long before the Members of Parliament returned to London that winter, Johnson and his countrymen were alerted to the course that the new session was likely to follow. Indeed, just a few days after the old session ended in May, the ministry announced its intentions to propose the repeal of all the Townshend duties except the tax on tea when Parliament recommenced that winter. The ministers realized that the Townshend duties were not producing enough income to support a military establishment in the colonies, and they were eager to free themselves from the problems the duties posed. Despite objections from the Duke of Grafton, who yearned for a friendly settlement with the Americans, the Bedfordites insisted that the tax on tea be retained as a symbol of Parliament's right to legislate in all matters, including a colonial revenue. That summer, Lord Hillsborough dispatched letters to all the colonial governors, relating the ministry's pledge for partial repeal.[1]

Johnson distrusted the administration's promise and urged his countrymen to disregard it. The government, he said, aimed to lure the Americans from their nonimportation resolves. If the ministers sincerely intended to repeal the duties, they would have announced their proposal to Parliament instead of waiting until the session had adjourned. Johnson cautioned that acquiescing to the tea duty would establish Parliament's right to tax, opening the way for more onerous burdens in the future.[2]

Johnson's admonitions could occasion no surprise. Months earlier, in a heated debate with the other colonial agents over a joint petition to Parliament, he had warned against any compromise on parliamentary taxation. What had changed was the conciliatory demeanor of Johnson's fellow agents, including Franklin and De Berdt. By the summer of 1769, they were no longer willing to lay aside the constitutional question to achieve a speedy Anglo-American reconciliation. Their patience had been tried to its limit when Parliament adjourned that spring without addressing America's grievances. But the agents' new firmness also reflected the growing strength of the nonimportation movement in America. In the summer and fall of 1769, the colonial agents received word that after two years of squabbling, America's three great ports—New York, Philadelphia, and Boston—had finally agreed on a joint pact to boycott British goods.[3] America's spokesmen in England would no longer be embarrassed by colonial irresolution. The merchants of Philadelphia assured Franklin that they would hold fast to the boycott until all the Townshend Acts, not just the most burdensome duties, were repealed.[4] In March, Franklin had advocated compromising with the ministry and laying aside the issue of Parliament's authority, but in July he applauded the merchants' determination and exhorted them to persist until all the duties, including the tax on tea, were defeated.[5]

Early in 1769, De Berdt, like Franklin, had insisted that America would win relief from the Townshend Acts only by forgetting the question of parliamentary jurisdiction and conciliating the ministry with less offensive arguments for repeal. By the end of the year De Berdt was filled with hostility toward the administration, and advised his constituents not to relent until they had secured a total victory. De Berdt's drastic change of heart was due in no small degree to the repeated expulsion of Wilkes.[6] But De Berdt was also enraged by the plans of Governor Bernard and Lord Hillsborough to subvert the Massachusetts charter. On this issue, Johnson and De Berdt were of one mind. Governor Bernard came to England in August 1769 to lay before the Privy Council his account of the supposed anarchy in Massachusetts. He had left the colony in July, after the Massachusetts House of Representatives had charged him with violating their charter and had petitioned the King to remove him from office. As soon as Bernard arrived in London, he joined forces with Hillsborough, who was still pressing his own plan to redraft the Massachusetts charter. Bernard also aired his complaints against the colony to his close associate, Thomas Whately, and to Hillsborough's Undersecretary, John Pownall.[7] De Berdt, like Johnson and Johnson's friend Thomas Pownall, had been apprehensive all year that Bernard's exaggerated and biased reports would instigate harsh actions against the colony. The Massachusetts agent repeatedly warned his constituents of the baneful consequences that might result from Bernard's misrepresentations. That the ministry seemed so willing to cooperate with the hated Governor and even reward him for his conduct in Massachusetts angered De Berdt.[8]

Johnson also closely watched Bernard's activities with the ministry that fall. He could probably have relied on reports from Whately and Thomas Pownall, but he also dined with Bernard on several occasions, and at least once attended a meeting between Bernard and Hillsborough.[9] Evidently Bernard complained to the American Department against Connecticut's five percent ad valorum tax on British imports. The tax had been enacted to boost Connecticut's nonimportation effort. Johnson waited all fall and winter to see whether punitive action would be taken against his colony.[10] He could not rely on Richard Jackson to alert Connecticut to this danger, for Jackson clearly was in the Bernard camp. Jackson owed his brief tenure as Massachusetts agent in 1765 to Bernard's influence, had served as Bernard's liaison with the Board of Trade, and was now working hard to secure a new appointment for Bernard should the Massachusetts House of Representatives win their case against the Governor.[11] Consequently, it was left to Johnson to report home faithfully on Bernard's transactions with the administration.

For a variety of reasons—including the failure of Parliament to address the American problem in the spring of 1769, the cooperation between Bernard and the American Department, and the promising growth of the colonial boycott—most of the agents were no longer willing to compromise with the ministry on American rights and refused to accept the ministry's May proposal for a partial repeal of the Townshend Acts. In January 1770, the agents would persuade the merchants to join with them in demanding repeal of all the Townshend duties.[12] The agents' new position was tactically unwise, for the political conditions that had persuaded them to compromise with the ministry in March 1769 still prevailed. No ministry could retreat from the principle of parliamentary taxation. Neither in 1769 nor in 1770 could the Townshend duties be repealed without asserting the principle behind them. In May 1769 the Grafton ministry had designated the tax on tea as a symbol of that principle, and the agents would be struggling against insuperable odds when they demanded full repeal the next year.[13]

Until Parliament reconvened in January, there was little for the agents to do. Every summer and fall, Westminster was nearly deserted and politics was at a standstill. In June and July, Johnson toured the Netherlands, and for the remainder of the season he took excursions into the English countryside, attended to the Mohegan case, and enjoyed the social life of the capital.[14] He made the acquaintance of his namesake, the noted lexicographer and essayist Samuel Johnson, who lived in the Strand, the artists' section of London. The Connecticut agent wrote home that, on first impression, the famous Englishman seemed "as odd a mortal, in point of behavior and appearance as you ever saw. You would not at first sight suspect he had ever read or thought, in his life, or was much above the degree of an idiot. But nulla fronti fides, when he opens himself after a little acquaintance, you are abundantly [delivered] from these first unfavorable appearances." Whatever else the two Johnsons discussed, they must have agreed readily on the disheartening state of British politics. In the words of the English Johnson, "Politics are now nothing more than a means of rising in the world. With this sole view do men engage in politics, and their whole conduct proceeds upon it."[15]

William Samuel Johnson was confident that when Parliament renewed its business in January 1770 some action would be taken on the American question, for he supposed that the growing strength of the nonimportation campaign could not be ignored in Britain much longer:

Our Ministers have long listened to the flattering, fallacious representations of their interested, wretched sycophants, and persuaded themselves that the opposition in America was no more than a petty, desperate, dying faction not worth their notice. . . . Now that they see all their measures ineffectual, and their designs frustrated, that the Colonies can neither be intimidated nor amused, they begin, I think, to believe the affair is of a much more serious nature than they were aware of and that it is necessary to act with more vigor or with greater moderation,—Prudence points out the one, Indignation dictates the other.[16]

When Parliament reconvened on January 9, it was obvious
that indignation had triumphed over prudence. Once again the
ministry had undergone a transformation, this time the resignation of the Duke of Grafton, who had opposed the retention
of the tea tax in May. A new First Lord of the Treasury, Lord
North, stepped in as chief minister. The quiet accession of
North signalled the final victory of the Bedfordite viewpoint
on colonial policy, a victory that had begun with the departure
of Chatham and Shelburne in 1768 and the creation of the new
American Department under Hillsborough. North's ministry
would prove to be the longest and most popular in many decades. North enjoyed great support in Parliament, where a con-
census was emerging that permissiveness in domestic and colonial affairs had gone far enough.[17] Johnson eyed the new
ministry gloomily:

Ld North who now leads the yet victorious ministerial squadrons
says he will yield us only the Repeal of the duties on Paper, glass and
Painters' Colours. . . . What seems most to influence against the repeal
[of the tax on tea] is the opinion many have formed (founded as they
pretend upon the extravagant demands of the people of Boston) that
America will not be satisfied with anything less than the repeal of all
the late Acts of Parliament relating to the Colonies, even that of navigation, and that therefore they had best make their stand where they
are now, disannulling only those duties which are anticommercial.[18]

Johnson surmised that the new chief minister could carry any
point he wishes in Parliament, for North was having no difficulty upholding the expulsion of Wilkes against the city's
remonstrances and the opposition's speeches.[19]

On March 4, Parliament opened the America question.
Johnson listened from the galleries on the following evening
when Lord North moved for repeal of the import duties on all
articles except tea.[20] North's motion occasioned a month-long
debate. Thomas Pownall advanced an amendment that revoked
virtually all the Townshend Acts, even the independent salaries
for royal officials in the colonies, but his amendment was defeated.[21] Edmund Burke and other partisans of the Rockingham
party censured the administration's colonial policy, but Johnson noted, "It is plain enough that these motions were not
made for the sake of the Colonies, but merely to serve the purposes of the Opposition, to render the Ministry, if possible,
more odious, so that they may themselves come into the conduct

of affairs, while it remains very doubtful whether they would do much better, if at all, than their predecessors." Chatham voiced his fears that Americans were carrying the notion of liberty too far and that they intended to disengage themselves from all paraliamentary regulation. Johnson reflected, "All this tends to evince what I have, I believe, often said, that America is to take care of herself."[22]

During the debates, North addressed the petition that the agents' merchant allies had presented to Commons in February. The merchants' petition depicted the distressing decline of the trade with North America and called for a repeal of all the Townshend duties, but Lord North responded that the tea tax was not a burden to British merchants or their American customers and was resisted only because it had been laid down by Parliament. It must remain, he said. North looked back over the past five years and took heed:

When the stamp act was first proposed, I saw nothing unjust, nothing uncommercial, nothing unreasonable in it—nothing but what Great Britain might fairly demand of her colonies. American took flame; America united against it. I still think, that if there had been a permanence of ministers—if there had been a union of Englishmen in the cause of England, that act would at this moment have been a subsisting act.[23]

On April 8, North's bill was read for the third time in Commons. The bill passed, went on to the Lords, who concurred on April 11, and received the royal assent the next day. The repeal of the Townshend duties, although the preamble to the Revenue Act and the tea duty remained, was a watershed in the struggle to regulate the colonies. Gone forever was the hope that an elaborate imperial government in America could be maintained at the Americans' expense. No one learned this lesson more thoroughly and painfully than George Grenville, who announced during the debates: "Nothing could ever induce me to tax America again, but the united consent of King, Lords, and Commons, supported by the united voice of the people of England. . . . Leave America to the Crown; do not let Parliament intermeddle."[24] Had Townshend lived to hear that speech, he would no doubt have seconded Grenville's sentiment. No party could tax the colonies so long as the opposition forces in Parliament stood ready to attack the ministry's every move. None had the means to enforce the taxes in America and stand by the honor of Parliament.

The repeal's significance, which was captured in Grenville's speech, eluded Johnson. He wrote to the Governor of
Connecticut: "We now see the end of another session of Parliament, very little I fear to the emolument of the Colonies, or of
this distracted country."[25] Johnson warned the colonists that if
they were ever to be safe from parliamentary taxation, they
must continue the nonimportation pacts until the tea tax was
withdrawn. "It will now be seen," he wrote,

whether America is really in earnest and resolved to preserve her liberty. The game (if I may be allowed the expression) is in their hands,
and whether they will play it well or ill depends upon themselves, but
without union and firmness they can do nothing. . . . I must yet believe
that there is wisdom, virtue, and patriotism in that country, not only
to save it from ruin but to fix its rights upon a firm basis.[26]

Franklin, like Johnson, exhorted the colonists to hold fast
to their nonimportation agreements.[27] That both men chose
this course is surprising, for they clearly saw that by rejecting
partial repeal, they risked an open rupture with the mother country. Franklin predicted that, should the colonists hold out for
total repeal, impatience would lead them to rash measures and
angry words, that the ministry might once again send troops,
and that mutual provocations would eventually lead to a complete separation. Yet the Pennsylvania agent could conceive
no alternative to resistance. "As to Relief from the Wisdom and
Tenderness of Administration," he wrote, "hope itself is gone,
even with our most sanguine Friends. We have no other Re-
sources but in our virtue and Resolution, which our Enemies
allow will prevail, if we can but persevere."[28] Johnson, too,
apprehended that continuing discord would bring both countries to "some deplorable crisis." "No matter," he said, "it will
still be better for America if she has but virtue and firmness and
if she has not she is not worth saving."[29] Where was the Connecticut agent's deep concern for preserving the empire? What had
happened to his grave apprehensions of the perils of political
independence? In the summer of 1770, frustration and hostility
toward the administration eclipsed Johnson's reasonable,
cautious regard for the imperial connection. The ministry's
unyielding stance on the tea tax did much to shape Johnson's
state of mind, but other forces were also at work.

Johnson still felt threatened by Bernard's intrigues with
the American Department. In March Johnson had assured Connecticut's Governor that Hillsborough was willing to drop the

complaint against Connecticut's five percent duty act.[30] But while Bernard agitated against the charter privileges of Massachusetts, Johnson trembled for his colony. "When the flames are so near," he would write home in November, "we should be stupid indeed not to be alarmed. When charters are called into question, we have certainly more to fear, because we have more to lose."[31] Surely Johnson's fear that the North ministry might attack the Connecticut charter heightened his anxious determination that the colonies win an unequivocal victory over the administration on the tea issue.

The threat to charter liberties that Bernard's transactions with the American Department posed and the ministry's refusal to repeal all the Townshend Acts eroded even the temperate and rational demeanor of Thomas Pownall, whose devotion to imperial harmony was known to all. Pownall wrote bitterly to the town of Boston:

The whole tenor of my correspondence with my friends in America and of my advice to those here who would give me hearing, has been trying to form some line of reconciliation and reunion. . . . But I find that I have been the dupe of my own good wishes. The great men here despise my advice, & I see enough both in the ignorance & in the bad temper of men never more to advise anything but that [you should entrench] yourselves in the rights of Englishmen as your citadel & within your charter rights as works that guard that citadel in America. . . .[32]

To the president of the Massachusetts Council, Pownall despaired, "Those of two contending parties who think they have the power will seldom have the candor & good sense to give up part, so as to retain the rest undisputed. . . . I have lost all hope of any accommodation."[33]

Americans like Johnson and Franklin and friends to America like Pownall, who had been most devoted to imperial union, left Parliament in the spring of 1770 determined that the colonies should secure a total victory against the tea tax, even at the risk of an imperial rupture. They were confident that the Americans would not disappoint them. On January 29, Governor Trumbull had assured Johnson that "The people of all the Colonies . . . are firmly united for the maintenance and support of their rights and privileges—unwilling to be taxed internally or commercially by any legislat[ure] but their own, or to have any commissioners of the customs to lord it over them, or drain

off their earnings."[34] Johnson's friend Joseph Chew had written
him in February that all the merchants in the colony were bound
by a compact to observe the nonimportation agreement established in New York, Boston, and Philadelphia.[35] These ardent
reports reached Johnson just as Parliament was deciding for
partial repeal, and the news from Connecticut bolstered his
belief that the colonies would hold out for a complete victory
over Parliament. Not until late August would he learn of his
countrymen's response to partial repeal.[36]

After Parliament adjourned in the spring, the agents could
do nothing but wait anxiously while the boycott was put to the
test. Their countrymen, however, did not permit the experiment
to run its course. In August, Johnson was crushed with disappointment when news arrived from North America that the
colonists had acquiesced in partial repeal and abandoned nonimportation. Word of Parliament's decision had reached the
colonies in early May. Rhode Island, New Hampshire, and
Albany, New York, deserted the boycott immediately. The fatal
blow to colonial resistance came late in June, when New York
City accepted the ministry's recommendation and opened its
port to British wares.

Some patriots deplored New York's decision. Connecticut
merchants were incensed, and they resolved in a colony-wide
meeting to sever all intercourse with the neighboring province.
But by mid-October, Philadelphia and Boston had also abandoned the cause.[37] Many merchants undoubtedly were eager to
resume their Atlantic trade, and found the ministry's concessions satisfactory from a commercial standpoint.[38] The majority of Americans, unconnected with trade, must have been
relieved to see the unhappy dispute at an end. Few were ready
in 1770 to risk a complete separation from the mother country.
Constitutional issues alone, such as taxation, could not thrust
the Americans into open warfare. Only when their suspicions
of a deliberate ministerial plot were heightened and confirmed
by the events of the next five years would the colonists hold
steadfast to the point of open warfare.

Johnson was enraged and embittered by the New Yorkers'
decision. By the summer of 1770 he was willing to hazard everything, even the dreadful chance of war, to put the ministry in its
place and demonstrate his countrymen's attachment to liberty.
Shortly after word arrived of New York's defection, Johnson
wrote rancorously to Governor Trumbull:

The Ministry are confirmed in their system, their prudence and firmness applauded, the advocates for the Colonies are confounded, and hardly dare show their faces. Is this, it is said, your American firmness? Are these the examples you give us of your fortitude, your patriotism, and perseverance? The eyes of all Europe were turned towards America, and on the issue of this controversy was to be formed their idea of your character. It is done; your character is now fixed; you will make a very contemptible figure in the eyes of all mankind and disgrace the fair page of history. What can an American say to this? Nothing. . . .[39]

New York's surrender jolted Johnson into remembering his earlier apprehensions over an American separation, for the downfall of nonimportation proved to him that his countrymen were too disunited and unsteady to take on the task of forming a separate nation. He told the Connecticut Governor:

The merchants of New York, it seems justify themselves on the ground of the breaches of the agreement by the merchants of the other Provinces. . . . how glorious would it have been for them to have persevered in their greater virtue! When men once begin to accuse and to recriminate, all confidence in each other is soon at an end. . . . Alas the fatal effects of disunion and discord! How many states and empires have they ruined and will yet ruin![40]

The stinging disappointment of 1770 wrought a permanent change in Johnson. Never again would he jeopardize the imperial connection to uphold his countrymen's boasted attachment to liberty. The Americans had shown themselves weak. divided, and irresolute.

Chapter Nine

The Long—Awaited
Passage Home

⟨⟨⟨⟩⟨⟩⟩

*T*he years of dispute over the Townshend Acts left Johnson weary and disappointed, and the repeated inexcusable delays in the Mohegan case added to his despair. In the fall of 1770, when the agents' struggle against parliamentary taxation reached its disheartening conclusion, Johnson was still waiting for the Mohegan hearing to begin.

When Johnson arrived in London in January 1767, he confidently expected to resolve the case before the end of the year.[1] But in January 1768, American affairs were shifted from Lord Shelburne's Southern Department to the newly created American Department, headed by Lord Hillsborough. "Thus it is in all affairs," Johnson exclaimed, ". . . when you have pursued them almost to a Close & think you are pretty sure of y^r point some change of System intervenes & oversets all y^r plans. So unsteady are their Counsels, so uncertain the Tenure of them in Power!"[2] An endless chain of more exasperating, less explicable delays followed, due mostly to the stubborn negligence of British officials, who constantly postponed the hearing or simply failed to appear. "Such is the hard fate of those who depend, for the despatch of affairs, on the caprice of these men in power," Johnson told Trumbull. "[They] seem to have no feeling for their fellow subjects, but think they are appointed to offices and employments solely for their own benefit and are under no sort of obligation to do the business of their offices if it at all interferes with their own convenience and amusements."[3] In 1768, Johnson considered abandoning the case and returning home, but the urgings of the Connecticut legislators and his intense involvement in the Townshend dispute held him in England.[4]

Ann Johnson grew impatient and distraught with her

husband's unforeseen and prolonged absence. In November 1769 Samuel Johnson warned his son that he must return by spring, "whatever comes to the colony or Mohegan case." Ann "has hitherto bore your absence and conducted with great bravery," Samuel Johnson wrote, "but your not being likely to return this fall seems a shock to her, as she had much dependence on it that you would, so that her patience seems to flag, as I doubt you will perceive by her letter here enclosed. She is however resolved to bear up through one winter more, but if you should fail coming immediately after the next equinox, I doubt it will be too much for her to bear."[5] Ann Johnson's impatience was understandable. Her children were growing up without the guidance and companionship of their father. That year, the Johnsons' eldest daughter, Charity, wed a young candidate for Episcopal orders, Ebenezer Kneeland. In December Samuel Johnson even appealed to Governor Trumbull to release his son from the seemingly endless task. One month later, William Samuel Johnson sent home hopeful promises that he would return by summer. But in April 1770, he reported another delay, and in July he wrote despondently that the attorney general had refused to leave his country home and return to the capital until after the summer vacation. "Never did disappointment affect me so deeply," he told Ann. "Never was I more unhappy than I am rendered by this unforeseen delay. All my patience had been exhausted long before this additional Misfortune almost reduced me to despair."[6]

Johnson learned in August that the case was postponed at least three months more. The Townshend dispute had reached its conclusion and Johnson longed to escape the capital, but he feared that by leaving the Mohegan case unsettled, he would incur the resentment of the Connecticut Assembly and ruin his law practice in the colony.[7] Ann's discontent troubled him deeply. "All my felicity in this world," he confided to his new son-in-law, "depends upon the felicity of my dear wife & family & that *all*, I see by y^r letter, now stands upon the brink of a most dangerous precipice in most imminent danger of being lost—What a tremendous Situation am I in—Cannot you, my Dear S[on] Interpose & do something to prevent the impending ruin."[8] Another year passed before Johnson boarded a ship bound for the colonies. In June 1771, he attended the final hearing on the case, and on August 2, after the busy formalities of bidding farewell to his friends and political colleagues, he set sail.[9] A host of uncertainties surrounded his departure. Eventually Johnson's diligence would be rewarded by a favorable decision in the Mohegan case, but he would wait two years for the final judgment.[10] Johnson also worried that he had lost his family's affection. To Ann, he confessed that he felt like "the Boy who has often played Truant, exhausted all his Excuses, [and] at last is afraid to go to School at all."[11] Johnson eyed his political future with uncertainty too. The Connecticut agency had drawn him into a number of controversial issues, and his confidence in his political support had steadily diminished. No issue had troubled him more than the volatile Susquehannah dispute.

Even before Johnson sailed for England in the winter of 1766, Eliphalet Dyer had enlisted the new agent to promote the Susquehannah cause, quietly mentioning that Johnson owed his good political fortunes to Dyer's friendship.[12] The Proclamation of 1763, which excluded settlers from Indian lands west of the Appalachians, the crown's instructions to Governor Fitch to halt the Susquehannah expeditions, and the massacre of the Susquehannah settlers later that year had abruptly halted the company's activities.[13] But Dyer had hastened to England to secure crown sanction for the Susquehannah scheme. After only a few months, he had given up hope of any immediate success and had returned home late in 1764, leaving the company's petition in the hands of a British attorney, John Gardiner. In 1766 Dyer still awaited word on the progress of the petition and urged Johnson to investigate the matter.[14] From England, Johnson reported in the spring of 1767 that Gardiner had totally neglected the petition. Johnson advised the company to appoint a new agent, but disclaimed any willingness to accept the task himself. "There are," he told Dyer, ". . . very many who think . . . that the pursuit of that Cause is prejudicial to the Colony, [and] who will at least make a Clamour about it sho'd I engage in it, while in the immediate service of the Govern^t."[15]

From Jackson, Franklin, and John Pownall, Johnson learned that British statesmen would not condone any settlement west of the proclamation line without a guarantee from the Superintendent of Indian Affairs that the Indians agreed to it.[16] Jackson, who owned shares in the Susquehannah Company, and Franklin, who regarded the Penns as his political enemies, had every reason to encourage the company's success. Yet both men had offered similarly discouraging advice to Dyer years earlier.[17] Undoubtedly Franklin and Pownall also told Johnson that the recent shift of American affairs from Shelburne's Southern

Department to Hillsborough's American Department boded ill for the company. Pownall and Franklin knew that Hillsborough was committed to enforcing the proclamation. Pownall, for many years the secretary to the Board of Trade, had drafted the proclamation in 1763, when Hillsborough was president of the Board.[18] Franklin's own speculative venture in western lands was meeting resistance from Hillsborough, who would not risk a frontier Indian war to gratify colonial land speculators.[19] In January 1768 Johnson cautioned Dyer against pressing the Susquehannah petition under such inauspicious circumstances.[20]

Johnson's admonitions involved him even more deeply in the company's fortunes. That January, the Susquehannah shareholders voted to send Dyer to England to present the petition before the crown. But, when Dyer received Johnson's dismal report, he decided that his journey would prove fruitless and persuaded the shareholders to delegate full responsibility for the company's business in England to Johnson. The politically circumspect Johnson had always managed to avoid any public involvement in Connecticut's partisan controversies, but in 1768 he saw no prudent means of escape. Already the stockholders had requested and received the Connecticut Assembly's approval for Johnson's agency on behalf of the company. Moreover, Dyer reported in July that the company's leaders agreed with Johnson that it would be best to keep silent on their petition while success appeared so unlikely.[21]

The company readily complied with Johnson's advice, because they saw a new opportunity to win the Susquehannah territory without a crown hearing. News reached Connecticut that summer that the Superintendent of Indian Affairs was negotiating a new frontier treaty with the Indians, in which the tribes would concede the lands east of Fort Stanwix. Sir William's negotiations promised to open up the vast expanse between Fort Stanwix and the proclamation line, including the Susquehannah tract. Although the Proclamation of 1763 was not repealed, the Susquehannah men, like land speculators everywhere, greated the treaty as a signal to recommence settlement in the trans-Appalachian region. In July Dyer related the promising event to Johnson. The Connecticut agent, in reply, agreed with the company's interpretation that the Fort Stanwix treaty rendered earlier prohibitions meaningless, but added that he would seek a legal confirmation of this interpretation from Jackson and other English counsel, as Dyer had instructed.[22] The harmony between the Susquehannah adventurers and their agent quickly broke down. In December the company, impatient with the delays of British officialdom, launched an expedition into the western territory without waiting for Johnson's report.[23] Their hasty action played into the hands of their Pennsylvania enemies and threw Johnson into a most disagreeable predicament.

In a letter to the company dated March 1769, Johnson expressed his shock at their proceedings and related the alarming consequences. The Pennsylvania proprietors were demanding a hearing before the Privy Council on the Susquehannah dispute, just when the company had decided that such a trial would prove disastrous. Everything, said Johnson, pointed to success for the Penns, should the hearing take place.[24] From his Connecticut friend and correspondent Joseph Chew, Johnson learned that, at Fort Stanwix, the Superintendent of Indian Affairs had negotiated a sale of the Susquehannah lands from the Indians to the Penn proprietors. The sale cast even more suspicion on the dubious deed secured from the Indians by the Susquehannah Company in 1754. "This they hope has laid a foundation to obtain an easy direction ag[ainst] you here," Johnson warned.[25]

In the spring of 1769 Pennsylvania law officers imprisoned twenty Susquehannah settlers on criminal charges. In reaction the company sent another large expedition to the disputed lands. Open warfare had begun. That autumn, Johnson reported that the Penns had petitioned the crown to settle the dispute, even with military force. Johnson added that the company's actions would "be represented to Ad[ministration] in as strong disagreeable light as they could be placed." He promised to appeal to the proprietors to drop the criminal charges and agree to a civil trial in the colonies in lieu of a Privy Council hearing, but he predicted little success.[26] To the proprietors, Johnson argued that the case involved only Pennsylvania and the Susquehannah Company and belonged in a civil court, but the Penns countered that Connecticut was deeply involved in the company scheme and that a dispute between two colonies ought to be settled by the Privy Council. In March 1770, Johnson notified the company that the Penns remained inflexible, and the decision for or against a Privy Council hearing now rested with the Board of Trade.[27] Four months later, Johnson would appear before that Board to rebut the proprietors' arguments for a crown hearing. He faced a difficult task. In 1763 the Board of Trade had interpreted the dispute as between two colonies.[28] Only the most persuasive arguments would reverse the Board's opinion that Connecticut stood behind the company's scheme. Moreover, the Penns enjoyed valuable connections with the ministry and the Board of Trade, and Connecticut had few.[29]

Events in Connecticut heightened Johnson's apprehensions. During 1769 the company repeatedly petitioned the General Assembly to assert the colony's claim to the wartorn region on the basis of Connecticut's ancient sea-to-sea grant. The company's leaders knew that the Assembly would not establish local government in the region until the claim was first acknowledged, and they also knew that unless the Assembly acted quickly to restore law and order along the Susquehannah, the company might dissolve. Already many stockholders, hearing of the violence that spring and summer and the forced evacuation of the settlers in November, began withdrawing their support, because they doubted that settlement could ever succeed without the assistance of the Connecticut government. But at year end, the Susquehannah partisans secured an important, though partial, victory that greatly alarmed Johnson. They persuaded the Assembly to appoint George Wyllys and Governor Trumbull to search for documents that would clarify the colony's title to the land and to request the opinion of Connecticut's agents in London on the validity and feasibility of that title. In February 1770, Trumbull's queries reached London.[30]

Johnson responded without equivocation or hesitation. Asserting Connecticut's claim, on the basis of the boundaries set forth in the charter of the colony, invited an examination of the entire charter at a most dangerous time. Johnson remembered Hillsborough's challenge to Connecticut's charter privileges and Bernard's invidious criticism of the colony's legislative autonomy. "We are watched with a very jealous eye," he warned, "and no occasion will be lost of increasing that jealousy. Such a constitution cannot but be envied, nor will any favorable pretences for subverting it be overlooked." Johnson also observed that a formal assertion of Connecticut's claim would impede rather than promote the company's fortunes. It would substantiate the Penns' argument that the dispute involved two colonies and belonged before the Privy Council. Johnson assured Trumbull that he held "a very high Opinion of the legal right of the colony to those western lands," but concluded that Connecticut should not assert its claim, extend its legal jurisdiction to the territory, attempt any settlement there, or in any other

way interfere in the company's dispute with the Penns.[31] Richard
Jackson dispatched equally cautious advice. Jackson and Johnson, like Ingersoll years before, also reported that British officials
gave little credence to the boundaries set forth in the original
colonial charters:

The Opinion however that in general prevails here . . . is, that all the
Ancient Charters & Patents in the Colonies, being Vague in their
descriptions, drawn by Persons often unacquainted with the Geography
of the Country, & Interfering frequently with each other, must be limited
by the Actual Occupation . . . & since this is their notion of the matter, it
seems plain that such Claim would not be very highly favor'd here & will
probably give much Offence, if made by the Colony.[32]

In the summer of 1770, Johnson won an impressive double
victory. From Connecticut, Trumbull reported that the Assembly
had ventured no further in support of the company's claim.[33] In
July, Johnson persuaded the Board of Trade to dismiss Penn's
request for a Privy Council hearing. The Board's decision rescued
the Connecticut charter from crown scrutiny and shifted the
burden of the dispute to the Penns, who would have to bring civil
suit against the company in a colonial court. To Trumbull,
Johnson confessed his great relief: "We are, I trust, happily
delivered from any Apprehension of further trouble or danger, at
present, from Mr. Penn's petition to the Crown relative to the
Susque[h] Lands."[34]

But Johnson's elation quickly vanished as he realized that his
successful efforts to protect the Connecticut charter had perhaps
destroyed his political following in the colony. Since February,
when Jackson and Johnson admonished the colony against
asserting its claim, the two agents had received no word from the
company. At the end of August, Johnson told his colleague:

The only thing I can guess at . . . is that they may be displeased at what
we have said relative to the Susq[h] Affair, for as I perfectly agreed with
you in the sentiments you express'd upon that Subject I wrote Strongly
(as I presume you did) ag[ainst] their Intermeddling at all in it. This I
know has been a party affair amongst them, & many who have a principal share in the Managem[t] of the Colony Affairs are zealously &
whimsically engaged in it perhaps Gov[r] T. himself (tho' I am not sure
of this) & have been very solicitous the Colony should Embark in it.
It had been several times tried in the Assembly & failed by a Majority
only of 2 or 3. It is possible that our opinions were only asked in view

to obtain an Authority by means of wh[ich] they might hope to carry their point in the Assembly, & as we attend[ing] only to the Int[eres]t of the Colony have disappoint^d them, they may have taken it amiss & Choose to leave us in this Embarrassment for want of Intell[igenc]e from them. . . . I am every way entirely at a loss & know not what to say of their Conduct but to Condemn it as absurd, stupid & cruel.[35]

No doubt Johnson remembered with apprehension the fate of the cautious Governor Fitch and Jared Ingersoll.

Two letters from Dyer, dated August 8 and December 15, soon confirmed Johnson's fears. Dyer complained that unless the Assembly would extend Connecticut law to the Susquehannah territory, all hope of settling the area would be lost, because the settlers faced repeated assaults and imprisonment. The Penns refused to bring the dispute before a civil court and relied on harassment and forcible eviction to win their point. They would never submit to a fair trial of the case, argued Dyer, until Connecticut asserted its claim to the land and backed the company's cause. Throughout 1770, an army of Susquehannah men waged a bloody battle to recapture the land from the Penn forces, but with no permanent success. More and more stock-holders refused to go to Pennsylvania or to pay their taxes to the company while its future looked so precarious. Dyer outspokenly blamed Johnson for the Assembly's cautious policy and the company's impending ruin.[36]

Dyer's own uncertain political circumstances added fuel to his anger. In the autumn of 1769, Governor Pitkin died and the Assembly elevated Lieutenant Governor Trumbull to the Governor's chair until the next election. Dyer had expected the Lieutenant Governor's seat, but his expectations were blasted, and rumors circulated that the Assembly had overlooked him because of his aggressive participation in Susquehannah.[37]

Dyer knew that his own fortunes would rise or fall with the company's. Throughout the winter of 1769 and all during 1770, the Susquehannah partisans and their political adversaries contended in the press and at the polls, with Dyer in the vanguard of the company's spokesmen. Unless the colony asserted its claim to the Susquehannah territory, Dyer warned, Connecticut would expire under the weight of an expanding population deprived of land. "What a figure must our towns and societies make," he exclaimed, "when instead of containing '*fields for grazing*,' there should not only [be] house join[ed] to house, but one house be erected upon the top of another, and all filled with inhabitants, till the upper lofts tumble down, and dash them in pieces, and the lower buried in ruins."[38] In angry rebuttal, the company's opponents attacked the plausibility of Connecticut's sea-to-sea claim, objected to the enormous cost of defending the claim in England, and imagined a colony drained of its population and wealth by the exodus to Pennsylvania. They openly accused the eastern politicians of fomenting the Susquehannah controversy to advance "party designs" rather than "with any reasonable prospect of acquiring and holding those lands."[39] Benjamin Gale, the company's most outspoken critic, had not forgotten the easterners' ruthless attack on Fitch and Ingersoll during the Stamp Act crisis. Susquehannah, Gale told Ingersoll, "has been Col. Dyer's Hobby Horse by which he has rose & as he has been unmerciful to Gov. Fitch & Yourself I never design to give him rest until I make his Hobby Horse throw him into the dirt."[40]

In May 1771, Dyer's political career took a promising turn and Johnson's grew more uncertain. The Assembly resolved that the Susquehannah lands were "well Contained within the Boundaries & Descriptions of the Charter granted by King Charles 2nd." The lawmakers appointed a committee to collect documents in support of the colony's title and to consult English legal counsel on the feasibility of asserting the title before the crown.[41] The vote signalled a dramatic victory for the Susquehannah interests and a glaring repudiation of the policy prescribed by Johnson. The Susquehannah men were fast gaining strength in the colony, and Johnson, removed from the political scene, could only worry that they now regarded him as their betrayer and political adversary.

For the previous four years, Johnson had been seeking a crown appointment as Chief Justice of New York, but his clash with the angry Susquehannah leaders in the summer of 1770 inspired Johnson to pursue the secure and lucrative appointment with new determination. In December, his Stratford neighbor wrote, "I again repeat it to you, if you can get any thing worth your while, accept it for some of your Eastern friends have repeated it that you are a pensioner to the Penns for your advice to the Assembly last spring."[42] Financial considerations also heightened his determination.

The costliness of London had reduced Johnson and his Stratford household to near poverty. Wherever Johnson turned in the capital, he had been surrounded by a maze of outstretched hands, from personal servants, bureaucratic underlings, and even the doorkeepers and messengers in Parliament. The sums were so fixed by custom that no economy was possible. Connecticut lawmakers promised their agent only £150 per annum, far below the £500 Pennsylvania awarded yearly to Franklin, and even Johnson's meager allowance rarely reached him on time. Johnson worried, too, that his long absence from Connecticut had cost him many clients. Reflecting on Ingersoll's profitable seat at Philadelphia, Johnson concluded that a crown post meant "the difference between living Idly upon Six hundred p^r Ann, & working hard for two." In fact, the chief justiceship of New York carried the slightly smaller salary of £500, but the rewards still seemed impressive. All the offices of Massachusetts' powerful royal official Thomas Hutchinson offered no greater profit.[43] By 1770 Johnson's financial and political insecurity made the New York post more attractive than ever, but in the previous four years he had learned that to win a crown preferment without arousing the suspicions of his countrymen or renouncing his stalwart defense of American rights was no simple task.

The overripe age and incompetence of New York's Chief Justice, Daniel Horsmanden, had attracted Johnson's attention even before he sailed for England in December 1766.[44] Upon reaching London in January, Johnson set out on two tasks—to secure the New York post for himself and a suitable appointment for his politically devastated friend Jared Ingersoll. He turned to Jackson and to Ingersoll's political associate, Thomas Whately, for assistance.[45] In May, Johnson learned that his own opportunities were small but that Ingersoll would receive some mark of royal favor, either the coveted New York post or another lucrative appointment. On May 15, George Grenville presented a resolution before the House of Commons that "His Majesty . . . will be graciously pleased to confer some Marks of His Royal Favour on those Governors and Officers in the several Colonies, who distinguished themselves by their Zeal and Fidelity in supporting the Dignity of the Crown, the just Rights of Parliament, and the supreme Authority of Great Britain over the Colonies, during the Late Disturbances in America." The House unanimously approved Grenville's resolution. Johnson concluded that neither the New York appointment nor any other crown preferment would be awarded to anyone who had not "given full proof of his firm attachment to the prerogative . . . by which I fear they mean such an absolute sovereignty as I am sure will be very disagreeable to all those who sincerely love that country."[46]

Johnson's discouraging prediction so dismayed his father that the elder Johnson appealed to the Archbishop of Canterbury to redress his son's reputation as an American rebel. "I am sorry to understand that he is represented as being a favourer of the late opposition to the Stamp Act," wrote Samuel Johnson, "and therefore not likely to have anything done for him. It is true that he was of the Congress at New York, but as his principles are truly English, I beg leave to assure your Grace that he was far from approving of everything that was said and done on that occasion."[47] The younger Johnson, who would have no part of his father's misrepresentations, set the matter straight in November.

I am sure I shall never regret having taken part with my Country & done the little I was able to do to defend its Liberties, when so imminently endangered as they were upon that occasion. Nor even here (whatever appearances they may think to put on [it] for political purposes) do I believe any of the sensible People really think the worse of any Americans who with Decency & Moderation, tho' with firmness and fortitude endeavour'd the Repeal of the Stamp Act, tho' they may not think it expedient to bestow any special favours upon them.[48]

That same month, Johnson learned that Whately had secured Ingersoll's appointment to the Vice-Admiralty Court at Philadelphia, one of the new courts established under the Townshend program. Johnson felt no spark of jealousy for his Connecticut friend's lucrative post, and reminded Ingersoll, "You have only to regret that it came from Mr. Grenville and proceeded from his Motion, which must be very odious in Am[eric]a and may seem to be the immediate reward of supporting his measures, which produced so much Indign[ation] in that Country."[49]

In the winter of 1768, Nathaniel Rogers, a Boston merchant, and Robert Temple, a member of the new American Board of Customs Commissioners, sent offers from Boston to secure a post for their friend Johnson, either as Solicitor to the American Board or as judge of the Vice-Admiralty Court at Halifax. Both posts entailed enforcing the odious Townshend Acts. One of the commissioners warned Johnson, "I fear it may have been said of you on that side of the water, as I heard our Collector and some Other high prerogative men say of you here, that you incline to the popular side." Johnson quickly put a stop to the commissioners' efforts: "I could not with firm principles, nor with peace of mind profess an office either detrimental or disagreeable to my fellow citizens and that you mention is I fear among the grievances as complained of in that country. I must live in peace or I cannot live at all."[50]

The Connecticut agent still eyed the lucrative, less controversial post in New York, but 1769 brought no success. Johnson asked his close friend and fellow churchman, the Rev. Dr. George Berkeley, to appeal to his influential parishioner Lord Dartmouth, but to no avail. "He would not, I am well persuaded," Berkeley told Johnson, "on *any* recommendation, forward the appointment of an American to such an office, unless such American should appear to be totally disunited from his country's case. This could not be supposed of you, an Agent, in the highest confidence of your constituents." Berkeley cautioned Johnson to give up his search for a crown office. "It would be using you very ill," he said, "to expose you to the jealousy of your countrymen at this ticklish time—and no application of this sort can now be kept secret, it being so obviously the interest of the administration to make you Americans afraid of each other."[51]

Johnson disregarded his friend's advice and pressed for the New York appointment with new determination in the winter of 1770-1771.[52] The angry resentment of the Susquehannah partisans and the financial strain of living in London compelled him to persevere. Undoubtedly he hoped that the North ministry, confident in victory, would regard American officeseekers with greater leniency and favor. That December, Johnson received the abusive letter from Dyer, in which the irate Susquehannah leader blamed the Connecticut agent for jeopardizing the company's fortunes. In the same letter, Dyer added that Johnson's pursuit of the New York post had occasioned talk in America.[53] Johnson immediately suspected Dyer of base political motives. From the beginning, Johnson had observed a careful distinction between royal favors that would compromise his fidelity to his countrymen and those that would not, but he knew that his search for preferment could easily be distorted by Dyer to discredit him at home. After the Stamp Act crisis, crown officeholders became objects of suspicion, and colonial agents who boasted crown posts as proof of their influence came under reproach for the very offices and intimate political ties that made them effective advocates. Even Franklin was assailed, at the instigation of a jealous political rival, for the lucrative appointments that he and his son enjoyed.[54] Johnson hastened to disarm Dyer and penned a reply that was false in point of fact, though true in principle. "It seems you have given me an Employment & sent me to N[ew] York . . ." Johnson wrote.

I hope this is not because you are weary of me, & want to get rid of me. Whatever the ground of the Report I assure you I know knothing of it. I have received no Appt. I expect none. I assure you my friend I have been much otherwise employed since I came to this Country tho' to my great Concern too unprofitably than in obtain^g Offices or Employm^{ts} for myself. . . . I doubt not indeed I might have obtained very good things in the way in which I have known them to have been obtained by some others . . . by deserting the Interests of the Country that gave them Birth, by abusing or Misrepresenting it & by licking the dust of the feet of Ministers or of the slaves of slaves of slaves of Ministers but I will say with an honest vanity that I have too much Integrity to do the one & too much spirit to submit to the other![55]

Throughout the spring and summer of 1771 Johnson appealed to his friends in government and high church positions to secure the New York post.[56] In August, he could wait no longer. The conclusion of the Mohegan hearing released him from his official duties, and the urgent pleas from his family compelled him to return home. After fifty-six days at sea and four days of overland travel, Johnson would arrive in Connecticut to learn the real state of his political fortunes.[57]

Chapter Ten

The Illusory Peace

❧⟨∕⟩⟨∕⟩∽

*O*n the night of September 25, 1771, Johnson's ship dropped anchor in New York harbor, and the next morning the homeward bound agent went ashore. But Johnson did not hasten to Stratford. Perhaps the disturbing reports from his son-in-law and father and Ann's impatient letters had inspired him to dread the approaching reunion. He spent several days conferring with his clients in the city, collecting the latest news on the bishop controversy from leading churchmen, and visiting old friends. At last, on October 1 he set out for Connecticut, dining with ex-Governor Fitch at Norwalk, and arriving at Stratford about seven that evening.[1] We can only wonder whether family resentment melted away in the warmth of a joyous reunion, or whether Johnson's prolonged absence left Ann permanently estranged.

The colony seemed in perfect political peace. The Americans had almost forgotten their grievances against the mother country, Johnson observed.[2] As the Anglo-American argument hushed, so had the anti-Episcopal clamor long heard from Pennsylvania and nearby New York.[3] Even Connecticut's noisy controversy over Susquehannah had quieted.

For years, the company's spokesmen had battled fiercely to secure the colony's support for the Susquehannah claim. Finally, in May 1771, they had persuaded the Assembly to declare Connecticut's right to the territory, in bold repudiation of Johnson's cautious advice. The Assembly had appointed a committee to draft a defense of the Connecticut claim and consult with English lawyers on the advisability of asserting the claim before the crown. Named to the committee were Governor Jonathan Trumbull, Secretary of the Colony George Wyllys, and Jabez Hamlin (all shareholders of the company), John Chester, who died soon after his appointment, and William Samuel Johnson, not yet returned from England.[4] Trumbull had seized the opportunity to draft the defense himself.

When Johnson returned from England that October, Trumbull presented the statement for his approval. Johnson kept silent on his objections to the colony's hazardous plan. Mindful that his earlier admonitions had angered the company's leaders and jeopardized his own political career, Johnson appended his signature to the statement, which he declared "very well drawn up."[5] The political apprehensions that had troubled him before his return quickly vanished. Whatever resentments the Susquehannah partisans had felt toward their agent were apparently forgotten after their victory in the Assembly that May. Johnson gladly signed Trumbull's paper to preserve this welcome harmony. In January 1772, the Governor sent the statement to the colony's new agent in London, Thomas Life, who would gather several legal opinions on its validity.[6] For the next two years, Susquehannah would excite little controversy. Despite anxious pleas from the settlers on the disputed lands, even the company's leaders agreed that the Assembly could not establish local government there until the legal opinions arrived from England.[7] Johnson sighed with relief. "I am heartily sick of politics," he exclaimed, where "the real object is wealth or power, or some other dirty selfish view."[8]

In January 1772, only three months after Johnson's return, his father died quietly one morning in Stratford at the age of seventy-five. Samuel Johnson's death must have grieved his son deeply, yet the new year also promised happy moments. The restoration of Anglo-American harmony, the lull in the anti-Episcopal campaign in nearby New York, and the temporary resolution of the Susquehannah dispute brought peace to the colony and political rewards to Johnson. In May 1772, the voters once again elected him to the Governor's Council. The following October, he secured his long-awaited appointment to Connecticut's Superior Court, the first Anglican ever to sit on that bench. The Assembly also commissioned him a major in the colonial militia.[9]

The apparent tranquility between mother country and colonies, even more than these personal triumphs, made Johnson rejoice. "Nothing was ever more unhappy," he recalled, "than the disputes and animosities which have arisen between two Countries which have been perpetually united."[10] He dreaded another contest with Great Britain. The collapse of the nonimportation movement had disheartened him, and, in his eyes, had disgraced his countrymen. The blame for Anglo-American discontent, he believed, rested on the instability and irresponsibility of British leadership. Until the summer of 1770, he had relied on America to resolve the dispute and establish colonial rights, but America's surrender to the partial repeal of the Townshend Acts had shattered his confidence in his countrymen. Thereafter Johnson had looked to the statesmanship of the new chief minister, Lord North. During his first year at the head of the government, North had demonstrated his capacity to win over important members of the opposition parties and achieve a degree of stability unprecedented in George III's reign.[11] In the autumn of 1770, Johnson had begun praising the skill and perseverence with which North subdued party turmoil and held a tight reign over Parliament. That October, Johnson had recorded that "the spirited conduct of Ld North"

has given him great reputation and tends strongly to secure him in his present situation, indeed everything at this moment seems to promise permanency to the present administration. My opinion of this minister's ability, assiduity & even integrity, increases the more I see and hear of him. I begin to think he is the best man considering all circumstances we could have in these times.[12]

In March 1771, several months before he departed for America, Johnson had concluded that the North ministry wanted nothing more than to keep Anglo-American disagreements hushed, trans-Atlantic trade flowing, and the antiministry forces in Parliament searching helplessly for an issue. He had written to Governor Trumbull that "the ministry is in perfect plenitude of power and seem to wish nothing so much as to continue undisturbed in their offices. . . . It is enough that they know that goods are going out [to America], this spring, to the amount of more than a million sterling and that they know, too (by their own experience) the wonderful political effects that luxury can produce."[13] The reports that reached Johnson, after his return to Connecticut, buoyed his confidence in the North administration. Lord North had quieted the opposition in Parliament, wrote Johnson's English friends, and British politics remained stable.[14]

Johnson's confidence that Lord North would preserve Anglo-American harmony overlooked one disturbing fact. The North ministry was determined to uphold Parliament's supremacy against any challenge from America. Even before

Johnson left England in the summer of 1771, events had shown that although North wanted to avoid another major contest with America, he did not intend to yield one iota of British authority to the colonies. In January 1770, the new ministry had dispatched a governor to New York with explicit instructions that all royal officers would be paid by the crown, not by the colonial legislature. These instructions echoed the policy set forth in the preamble to the Townshend Acts, a policy that Johnson and his countrymen abhorred.[15] Three months later the Privy Council had annulled the South Carolina Assembly's resolution to send a financial contribution to Wilkes. This action simply repeated Townshend's attacks on the legislatures of Massachusetts and New York in 1767, incidents that Johnson had outspokenly deplored.[16] Finally, Johnson had expected that American submission to partial repeal would be answered by an equally conciliatory gesture from the North ministry, namely, the repeal of the duty on tea. Other Americans had shared Johnson's expectation. One Massachusetts man had told Franklin, "the agreement of the Merchants is broken. Administration has a fair opportunity of adopting the mildest and most prudent Measures respecting the Colonies without the Appearance of being threatened or drove."[17] But in 1771, the ministry still had not relented. During his last year in England, Johnson had ignored all these indications of an unyielding colonial policy. Perhaps he had found it easier to accept defeat in the Townshend Acts contest and abandon his uncompromising defense of American rights once he believed that his irresolute countrymen had little to fear from the victorious Lord North.

The mood of tranquility that greeted Johnson on his return to Connecticut heightened his false confidence in peace. Reporting on the apparent contentment of his countrymen, Johnson wrote, "They know how prone Englishmen are to Party & disunion in their Councils and affirm that it was never known that an old lascivious dissipated divided Nation ever was very formidable."[18] Yet the quiet spirit that Johnson celebrated merely veiled the distrust and suspicions that had developed in the colonists' minds over the past five years. Americans had not forgotten their fears of a diabolical ministry, and any provocation would bring these deep-seated feelings to the surface again. Massachusetts, no doubt, would lead the colonies into the coming crisis.

For over a decade, that colony had suffered under a royal

governor whose exaggerated and malicious reports to anti-American politicians in England and concerted efforts to subvert the Massachusetts charter infuriated the citizenry. This fact alone made Massachusetts the watchdog against British tyranny. Then, on March 5, 1770, when the colony's impatience with everything British had reached fever pitch, His Majesty's soldiers opened fire on an angry horde in Boston, killing five townspeople. The "massacre" of March 5 magnified the Bostonians' suspicions of ministerial tyranny.[19] Recent events, the Town Meeting declared, "afford great reason to believe that a deep laid and desperate plan of imperial despotism has been laid, and partly executed for the extinction of all civil liberty."[20] Lieutenant Governor Thomas Hutchinson's response to the "massacre" raised the citizens' apprehensions still higher. Hutchinson, who would soon succeed Barnard as governor, testified to the home government that Boston was totally ungovernable and that strong support from England was essential. The Bostonians frantically anticipated the most severe repercussions from Hutchinson's reports. "The Measures which have been taken in Consequence of Intelligence Managed with such Secrecy, have already to a very great degree lessened that mutual confidence which had ever subsisted between the Mother Country and the Colonies, and must in the Natural Course of things totally alienate their Affections towards each other and . . . in the End destroy the power of the Empire."[21] Finally, in the summer and fall of 1772, news reached Boston that the British government, determined to maintain its authority over the ungovernable colony, had ruled that the salaries of the Governor and the judges of the Superior Court should henceforth be paid by the crown. The decision removed these officials from the oversight of the Massachusetts legislators, enraged the colony's patriots, and provoked a public debate between the Massachusetts General Court and Governor Hutchinson. The colony's lawmakers boldly declared that America owed no obedience to Parliament.[22]

Johnson reacted with horror to the "bold doctrines" heard in Boston. The open debate over parliamentary authority promised to carry the Anglo-American dispute to a disastrous deadlock. "For my part," he told Jackson,

I think that certain nice political questions like some intricate points in Divinity had better never be meddled with. The discussion of them can hardly do any good and will certainly produce much mischief. While they serve to whet the wits of men they more surely sharpen their tempers toward each other and are equally fatal in the one case to virtuous practice in the other to due subordination and in both to the peace of society.[23]

Franklin, too, reacted with alarm. He urged the new head of the American Department, Lord Dartmouth, not to present the colony's bold statement to Parliament, and he admonished his constituents in Massachusetts "that as between friends every affront is not worth a duel, so between the governed and the governing every mistake in government, every encroachment on rights, is not worth a rebellion."[24] Franklin entertained no false confidence that the North ministry would respect American liberties. He felt sure that colonial submission to the tea tax had opened the way for heavier burdens in the future. In fact, he was convinced that "in the system of Customs to be exacted in America by act of Parliament, the Seed [were sown] of a total disunion of the two countries, though as yet, that event may be at a considerable distance."[25] But, like Johnson, Franklin had been bitterly disillusioned by the collapse of the nonimportation movement, and he no longer felt confident that his countrymen would stand behind their bold declarations. The Massachusetts agent repeatedly cautioned his countrymen against any "open Denial and Resistance" to Parliamentary authority, which might "bring on prematurely a Contest, to which, if we are not found equal, that Authority will by the Event be more strongly established."[26]

Johnson worried that Massachusetts' bold spirit would infect the other colonies.[27] Events soon confirmed his apprehensions. In December 1772, the British ship *Swan*, dispatched to colonial waters to rout out smugglers, seized a contraband cargo and deposited it at New London. Three months later, a band of Connecticut patriots daringly stole the illicit goods. The customs officers charged with arresting the robbers appealed to the Superior Court for writs of assistance. Their request excited a noisy protest against the general search. All through the spring and summer of 1773, the Connecticut judges debated whether to award the writs to the officers or disobey a law of Parliament.[28] Johnson saw every skirmish as a step toward open conflict. He dreaded nothing more. That June, the Assembly renewed his appointment to the Superior Court, but Johnson excused himself, pleading that his poor finances prevented him from accepting such an unprofitable post. To Jackson, he confided his true motives, explaining that the judges faced two "disagreeable" alternatives, either "disobeying an Act of Parl[iament] and thereby exposing the Colony to the resentment of the Government at home, or of incurring the Indignation of the People and exposing themselves to insult or abuse."[29] Only five years earlier, at the height of the Townshend dispute, Johnson had urged the Superior Court to withhold the writs.[30] But the disheartening climax of that dispute had tempered his fervent defense of American rights.

Johnson was determined to take no part in the contest between his countrymen and the customs officials. Connecticut's bold affront to British authority alarmed him, but so too did the severe enforcement measures adopted by the North ministry the following year. When angry patriots in nearby Rhode Island burned the customs schooner *Gaspee* in the summer of 1772, the ministry appointed a commission to search out the culprits and send them to England for trial. The commission's instructions, Johnson told one Englishman, enraged the colonists, who were "shocked at the idea of their fellow subjects being transplanted to England."[31] Since returning to Stratford in 1771, Johnson had continued to press his influential friends in London for the chief justiceship of New York. His requests met with no success.[32] But when John Pownall lamented to Johnson that the Connecticut lawyer had been overlooked for a seat on the *Gaspee* commission, Johnson retorted that he would not have accepted a post so odious to his countrymen.[33]

As Anglo-American tensions worsened, Johnson's opportunities for crown preferment diminished. British officials, he would soon be told, were loath to consider an American for an important office so long as the colonies persisted in their disobedience. Long before the final crisis, Johnson would discard any expectation of royal favor.[34] But the approaching crisis posed a greater problem for the ambitious Connecticut politician. Johnson owed his handsome political standing to the colony's voters, not to the British government. How long could he silently protest their resistance to British authority without losing their trust and support? Each incident would draw America and England closer to armed conflict, and in war there would be no middle ground between patriotism and treason.

The most crushing blow to Johnson's hopes for peace came not from the rash patriots but from Lord North and his majority in Parliament, on whom Johnson relied for a just and prudent colonial policy. In April 1773, Parliament granted a special concession to the East India Company, allowing the company to pay no British import duty on the tea it reexported to America. The American duty on tea, established by the Townshend Acts, would still be paid when the tea reached the colonies, but the concession enabled the company to undersell other British exporters and the Dutch merchants who traded illicitly with America. The Tea Act of 1773 promised to revive colonial resentments against the six-year-old tea duty. The ministry seemed less concerned with quieting America than with saving the nearly bankrupt company, on which the British government virtually depended for imperial control in India.[35]

First word of the Tea Act reached America in July, and by October the news had spread to every province. Americans assailed the British for trying to hide the old tea duty insidiously beneath the new lower price charged by the company. Colonial merchants accused the ministry of giving the East India Company an unfair monopoly on the tea trade. In October, mass meeting in Philadelphia and New York condemned the act and demanded the resignation of the company's local representatives. By December the indignation had spread southward to Charlestown, where the patriots forced that city's tea consignees to resign.[36] But in Boston public protests and threats of violence proved insufficient. The consignees, including two sons and a nephew of Governor Hutchinson, stubbornly held their posts. On December 1, the first of three ships entered the harbor. The patriots insisted that the ships turn back without paying the tea duty or unloading their cargo, but Hutchinson insisted that the customs regulations be obeyed. After sixteen days of bitter debate, a band of Boston citizens disguised as Mohawk Indians rushed to the wharfs and dumped the tea into the briny water.[37]

Americans everywhere were determined to prevent the sale of the company's tea, but many condemned the wanton destruction of property at Boston. No one was more horrified than Johnson. The Tea Act, he observed, "at Boston particularly has produced most fatal and pernicious and violent effects."[38] During his years in England, Johnson had learned that colonial lawlessness only antagonized America's friends in Parliament and frustrated their attempts to win concessions from the British government. The colonial agents in London deplored the outrage at Boston and warned their constituents against further rash measures. Franklin denounced the tea party at Boston as "an act of violent injustice" and implored the Massachusetts General Court to pay for the tea immediately, "for such a step will remove much of the prejudice now entertained against us, and put us again on a fair footing in contending for our old privileges."[39]

Johnson aimed his anger at Parliament as well as at his unruly countrymen. Lamenting the impolitic revival of the dispute over American rights and parliamentary authority, he asked:

When shall we come to a right understanding about these great, or at least curious questions of right of Parliamentary power and provincial liberty? or rather when shall we see that it is dangerous or at least unnecessary to define precisely these deep and difficult objects and wisely on both sides pursue such a conduct as may cement and secure that connection between us and that just subordination on our part which is so necessary for both. To continue in this state will ruin us all.

Above all, Johnson wanted peace. "Any settlement," he declared, " . . . would be preferable to this state of uncertainty and contest."[40]

By year's end, the Tea Act had aroused opposition in nearly every colony. Only Connecticut, of all the New England provinces, had adopted no official protest against the act. A few vigilant patriots celebrated Boston's boldness and urged their own colony to defend its rights, but most Connecticut men were busily preparing for a different contest. The spring election neared, and on the outcome hung the future of the Susquehannah Company.[41] In the summer of 1773, just when news of the Tea Act excited anger and alarm in America, reports from Connecticut's agent in London broke the uncertainty that had silenced the Susquehannah controversy for nearly two years. To Governor Trumbull came the official opinion of agent Thomas Life and four eminent lawyers on the justice of Connecticut's claim. The opinion stated that, "As the charter of Connecticut was granted but eighteen years before that to Sir William Penn, there is no ground to contend that the crown would at that period make an effective grant to him of that country which had been so recently granted to others." The Susquehannah men seized the report to justify asserting Connecticut's claim and erecting townships on the disputed land under the colony's protection and jurisdiction.[42]

Johnson had worked closely with all four of these lawyers in England, and their official statement shocked him. He and Jackson had reached a perfect agreement on the dangers impeding

Connecticut's claim. The other three lawyers, Alexander Wedderburn, E. Thurlow and John Dunning, had represented the Penns
before the Board of Trade in 1770. Thurlow and Wedderburn
enjoyed important positions in government and knew, as Johnson and Jackson did, that crown policy discouraged the extensive
territorial pretensions of the seaboard colonies.[43] Johnson had
hoped and expected that the lawyers would advise the colony
against submitting its charter to crown scrutiny.[44]

Confidential letters from Jackson and Life shed light on the
unexpected statement submitted to Trumbull. Life confessed to
Johnson that Wedderburn and Thurlow privately opposed
Connecticut's claim, but Life refused to communicate this information to Trumbull, leaving the matter to Johnson's discretion.
In a second letter, Life repeated the story, adding that the
information should remain "entre nous." Jackson assured Johnson, "I have not changed my opinion which is indeed perfectly
the same as yours, in short, I conjecture we shall not finally
succeed." But Jackson too left Johnson to decide whether and
how the official opinion should be countered.[45] Apparently
the lawyers feared arousing the disfavor of Connecticut's most
powerful politicians and losing their official business with the
colony. Their fears were well founded. Jackson had only to
remember Dyer's stinging accusations in 1770. Two years later,
Jackson had warned Trumbull that the colony's claim appeared
unpromising, but Trumbull had countered that the company's
supporters had incurred a "very great Expense" and "the failure
of the Colony in this case might prove ruinous."[46] By 1774, it was
widely known in Connecticut, and no doubt in England too, that
Trumbull was determined for financial and political reasons to
support the Susquehannah Company, whatever dangers threatened the colonial charter.[47] Since 1761 Trumbull had owned
shares in the company, and his defense of the Susquehannah
interests had carried him to political prominence on the votes of
the eastern faction. From the Governor's seat, Trumbull had
participated intimately in the Company's highest councils and
had defended its activities against the accusations of the Pennsylvanians. In June 1773, the company had awarded him five
hundred acres of the disputed land in return for his "Sundry
services."[48]

Johnson advised Trumbull on the unreliability of the
lawyers' official opinion, but the Governor turned a deaf ear.[49] In
October 1773, the Susquehannah men hurried to the General

Assembly, confident that the official opinion would silence their opponents. Johnson assessed the scene cautiously. He realized that challenging the opinion before the legislature would sway few minds and cost him many friends. When the Assembly balloted whether to assert the western claim and negotiate with the Penns on the company's behalf, Johnson withheld his judgment and his vote. Johnson told Jackson, "I own I was not in the Vote having never alter'd the Opinion I settled when I had the happiness to visit with you upon the subject. I am not satisfied that it would be of any use to have those Lands, if we could obtain them, nor can [I] bring myself to believe that we stand much chance . . . of recovering them. However y^r Opinion & that of the att^y [Thurlow] & Sol^r Gen'l [Wedderburn] & Mr. D[unnin]g in fav^r of the Colony Title has silenced every objection & a large Majority of the Assembly have determ^d to make the most of the Claim."[50] Days later, the Assembly appointed a committee to open negotiations with Governor Penn and, in case Penn remained unmoved, to prepare the colony's appeal for crown arbitration. "I have no Expectation that Govr Penn will accede to any proposals for an Accommodation," Johnson observed. He predicted that the Assembly's plan of action would lead to another "tedious controversy" before the home government, yet when the Assembly appointed him to the committee, he prudently accepted.[51] The naming of the committee occasioned an open debate between the Council and the lower house. The Council, eager to appoint Susquehannah partisans, named eight men, including Johnson. The lower house, more divided on the issue, rejected three of the nominees, but accepted Johnson and four others.[52] In the months to come, as the Susquehannah controversy swelled, Johnson would struggle to maintain his politically advantageous position, trusted by both sides, yet committed to neither.

In mid-December Johnson, Dyer, and a third committeeman, Jedidiah Strong, journeyed to Philadelphia to treat with Governor Penn. As Johnson had predicted, Penn rejected every overture for negotiation.[53] Soon after the Connecticut mission returned home, the Assembly reconvened to take decisive action on behalf of the company. The legislators established the township of Westmoreland on the disputed land under the protection and jurisdiction of Connecticut, declared that no one could settle on the territory without the colony's permission, and instructed Life to defend Connecticut's claim "in all courts and in all causes."[54] The Assembly's action played directly into the hands of the Pennsylvanians, who had clamored for years that the Susquehannah dispute merited a crown hearing as a case involving two colonial governments. In April, Thomas Penn would retain Wedderburn and Thurlow as his legal counsel and petition the Privy Council to compel Connecticut to appear for a trial.[55]

The Assembly's drastic measures also evoked unprecedented fury from the company's foes. The spring election lay five months ahead, and in the interim, while patriots in every other colony agitated against the odious Tea Act, Connecticut men campaigned against one another. "This controversy relative to the Western Claim of our Colony is much more warmly Agitated between you & the colony," Johnson explained to a Pennsylvania friend.

Efforts have been made to displace some of the Leading Men in Office in these Affairs & both sides are waiting with anxious suspense for the Event of our Gen[l] Election. . . . This Ferment will no doubt induce the Assembly to revive & reconsider the steps they have already taken, but whether they will perservere or retract it is impossible to determine at present, & will depend probably more upon the prevalence of Party than the Merits of the Cause. Either way I think it extremely unhappy that the Peace of our Colony should have been thus Disturbed.[56]

The company's opponents fired their entire arsenal of arguments, most of which had been heard many times before.[57] Their boldest attack came from the pen of "Many," who complained that

by *selling* rights to *some,* and giving to *others* [the Company partisans] have so increased their numbers, that the General Assembly could not procure a vote of the House to exclude the Members of the Susquehannah Company for *sitting* and *voting* in that very case in which they were *immediately* interested, by which means a vote has been obtained for the Government to take upon themselves the defence of our title to those lands.

"Many" urged every town to elect delegates to a convention at Middletown, where "on the last Wednesday of March" a strategy would be devised "to evade the evils which we apprehend will attend our present measures."[58] Heeding the call, twenty-three towns dispatched representatives to Middletown on March 30. The convention addressed a remonstrance to all the towns and drafted a petition to the General Assembly reminding the lawmakers that asserting the claim to the western lands en-

dangered the colonial charter at a time when "Debates run high
between the parent State and her Colonies, and we may presume
every Opportunity will be watched and greedily seized by
Administration, to enlarge and extend the Power and Influence of
the Crown in America." After the convention completed its
official business, some of the delegates drafted a list of candidates
for the coming election, and among those chosen was William
Samuel Johnson.[59]

   The company's advocates fired back unrelentingly. Most of
their arguments, too, had been rehearsed many times in the past
decade.[60] The fortuitous resurgence of Anglo-American tensions
again invited the eastern faction to brand their foes as British
sympathizers and traitors. A pamphlet written by the Philadelphian William Smith in January proved most advantageous.
Smith's assault on the Connecticut claim revealed an intimate
knowledge of the company's history, the colony's political
divisions, and even the legal advice recently sent from England. The Susquehannah politicians immediately charged Ingersoll with having written the piece. The accusation was not
wholly false. Ingersoll, a frequent visitor to Connecticut, had
imparted valuable information to the real author.[61] Ingersoll's
seat on the Vice-Admiralty Court at Philadelphia made him the
perfect villain, and the Susquehannah partisans quickly expanded their attack to defame all the company's critics as
"placemen or pensioners" and "traitors to the [Connecticut]
government." One Susquehannah spokesman, calling himself
"Philanthropus Redivuvus," invoked the memory of an election
long past to support this contention. "Our present freedom from
the Stamp act under God," he wrote,

was owing very much to . . . the vigorous intrepid exertion of *the wise
men of the east* in our colony, and not to the mean, mercenary conduct of
a number of courtiers, that appeared ready and willing to resign all our
natural rights and charter privileges, under the vain and groundless
pretence of saving our charter, though truly for the sake of some petty
post or honor, that comes from home. Upon examination, you'll find,
perhaps, the same men and their tools, as willing to give away part of our
colony now, as they were all our rights and privileges then.[62]

   In 1774, as in 1765, the eastern faction's claim to be the sole
defenders of American liberty made powerful propaganda but
inaccurate political analysis. A multitude of factors, unrelated to
the Anglo-American dispute, inspired men to cast their votes for

the advocates of Susquehannah. The inhabitants of Hartford perceived the contest of 1774 not as a struggle between the company and its foes or between American liberty and British slavery, but as a time to support political decency against "the mad proceedings" at Middletown. Days earlier a Hartford town meeting had endorsed the resolutions of the Middletown convention, but on May 11 the inhabitants assembled again and declared "That it is the sense and Opinion of this Town that the aforesaid Convention and the extraordinary . . . Petition and Remonstrance as well as their circulating the same through this Colony at the Juncture and in the Manner they did accompanied with certain Nominations, different from those published by Order of the Assembly in October last, are Measures of a most dangerous Tendency, subversive of all Order & Government and destructive of the Peace and Prosperity of this Colony."[63] Ambition impelled other men to speak out against the company's critics. Roger Sherman, a conspicuous defender of American rights since the Stamp Act crisis, had kept aloof from the company's cause for nearly a decade, but in 1774 he judged that the political majority favored the company, and his continued silence might imperil his quest for high office.[64] No one worked harder or longer to promote the company than did the prominent Connecticut lawmaker George Wyllys, yet Wyllys took no part in the American resistance in 1765 or 1774, and when war broke out, he would continue his silent protest.[65]

Those who opposed the Susquehannah scheme also shaped their stance without regard to the impending imperial crisis. Ever since the expulsion of Governor Fitch in the election of 1766, many of the colony's western voters had resented the aggressive tactics of the eastern politicians and their leadership of the patriot cause. But opposition to New Light religion, land expansion, and eastern politicking would not make the colony's western Congregationalists into loyalists. Even Benjamin Gale, the easterners' most outspoken adversary, would discard his partisan jealousies in 1775 and declare that he had always been "firmly attached to the cause of Liberty."[66] No one better exemplified the separateness of the two issues—Susquehannah and American liberty—than William Samuel Johnson. Johnson had opposed Connecticut's involvement in the Susquehannah scheme as firmly in 1768, when he defiantly resisted Lord Townshend's taxes, as in 1774, when he deplored the boldness of his patriot countrymen.

Political prudence spared Johnson from the wrath of the Susquehannah propagandists. Even as the controversy raged in the spring of 1774, Johnson held to his resolve against entering the public fray. His caution was well rewarded. As in the past, both sides claimed the Stratfordite as their ally. The Middletown delegates named Johnson to their slate of candidates for the coming election, but Johnson's name was also circulated by the Susquehannah partisans and Benjamin Trumbull pronounced him a true advocate of the western claim.[67] When the votes were tallied in May, Johnson once again took his seat on the Governor's Council.

The election also brought victory to the Susquehannah men. The new Assembly quickly ratified the perilous course adopted in January.[68] The controversy was closed, at least temporarily. All eyes now turned to the graver contest that America faced. To Johnson, the Anglo-American dispute posed a far greater challenge than the Susquehannah controversy. Johnson had not invested in the company, nor had he built his political prominence on the company's cause. He had privately doubted that the western scheme could succeed, but he had long ago determined that opposing the scheme would accomplish nothing. Instead he had steered his way cautiously through the turmoil, bending to the public will when necessary and remaining silent whenever possible. But Johnson was firmly committed to peace with England, even to risking his political career. Before year's end, he would confide to Richard Jackson, "though a moderator is indeed an unpopular character at present, I am resolved to adhere to it, and do everything possible to keep the ardor of my countrymen within bounds, though it is more than probable that I shall thereby forfeit their esteem."[69]

Chapter Eleven

The Moment of Decision

*N*ews of the Boston Tea Party reached London in January 1774, enraging the ministry, Parliament, and the British public. "The Resistence Made by the Colonies to Receive the Comp[any] Tea and Particularly the destruction of it at Boston," one Englishman reported to Johnson, "has Raised a Greater Clamour here without doors against the Americans than Ever I have known, and the papers are every day filled with Scurillity and abuse. Hypocrates, Traytors, Rebels, Villians are the Softest Epithets Now bestow[ed] on the Colonies."[1] The North administration responded with force. That spring, the ministry pushed through Parliament four punitive bills against the unruly colony, closing the port of Boston and stripping Massachusetts of its cherished privileges of self-government. Lest Great Britain's determination to uphold her authority seem halfhearted, the ministry dispatched four regiments of British regulars to Boston and named the Commander in Chief of all British forces in North America, General Thomas Gage, as the new governor of the rebellious colony.[2]

The so-called Coercive Acts produced a sudden, dramatic revolution in colonial sentiment, convincing many Americans that they must resist or submit to British tyranny. Only months before, men in Connecticut and elsewhere had denounced Boston's imprudent, destructive assault on the East India Company, but in the summer of 1774 the Connecticut towns sent gifts of sheep and cattle, oats and rye to the besieged Bostonians and framed fiery resolutions against the ministry's retaliatory measures.[3] One Connecticut penman, Rev. Ebenezer Baldwin, set forth his countrymen's fears in the plainest terms: "If we view the whole conduct of the ministry and Parliament," he wrote, "I do not see how anyone can doubt but that there is a settled fix'd plan for *enslaving* the colonies. . . . "

Notwithstanding the excellency of the British constitution, if the ministry can secure a majority in Parliament, who will come into all their measures, will vote as they bid them; they may rule as absolutely as they do in *France* or *Spain*, yea as in *Turkey* or *India*. . . . The more places or pensions the ministry have in their gift the more easily they can *bribe* a majority of Parliament by bestowing those places on them or their friends. . . . This doubtless is the great thing the ministry are driving at, to establish arbitrary government with the consent of Parliament. And to keep the people of England still, the first exertions of this power are upon the colonies.[4]

To resist the growing danger, the united cooperation of all the colonies was vital. On June 17, the Massachusetts patriots called upon the other colonies to select delegates for a general congress at Philadelphia, which would commence on the first day of September.[5] Less than one month later, Connecticut's Committee of Correspondence gathered to select the colony's delegates and named five, including Johnson.[6] Johnson refused. To the committee, he pleaded that a pressing legal suit would detain him in Albany on the appointed date of the congress, but to his two English correspondents, Benjamin LaTrobe and Richard Jackson, Johnson confided his true reasons. The proposed congress "would I fear in the present State of things but tend to widen the Breach already much too great between the Parent State & her Colonies." It was being said, wrote Johnson, that the congress will propose an accommodation. "Were this to be the Case I should very gladly assist at their Consultations but while the Passions of Men are so awakened as they seem to be at present, little [room] I fear will be found in that Assembly for Moderate Men or Moderate Measures & with no other will I be Concerned." He observed that "the minds of people are greatly alarmed and highly inflamed," and despaired that for peace "the Prospect is very gloomy."[7]

Johnson had good reasons to dread an immoderate response from the intercolonial congress. In every colony, patriots inflamed their neighbors with the same tale of ministerial conspiracy that Baldwin portrayed to his Connecticut listeners.[8] More alarming, colonial writers and local conventions boldly declared that a corrupt Parliament had no legal authority over the colonies, that Americans were bound by "no laws to which they have not given their consent by Representatives freely chosen by themselves."[9] Even more ominous, the Connecticut General Assembly and the other colonial legislatures were instructing the citizens to ready their armaments and exercise their militia.[10] Finally, newspapers everywhere talked of nonintercourse with Great Britain, and the very idea of an intercolonial congress had emerged around that plan.[11] Johnson must have feared that a second colonial boycott would bring the same humiliating defeat as the first had in 1770. Reports from England told him that the ministry, with strong support from Parliament, would stand firm against any American challenge.[12] The reports were accurate. When Lord North presented the Coercive Acts to Parliament in the spring, he had encountered only a weak and divided opposition. All the bills had passed by substantial majorities.[13]

Dread that an open debate on parliamentary authority would aggravate the conflict, fear that an American boycott would end in another humiliating defeat, and apprehensions that rash American measures would provoke an angry British retaliation kept Johnson away from the congress. So, too, did the essence of his personality, shaped long before the Anglo-American dispute began. Born an Episcopalian in a Puritan colony, educated by his staunch Anglican father, Johnson had been taught in his earliest years to hold to his convictions even against an overwhelming majority. His Yale education and superior legal training had carried him swiftly to political prominence, and he had quickly realized that to guard his political opportunities from the ravages of sectarian warfare he must shun public debate and pursue his objectives only when quiet methods could be used. From these two principles he had never swayed, as he adhered steadfastly to the Church of England and privately campaigned for an American episcopate, all the while staying clear of the public contest between the churches. In the summer of 1774, when political as well as religious issues divided Johnson from his countrymen, these principles again shaped his conduct. Confronted with three choices—to join the fervent cry of the majority for immediate resistance, to speak out against such rash measures, or to do nothing—Johnson chose inaction.

How different were the personalities of men like James Duane and John Jay of New York, Joseph Galloway and John Dickinson of Pennsylvania, who would hurry to the congress to thwart rash measures and search for peaceful resolution! Like Johnson, they sensed that public outrage was swelling to crisis proportions, but they were determined to moderate the tempers of their fellow delegates and take part in shaping the coming events.

Congress convened on September 5, with fifty-six delegates

from twelve colonies assembling at Philadelphia.[14] The course
they would follow was plainly revealed twelve days later, when
they approved and ordered printed in the newspapers the "Suffolk
County Resolves," which had been drafted earlier that month by
the patriots of Suffolk County, Massachusetts. The resolves,
which were aimed at "the arbitrary will of a licentious" ministry,
condemned the recent acts of Parliament against the colony
"as the attempts of a wicked Administration to enslave America."
The resolves alerted the citizens of Massachusetts "to acquaint
themselves with the art of war as soon as possible," and declared
that the people of Suffolk County were "determined to act merely
upon the defensive so long as such conduct may be vindicated by
reason and for the principles of self-preservation, but no
longer."[15] The delegates at Philadelphia soon showed themselves
equally determined to obstruct the wicked plans of a licentious
ministry. On September 27, they voted to ban the importation,
purchase, or use of any goods exported from Great Britain or
Ireland, beginning on December 1. Three days later, the delegates
forbade the exportation of any colonial wares to Great Britain, the
West Indies, or Ireland after September 10, 1775.[16]

The delegates' apprehensions of a diabolical plan to enslave
America impelled them to quick and drastic action, and moved
them also to venture farther than ever before in challenging
Parliament's authority over the colonies. But how far? On this
question, they were divided and reluctant, debating for twenty
days. Some delegates, including the Connecticut representative,
Roger Sherman, insisted that the recent attack on colonial
liberties compelled America to reject Parliament's authority
entirely. Patrick Henry declared that the bonds of government
were dissolved and a new governing body should be formed. But
John Jay retorted that "the measure of arbitrary power is not full,
and I think it must run over, before we undertake to frame a new
constitution."[17] James Duane proposed that Congress recognize
the authority of Parliament to regulate colonial trade, but his
proposal failed by a tie vote.[18] In the final compromise, which
passed by a narrow margin in mid-October, the powers left to
Parliament were so restricted as to be practically meaningless.
Galloway fumed that they "concede nothing."[19]

The debates in Congress over military preparations, like the
discussions on the extent of British authority, revealed not only a
struggle between fiery and cautious personalities but also a
hesitant recognition that if the British government had fallen

under the control of evil and selfish men, as an increasing number of colonists believed, America must defend herself and free herself, or fall victim to slavery and vice. On the first three days of October the Congress debated and finally rejected a motion by Richard Henry Lee to alert the colonies to prepare their militias in case economic coercion failed. In fact, the Congress would rise before taking any decisive steps toward military readiness. Yet the dread anticipation of war colored all their proceedings. In a formal address to their countrymen, the delegates again warned against the "regular system" for "subjugating the Colonies" to "the uncontroulable and unlimited power of Parliament" and admonished that, should economic coercion fail, "the schemes agitated against these colonies have been so conducted as to render it prudent . . . [to] extend your views to the most mournful events, and be in all respects prepared for every contingency."[20] On October 26, the Congress adjourned, and John Dickinson rose from his seat gloomily. "I wish for peace ardently," he reflected, "but must say, delightful as it is, it will come more grateful for being unexpected."[21] To William Samuel Johnson, watching his own colony's response to the Coercive Acts, the prospect for peace seemed no more promising.

Johnson had no reason to hope that Connecticut would reject the Congress's measures in favor of a less forceful appeal to the home government. In September, even before the delegates at Philadelphia had announced their program, Connecticut patriots had gathered in local and countywide meetings to urge military readiness and a boycott against British goods.[22] A feverish impatience pervaded the colony. On October 20, the Congress had adopted formal procedures to enforce its proposed boycott, and had ordered the rules of this so-called association to be published in the newspapers. The association required "that a committee be chosen in every county, city, and town . . . whose business it shall be to observe the conduct of all persons," and that when violators of the boycott were discovered, their names should be publicized in the newspapers so that "all such foes to the rights of British-Americans may be publicly known, and universally condemned as the enemies of American liberty; and thence forth we respectively will break off all dealings with him or her."[23] The Connecticut General Assembly immediately endorsed the association and urged quick compliance by every town.[24] The Assembly also responded without delay to the Congress's admonition to prepare "for every contingency." The first steps toward military preparedness had been taken in May, but in the fall the legislators redoubled their efforts, ordering the towns to exercise their companies and increase their stores of ammunition. "Now if the British parliament and ministry continue resolved to prosecute the measures they have entered upon," declared one patriot preacher, "it seems we must either submit to such a dreadful state of slavery as hath been shown will be the probable issue of their measures, or must by force and arms stand up in defence of our liberties."[25]

Johnson's heart sank as he sat in the Assembly listening to the preparations for war. In January 1774, his fellow lawmakers had raised him to Lieutenant Colonel of the Fourth Regiment,[26] but sometime between May and October he submitted his letter of resignation from the militia. He would take no part in warlike measures, but neither would he expose his convictions to public ire. Instead he pleaded that old age and infirmity had made him indifferent to public offices and honors. "These are not the Sentiments of a Soldier," Johnson explained. "Under so calm a [state] of Soul, it is impossible to animate the placid Heart, or invigorate the feeble Arm to deeds of danger."[27] Johnson had suffered long attacks of gout and other illnesses during his mission in England,[28] and no doubt the last thirty years had tempered his youthful longing for military adventure. But the Stratford politician, then forty-seven years old, had lost none of his ambition for public leadership, whether in the legislature, on the bench, or in the militia. Dread of war, not old age, would impel him to gradually withdraw from every phase of public life during the next two years.

In November and December, patriots in Connecticut and every colony subscribed to the association and chose their committees of inspection. By year's end, twenty-eight or more Connecticut towns had answered the Congress's call.[29] The spirited support of the majority was impressive, but so was the unprecedented boldness of the dissenting minority. In the winter of 1774-1775 a literature of loyalism suddenly emerged. Daniel Leonard of Massachusetts, Joseph Galloway of Pennsylvania, and a number of New York Anglicans including Samuel Seabury, Thomas Chandler, and Myles Cooper, accused Congress of violating its mandate by rejecting every course of action that might produce a reconciliation. The Congress, they protested, was luring an unsuspecting public into rebellion and inde-pendence, which could lead only to anarchy in government and desolation in war.[30] The loyalist outcry would be crushed almost as suddenly as it had emerged. Within a year after the first loyalist tirades appeared, a band of Connecticut vigilantes would smash the presses of a notorious loyalist printer in nearby New York, and the Connecticut Assembly would outlaw all criticism against the Continental Congress and the colony's resistance efforts.[31]Loyalist penmen and printers were not the only ones to suffer intimidation and violence from the patriots. The association made it impossible to oppose the Congress's policy of economic coercion without being branded as a friend to British tyranny. Men who might have sought some middle course were forced to choose between the two extremes. Let all violators of the association "feel the weight of [America's] vengeance and rue the day they ever suffered a selfish spirit to banish all love to their country from their breasts," exhorted the patriot preacher Baldwin. In most Connecticut towns, where committees of inspection sprang up quickly, nonassociators were condemned, ostracized by their neighbors, and in some cases persuaded to repent their errant ways. Patriot vigilantes would soon take matters into their own hands, disarming and jailing the recalcitrants in towns such as Newtown and Woodbury, which refused to adopt the association.[32]

Johnson assessed the situation cautiously. In December 1774, the Stratford town meeting approved the association and selected a committee of eighteen to enforce it. Named to the committee were the town's leading citizens, including Stratford's two deputies in the Assembly and the only Stratfordite who held a seat on the Governor's Council, William Samuel Johnson.[33] Johnson made no protest. Undoubtedly he recalled the friendly advice of his political associate, Silas Deane, who had told Johnson in August that his refusal to attend the Congress had occasioned malicious rumors. Deane had warned that "a Report has been circulated that you rather disapproved the Measure & professed an Unwillingness to attend through Fear of disobliging your Friends in England . . . such a story must give a Gentleman of Character and Sensibility some uneasiness." From Deane had come the admonition that, "in Times such as the present, where a Man's Actions or words will admit of two constructions, the world are disposed to prefer the unfavorable."[34] In the months of intense excitement following the adjournment of Congress, public sentiment would recognize no middle position between supporting Congress and betraying American liberty. Men like Galloway and

Leonard and the citizens of Woodbury and Newtown protested
Congress's course only at great risk to their reputations and
personal safety. To them, that course spelled treason and war. But
other men, who would ultimately oppose independence, still
shared the hope of their patriot neighbors that American resistance would stop short of war, and indeed produce a negotiation.
For these men, including Johnson, the times did not yet require
open dissent.

During the winter of 1774-1775, as townsmen everywhere
routed out nonassociators and prepared their militia for the
dreadful extreme, Johnson and his fellow legislators labored over
an address to Lord Dartmouth. In the fall of 1774, Governor
Trumbull had received from the Secretary of State for the
American Department a plea to abandon any plans for another
intercolonial congress. Trumbull had appointed a committee of
five, including Johnson, to pen a response. After collecting the
sentiments of all the colony's towns, the five committeemen
drafted a reply and submitted it to the Assembly in March. The
letter, quickly approved by the Assembly stated:

On the one hand, we do assure your Lordship that we do not wish to
weaken or impair the authority of the British Parliament in any matters
essential to the welfare and happiness of the whole Empire. On the other
hand . . . it is our duty . . . [to] maintain the constitutional rights and
liberties derived to us as men and Englishmen. . . . British supremacy
and American liberty are not incompatible with each other. They have
been seen to exist and flourish together for more than a century. What
now renders them inconsistent? Or, if anything be further necessary to
ascertain the one or limit the other, why may it not be amicably adjusted,
every occasion and ground of future controversy be removed, and all that
has unfortunately passed be buried in perpetual oblivion?

A partial answer to that question was given by the legislators
themselves, when they told Lord Dartmouth that "the unlimited
powers lately claimed by the British Parliament drove them to the
borders of despair."[35] Colonial suspicions of a malign conspiracy
against American liberty made any concessions to parliamentary
supremacy seem fraught with peril. The rest of the answer came
from Great Britain that spring, in a letter to Johnson and in the
official response of the ministry and Parliament to the addresses
and boycott of the Congress. The answers showed that the increase
of distrust and fear on both sides of the Atlantic was carrying
Great Britain and her colonies to a disastrous deadlock. Benjamin

LaTrobe wrote to Johnson from England that "those at the head of affairs here would gladly come into conciliatory measures, if they could believe that there were not leading men on your side of the Atlantic who aim at more than an exemption from taxation by a British Parliament."[36] The actions of the ministry and Parliament that spring confirmed the truth of LaTrobe's report, that the British government was convinced that America aimed at nothing less than total independence—in short, rebellion.

On February 2 the ministry moved in Parliament for an Address to the King stating that "a rebellion at this time actually exists" in Massachusetts and requesting the King "to take the most effectual measures to enforce due obedience" to Parliament. The motion was adopted by large majorities in both houses, and the government dispatched six thousand reinforcements to the colonies. Next, the ministers responded to the American boycott with their own commercial countermeasure. They introduced a bill which became law on March 30, forbidding the New England colonies from trading with any nation but Great Britain and the British West Indies and barring New Englanders from the North Atlantic fisheries. Soon afterward Parliament imposed the same restrictions on the colonies south of New England.[37] Clearly a majority of Parliament, as well as the ministry, favored forceful submission rather than conciliation.

By the spring of 1775, the British and American positions had polarized, and no one recognized the dire consequences of this fact better than the colonial agents. In the 1760s, when Johnson was in England, the frequent changes of ministers and the confusions and divisions in Parliament had frustrated the agents' attempts to lobby effectively. But in the 1770s the agents encountered a more difficult obstacle. The prolonged stability of the North ministry in that decade rested upon a consensus in Parliament that permissiveness toward the colonies had reached its limit and that no challenge to the authority of the supreme legislature could be tolerated. As America's complaints extended beyond British taxation to include a whole range of laws made by Parliament and as the Americans became bolder in declaring their grievances, the agents found themselves excluded from the halls of Parliament, harassed, unheard, and powerless. As a channel of communication between America and the home government, the colonial agencies had become, in the words of William Bollan, "a rope of sand." The polarization of American and British positions over the issue of Parliament's powers also created divisions among the agents themselves. Only three, Lee, Bollan, and Franklin, all American-born, would agree to present the Congress's "Statement of Rights and Grievances" to the King. The other agents— unsympathetic to any challenge against Parliament or convinced that such a challenge would meet failure—refused, including Thomas Life, who reported to Johnson that he had taken no part in the presentation "thro' caution."[38] The harsh commercial and military measures adopted by the government and the Declaration of Treason and Rebellion left the three American-born agents with a sense of bitterness and futility. To Franklin, the possi- bility—indeed, even the desirability—of peace had vanished. In October 1774, Franklin had urged his constituents to conduct the association prudently and quietly, lest an "accidental quarrel" or "personal insult . . . produce a tumult, unforeseen and therefore impossible to be prevented in which such a carnage may ensue as to make a breach that can never afterwards be healed." But in March 1775, Franklin left England carrying a very different message to the Continental Congress, where he would take a seat in May at the opening of the second session. "When I consider the extreme corruption prevalent among all orders of men in this old rotten state, and the glorious public virtue so predominant in our rising country, I cannot but apprehend more mischief than benefit from a closer union . . . to unite us intimately will only be to corrupt and poison us also."[39]

For the past five years, Johnson had worried that pulling one loose thread would unravel the whole fabric of empire. Now he saw each side tearing carelessly at the fraying cloth. Around him, he could see his neighbors growing enraged by the British retaliation. When news of the Declaration of Treason and Rebellion reached Connecticut, Ezra Stiles exclaimed that "the Friends of Liberty are hereby exasperated & declare themselves ready for Combat, & nothing is now talked of but immediately forming an American Army at Worcester & taking the Field with undaunted Resolution."[40] Stiles's words foreshadowed the heated response of the Second Continental Congress, which would convene on May 10. But twenty-one days before the delegates reached Philadelphia, British shots fired at Lexington pushed the Anglo-American dispute to the long-dreaded extreme, open warfare.

On April 20, the earliest word of the battle reached Con- necticut, and by the twenty-third all the colony had been aroused. In some towns men left their plows, their household chores, and even their Sunday meetings to join their regiments and march to the aid of Boston. But other towns responded with a cautious dread. The town meeting at New Haven, for example, refused to take any immediate action. On the twenty-sixth, Johnson and his fellow legislators hurried to Hartford for an emergency session. There, also, the awful anticipation of war delayed an immediate call to arms. One legislator, probably Roger Sherman, proposed that the colony dispatch a letter of inquiry and peaceful overture to General Gage, and the Assembly appointed Johnson and Erastus Wolcott as emissaries. The letter, composed by Governor Trumbull on April 28, warned that the people of Connecticut "are most firmly resolved to defend their rights and privileges to the last extremity; nor will they be restrained from giving aid to their brethren if any unjustifiable attack is made upon them. Be so good therefore," the letter implored,

as to explain yourself upon this most important subject. . . . Is there no way to prevent this unhappy dispute from coming to extremities? Is there no alternative but absolute submission, or the desolations of war? . . . Will it not be consistent with your duty to suspend the operations of war on your part, and enable us on ours to quiet the minds of the people, at least till the result of some further deliberations may be known?[41]

Johnson and Wolcott set out immediately for Boston, but before they could complete their mission and return Gage's answer to the Assembly, their fellow legislators discarded any hopes for immediate peace and readied the colony for war. The Assembly's sudden shift of purpose apparently owed much to the noisy indignation of the Massachusetts patriots, especially John Adams. One Connecticut man reported from Roxbury, outside Boston, that "the Negotiation with which Doct. Johnson and Col. Wolcott is charged has thrown a Chagrin upon the leading Men here which they do not know how to throw off."[42] On the twenty-eighth or twenty-ninth, Johnson and Wolcott lodged at a tavern at Springfield, where they met John Adams.[43] The next morning the two Connecticut emissaries proceeded on to Boston, while Adams seems to have hurried to Hartford to dissuade the Assembly from negotiating with Gage. Adams recorded on the night of the thirtieth that "the Assembly of this Colony is now sitting at Hartford. We are treated with great tenderness, sympathy, friendship, and respect. Everything is doing by this Colony that can be done by men, both for New York and Boston."[44]

Before the legislators adjourned on May 6, they ordered one-fourth of the militia "inlisted, equipped, accoutred and assembled for the special defence and Safety of this Colony" and required that "three thousand stand of arms be procured as soon as may be, and held in readiness."[45] Soon afterward, Johnson arrived in Hartford carrying Gage's reply. But, as Johnson later recorded in his memoirs,

I found that our Legislature had risen without leaving any directions for their Committee or saying any thing about them. I applied to the Secretary & found that no directions had been left for us but, that they had come to resolutions of a very contrary nature & tendency—having voted men & money for the war. (The change was effected by the Massachusetts delegation.) Finding myself thus deserted I returned solitarily home full of reflection & consideration.[46]

The warlike measures decided upon at Hartford, the similar preparations made in the other colonies, and the steps soon to be taken at the Second Congress promised to transform the skirmishes at Lexington and Concord from a dreadful but isolated incident into the first exchange in a long and bloody war. Everywhere patriots and future loyalists alike disavowed rebellion, but the horror of the British attack impelled the majority to prepare for combat. Nowhere was the struggle between conflicting emotions—the desire for peace and the determination to defend American liberty—more dramatically acted out than at Philadelphia, where Congress convened on May 10. In mid-June, news reached Philadelphia that British and American forces had again clashed outside Boston, at a place called Bunker Hill, leaving one hundred Americans dead. Fear of a British invasion of New York and the bitterness of defeat at Bunker Hill impelled the delegates to immediate action. By the end of the month, Congress had appointed a military commander in chief, George Washington, and had organized two armies, one under Washington's direct command to surround Boston, and a second, led by General Philip Schuyler, to seize Montreal against an invasion of New York from the north.[47] Johnson and the other Connecticut legislators learned quickly of the military measures adopted at Philadelphia. Time and again that summer, Congress called upon Connecticut to send men and powder to New York and Boston. In May and again in July the Assembly hurriedly convened to call out additional regiments and requisition more supplies.[48]

To nearly every colony came similar appeals from the Congress, and everywhere, as local governments joined the war effort, a number of prominent men unalterably opposed to imperial separation decided that armed conflict had made that inevitable. For these men, the time to dissent had come. Peter Van Schaack of New York, for example, abhorred the Stamp Act, the Tea Act, and the Coercive Acts. He had actively participated in New York's resistance and had supported the Congress until the outbreak of a shooting war. But in the summer of 1775, Van Schaack retreated to the seclusion of Kinderhook. "I cannot see any principle of regard for my country," he reasoned, "which will authorize me in taking up arms, as absolute dependence and independence are two extremes I would avoid; for should we succeed in the latter, we shall still be in a sea of uncertainty and have to fight among ourselves for that constitution we aim at." None of the acts of Parliament, no matter how onerous and unconstitutional, justified armed rebellion, he believed, because "taking the whole of the acts complained of together, they do not, I think, manifest a system of slavery, but may fairly be imputed to human frailty and the difficulty of the subject."[49] Van Schaack's words echoed the same convictions that would soon thrust Johnson into the loyalist camp: a belief that independence would produce insurmountable difficulties and civil chaos, and a repudiation of the widespread notion that the British government had conspired maliciously to enslave America. Yet, while Van Schaack deserted his public posts, Johnson remained in his seat on the Council as his fellow legislators prepared for war. Unlike Van Schaack, he still hoped that peace could be won.

This same hope inspired a majority of the delegates at Philadelphia, patriots and future loyalists alike. On July 6, the Congress issued a "Declaration on Taking Arms," drafted almost entirely by John Dickinson. The Parliament of Great Britain, Dickinson charged, stimulated by the "cruel and impolitic purpose of enslaving these Colonies by violence," had "rendered it necessary for us to close with their last appeal from Reason to Arms." "We are reduced to the alternative of chusing an unconditional submission to the tyranny of irritated ministers, or resistance by force. The Latter is our choice." Yet Dickinson closed with an unequivocal statement of the limited purpose of the Congress's warfare:

Lest this declaration should disquiet the minds of our friends and Fellow-Subjects in any part of the empire, we assure them that we mean not to dissolve that Union which has so long and so happily subsisted between us and which we sincerely wish to see restored. Necessity has not yet driven us into that desparate measure, or induced us to excite any other nation to war against them. We have not raised armies with ambitious designs of separating from Great Britain, and establishing independent states. We fight not for glory or for conquest.[50]

Two days later, the delegates signed a petition to King George III, again the work of Congress's foremost spokesman for conciliation. Once more John Dickinson blamed wicked ministers for fomenting discord between Great Britain and her colonies, but again he set forth the limited objectives of the Congress, assuring the King that "we not only most ardently desire the former harmony between her and her colonies may be restored, but that a concord may be established between them upon so firm a basis as to perpetuate its blessings, uninterrupted by any future dissentions, to succeeding generations."[51]

In the summer of 1775, a small number of delegates, like a minority of patriots outside the Congress, recognized and even celebrated the inevitability of independence. For men like John Adams of Massachusetts, the South Carolinian John Rutledge, and Connecticut's Roger Sherman, the overtures for peace, the search for negotiation, were futile. "I am myself as fond of Reconciliation, if we could reasonably Hope of it upon a Constitutional Basis, as any Man," Adams confessed. "But . . . the Cancer is too deeply rooted, and too far Spread, to be cured by anything short of cutting it out entirely." Despite his impatience, Adams realized that the majority, in and out of Congress, could not be pushed prematurely to the final breach. "You will see a Strange Oscillation between love and hatred, between War and Peace—," he observed, "Preparations for War and Negotiation for Peace. . . . This Negotiation I dread like Death. But it must be proposed. We can't avoid it. Discord and total Disunion would be the effect of a resolute Refusal to petition and negotiate."[52] The ardent desire for reconciliation voiced that summer, in Congress and from the pulpits and presses of every colonial town, undoubtedly kept alive Johnson's hope for peace. Indeed, like Johnson, many men in public positions throughout America who would join the loyalist camp within the year acquiesced to the war preparations that summer, trusting that a restored harmony would render them unnecessary. But by winter, Johnson's hope had vanished. The stubborn refusal of the British government to answer Congress's overtures for negotiation offered no promise that a prolonged and bloody war would be averted. Late in the summer, Johnson had received dismal news from Thomas Hutchinson in London. "I hear one and another of the King's Ministers say—there is no receding—And yet, to think of going on makes me shudder."[53] In November, America learned that the King had refused to answer the Congress's olive branch petition and had declared the colonies in a state of rebellion. "The King's Proclamation," exclaimed Governor Trumbull, "is decisive. We are now fully assured of the Inefficiency of Petitions."[54] In December, as the delegates at Philadelphia considered retaliatory measures, the Connecticut Assembly gathered in New Haven to alert the colony to immediate military readiness and to pass the colony's first law declaring treasonous any assistance, in word or deed, to the forces of Great Britain.[55] For Johnson, the time to dissent and to withdraw from his last public post had arrived. There would be no room in Connecticut's wartime government, on the colony's law books, or in the hearts of his countrymen, for a man of divided loyalties. Johnson resigned his seat on the Governor's Council,[56] and retreated to Stratford, still committed to American liberty and British rule, still convinced that no malign ministerial conspiracy had rendered the two incompatible.

William Samuel Johnson, attributed to Robert Edge Pine (Ca. 1788)
Columbiana, Columbia University and Frick Art Reference Library

Chapter Twelve

The War Years

That winter, signs appeared everywhere that the war would not end before the empire had been torn apart. Men who had long supported the patriot cause withdrew from public leadership, convinced that their countrymen had forsaken the quest for peace. Soon after Johnson abandoned public office, his friend of thirty years ago William Smith, the famous Triumvirate penman and vocal champion of American rights, chose the same course.[1] Yet many other men who adamantly opposed independence continued to participate in the American resistance, clinging to the hope that Johnson and Smith had discarded. Nowhere was the tense drama of waging war and searching for peace more visible than at the Continental Congress. For a number of men in Congress, as in every colony, the final decision between independence and loyalism lay months ahead.

For fourteen months the Congress had equivocated and shunned the issue of parliamentary authority, but in December, the delegates issued their first forthright denial of that authority. "Allegiance to Parliament? We never owed—never owned it. Allegiance to our King? Our words have ever avowed it—our conduct has ever been consistent with it," the Congress asserted.[2] Weeks later Thomas Paine's masterly philippic attacked America's last acknowledged tie with Great Britain, allegiance to the monarch.[3] Bold disclaimers against British authority were fast leading to a declaration of independence, and so too were the war measures adopted in Congress. Yet in the spring of 1776, a majority of the delegates, patriots and future loyalists alike, refused to debate the crucial question. "I can only answer at present that nothing seems wanting but that 'general consent.' The novelty of the thing deters some, the doubt of success others, the vain hope of reconciliation, many," observed Franklin.[4] The situation exasperated the radical minority. "Have we not been independent these twelve Months, wanting three days," exclaimed John Adams, who counted independence from the first shots fired at Lexington and Concord. "Have you seen the Privateering Resolves? Are not these Independence enough for my beloved Constituents? Have you seen the Resolves for opening our Ports to all Nations? Are these Independence enough? What more would you have?"[5] "Every day's Delay trys my Patience," confessed Sam Adams in April. "Reconcilation upon reasonable Terms is no Part of their [British] Plan. The only alternative is Independence or Slavery."[6]

The pressure for independence was mounting in and out of Congress. In March and early April, South Carolina and Georgia released their delegates from any obligation to pursue reconciliation. On April 21, North Carolina explicitly instructed its delegates to vote for independence. Finally, on May 10, Congress advised each colony to establish a government free from royal governors and crown authority.[7] The Congress's decisive step toward an open avowal of separation compelled two delegates to withdraw from the American resistance. Convinced that they could do nothing more to avert a declaration of independence, Robert Alexander of Maryland and Andrew Allen of Pennsylvania left their seats.[8] Yet not all the delegates who remained accepted the necessity of disunion. For a number of men, only the final vote in July would force them to abandon their hopes for reconciliation and their leadership of the patriot cause. Throughout May and June they carried on their struggle.[9]

By July every colony except New York had released its delegates to vote for independence.[10] On July 1, the delegates from twelve colonies cast their initial ballots. Three colonies dissented—South Carolina, Pennsylvania, and Delaware—but the pressure for unanimity prevailed. When the final vote was taken on July 2, a majority of the delegates from these three colonies joined their colleagues in the affirmative. By August 2, when the parchment Declaration of Independence was laid before Congress for signing, New York had reached its decision, and that colony's delegates, including John Jay, affixed their names with the rest.[11] Throughout the provinces, the declaration was celebrated with huzzas, cannon fire, speeches, and elegant dinners.[12] Yet for a number of the signers at Philadelphia, the event was disheartening. No one had pressed harder for conciliation or dreaded independence more than John Jay.

His attachment to American rights, his commitment to reunion, and his pessimistic view of the perils that independence would bring, closely resembled the convictions of William Samuel Johnson. But unlike Johnson, Jay had not receded from public responsibility. It was Jay's presence in the Congress, his intimate involvement in the rush of events, and his vulnerability to the persuasive force of the common will, that explain his acquiescence to independence.[13] From these very pressures Johnson had fled by refusing to attend the First Congress, resigning from the militia, and finally leaving the Council.

The cries for independence heard from every colony, the eruption of open war, and the impulse for unanimity in Congress persuaded most of the delegates who had long disavowed independence to vote affirmatively on July 2, but the dramatic vote on that day also evoked declarations of loyalism from a small minority of delegates. On July 1, Dickinson had cast his ballot against independence, and the next day he withdrew from the voting.[14] Until the appearance of Paine's *Common Sense*, Dickinson's famous writings had articulated the American position. But Dickinson dreaded independence. For years factional squabbling had convulsed Pennsylvania politics, and as early as 1768, in his *Farmer's Letters*, Dickinson had predicted that without the strong support of the British government, the colonies would fall into confusion and self-destruction. In 1776, he would not sanction the perilous course.[15]

The American revolutionaries opprobriously branded their loyalist neighbors as Tories, a term that misrepresented the convictions of many opponents of independence. Toryism harkened back to the seventeenth-century British political tradition that upheld the divine origins of monarchical government and denied the right of resistance for any reason. By the eighteenth century most Englishmen, at home and in the colonies, had discarded that tradition and heartily embraced the Lockean notion that government was founded on the consent of the governed. In 1776 the vast majority of Americans, patriots and loyalists alike, were Whigs. They believed that every British subject possessed certain constitutional rights on which government could not encroach.[16] For the small number of American Tories, the crisis of dissent had come in 1765, when their neighbors resisted the Stamp Act and denied Britain's right to tax the colonies. In that year Martin Howard of Rhode

Island, for example, had outspokenly defended Parliament's supremacy in all matters including taxation, a doctrine that cost him his reputation, his home, and nearly his life.[17] For the majority of American loyalists, including William Samuel Johnson, the time to dissent came much later. Only their opposition to independence compelled these men to abandon the patriot cause.

Two convictions impelled Johnson to oppose independence, and both had taken shape during his mission to England: war was unnecessary, and political independence posed grave perils. In 1766, Johnson had outspokenly denounced the Stamp Act as evidence that British statesmen "had a formed design . . . to reduce the Colonies to the State & Condition of the Roman Provinces in the Times of the Cesars. . . ." The ministry's measure, he had declared, has "given such an Alarm as will forever keep America upon her guard."[18] The following year, Johnson had embarked for England, and his experiences there had drastically altered his understanding of the Anglo-American dispute. The Connecticut agent had been horrified by the rampant factionalism, selfish political motives, ignorance and neglect that prevented a prudent and just colonial policy. Yet beneath the scene of confusion, he had found no deliberate plot to defraud Americans of their liberty. In 1771, Johnson had returned to Stratford convinced that ignorance, irresponsibility, and partisan jealousies—not the sinister designs of a wicked ministry—were to blame for the Anglo-American discord.[19] And without the threat of a malicious, well-laid plan to enslave the colonies, war against England was unnecessary.

Independence was more than unnecessary. It was fraught with peril. The bitter factionalism that rocked Connecticut's once stable polity had distressed Johnson and made him doubt that his countrymen could ever unite in self-government on a lasting and lawful basis. In the middle of the Townshend dispute, when fear and suspicion first impelled Americans to contemplate independence as their ultimate defense, Johnson had apprehended that "If we were wise and could form some system of free government upon just principles, we might be very happy without any connection with this country. But should we ever agree upon anything of that nature, should we not more probably fall into faction and parties among ourselves, destroy one another and become at length the easy prey (and property) of the first invaders?"[20] After the partial repeal of the

Townshend Acts, Johnson had exhorted the colonists to hold
fast to their nonimportation agreements until the duty on tea
had been removed.[21] But the collapse of the colonial boycott in
the summer of 1770 had enraged and embittered him. His countrymen had shown themselves weak, divided, and irresolute.[22]
The stinging disappointment of 1770 had brought personal
humiliation to Johnson and, more than any other event in the
prewar decade, had convinced him that his countrymen were
too divided and unsteady to contest British authority and unite
in self-government

From his return to Stratford in 1771 until the outbreak of
the war, Johnson had never reassessed the possibility of Anglo-
American reconciliation or appreciated the growing, fear-
inspired fortitude of his countrymen. He had not seen that
increasing distrust on both sides of the Atlantic was making
negotiation on the legitimate extent of Parliament's authority at
once necessary and impossible. To the North ministry and a
majority of Parliament, the Americans aimed at nothing short
of rebellion, and any concessions to colonial demands would
prove fatal to the empire. The ministry refused to hear American
grievances, negotiate with the colonial agents, or consider a
constitutional settlement limiting Parliament's lawmaking
powers over the colonies. But to the Americans, who were frantic with suspicions of an evil-minded ministry and a corrupt
legislature, submission to Parliament spelled slavery.[23] During
the 1770s, Johnson had remained insensitive to his countrymen's mounting alarm and had repeatedly insisted that disputing the sovereignty of Parliament raised tempers on both sides
to no real purpose.[24] Finally, Johnson had failed to understand
that the passionate anger and indignation impelling his countrymen to wage the long-dreaded war would also make them
equal to the tasks that lay ahead.

For many loyalists, the war years brought imprisonment,
banishment, and even death. The fortunate, including William
Samuel Johnson, suffered only painful isolation. Long before
Congress declared independence, Connecticut's magistrates
had begun purging loyalists from civil and military posts. In
May 1775, the Assembly stripped nine justices of the peace of
their commissions and dismissed a number of militia officers
who were suspected of disaffection. In November, one month
after Congress recommended the disarming and arrest of dangerous suspects, Stratford's deputy, Ichabod Lewis, led a posse

through Danbury, Newtown, Redding, Ridgefield, and Woodbury to disarm loyalists in each town and jail anyone who resisted. The number of interrogations and arrests soared in the
early months of 1776, and the Assembly passed increasingly
harsh laws to confine loyalists and restrict their travel.[25] Yet
Johnson had little to fear from patriot lawmakers and vigilantes. Personal conviction, not public suspicion, had compelled him to withdraw from public life. His refusal to join the
Continental Congress and his unpopular embassy to General
Gage had cost him about five hundred or more votes in the
spring election of 1775, but the support of 2582 freemen had
secured his seat on the Governor's Council. Although his popularity had fallen further by autumn, he still had won 991 votes,
enough to place him among the nominees for the next year.
Even in the spring of 1776, after he had resigned his seat on the
Council, 1272 voters had continued to support him.[26] Deference
to long-esteemed rulers was still the abiding rule for many
Connecticut patriots, and Johnson's quiet demeanor throughout the final crisis invited the support of these men. In May
1776, a full year after the Assembly had stripped loyalist suspects
of every military and civic responsibility, Connecticut's lawmakers once again appointed Johnson a justice of the peace for
Fairfield County.[27] But in 1777, an Oath of Fidelity Act was
passed that required every voter, every civil and military officer,
and every lawyer who pleaded before a Connecticut court to
swear allegiance to the new state government.[28] The law compelled Johnson to abandon his legal practice. For a man who
had long enjoyed leadership in his profession and a voice in the
public councils of his community, isolation and inactivity were
the high cost of dissent.

Johnson renounced any participation in the war, but thousands of other loyalists throughout the colonies boldly defended
the empire by joining the British army or one of the provincial
loyalist regiments.[29] Patriot magistrates and vigilantes showed
them no mercy. Enlisting men in the British army and accepting a captain's commission for himself cost Moses Dunbar his
life in 1777, when he was hanged at Execution Hall in Hartford
for treason.[30] In Connecticut, the Anglican clergy were the other
main target of patriot wrath. Their lives and property were in
constant peril throughout the war.

Not all Connecticut Anglicans became loyalists, but most
of the colony's loyalists worshipped in the Church of England,

which explains the heavy concentration of British sympathizers in the western counties. Fairfield and New Haven County
Congregationalists, who had long battled wits with Connecticut's eastern politicians, supported the patriot cause in the final
crisis.[31] By 1775, even Benjamin Gale judged that "we are now
come to that period when different sentiments . . . must not
divide us in making opposition, the mode which shall be universally agreed upon, must be universally adopted and pursued."[32] It was the colony's Anglicans, living primarily in the
western counties, who dreaded losing the protection of the
mother church and state. The testimony of Samuel Johnson
and his fellow missionaries to the SPG, especially in the years
after the Stamp Act crisis, dramatized the fear of New England
Anglicans that their church, their freedom, and their very lives
would be lost once the ties to England were severed.[33] Of Connecticut's twenty-one Episcopal divines, fourteen openly opposed independence, including Ann Johnson's uncle, Rev.
John Beach of Newtown, and Charity Johnson's husband,
Rev. Ebenezer Kneeland of Stratford. Little is known about the
remaining seven missionaries, but not one became a conspicuous patriot.[34]

The fear that impelled many New England Anglicans to
oppose independence played little part in William Samuel
Johnson's decision. Johnson had long envisioned an "American Church upon the pure principles of the Chh. of England
but unconnected with it & independent of it."[35] The venality,
formalism, and impiety of British church life had shocked and
disillusioned him.[36] But even in 1766, before he journeyed to
England, he had suggested to Myles Cooper that, if all appeals
for an English bishop failed, the Americans might turn to
Sweden, Denmark, or any other Episcopal outpost that could
dispatch a bishop to lay a foundation for America's own Episcopal hierarchy.[37] Johnson's confidence that an independent
Episcopal Church could survive in America reflected his own
trust and affection for his New England neighbors. Throughout his childhood, education, and rapid rise to prominence as a
lawyer and public leader, he had met success and friendship in
the Puritan society. The opening of an Episcopal mission at
Stratford had created tensions and hostilities at the outset, but
these difficulties had subsided in the years before Johnson's
birth, when ties of neighborliness and kinship bound Stratford's Anglicans and Puritans together in harmony. Johnson's

schooling at Yale antedated Clap's notorious crusade for Calvinist orthodoxy, and both the rector and Johnson's Puritan classmates had befriended him. The colony's freemen had given him their votes, and his fellow legislators had bestowed on him impressive honors and responsibilities. Samuel Johnson had waged a lifelong campaign against the Connecticut government, but his son had seen no inconsistency between worshipping in the Church of England and serving his colony well. On the day that William Samuel Johnson left the pulpit to prepare for the bar, he had set himself apart from the sectarian controversy and the rancorous churchmanship of his family. For two decades, he had remained faithful to his colony and his church. And on the eve of independence, political conviction, not family pressures or sectarian bitterness, compelled him to renounce his countrymen's cause.

A decade after the war, Johnson's vision of an independent Episcopal Church, safely at home in America, would reach fruition. But during the harsh war years, the fears that had impelled many Anglicans to oppose the Revolution became a terrible reality. The clergy's sufferings must have shocked and distressed Johnson deeply. In 1777 the patriots held Johnson's son-in-law, Ebenezer Kneeland, a prisoner in his own home, and the terrors of war led quickly to his physical collapse and death. For the next seven years, Stratford's Christ Church remained shut. Most of Connecticut's missionaries left their pulpits for the duration of the war, but Ann's uncle, Rev. John Beach, delivered his sermons until 1782, when an angry patriot aimed his gun at the pulpit and felled the aged stalwart.[38]

Connecticut patriots reserved no vengeance in punishing the active supporters of the British military and the colony's brazen Anglican missionaries. Yet most of the colony's quiet loyalists, including William Samuel Johnson, escaped harassment and personal danger in the early years of the war. In Connecticut, and wherever Americans were spared the hardship of fighting the enemy on home ground, loyalists suffered less than in colonies that hosted the war.[39] But in February and again in July 1779, General Tryon led his British forces in the first major assaults against Connecticut towns. The attacks raised antiloyalist feeling to new heights, imperilling even the safety of the colony's passive loyalists. That summer, Johnson was thrust into an open and decisive confrontation with Connecticut's wartime government.

On July 7, three thousand British troops under General Tryon's command plundered New Haven and four days later burned Fairfield. Terror spread through Stratford, which lay halfway between the two ravaged towns and seemed the next likely target. Forty-eight British ships still threatened the Connecticut coast.[40] Stratford's patriots argued over the best means of defense. Some believed that the town should be evacuated, but others refused and devised a secret plan to save it from attack. Tryon, a Yale graduate, was well known in Connecticut. Several Stratford leaders, including two justices of the peace and a militia officer, privately asked Johnson to intercede secretly with the British general. Johnson felt trapped. On the one hand, he feared engaging in any clandestine act that might be construed as treason. On the other hand, he worried that "this was not a time to disobey the people." Johnson agreed to intercede, but only if his fellow townsmen would sign a pledge to support the scheme and defend him from injury and abuse. On July 12, the subscription circulated.[41]

The proposal to negotiate with Tryon enraged many of the townspeople, horrified Governor Trumbull, and impelled the state's militia commander, Major General Oliver Wolcott, to take immediate action. On July 12 Wolcott dispatched Lieutenant Colonel Jonathan Dimon to the scene, instructing him to prepare the town's defenses and "prevent any people from carrying on any traitorous Correspondence with the Enemy."[42] For the next three days, Dimon interrogated Johnson and the signers of the subscription. The lieutenant colonel assured Wolcott that most of the subscribers, including the originators of the scheme, were "firm Friends to the Independency of these States" who had been "deluded by their designing Enemies." He urged Wolcott to distinguish between these erring patriots and Johnson, a known loyalist.[43]

On the eighteenth, Wolcott ordered Dimon to arrest Johnson and deliver him into the custody of the magistrates of Farmington. Farmington lay inland, away from the threat of a British assault. Wolcott probably worried that the presence of known loyalists in any coastal town imperiled the Connecticut shoreline. Tryon's assault on New Haven two weeks earlier had owed its success, in part, to the information and support of the town's loyalists.[44] Nevertheless, Wolcott apparently regretted having to order Johnson's arrest. For years, the two men had sat together in the colony's highest offices. In his instructions to Dimon, Wolcott lamented that "these are the times when the usual forms of proceeding are to give place to a regard for public safety, and the love of country is to be preferred at all times to the friendship of youth."[45]

Unlike Wolcott, the Farmington magistrates refused to confine a man of Johnson's public stature. When the prominent loyalist appeared in Farmington on the twenty-third, the town fathers heard his case and released him on parole. But Johnson feared returning to Stratford without an explicit acquittal, and for good reason. Just two days earlier, a Stratford town meeting had publicly denounced the allegedly traitorous scheme in which Johnson took part. As Johnson later recorded in his "Memoirs," more than a parole was needed to "quiet the People." He therefore set out for Lebanon to present his case to Governor Trumbull and, two days later, on July 28, he appeared before the Governor's Council and the Council of Safety.[46]

Many of the patriot lawmakers who heard Johnson's case had served with him in the colonial legislature or the courts of law a few years before. The Revolution had brought no upheaval in Connecticut's constitution or leadership. It was not surprising, therefore, that Johnson received a sympathetic hearing. The Governor's Council voted to release Johnson immediately. Nine of the twelve men who sat on the Council had held their seats in the 1770s, when Johnson too was a member. Three, Roger Sherman, Eliphalet Dyer, and William Pitkin, had also shared the Superior Court bench with him in 1772 and 1773.[47] But Johnson counted fewer allies on the new Council of Safety, a wartime advisory board created in 1775 to assist the Governor during the Assembly's adjournments. Only four of the thirteen members of the Council of Safety had served with Johnson on the Governor's Council or on the bench before the war. The Council of Safety refused to release Johnson until he had sworn an oath of allegiance to the independent state of Connecticut.[48]

Johnson left no personal reflections on this difficult decision, and we can only conjecture that the past years of isolation and inactivity, and the sudden threat of dangerous antiloyalist feeling in Stratford, persuaded him to take the oath. The ordeal that had begun so perilously two weeks earlier concluded auspiciously. Johnson's decision to acknowledge Connecticut's revolutionary government no doubt caused him much personal anguish, but the oath allowed him to return safely to Stratford and resume his law practice. More promising still, the oath made him eligible again for public office, and his sympathetic treatment by the Governor and his assistants boded well for Johnson's political future.

According to Johnson's later recollections, he lived in peace after his return to Stratford.[49] But for a man who had long stood at the center of public affairs, only a return to political prominence could heal the wounds from his wartime ordeal. In 1782, Johnson's opportunity appeared. It seems ironic that the Susquehannah controversy, which had tried his patience and imperiled his political support so many times before the war, occasioned his return to public life.

With the outbreak of Revolution, any possibility that the Privy Council would render a final decision in the contest between Pennsylvania and Connecticut had vanished.[50] The responsibility rested with America. In 1775 and again in 1776, the Continental Congress had appealed to the two states to quiet the bloody hostilities in the disputed territory until a settlement could be reached at war's end. The appeals had proved ineffectual.[51] Three years later, Pennsylvania had urged the Congress to decide the issue. The Articles of Confederation empowered Congress to adjudicate boundary disputes between states. But Connecticut had objected, and until the Articles were ratified and the powers of Congress were thereby legalized, no one could require Connecticut's surrender to a congressional hearing.[52] At last, in 1781, the Articles won full ratification, and Pennsylvania immediately seized the moment to petition again for a congressional trial. On November 14, Congress announced its intention to settle the dispute, and invited Connecticut and Pennsylvania to dispatch agents to Philadelphia in June 1782.[53] The agents' duties would be twofold: first, to agree on a location and date for the trial and select judges from among the delegates in Congress, and secondly, to plead their state's case when the court convened.

In January, the Connecticut Assembly named three agents: Eliphalet Dyer, Jesse Root, and William Samuel Johnson.[54] Dyer and Root, the state's two delegates in Congress, boasted experience in the national government and the support of Connecticut's voters. Johnson had neither, but the Assembly apparently regarded his expertise on the Susquehannah issue as vital to the state's cause. The same public leaders, such as Governor

Trumbull, who had originally involved Connecticut in the Susquehannah controversy and had enlisted Johnson as their legal spokesman before the Revolution, remained in power throughout the war. In 1779 these men had spared Johnson from imprisonment and personal danger, and three years later they welcomed his return as a spokesman for the western claim.[55]

Johnson did not proceed to Philadelphia in June as Congress had directed. There is no evidence that he hesitated to accept the appointment, but it seems that his legal business detained him in Connecticut until late autumn.[56] To Dyer and Root fell the task of negotiating with the Pennsylvania agents that summer. At last, in August, the agents agreed upon five judges and consented to hold court at Trenton, New Jersey, the following November.[57] Johnson set out for Trenton on November 8, arriving six days later. After conferring with the judges and other agents, and searching for comfortable lodgings, he attended the opening day at court on the eighteenth.[58]

For nearly a month, one state and then the other took the floor to present evidence. On December 10, after both sides had set forth their claims, the judges invited each agent to deliver his own summary.[59] Johnson, the fifth speaker, opened his argument on December 29. Like his two Connecticut colleagues who had already addressed the court, he relied on Connecticut's century-old charter to support the state's claim and barely mentioned the dubious Indian deed purchased by the Susquehannah Company just three decades before the trial.[60] After Johnson, Pennsylvania's Joseph Reed took the floor, the last agent to speak. Reed assailed Johnson's argument point by point, and fired again and again against the crucial weakness of the Connecticut claim: the fact that for over one hundred years, until 1774, Connecticut had neglected its sea-to-sea claim and testified that its territory extended only to the New York line.[61]

On December 30, the judges awarded jurisdiction of the disputed land to Pennsylvania.[62] The reasons for Connecticut's defeat can only be conjectured, because the court had agreed at the outset to render a unanimous decision and issue no justifying statement. Eliphalet Dyer's account of the trial suggests two likely causes for the defeat. The judges, speculated Dyer, "took up the long Silence of Connecticut" regarding the sea-to-sea claim, "the contest in Connecticut against the Claim, Govr. Fitches letters calling of it a wild scheem in our people & the cautious manner in which our assembly first treated the affair." Dyer also blamed the allegiances of the five judges, four of whom hailed from states that claimed no land to the west of their recognized border.[63] Dyer's reasoning was sound.

Jealousy between the landed and landless states had provoked hostilites in Congress for years. States that claimed vast expanses of western territory under their original royal patents or charters had persistently refused to cede this uninhabited land to Congress. The debates over cession had even delayed ratification of the Articles of Confederation. By 1782 the bitter divisions on the issue had worsened. Congress desperately needed a revenue to pay its army and finance its debt. Until the landed states awarded clear title to the western lands, the territory could not be sold, yet all other means of securing an income for the nation had failed. Delegates from the landless states no doubt felt little sympathy for the sea-to-sea claim on which Connecticut based its pretensions to the Susquehannah territory, because Connecticut was one of the states that still denied Congress an unimpaired title to the territory west of settlement.[64] In October, Dyer had warned Governor Trumbull that the state's continued refusal "may be productive of great animosity & Contention," while a generous cession "might operate kindly & beneficially in our Cause." Dyer had urged speedy reconsideration, but Connecticut had not acted.[65] Of the five judges at Trenton, only Cyrus Griffin hailed from a landed state, Virginia.[66] Griffin may have dissented from the judgment of his four fellow judges, but his dissent could not be heard under the terms of the trial.

Connecticut's defeat at Trenton, rather than impeding Johnson's political future, greatly enhanced his opportunity to launch a new public career. No one blamed him for the adverse decision. "The Cause by Doctr. Johnson & Col. Root was placed in every advantageous point of Light," Dyer reported, "[and] they were intent upon it for more than 40 days. They never exerted themselves better nor to more advantage."[67] More important, the longer the Susquehannah dispute burned on, the greater became Johnson's opportunity to reestablish himself as the spokesman for Connecticut's cause. The decision handed down at Trenton, far from extinguishing the controversy, added new fire to Connecticut's longstanding grievances and even ignited new ones. First, the Company's leaders sent home complaints that the Pennsylvania agents had suppressed evidence vital to the trial.[68] Secondly, although the judges at

Trenton awarded Pennsylvania jurisdiction over the disputed
territory, they rendered no final decision on whether Connecticut settlers who submitted to the laws of Pennsylvania could
remain the bona fide owners of the land. The judges left the
Pennsylvania government and the Connecticut settlers to negotiate the question of soil rights, and merely urged Pennsylvania
to treat the settlers fairly until an agreement was reached. But
the following year brought more bloodshed and no agreement.[69]
Thirdly, the defeat at Trenton made Connecticut more determined than ever to retain its claim to the land west of Pennsylvania. Two months before the trial, Dyer had urged Connecticut
to offer a generous cession to Congress, hoping that the offer
would quiet the jealousies of the landless states, but immediately after the Trenton defeat, Dyer warned the Assembly against
making any concessions.[70]

In October 1783, the Connecticut Assembly, acting on the
complaints of unfairness at Trenton and on the undetermined
fate of the Susquehannah settlers, appointed Dyer, Root, and
Johnson to press for a new hearing on the Connecticut claim
and a speedy trial of the settlers' soil rights.[71] Soon after, the
Assembly treated the third issue raised by the Trenton decision,
cession of the vast territory west of Pennsylvania. Once before,
in 1780, Connecticut had framed its conditions for relinquish-
ing the land, but the rigid conditions had rendered the cession
useless, and Congress had rejected it. In January 1784, the Assembly revoked this prior cession and drafted a new, even more
restricted one that reserved for the state an expanse of 250,000
acres west of Pennsylvania to compensate for the territory lost
at Trenton.[72] Although Congress would quickly deny Connecticut a new hearing on the jurisdiction of the Susquehannah
territory, the two other issues—the soil rights of the settlers and
the lands west of Pennsylvania—would provoke disagreement
in Congress throughout 1784 and remain unresolved at year's
end.[73] This prolonged contention proved crucial for Johnson's
reentry into Connecticut politics.

Connecticut's political leaders had already forgiven Johnson's loyalist past and welcomed the Susquehannah expert into
the state's public councils, but in the state of Connecticut, as in
its colonial predecessor, political success required the support
of the voters. By 1783 the war was over, but peace with Great
Britain brought no sudden harmony between patriots and loyalists. Throughout 1783 and most of 1784, the treatment of former

loyalists occasioned heated debate among Connecticut's voters. On the resolution of this issue hung Johnson's political future. Time was needed to subdue the passions of civil conflict. The ongoing dispute in Congress over Connecticut's land claims sustained Johnson's role as a vital counselor to the state's leaders until the voters were ready to support him. Not until the spring of 1785 could Johnson make the critical leap from appointed agent to popularly elected official.

Connecticut townspeople resisted every attempt by their national leaders and state officials to dictate local policy regarding former loyalists. In conformity with the articles of peace accepted by the United States in April 1783, Congress urged the states to restore the loyalists' confiscated property and cease all harassment and punishment.[74] Even before the peace treaty became official, Connecticut's rulers set a precedent for leniency. In January, the loyalist Boston merchant Richard Smith requested permission to enter Connecticut with his property. Although Massachusetts had banished Smith and Connecticut had confiscated his share of a local mine during the war, the Assembly granted his request. Towns everywhere responded with protests. Especially in New London, New Haven, Fairfield, Danbury, Norwalk, and Stratford, which had felt the hardest blows from British assaults, the Assembly's decision created an uproar.[75] Other issues aggravated the displeasure with the state's leadership. A number of Connecticut voters had grown restive under the long rule of Governor Trumbull and his assistants, most of whom had held office since colonial times. High wartime taxes, inflation, and price regulations had added to the discontent.[76] In the spring of 1783, all this impatience coalesced around the single issue of returning loyalists. At the statewide election in April, lenience would be accepted or rejected, and with it the continued leadership of Trumbull and his colleagues.[77]

The April election brought a narrow victory for Connecticut's established rulers and the first promising signs for the state's former loyalists. Governor Trumbull, Lieutenant Governor Griswold, and all twelve assistants were returned to office. In May, the Assembly repealed most of Connecticut's wartime laws against loyalists and rejected demands from some towns that loyalist exiles be denied reentry into the state.[78] The May legislation did not extinguish all local animosity toward wartime enemies. A few towns continued to exclude former loyalists, and Yale students debated the justice of amnesty in 1784, as they had in 1783.[79] The issue was not closed, but late in 1783 and especially the following year, signs appeared everywhere that the passions of the war years were subsiding.[80]

The narrow victory for the state's lenient policy in April 1783 and the gradual abatement of local antiloyalist feeling over the next year served as a barometer for Johnson's own rising political fortunes. Despite his service on behalf of Connecticut's western claim in 1782 and 1783, the voters had passed him over for any state office. But in October 1784, freemen in every town cast their nominations for Connecticut's delegates in Congress. For the first time, Johnson's name appeared on the list of fifteen nominees, and in the spring of 1785, Connecticut voters sent him to Congress.[81]

Chapter Thirteen

The Quest for Union

∽∂)(ᗧ∾

*I*n January 1785, several months before the Connecticut freemen elected their delegates to Congress, Johnson set out for New York to take his seat among the nation's leaders. The Connecticut Assembly, which reserved the right to make interim appointments to Congress, had selected Johnson to replace Charles Church Chandler,[1] who had resigned.

The scars of war in New York could be seen everywhere. Congress met in the old City Hall, close to the "burnt district," where the skeletons of old brick ruins "cast their grim shadows upon the pavement, imparting an unearthly aspect to the street." Nearly every landmark had been defaced or destroyed during the British occupation. Yet New York, unlike any other American city, boasted a gaiety and extravagance that must have reminded Johnson of London. Taverns sprang up so quickly in the decade after the war that even the city magistrates tried unsuccessfully to curb the increase. Pleasure gardens modeled after London's famous Vauxhall and Ranelagh invited New Yorkers to parade in their finest dress and attend the entertainments. Although public theatres were banned in Philadelphia, the American Company launched its first regular season in New York a few months after Johnson's arrival. Foreign visitors exclaimed at the extravagance of the New York women's fashions and observed that "if there is a town on the American continent where English luxury displays its follies, it is New York."[2]

The high spirits of the city contrasted starkly to the languor and despair of Congress. After the war, the states turned inward, depriving Congress of the authority and funds necessary to meet its peacetime obligations. Time and again in 1784 the insufficient attendance of the states' delegates had embarrassed Congress and suspended its proceedings. Johnson's ar-

195

rival on January 13 made possible a quorum, but over the next three years the delinquency of the delegates would be a persistent problem.[3] Even more distressing was the reluctance of the states to invest the Confederation with adequate powers over the new republic's commerce. Without this authority, Congress could neither tax trade to pay its enormous domestic and foreign debts nor defend American shipping against the discriminatory restrictions imposed by other nations. Soon after Johnson took his seat, Congress appointed him to several committees charged with solving these two difficult problems—securing a national revenue and protecting American commerce.

In April 1783, the financially destitute Congress had asked the states for the power to levy various import duties, but even in 1785 Congress still awaited the compliance of Rhode Island, New York, and Georgia. Johnson exclaimed in March that the nation "seems already destined to ruin thro the persis't narrowness timidity and obstinacy of some of our Countrymen." He lamented that "the feeble Finances of the United States give a check to every liberal and enlarged Idea. They damp the Ardor of the generous, and are an effectual screen for the illiberal and contracted."[4] In March a committee of four, including Johnson, urged Congress to send a deputation to the three recalcitrant states, but no action was taken on the suggestion for more than a year.[5]

Congress's inability to regulate the republic's commerce also imperilled the solvency of the new government. A national revenue depended upon a prosperous citizenry, but British trade restrictions excluding American vessels from the British West Indies dealt a heavy blow to America's economy. The New England carrying trade languished, southern agricultural exporters stood at the mercy of British shippers, and the republic's balance of trade worsened. In April 1784, Congress had applied to the states for the necessary authority to retaliate against the British Orders in Council. Sectional jealousies and distrust of the central government had defeated the effort. Instead the individual states tried to impose their own retaliatory restrictions on British trade, attempts that produced chaos and ill will among the states but no concessions from abroad. Connecticut was among the worst sufferers; its West Indian trade declined, and its money poured into the treasuries of neighboring New York and Rhode Island, where British goods were received and taxed before reaching Connecticut.[6]

On the motion of the Virginia delegate James Monroe, who was an ardent advocate of strong commercial regulation, a committee was formed in January 1785 to consider enlarging the powers of Congress. Three months later the committee of five, which included Johnson, proposed a ninth Article of Confederation, awarding to Congress the sole power to negotiate with foreign nations, regulate interstate and foreign trade, and lay "such imposts and duties upon imports and exports, as may be necessary for the purpose."[7] Monroe apparently designed the proposal and, from the committee's earliest days of deliberation, Johnson supported it. The idea, Johnson told a Connecticut colleague in January, is "to invest Congress with the Power of regulating the Trade as well with foreign Nations *as with each other.* The first is conciev'd necessary in order to carry into effect the Treaties made and to be made with foreign Powers, the other to prevent Dissentions between State and State which might indanger the union."[8] In June, a month before Congress opened debate on the proposed article, Johnson, Monroe, and three other delegates presented a series of principles on which to negotiate with Great Britain. They warned that the United States could not secure a mutually advantageous commercial treaty with her trans-Atlantic rival until the Confederation possessed the authority to regulate the trade, granting commercial advantages to friendly nations and meeting foreign restrictions with equally severe penalties. They admonished Congress against sanctioning any treaty with Great Britain until she opened the West Indies to American vessels, and they warned that no treaty on these terms could be expected while the Confederation remained subservient to the states in matters of trade.[9]

The ninth article encountered an angry opposition in Congress that July. A number of southern delegates, with Richard Henry Lee as their foremost spokesman, protested that the power to exclude British vessels from American ports would put the five southern agricultural states at the mercy of the northern shippers. But the conflict was not only sectional. The Virginia delegation divided over the proposed article, while the Massachusetts delegates complained that congressional power over trade should be temporary, lest a permanent enlargement of the Confederation's authority invite tyranny.[10] Monroe, recognizing that continued debate on the article would only aggravate divisions in the Congress, decided against pressing

his proposal. He was confident that eventually the "embarrassments" imposed on American trade by foreign sovereignties
would "operate more powerfully than the utmost force of argument co'd do for the strength'ning our Govt."[11]

The unwillingness of the states to grant Congress the powers to tax and regulate commerce compelled the delegates to
look elsewhere for a national revenue, and the sale of the vast
unoccupied western lands seemed most promising. "Our only
actual resource is the Western Territory, (for I consider Requisitions as extremely precarious)," Johnson observed. Delegates
of every persuasion and from every section agreed.[12] The invasion of squatters and lawless speculators into the region impelled Congress to act quickly in the spring of 1785. On
March 16, a committee of twelve delegates, including Johnson,
began deliberation on a plan to sell the enormous tract between
the western boundary of Pennsylvania and the Mississippi
River, bordered on the south by the Ohio River and on the north
by the Great Lakes.[13] In the committee and in Congress, the
issue provoked "warm and unexpected disputes," Johnson
reported.[14] He and the other northern delegates insisted that
the land be surveyed and sold in thirty-thousand-acre townships, to be offered in an orderly and equitable fashion to settlers from every state. The township system would enable like-
minded New Englanders to transplant their tradition of closely
knit, homogeneous communities to the uninhabited territory.
The Southerners pressed for the random sale of the land in small
parcels, but the New Englanders retorted that a random sale
would allow the best of the uninhabited lands to be quickly over-
run by migrants from the states closest to the new territory.[15]

From mid-April to early May the New Englanders and their
rivals waged a stubborn debate. A stalemate seemed to threaten
the most promising remedy for the nation's burdensome domestic debt. At last, on May 20, the delegates agreed to a compromise, probably devised by William Grayson of Virginia. It
called for the survey of townships six miles square, each containing thirty-six sections. Half of the land would be sold in
townships and half in smaller sections, alternating systems as
each strip of land was offered at public auction.[16] Neither the
New Englanders nor their adversaries were pleased with the
compromise. But on May 8 Grayson predicted that his proposal
would win approval, relying on "the opinion of most gentlemen that it is better to pass it in its present form nearly, than

to delay it much longer and incur the risque of losing the country altogether . . . . if the importunities of the public creditors and the reluctance to pay them by taxation either direct or implied had not been so great I am satisfied no land Ordinance could have been procured."[17]

On the twenty-seventh, Connecticut's delegates told the state's Governor that the ordinance was "not such as we could have wished and long hoped it would have been done, but such as after the utmost efforts of publick Argument and private solicitation it could alone be. . . . The Necessity there was for doing something upon a subject of so much importance to the Interest of the United States, will we hope Apologize for our consenting to a mode of disposition which we could not perfectly approve."[18]

The urgent need for a national revenue compelled Congress to reach a quick compromise not only on the mode of selling the Northwest Territory but also on Connecticut's claim to part of that land. Although a number of southern states had not yet relinquished their claims to lands in the west, only Connecticut's claim impeded the sale of tracts northwest of the Ohio River. Soon after Johnson's arrival at Congress, the Connecticut delegation moved for the acceptance of the state's cession, including a provision acknowledging Connecticut's right to a 120-mile strip west of Pennsylvania. A committee of four, including Johnson, was appointed to consider the motion. At that time Johnson observed that his fellow legislators "contest it with vigour," but reflecting on the failure of the impost and the urgent need for a national revenue, he felt confident that the state's cession, including the 120-mile reserve, would win acceptance.[19]

By 1786 the worsening financial crisis in Congress made the success of the Connecticut cession seem even more likely. All during 1785 the delegates had squabbled over the apportionment of that year's requisition on the states, and not until September had the official request for the states' contributions been approved. This prolonged contention, and the dissatisfaction of many delegates with the final requisition, suggested that few states would comply. On February 2, 1786, Johnson and four other members of Congress reported that no reliance could be placed on the requisition, that additional borrowing was unfeasible, and that Congress must turn all its efforts to securing the power to tax imports "as the means of relieving them from their present embarrassment.''[20] But six months later Congress would still await New York's approval of the impost, and even at year's end, the Confederation would have no taxing power.[21] Only the sale of the Northwest Territory seemed to offer an immediate remedy, and the delegates realized that a long dispute with Connecticut over the state's 120-mile claim would obstruct the sale of the entire expanse. Monroe apprehended that "unless we accept this cession, Connecticut will open an office for the whole degree claim'd by her to the Mississippi, for sale.''[22]

An emerging understanding between Connecticut and Pennsylvania also boded well for the cession and Johnson's own political future. Connecticut's land hunger had provided Johnson's opportunity to reenter public life after the war, and his continued leadership undoubtedly depended upon the success of the Connecticut claim. But in 1785 Pennsylvania had proved itself a powerful adversary in Congress. Three times that autumn, the Pennsylvania delegates had won sufficient support to defeat Johnson's request for a trial on the soil rights of the Connecticut settlers along the Susquehannah River. That year it had also seemed likely that Pennsylvania would oppose the terms of the Connecticut cession, because Connecticut's demand for explicit recognition of the state's right to all lands not ceded endangered the Trenton decision. In October 1785, the Connecticut Assembly had revised its cession, omitting any explicit claim to the lands not ceded, but its pretension to the reserve west of Pennsylvania and to the Susquehannah lands was still implied.[23] Yet in 1786, the Pennsylvanians abandoned their adversary position. The state was desperate to quiet the unceasing bloodshed and lawlessness along the Susquehannah. The major resistance to Pennsylvania rule came not from the Connecticut settlers but from the nonresident Susquehannah shareholders who invaded the region solely to wage war against the Pennsylvania authorities. The settlers desired only a confirmation of their soil rights under Pennsylvania law. The invaders aimed to defeat the Trenton decision by force and seize the disputed land for themselves. Connecticut's claim to the land west of Pennsylvania offered a way to lure the troublemakers westward out of the state. The settlers would never leave their homes for a western wilderness, but Pennsylvania was willing to recognize the settlers' soil rights if peace could be restored.[24] The state awaited only a suggestion from Connecticut that the success of the cession in Congress would remove the company agitators from the war-torn Susquehannah. On March 13, Pelatiah Webster of Connecticut wrote to Johnson that James Wilson, a recently elected member of Congress from Pennsylvania, had just visited Connecticut and "thinks he can Settle a plan with you that will Quiet & Satisfy all Parties."[25]

Connecticut was also eager for a compromise. Since the Trenton decision, Connecticut expansionists had gradually shifted their aspirations from the Susquehannah region to the land west of Pennsylvania. The state's leaders continued to defend the soil rights of the settlers but refused to support the pretensions of the company speculators to the land lost at Trenton.[26] The state's changing political sentiments on the Susquehannah dispute freed Johnson and his fellow Connecticut delegates to negotiate with Pennsylvania without jeopardizing their own public careers. Johnson made it widely known in Congress that the acceptance of the cession, including recognition of Connecticut's 120-mile reserve, would quiet the turmoil along the Susquehannah.[27]

The other legislators were as eager as the Pennsylvania and Connecticut delegates to resolve the dispute between the two states. William Grayson of Virginia noted that the supporters of the Connecticut cession "urged in favor of its adoption that the claim of a powerful State although unsupported by right, was under present circumstances a dangerous thing; and that sacrifices ought to be made for the public tranquility." On April 10, 1786, a committee of five charged with considering the cession reported that Congress should accept Connecticut's terms. According to the Pennsylvania delegates, the committee urged "as a special motive for our agreeing to it that it will induce the state of Connecticut to discountenance the further pretensions of the Delaware and Susquehanna Companies to lands in Penn'a and tend to detach the Real settlers at Wyoming from the more disorderly Partezans of these Companies." The Pennsylvanians predicted that "from the warmth with which an early decision is urged for we imagine a decision will be obtained in the course of this week, and from present appearances it will probably be in favor of the Report."[28]

In fact, the committee's report provoked a heated debate in Congress, and no agreement was reached until the twenty-sixth. Although Congress felt the urgency of quieting the Susquehannah turmoil and opening the Northwest Territory for sale, a host of jealousies and conflicting interests threatened to obstruct the cession. The final acceptance of Connecticut's offer attested to the political finesse of the Connecticut and Pennsylvania delegates.

On the twenty-second and the twenty-fourth, the Pennsylvania delegates moved to accept the cession under terms that explicitly protected the Trenton decision and guaranteed Connecticut's right to the reserve west of Pennsylvania. Both motions failed. Johnson had anticipated Congress's objections a year earlier, noting that Connecticut's western claim comprised land already ceded by Virginia in 1784 and sold to the United States by the Indians as well. Few congressmen were willing to offer such large guarantees to Pennsylvania and Connecticut in exchange for territory already twice acquired.[29] Later on the twenty-fourth, the Pennsylvania delegates abandoned their Connecticut allies to court the landless states. The Pennsylvanians moved that acceptance of the Connecticut cession or of any other state cession should not be "construed nor understood as confirming or in any wise strengthening the claim of such states to any such territory not ceded." The motion failed, as the landed states rallied to Connecticut's defense: Virginia, North Carolina, South Carolina, Georgia, and Massachusetts joined Connecticut in the negative.[30] A third motion, guaranteeing the sanctity of the Trenton decision without asserting the claims of the United States to land not ceded from the states, encountered the resistance of the landless states, which saw no reason to support Pennsylvania unless their own interests were also protected.[31] Toward the close of the day, Pennsylvania and Connecticut reached an understanding—crucial to the final success of the Connecticut cession—that neither Connecticut's right to the western reserve nor Pennsylvania's jurisdiction over the Susquehannah region could be articulated without arousing the conflicting jealousies of the landed and landless states and endangering the cession altogether.[32]

On April 26, Congress voted on a motion offered by Johnson and his Connecticut colleague, Samuel Mix Mitchell, that omitted any reference to the western reserve or the Trenton decision, although Connecticut's claim was clearly implied and the sanctity of the Trenton verdict was privately acknowledged by Pennsylvania and Connecticut. The motion passed with the support of ten states. The omission of any explicit guarantees to the two states had quieted the resentments of the landed and landless interests. The Pennsylvania delegate Charles Pettit reflected that the "Interests and Views of Parties whetted the Jealousy of each other in a high Degree & called forth great Exertions in various Modes of Attack & Defense." Connecticut and Pennsylvania, he explained, had finally agreed "to meet each other on the ground of reciprocal Confidence & Generosity." "In Compromises of this kind," he cautioned a Connecticut man, "it is [found] dangerous to go too minutely into Explanations." A public examination of the private agreement between the two states would "bring on an unprofitable Discussion, and occasion the Revival of Disputes which ought never again to be unveiled."[33] The vote on the twenty-sixth signalled a victory for Connecticut and Pennsylvania, and a political triumph for Johnson. In June, Mitchell reported from Connecticut on the state's happy reaction to the acceptance of the cession, and added "I think the people are more fond of you than ever."[34]

The burdensome domestic debt had impelled Congress to act quickly on the organization and sale of the Northwest Territory, contributing to the final acceptance of the Connecticut cession, but the disposal of the western lands promised no remedy for the enormous foreign debt. The refusal of the states to comply with the annual requisition or to sanction an impost impelled treasury officials to declare in February 1786, "The Crisis is arrived when the People of these United States . . . must decide whether they will support their Rank as a Nation by maintaining the Public Faith, at home and abroad; or whether for want of a timely exertion in Establishing a General Revenue and giving Strength to the Confederacy, they will hazard not only the existence of the Union, but of those great and invaluable privileges, for which they have so arduously and honorably contended." The congressmen were amazed and frustrated by the inattention and complacency of their constituents who, Rufus King exclaimed, "do not know their dangerous situation." "Our affairs," reported the Connecticut delegates, "seem to indicate the approach of some great crisis."[35]

In July the Congress organized a grand committee—one delegate from each state—"to report such amendments to the Confederation . . . as will render the federal government adequate to the ends for which it was instituted." Johnson embarked upon the task with great expectations.[36] On August 7, the committee submitted seven additional articles, drafted primarily by Charles Pinckney. Among the new powers proposed in the articles were "the sole and exclusive power of regulating trade," both foreign and domestic, the authority "to establish any new system of Revenue" for a period of fifteen years upon the approval of eleven rather than all thirteen states, and the ability to enforce compliance with congressional requisitions. The delegates agreed to debate the proposed articles on the fourteenth, but before any action could be taken, a dispute over America's commercial negotiations with Spain split the Congress into two hostile factions and motivated even such ardent advocates of strong central government as James Monroe to speak out against increasing Congress's authority.[37]

In the summer of 1785 Don Diego de Gardoqui had arrived in New York from Spain to negotiate a treaty of commercial reciprocity with the United States. Spain offered unrestricted importation of American goods, in American as well as Spanish bottoms, and the purchase of American masts for the Spanish navy in exchange for gold and silver. The offer promised new ports for America's languishing commerce and a supply of much-needed specie. In August 1785, Congress had instructed John Jay to negotiate with Gardoqui, but had stipulated that any commercial agreement with Spain must include free American navigation on the Mississippi River. Spain had closed the river to United States shipping the previous year. Southerners, anticipating the decline of their seaboard agriculture and eyeing the western territory for expansion, realized that navigation of the river was vital to their future. But when Jay returned to Congress in the summer of 1786, he reported that Gardoqui would not surrender Spanish control of the Mississippi under any conditions and he urged Congress to retract its demand. Jay advised that the United States lacked the military strength to seize control of the Mississippi, and that to refuse Spain's offer would lead to defeat in war or disgrace for having sacrificed commercial advantages while gaining nothing.[38]

Jay's request pitted southerners against northerners in a passionate debate that raged throughout August. "It is confessed our government is so feeble and unoperable," warned Charles Pinckney, "that unless a new portion of strength is infused, it must in all probability soon dissolve. Congress have it in contemplation to apply to the States on this subject. . . . Is it to be supposed that if . . . a treaty is formed upon principles calculated to promote the interests of one part of the union at the expence of the other, that the part conceiving itself injured will ever consent to invest additional powers?" Monroe and Grayson repeated the warning.[39] Johnson and the two Massachusetts delegates, Rufus King and Theodore Sedgwick, defended the northern position, arguing that under the proposed treaty with Spain the United States sacrificed nothing, because navigation of the Mississippi was unobtainable. Johnson took the floor on the twenty-first, exhorting the five staple states to sacrifice their interest in the western lands for the welfare of the republic as a whole. Delegates from the landed states especially, recollecting the long struggle over the Connecticut cession, must have listened with some skepticism to Johnson's plea that "General Good must be attended with partial evil and Inconvenience. . . . If I verily thought it would Depreciate in a degree the Connecticut lands," he declared, "yet I Should conceive we ought to sacrifice the additional Profit we might make to so beneficial a Treaty and to the general good."[40] On a vote to repeal the demand, the seven states north of Virginia scored a victory, but the vote seemed to spell defeat rather than success for the Confederation. Timothy Bloodworth of North Carolina reflected that "if seven States can carry on a treaty, or in other words will persist in the measure, it follows of course, that the Confederated compact is no more than a rope of sand, and . . . a disolution of the Union must take place."[41]

Other events that fall and winter augured further ills for the fragile government. On September 7 Congress appointed Johnson chairman of a committee charged with preparing an address to the states, urging them to comply with the annual requisition. "Pray speak plain Language to the states, paint your Situation and your feeling without Disguise," Mitchell urged Johnson, "and let them know you are or soon will be, the most contemptible political Body which ever conven'd." But a few days later, Mitchell confessed to Johnson that "Your Address to the States will (I fear) prove like Water spilled upon the Ground and have no Influence to awake us from our Stupor." In October, the pessimistic Congress decided against sending any appeal.[42]

The opening of the new federal year in November brought no promising signs. Not a single state had complied with the requisition. So few delegates attended in the opening weeks that the Congress could not elect a president until February 2.[43] Lawlessness and bloodshed in Massachusetts inspired the legislators to fear that all government was near its end. From September until February debt-ridden farmers, angered by the scarcity of money and burdened with taxes, resorted to mob action to close the courts and even took up arms to attack the federal arsenal at Springfield. From Connecticut Mitchell warned Johnson that "ye flame may catch in this State." Henry Lee of Virginia apprehended that "The period seems to be fast approaching when the people of these U. States must determine to establish a permanent capable government or submit to the horrors of anarchy and licentiousness."[44]

Congress was ripe for radical measures. On February 12, 1787, the delegates opened debate on a proposal for a general convention of the states "to render the constitution of the federal government adequate to the exigencies of the Union." The proposal had originated in the report of the Annapolis Convention, held the previous September, when representatives from five states gathered to consider "requisite augmentations of the power of Congress over trade." They had found that "the power of regulating trade is of such comprehensive extent that to give it efficacy . . . may require a corresponding adjustment in other parts of the system." The poor attendance at Congress had delayed discussion of the Annapolis proposal until February, but the states had acted sooner. Already seven had chosen representatives to meet at Philadelphia in May.[45]

Several members of Congress feared that a constitutional convention would fatally weaken rather than strengthen the federal government. In 1785, when the Massachusetts legislature petitioned Congress to call a convention for increasing the commercial powers of the Confederation, the state's delegates to Congress had opposed the petition, arguing that "such a measure must have implied more than at first the State might be aware of—that she disliked [the Confederation] in all its parts and had given a kind of legal toleration to every quibbling party to attack it." They had warned that "an Administration of the present Confederation with all its Inconveniences, is preferable to the Risque of general Dissentions and Animosities, which may approach Anarchy." The Massachusetts delegates raised the same protest against the proposed constitutional convention, urging that "amendments . . . originate with Congress [rather than a convention] and, be agreed to by the States, and that it would derogate from the dignity and weight of that body to take a secondary position in the business."[46]

Johnson and Mitchell felt similar apprehensions, and the political conflicts in Connecticut explained why. Connecticut's highest leaders—the Governor and his assistants—had long supported the Confederation, but since 1783 they had suffered repeated assaults from the state's antinationalists. Distrust of governmental power, suspicion of privilege, especially in the military, and resistance to the heavy postwar taxes lay behind the antinationalist movement.[47] The two factions had first clashed in 1783 over Congress's request for an impost. That same year Congress had voted to grant officers of the Continental Army five years' full pay in lieu of lifetime pensions. The army grant had excited furious opposition in Connecticut, heightening antinationalist feeling against the impost. Not only had New Englanders long distrusted standing armies and military privileges, but Connecticut had provided for the reimbursement of its own officers in the Continental line four years earlier and opposed assuming the burden of the other states. In June and October 1783, and again in January 1784, these volatile issues had divided the Assembly, the lower house opposing the army grant and the impost, and the Council supporting both. Four times between September 1783 and the following April, the antinationalists had called extralegal conventions at Middletown, where the enemies of military privilege and federal taxes demanded the expulsion of the Governor and his Council at the spring election. The Middletown meetings had made conventions synonymous with lawlessness and antinationalism in the eyes of Connecticut's nationalists. Governor Trumbull and his assistants had answered the antinationalists' arguments with pleas for orderly government and a strong Confederation. The state's long-respected leaders had triumphed over the protesters in the April 1784 election, and in May the Assembly had consented to the impost with no prohibition on the use of the revenue to reimburse the army.[48] But the bitter struggle in the winter of 1783–1784 had divided the state into two hostile camps and alerted the state's leaders to the seriousness of the antinationalist challenge.

It is not surprising, then, that Johnson and Mitchell spoke out in Congress against the proposed constitutional convention. In Connecticut, conventions spelled antinationalism. The Connecticut delegates undoubtedly feared that the very call for a convention would undermine the authority of Congress and that antinationalists would dominate the proceedings.

The growing strength of the antinationalists in their own state had prevented the Assembly from answering the invitation to Annapolis in September and from considering the call to Philadelphia that winter. The proposed convention ignited a heated controversy in the Connecticut press, and both the nationalists and their adversaries looked to the spring election for a decisive victory.[49] Troubled by Connecticut's uncertain support for a stronger union, Johnson told Congress in February that the convention would deal a fatal blow to the existing Confederation, and Mitchell insisted that he would take no part in conventions of any sort.[50]

Despite the apprehensions of the Massachusetts and Connecticut delegates that the convention might fatally weaken the already tottering government, all the congressmen seemed to agree that inaction posed even greater perils. Shays' Rebellion in Massachusetts alarmed everyone. Massachusetts Congressman Rufus King voiced his fear that "Events are hurrying to a crisis: prudent and sagacious men should be ready to seize the most favourable circumstances to establish a more permanent and vigorous government."[51] On February 21, the Massachusetts delegates moved that Congress lend its support to a convention for the "sole and express purpose of revising the Articles of Confederation and reporting to Congress and the several state legislatures such alterations and provisions therein as shall when agreed to in Congress and confirmed by the States render the federal Constitution adequate to the exigencies of Government and the preservation of the Union." The wording of the motion suggested both due recognition of the final authority of Congress and safeguards against any total departure from the federal system. The motion was accepted, and one delegate observed afterward that the opposition of the eastern delegates had made the resolution "a piece of patchwork, but this was thought better than to keep up the smallest appearance of opposition to public view."[52] The same apprehension— that a show of disagreement might undermine the people's confidence in their leaders—would guide the men who convened in Philadelphia in May. After the vote, James Madison observed that "In general I find men of reflection much less sanguine as to the new than despondent as to the present System." Johnson concluded that "our Affairs are daily growing worse and worse. . . . If we can derive no succor from the Convention at Philadelphia which I consider as a very doubtful

Measure at best I fear We shall soon be in a deplorable situation."[53] Johnson turned his attention to Connecticut, awaiting the verdict of the state's voters, who would decide in May whether to support the effort for a stronger union.

Neither Connecticut's nationalists nor their rivals won a decisive victory in the spring election, and when the Assembly began its new session, the tense equilibrium persisted. But two days later, the nationalists and their adversaries began a heated debate on the proposed convention, and the nationalists had every advantage. Commerce languished, Connecticut money poured into the treasuries of Rhode Island and New York, and the state's merchants clamored for congressional regulation of foreign trade. Even more important, Shays' Rebellion raised the spectre of anarchy, and news of a Shaysite plot in Sharon, Connecticut, reached the Assembly during the debate. The nationalists quickly linked their opponents with these democratic excesses.[54] Finally, Congress and several of the states had already endorsed the convention, investing it with too much importance for Connecticut to be unrepresented.[55]

By midday a number of antinationalists had given their support to the convention, and the Assembly proceeded to select Connecticut's spokesmen, naming Johnson first, then Oliver Ellsworth, and finally Erastus Wolcott.[56] The antinationalists had not surrendered their voice in the deliberations. In Congress Johnson had proved himself an ardent advocate of strong federal government, but in Connecticut antinationalists as well as nationalists considered him their ally. Two days earlier, Johnson had placed first both in the election of the Governor's assistants and in the selection of delegates to Congress.[57] Undoubtedly Johnson owed his diverse political support primarily to the success of the Connecticut cession. But a number of antinationalists had mistakenly interpreted Johnson's admonitions in Congress against the convention as an expression of their viewpoint.[58] The politically astute Johnson, eager to maintain his following in both factions and to avoid any part in the heated debate over the convention, stayed away from the Assembly until the issue had been decided.[59]

The antinationalists once again unknowingly supported a stronger union when they agreed to the selection of Oliver Ellsworth. A man of little political ambition, Ellsworth had retired from Congress in 1783 after four years' service, and had taken no part in the state's political controversies since then.

But Ellsworth's experiences in Congress would make him a vigorous supporter of a strong union at the convention. Unlike most congressmen, who had served many years in their state governments before taking a seat in the federal government, Ellsworth had begun his public career in Congress. This formative experience had undoubtedly taught him to favor national over local interests and to support strong federal government over the jealous protests of the states. Ellsworth had deplored Connecticut's "horrid clamour" against the impost. The measure, he had told Governor Trumbull, may produce "abuses and misapplication, still it is better to hazard *something*, than to hazard *all*."[60]

The third representative chosen, outspoken antinationalist Erastus Wolcott, refused to attend. In his place the Assembly elected Roger Sherman. One historian attributes Sherman's election to his political astuteness, especially his reticence during the heated debate.[61] But it seems that Wolcott's refusal weakened the antinationalists' position, allowing their rivals to seize the initiative. Sherman's vigorous support of the federal government was known to all. Despite his failure to win reelection to Congress in 1779, the state's nationalist leaders had returned him to Congress in 1780, 1781, and 1784 on interim appointments.[62] His defense of army pensions as an implied power of the Confederation had created such outrage among Connecticut's antinationalists in 1783 that a popular gathering at Middletown had called for his dismissal from the Council at the spring election. Jeremiah Wadsworth, an enthusiastic advocate of the proposed convention, cast his ballot for Sherman as a vote for a stronger frame of government.[63] Together Sherman, Ellsworth and Johnson would labor hard for a more durable union.

Chapter Fourteen

The Great Debate

On May 27, 1787, Johnson set out from Stratford to attend the Federal Convention. After stopping at New York for two days and then crossing to Elizabethtown by ferry, he continued on to Philadelphia, arriving June 1. The next day he took his seat among the delegates.[1] Many of his apprehensions must have vanished immediately. The Convention, he could plainly see, had attracted energetic nationalists. Like Erastus Wolcott, most antinationalists had refused to attend. Independent-minded Rhode Island, long notorious for defying Congress, sent no delegates, but the twelve other states answered the call, a sufficient number to endow the Convention with legitimacy.[2] The fifty-five men assembled were impressed with the seriousness of their endeavor. Forty-two had served in Congress, witnessing daily the inadequacies of the Confederation. George Mason of Virginia judged that "the revolt from Great Britain and the formation of our new governments at that time, were nothing compared to the great business now before us." The Convention brought together "many of the most able Men in America," Johnson observed. Even Benjamin Franklin, renowned in Europe and America for his achievements in science, art, literature, and public service, and at eighty-one the oldest statesman present, declared it "the most august and respectable Assembly he was ever in in his life." Many of the delegates had anticipated Johnson's election to the Convention.[4] "He was once employed as an Agent for the State of Connecticut," the Georgia delegate William Pierce explained, and "discharged [the office] with so much dignity, and made such an ingenious display of his powers, that he laid the foundation of a reputation which will probably last much longer than his own life." Pierce, who wrote short sketches of all his fellow delegates, made no mention of Johnson's loyalism.[5]

Despite their distinguished reputations, most of the framers were young, their average age only forty-three. The two Virginians who would steer the deliberations with their bold strategy and radical proposals for a truly national government were even younger, James Madison only thirty-six and Edmund Randolph just thirty-three.[6] Four of the senior delegates, Benjamin Franklin, John Dickinson, Roger Sherman, and Johnson (who had reached the age of sixty), would play another role—as mediators and practical statesmen. Young Madison and men of his persuasion, who had come of age during the Continental war effort, were determined to lead the country from a loose confederation into a strong national government.[7] The four elder statesmen, whose political careers long antedated the struggle for American unity, were mindful of the local prejudices and fears that impeded union. They were determined to model a practical government acceptable to all thirteen states. They saw the necessity to listen as well as to lead.

The Convention had begun its deliberations seven days before Johnson's arrival. On May 29, Edmund Randolph presented fifteen resolutions that together constituted a new frame of government and a radical departure from the Articles of Confederation. The Virginia plan called for a two-house legislature with representation in each house proportional to the populations of the member states, a national executive charged with executing the laws, and a national judiciary. The plan, drafted chiefly by James Madison, provided for the direct election of the lower house by the people, but removed the other institutions of government from popular influence. The upper house, executive, and judiciary would be chosen by the lower house. Advocates of the Virginia plan were "for raising the federal pyramid to a considerable altitude, and for that reason wished to give it as broad a basis as possible. No government could long subsist without the confidence of the people." Far from merely revising the Articles of Confederation, the Virginians had completely abandoned the principle of confederation. The new government would be a direct compact with the people, because the states had failed to meet their obligations to the federal government or even maintain law and order within their own boundaries. To Gouverneur Morris, a firm supporter of Madison's scheme, "State attachments, and State importance" had been "the bane of this Country. We cannot annihilate; but we may perhaps take out the teeth of the serpents."[8]

Even before Johnson took his seat at the Convention, Sherman and Ellsworth voiced their opposition to the Virginia plan. Their objections reflected the political situation in Connecticut, and established the position that all three Connecticut spokesmen would defend throughout the proceedings. On May 30, Sherman warned against making "too great inroads on the existing system," because the support of the states would be lost, and with it, the opportunity for reform. The next day Sherman proposed that the state legislatures, not the people, elect the republic's lower house. Mindful that Connecticut's lawmakers had supported the Confederation against the assaults of the Middletown protesters—even sending nationalists to Congress under interim appointments when popular sentiments opposed them—Sherman declared that the people "should have as little to do as may be about the Government." Elbridge Gerry of Massachusetts, no doubt recalling the horrors of Shays' Rebellion in his own state, agreed, but the Virginia resolution for popular election of the lower house passed.[9] To Sherman and Ellsworth, any frame of government that abandoned the principle of confederation was doomed to failure. The cooperation of the state governments, they believed, was vital to the union, and the Virginia plan would not achieve this. "If we are so exceedingly jealous of state legislatures," Ellsworth apprehended, "will they not have reason to be equally jealous of us. If I return to my state and tell them, we made such and such regulations for a general government, because we dared not trust you with any extensive powers, will they be satisfied? nay, will they adopt your government? and let it ever be remembered, that without their approbation your government is nothing more than a rope of sand." On May 31, Sherman and Ellsworth pressed hard for the election of the upper house by the state legislatures, and gathered sufficient support to defeat Randolph's proposal that the second house be chosen by the first.[10] When Johnson took his seat on June 2, the mode of selecting the second house was still undecided.

Five days later John Dickinson spoke out in favor of election by the state legislatures, and Sherman again urged that "the particular States would thus become interested in supporting the National Governmt. and that a due harmony between the two Governmts. would be maintained."[11] The measure won unanimous approval. But if the supporters of the Virginia plan hoped that this concession would quiet all opposition to their system, they were mistaken. The advocates of confederation were ready to consider an even more divisive question: whether representation in the two houses would be granted to every state equally or according to population and wealth.

On May 30, when the discussion of the Virginia plan began, Randolph had moved that in lieu of the one-state-one-vote rule observed under the Articles of Confederation, "an equitable ratio of representation ought to be substituted." George Reed of Delaware, the smallest state to attend the Convention, had quickly urged that the motion be postponed, "reminding the [Convention] that the deputies from Delaware were restrained by their commission from assenting to any change of the rule of suffrage, and in case a change should be fixed on, it might become their duty to retire from the Convention." Even Madison had prudently endorsed the postponement, recognizing that his opportunity to present the Virginia plan as the basis for the Convention's discussions would otherwise be lost, or worse still, that the Convention would dissolve.[12]

On June 9, New Jersey's William Paterson, impatient under the leadership of the aggressive Virginians, raised the issue of representation. In the angriest speech heard since the opening day, Paterson warned that "N. Jersey will never confederate on the [Virginia] plan. . . . She would be swallowed up. He had rather submit to a monarch, to a despot, than to such a fate. He would not only oppose the plan here but on his return home do everything in his power to defeat it there." The delegates, he insisted, had no authority to abandon the Articles of Confederation and form a national government. Their sole task was to augment the powers of the existing government.[13]

The Madisonians ignored Paterson's warning. On June 11 they mustered a majority of seven states to adopt proportional representation in the lower house. The Connecticut delegates cast an affirmative vote, hoping that their action would set a precedent for a compromise on suffrage in the upper house. They proposed that proportional representation in the first house be combined with an equality of the states in the second house, a remedy that the Connecticut spokesmen would raise time and again as a meeting ground between the adamant Virginians and the recalcitrant New Jerseyites. (As early as June 2, the conciliatory John Dickinson had reminded the Convention that the thorny question of representation required mutual concessions, with states voting equally in one house and proportionally in the other.) But the advocates of the Virginia plan rejected any compromise. Before the day ended, a narrow majority approved a resolution that "the right of suffrage in the second branch of the national Legislature ought to be according to the rule established for the first."[14] Despite Paterson's angry warnings, none of the small-state delegates left their seats after their defeat, a promising sign that the Convention would remain intact until its work was completed.

Two days later, the Convention agreed to review the proposals framed thus far. Despite the bitter dispute over representation, the delegates had drafted nineteen resolutions that were a confirmation and extension of the Virginia plan. These included a national government with a two-house legislature, direct popular election of the lower house and election of the upper house by the state legislature, an executive and a judiciary, and most important, a broad enlargement of the government's lawmaking powers to include all cases in which "the separate States are incompetent: or in which the harmony of the United States may be interrupted by the exercise of individual legislation . . . to negative all laws passed by the several States contravening, in the opinion of the national legislature, the articles of union; or any treaties subsisting under the authority of the Union." The resolutions also provided for proportional representation in both houses, as voted upon two days earlier, and once again Paterson raised the opposition.[15]

On June 14 Paterson moved that the Convention postpone consideration of the nineteen resolutions in order to hear the New Jersey plan, "one purely federal," and the next day the plan was read. Like the Virginia plan, it enlarged the lawmaking and law enforcement powers of the union, and stipulated that the laws of the federal government would be supreme: "any thing in the respective laws of the Individual States to the contrary notwithstanding; and that if any State, or any body of men in any State shall oppose or prevent ye carrying into execution such acts or treaties, the federal Executive shall be authorized to call forth ye power of the Confederated States . . . to enforce and compel an obedience." New Jersey ardently supported a stronger union, and had elected delegates to the Convention three months before Congress endorsed the proposed meeting. But the state's delegation warned that New Jersey would never accept the Virginia plan. "Our object," Paterson reminded the body, "is not such a Govermt. as may be best in itself, but such as our Constituents have authorized us to prepare and as they will approve."[16]

On the nineteenth the Convention voted to reject Paterson's plan and resume consideration of the nineteen resolutions that followed the Virginia system. Although Paterson's plan answered Connecticut's main grievance against the Virginia design—by preserving the confederation principle and allowing each state an equal vote in the legislature—the Connecticut delegation joined the majority. Once again, the Connecticut men showed their confidence that a compromise could be reached. Heeding Madison's warning that the small states' "pertinacious adherence to an inadmissable plan [would] prevent the adoption of any plan," they resumed their effort to remedy the objections of New Jersey, Delaware, and Maryland while preserving the considerable progress already made in the Convention.[17] On the twenty-first, Johnson addressed the Convention for the first time. Illness sapped his energy, and despite his reputation for eloquence he usually deferred to Sherman and Ellsworth. But on that day he took the floor to advise the Convention that "If [it] could be shewn in such a manner as to satisfy the patrons of the N. Jersey propositions, that the individuality of the States would not be endangered, many of their objections [to the Virginia plan] would no doubt be removed." He doubted that this could be done "without giving them each a distinct and equal vote . . . in the general Councils," and he urged the Convention to grant the state governments "the right of appointing the second branch of the legislature to represent the states individually."[18]

Throughout the following week, as the Convention resumed its discussion of the nineteen resolutions, the Connecticut delegation anticipated the moment when the divisive issue of representation would again occasion debate. Although the New Jersey plan had met defeat, the Connecticut men realized that no simple majority on behalf of Madison's plan would suffice. The task before the Convention was to preserve the union, and the framers had to devise a government amenable to all the states. On Friday, June 29, Johnson rose again to remind his colleagues that compromise was imperative. "The controversy must be endless," Johnson exclaimed,

whilst Gentlemen differ in the grounds of their arguments; Those on the one side considering the States as districts of people composing one political Society; those on the other considering them as so many political Societies. The fact is [Johnson explained] that the States do exist as political Societies, and a Govt. is to be formed for them in their political capacity, as well as for the individuals composing them. [He urged that] the two ideas embraced on different sides, instead of being opposed to each other, ought to be combined; that in *one* branch the *people*, ought to be represented; in the *other*, the *States*.

Ellsworth assured the Convention that "some good plan of Govt. wd. be devised & adopted."[19]

The Madisonians secured the first victory, winning a majority of six states in support of proportional representation in the lower house. Ellsworth again appealed for moderation:

He was not sorry on the whole . . . that the vote just passed had determined against [equality of the states] in the first branch. He hoped it would become a ground of compromise with regard to the 2d. branch. . . . The proportional representation in the first branch was conformable to the national principle & would secure the large States agst. the small. An equality of voices was conformable to the federal principle and was necessary to secure the Small States agst. the large. He trusted that on this middle ground a compromise would take place. He did not see that it could take place on any other. And if no compromise should take place, our meeting would not only be in vain but worse than in vain. . . . Let a strong Executive, a Judiciary & Legislative power be created; [he admonished] but Let not too much be attempted; by which all may be lost.[20]

The next day Benjamin Franklin lent his support to the Connecticut compromise, and proposed as an additional measure, that "in all appropriations & dispositions of money" the legislators "shall have suffrage in proportion to the Sums which their respective States do actually contribute to the treasury." Franklin admitted that "The diversity of opinion turns on two points. If a proportion of representation takes place, the small States contend that their liberties will be in danger. If an equality of votes is to be put in its place, the large States say their money will be in danger." He cautioned the Convention that "both sides must part with some of their demands" to make an accommodation.[21]

When the Convention reconvened on Monday, July 2, it was apparent that the appeals for compromise had not been in vein. On Ellsworth's resolution that "in the second Branch of the Legislature . . . each state shall have an equal vote," the states voted five against five, with Georgia divided. More important, the delegates agreed to appoint a grand committee—one delegate from each state—to devise a remedy. "We are now at a full stop," said Sherman, "and nobody he supposed meant that we shd. break up without doing something." Three days later, the grand committee reported their plan, which embodied the points of compromise first raised by Dickinson, Franklin, and the Connecticut delegates. First, the lower house would have one representative for every 40,000 inhabitants and exercise exclusive control over taxation and expenditures, always apportioning taxation according to representation. Secondly, the upper house would abide by the one-state-one-vote rule.[22] Eleven more days would pass before the bargain was sealed in the Convention, but its success was predictable that first Monday, when Elbridge Gerry of Massachusetts, previously a strong supporter of the Virginia plan, announced: "The committee were of different opinions . . . and agreed to the Report merely in order that some ground of accommodation might be proposed. Those opposed to the equality of votes have only assented conditionally; and if the other side do not generally agree will not be under any obligation to support the Report." Despite the ominous sound of Gerry's warning, it was clear that he would not retreat from the bargain. "If we do not come to some agreement among ourselves," he warned, "some foreign sword will probably do the work for us."[23]

The formation of a grand committee was a clever device, for it had enlisted reasonable large-staters such as Gerry who would support a compromise of their own devising. On the ninth, the Convention appointed a second grand committee to draft an exact schedule of representation in the lower house, and the committee presented its report the next day, apportioning 65 seats among the thirteen states and allowing a slave to count as three-fifths of a person for the purpose of apportionment. When the final vote was called for on July 16, the compromise passed by a narrow majority of five to four. William Davie (a member of the first grand committee) and Hugh Williamson (who sat on the second) swung the North Carolina vote to support the bargain. The Massachusetts ballots were divided between the conciliatory Gerry and Caleb Strong and the stalwart Madisonians, Rufus King and Nathaniel Gorham.[24]

Only five states cast their votes for accommodation on July

16, but in the following days it became apparent that the struggle for compromise had influenced everyone. First, all but the most recalcitrant Madisonians recognized that the bargain struck that day could not be reversed without sacrificing the entire work of the Convention. Madison recorded that on the morning of the seventeenth, "before the hour of the Convention a number of the members from the larger States, by common agreement met for the purpose of consulting on the proper steps to be taken in consequence of the vote in favor of an equal Representation in the 2d. branch, and the apparent inflexibility of the smaller States on that point—Several members from the latter also attended. The time was wasted in vague conversation on the subject, without any specific proposition or agreement."

In fact, the time was not wasted. Madison continued that although a few states were unalterably opposed to the compromise, "Others seemed inclined to yield to the smaller States, and to concur in such an Act however imperfect. . . . It is probable that the result of this consultation satisfied the smaller States that they had nothing to apprehend from . . . any plan whatever agst. the equality of votes in the 2d. branch."[25] Although the issue of representation would be raised again before the Convention completed its deliberations, the Connecticut compromise would not be overturned.

Secondly, the accommodation allayed the fears of many members that the states would reject the Convention's radically new frame of government. "Whether we shall be able to agree upon any Plan which will be acceptable to the People I cannot determine," Johnson reflected in a letter to a Connecticut friend, "but there appears at present many circumstances in our favour."[26] The Connecticut delegates, previously reluctant to sanction bold measures that might arouse the jealousy of the state governments, were now ready to invest the new government with extensive powers, confident that they had thwarted the most objectionable aspect of the Virginia plan. For example, on June 5 they had voted against a resolution establishing "inferior tribunals" in addition to a supreme court of appeal. They had agreed with South Carolina's Pierce Butler that the national judiciary should not assume such far-reaching powers, which would seem to imperil the state courts. "The states will revolt at such encroachments," Butler had admonished. "Supposing such an establishment to be useful, we must not venture on it. We must follow the example of Solon, who gave the Athenians

not the best Govt. he could devise; but the best they wd. receive."
Yet, on July 18, just two days after the final compromise on
representation, Connecticut and South Carolina joined the other
states in a unanimous resolution that "the national Legislature
be empowered to appoint inferior Tribunals." Connecticut
"was willing to give the power to the Legislature but wished
them to make use of the State Tribunals whenever it could be
done with safety to the general interest."[27] A readiness to try
radical innovations, entrusting their prudent exercise to the future leaders of the new government, inspired the constitution
makers after mid-July. Even Madison would admit in retrospect
that, once the dispute over representation had ended, the small
states "exceeded all others in zeal."[28]

Finally, the successful resolution of the acrimonious debate over representation prepared the Convention for the even
more difficult task that lay ahead. As the unrestrained arguments in Congress over the Jay-Gardoqui negotiations had for-
boded, the most serious division that would imperil the success
of the Convention was not between small states and large, but
between North and South. The first sign of this impending division had appeared during the final bargaining over representation, when Gouverneur Morris of Pennsylvania spoke out
against the inclusion of slaves in the lower house ratio. Ellsworth and Johnson had rushed to the defense of the southern
interest (realizing that the Connecticut compromise was at
stake), and the deep-seated northern opposition to slavery had
been silenced, but only temporarily.[29]

On July 23 the Convention appointed a committee of de-
tail—one delegate from each state—to draft a constitution conformable to the resolutions already adopted, allowing the committee considerable latitude to work out the details of the general
plan. South Carolina's General Charles Pinckney seized the
occasion to alert the Convention "that if the Committee should
fail to insert some security to the Southern States agst. an eman-
cipation of slaves, and taxes on exports, he shd. be bound by
duty to his State to vote agst. their Report." The committee
heeded Pinckney's threat, in fact too generously to escape protests from the stalwart antislavery men of the North. The committee's report barred the national legislature from taxing exports or prohibiting the importation of slaves, and provided
that navigation acts would pass only with "the assent of two

thirds of the members present in each house."[30] Massachusetts delegate Rufus King and Pennsylvania's Gouverneur Morris rushed to attack the proposal. "The admission of slaves," said King, "was a most grating circumstance to his mind. . . . He never could agree to let them be imported without limitation & then be represented in the Natl. legislature." Morris moved that only "free" inhabitants be represented. "He never could concur in upholding domestic slavery. It was a nefarious institution—It was the curse of heaven on the States where it prevailed." But Rutledge retorted that "The true question at present is whether the Southn. States shall or shall not be parties to the Union."[31]

King rejected the committee's plan as unfairly biased toward southern interests. "There was so much inequality & unreasonableness in all of this, that the people of the Northern] States could never be reconciled [to it]."[32] Yet Connecticut immediately defended the plan. The state's economy favored a ban on export taxes. Connecticut depended upon the exportation of agricultural produce and livestock to the West Indies.[33] More important, the Connecticut delegates realized that the northern attack on slavery endangered the bargain on representation, which King and Morris had never approved. The delegation urged their colleagues to put aside dangerous moral questions. "The morality or widsom of slavery are considerations belonging to the States themselves."[34]

A majority of the members found this pragmatism overly distasteful, but the Convention had progressed too far and struggled through too many divisive issues to accept defeat now. The framers, now practiced in the art of compromise, resorted to their tested device, a committee of the states. Johnson took his place as Connecticut's spokesman on the committee. At last, on August 29, after far less contention and wearisome debate than the Connecticut compromise had required, the delegates sealed the agreement. The importation of slaves would not be banned before 1808, but a tax could be imposed "at a rate not exceeding the average of the duties laid on imports." A simple majority in each house could pass navigation acts binding on all the states, but no tax would be laid on exports. Northern consciences were soothed, southern fears were temporarily assuaged, and Connecticut's own economic interests, as well as those of the staple states, were recognized. The Convention had

invested the national legislature with the vital power to regulate commerce, had preserved the Connecticut compromise,
and, most important, had hurdled the highest barrier to union.[35]

The constitution makers hastened to complete their work.
The Convention, one member later recalled, "was not exempt
from a degree of the hurrying influence introduced by fatigue
and impatience in all such bodies."[36] On September 8, they
appointed a committee of style to bring in a final draft, and
only four days later the committee, of which Johnson was a
member, reported. To Gouverneur Morris belonged most of the
credit for the elegantly simple document.[37] The last changes
were made on the fifteenth, and these carried great symbolic
weight. Morris, a firm advocate of the large-state interests,
moved that a proviso be added that "no State, without its consent
shall be deprived of its equal suffrage in the Senate." Madison
predicted that the Constitution, "should it be adopted, will
neither effectually answer its national object, nor prevent the
local mischiefs which everywhere excite disgusts agst. the State
Governments." But Morris's motion, which was "dictated by
the circulating murmurs of the small States," was "agreed to
without debate, no one opposing it, or on the question, saying
no."[38] Not even Madison dared raise an objection, and never
again would a jealousy between small and large states threaten
the union.

Virginia's George Mason, noting the Convention's eager-
ness to relieve all lingering doubts and divisions, proposed
"that no law in nature of a navigation act be passed before the
year 1808, without the consent of 2/3 of each branch of the
Legislature." Mason's motion won the approval of only three
states, and two days later, when the Convention met for the last
time to sign the Constitution, Mason withheld his signature.
Madison regarded his fellow Virginian's dissent as "a subject of
regret," and indeed it was, for it symbolized the unassuageable
southern distrust that would one day shatter the union.[39]

William Samuel Johnson and forty other delegates assembled in the State House on that last day, and all but three signed
the Constitution. The framers, far from despairing over the dissent of a few, marvelled at the accomplishment of the majority.
Madison called it "a real wonder," confessing that "It is impossible for any man of candour to reflect on this circumstance
without partaking of the astonishment."[40] Although not all
of the original fifty-five delegates were present, only four of

those absent had departed in protest: John Lansing, Jr. and Robert Yates of New York, and Luther Martin and John Francis Mercer of Maryland. On August 23, Ellsworth had hurried back to his duties on Connecticut's Supreme Court. Illness and exhaustion kept another of the Convention's great conciliators, John Dickinson, from participating in the ceremony. He had returned to Delaware just days earlier.[41]

Anticipation of the enormous task ahead, to win the approval of the thirteen states, must have tempered the joyousness of the occasion. Johnson and Sherman must have felt especially apprehensive over the challenge that awaited them in Connecticut. Nowhere in the Constitution did the word "national" appear—Ellsworth had moved to drop it on June 20 and his successful motion was never reversed—but the new frame of government was undeniably national in structure and purpose. It was a testimony to the belief of its creators that not only a small, homogeneous country, but even a vast republic embracing diverse interests and local allegiances could be governed as one nation.[42] They had worked pragmatically to devise a government acceptable to the people. Yet the end product was a radical departure from the principles of the Confederation (despite the equality of votes in the Senate) and from the mandates of the delegates, who had been instructed merely to revise and amend the Articles.[43] In mid-summer the Governor of Connecticut had advised the state's delegation that should the Convention "be so happy as to unite in their doings without attempting too much," their labors would be well received. In July Stephen Mix Mitchell had alerted Johnson that "no tho'ts are entertain'd of any great Alterations in the form or force of the foederal government by the people at large." "When Congress met in 1774," Mitchell explained, they had "the strong impression of Fear to support their Influence." But now is "a time of profound peace" and "Subjects will at such a time be cautious how they give power to their Rulers, will deliberate with Coolness & Circumspection & with great Reluctance alter their old forms of Government."[44] The mode of ratification devised by the Convention was also a cause for concern to the Connecticut delegates. All summer they had urged their colleagues to submit the plan of government to the state legislatures, but the majority had supported ratification by special conventions elected in each state. In Connecticut, popular conventions spelled antinationalism. The Connecticut delegates "did not like these conventions. They were better fitted to pull down than to build up Constitutions."[45]

After the final adjournment, Johnson joined the convivial gathering at the City Tavern, and the next morning he set out for New York. Two days later, on the twentieth, he and twelve other participants at Philadelphia took their seats in Congress, just in time to hear the Constitution read.[46] On September 26 the debate began, some congressmen protesting that the new frame of government was too weak, others objecting that such a strong national government endangered liberty. At last, on the twenty-eighth, the same concern for a public appearance of unanimity that had influenced the men at Philadelphia prevailed in Congress. To avoid any dissent, the delegates agreed to forward the Constitution to the states, but without a warm recommendation for its ratification.[47]

The cautious mood of Congress contrasted starkly to the energetic spirit of Connecticut's Federalists, who launched their campaign for ratification even before the Constitution was officially publicized. Their letters, satires, and forthright appeals filled the newspapers. They hurled invective at the Constitution's critics and eulogized the framers as "a chosen band of patriots and heroes, arresting the progress of American anarchy." They defended the new frame of government as the only safeguard against the dreadful extremes of monarchism or Shaysism. Farmers, merchants, and debtors alike, they argued, would benefit from the financial stability that the Constitution promised.[48] No one was more outspoken on behalf of the Convention's work than Sherman and Ellsworth, whose appeals to the public circulated widely in the Connecticut press.[49] The Federalists won their first victory on October 16, when the state's lawmakers agreed nearly unanimously to call a ratifying convention. The Assembly authorized town elections for delegates in November, and set the date of the convention for January 3.[50]

Johnson arrived in New Haven and took his seat in the upper house on October 17, one day after the Federalist victory. Why Johnson took no part in the campaign and failed to appear for the important vote of the previous day can only be conjectured. Perhaps ill health still constrained him, or family concerns had delayed him in Stratford on his way to the Assembly. Surely it was not political caution that kept Johnson from speaking out for the Constitution that October.[51] A prudent avoidance of controversy had contributed greatly to Johnson's political success, but by autumn he had already decided to leave politics behind and embark on a new calling, as president of Columbia College. On November 1, he resigned from the assembly and returned home to Stratford, sailing for New York nine days later. On the twelfth, he appeared before the Columbia trustees to accept his new office. The trustees had elected Johnson to the presidency on May 21, but Johnson had delayed his decision, conferring first with his wife and children.[52] He considered retiring to Stratford but his eldest son, Samuel William, cautioned him that such a course would bring "heavy and dull moments." Samuel William Johnson felt that the New York post would afford a more sensible escape from the rigors and fatigue of politics. "When a Person is master of his own time," he advised his father, "the society of Friends of liberal and improved Sentiments must at times give a relish in Life, that perfect retirement is unable to produce." Ann Johnson urged her husband to take on the presidency, hoping that at last the family could be reunited in a permanent home at the college. The small salary of £400 attached to the office and the considerable expense of living in New York caused Johnson to hesitate. But finally, in October, shortly before the Connecticut Assembly convened, Johnson reached his decision.[53].

When Johnson resigned from Connecticut politics, his popularity had never been higher. The previous May he had placed third in the election for Governor and first in the selection of the state's twelve assistants. "You dont know how much you have disappointed many of your old friends and [colleagues] this way as also at the Eastward," wrote one man, "who for years past have had hopes of your filling the first chair in this state." But few Connecticut voters resigned themselves so readily to Johnson's retreat from public service. At the election the following spring, Johnson would be recalled to the Council. The citizens of Stratford acted even sooner, drafting Johnson, only days after his return to New York, to represent them at the coming ratifying convention.[54]

The Constitution provoked a noisy debate at the Stratford town meeting. Johnson's youngest son, Robert Charles, who had graduated from Yale five years earlier, told his father that just when "a powerful opposition" was about to prevail, he "jumped over the seats, mounted the pulpit stairs and succeeded beyond my expectations, equal to my wishes, and closed, with launching an empire on the sea of glory, amidst a general clap of hands." William Samuel Johnson regretted that the meeting had not elected Robert Charles to the convention "which would have given me much Satisfaction & [saved] me from a tedious winter Journey." The Columbia trustees, he noted, "think it of so much consequence that they wish me to attend it, notwithstanding the prejudice it may be of to their affairs, so that you see I cannot disengage myself from Politicks."[55]

On December 27, Johnson left New York by stage, and after stopping briefly at Stratford, he reached Hartford on January 2, one day before the ratifying convention assembled. The galleries were crowded on January 3, as the convention organized, and before the day ended the members moved to the North Meeting House to accommodate the spectators.[56] Ellsworth and Johnson opened the next day's proceedings with speeches in praise of the Constitution. Their presentations were cleverly designed to conceal the doubts and divisions that had appeared at the Constitutional Convention and, at the same time, to appeal to Connecticut's deep distrust of the military.

Rather than stressing the similarities between the Articles of Confederation and the new plan, especially the equality of the states in the Senate for which the Connecticut delegation had struggled unrelentingly, Ellsworth and Johnson argued forcefully for the very nationalist principles on which Madison had drafted the Virginia plan. "Such is the nature of . . . confederacies," Johnson told the Connecticut convention, that only the force of arms can compel the compliance of delinquent members.

The Convention saw this imperfection in attempting to legislate for States, in their political capacity; that the coercion of Law can be exercised by nothing but a military force. They have therefore gone upon an entirely new ground. They have formed a new nation out of the individual States. . . . The force which is to be employed, is the energy of Law, and this force is to operate only upon individuals, who fail in their duty to their country.

Contending that a direct compact between the national government and the people must replace the Confederation, Ellsworth and Johnson reiterated the numerous instances in which the states had evaded their duties to the union. "The states," Johnson continued,

were sensible to this, to remedy the evil they appointed the convention. . . . I cannot but impute it to a signal intervention of divine providence, that a convention from States differing in cirumstances, interest, and manners should be so harmonious in adopting one grand system. If we reject a plan of government, which with such favorable circumstances is offered for our acceptance, I fear our national existence must come to an end.[57]

After Johnson spoke, the Hartford meeting began an article-by-article debate on the Constitution, continuing until January 9. Despite the length of the deliberations, the ratificationists were confident of victory. The eyes of the entire country had been focused on the proceedings at Philadelphia, and the prestige of the Convention favored a victory for the Constitution.[58] Moreover, the issues on which the antinationalists had gained their strength in Connecticut—military pensions, the impost, and the Society of Cincinnati—were dead by 1787. Connecticut had long resented paying import duties to New York and Rhode Island for British goods. Under the Constitution, the duties would be collected by the general government and benefit all the states, not just Connecticut's two neighbors. And the general taxing power promised financial stability for the new nation, inviting the support of state and continental creditors alike.[59] Finally, the Federalists had a complete plan, and their rivals had none. When Richard Law announced to the ratifying convention on January 9 that "A free government now presents itself for acceptance," few could resist the call.[60]

The Hartford meeting approved the Constitution by a vote of 128 to 48. Two of Connecticut's most outspoken antinationalists, William Williams and Joseph Hopkins, prudently joined the majority. Both were prominent politicians who depended on the state's voters and the nationalist-minded Assembly for their public posts. But the third antinationalist spokesman, James Wadsworth, stood firm against the Constitution, and in the coming May election he would lose his political office.[61] Once the Connecticut freemen had ratified the Constitution they were determined to supply the new government with proven nationalists, including the weary and reluctant statesman William Samuel Johnson.

By mid-January, when Johnson embarked for New York to resume his duties at the college, five states had ratified the Constitution. Throughout the following months, he pursued his fatiguing schedule, presiding at Columbia, journeying by sail or stage to Stratford for brief visits, and then on to the Connecticut Assembly.[62] All the while he waited anxiously for the verdicts of the other states. On June 21, New Hampshire gave the framers their ninth victory, the requisite number to launch the new government. The assents of Virginia and New York, crucial to the solidarity of the Union, quickly followed, and by the autumn every state except North Carolina and Rhode Island was deliberating on the selection of the wisest statesmen to implement the grand experiment. In October, the Connecticut Assembly appointed Johnson and Ellsworth as the state's first two senators. From New Hampshire came congratulations that Connecticut had sensibly supplied the nation with "staunch Federalists."[63]

On March 4, 1789, the appointed day for the new government to begin, Johnson once again entered the old City Hall, where the Continental Congress had sat out its last hours. The building wore a fresh appearance and a new name, Federal Hall. New York's wealthiest citizens had contributed the awesome amount of $32,000 to renovate it, hoping that their city might be honored as the republic's permanent capital. Cannons fired and bells rang in celebration of the opening day, but only seven other Senators and thirteen Representatives appeared. The delay occasioned murmurs of curiosity and alarm. "The good people of this Region," Samuel Mix Mitchell wrote from Connecticut later that month, "are impatient with the Tardiness of the new government & conjecture there must be a defection in the friends of it. Why are the Chariot Wheels from the South so slow?" At last, on April 1, the House of Representatives gathered a quorum, and five days later, when Richard H. Lee of Virginia took his seat in the Senate, the Congress was ready to proceed.[64]

New York now awaited the arrival of the nation's new chief executive, George Washington. On April 22, Johnson and two fellow Senators set out for Elizabethtown, New Jersey, to prepare for Washington's grand welcome. The next morning the three Senators, a similar committee from the House of Representatives, and a host of New York officials greeted the President and embarked on a lavish progress across the Hudson. Cannons roared from both shores as Washington and his entourage crossed the river in barges decked with naval ornaments and manned by uniformed pilots. The procession, Johnson recorded, landed about three o'clock and paraded past the Federal House (where Washington would be inaugurated seven days later) and on to the President's house "amidst the acclamat[io]n of an immense Concourse of People."[65]

The regal display that surrounded Washington's arrival and inauguration no doubt caused concern among the advocates of republican simplicity. Americans were initiating their second frame of government after only fourteen years as a republic, and they were nervously aware that the ability of republican government to resist monarchical subversion, as well as popular tumult, remained to be proved. Nowhere was this apprehension more visible than in the First Congress, which debated heatedly over a suitable title for Washington and his successors. A Senate committee on which Johnson sat favored "His Highness the President of the United States and Protector of the Rights of the Same." The epithet aptly suited Washington's solemn, formal, and aloof demeanor, but the House of Representatives rejected it. The Representatives, obeying the prejudices of their countrymen as well as their own distaste for any vestiges of monarchism, resisted even the word "Honorable." The Senate's efforts to endow the office with a title conforming to "the opinion and practice of civilized nations" was defeated. To Senator William Maclay of Pennsylvania, whose views found more sympathy in the lower house, Johnson epitomized the "thoroughpaced courtier."[66]

Except for the fruitless wrangling over a presidential title, Congress pursued its chief task—transforming the paper Constitution into a working government—with impressive energy and little discord. Nineteen of the congressmen had participated in the great debate at Philadelphia, and twenty-three others had joined the Federalist campaigns for ratification. When the legislators undertook to establish the departments of the executive branch, no serious disagreements on the meaning and intent of that branch thwarted their progress. By autumn 1789, the lawmakers had created the Departments of War, State, and the Treasury, all responsible to the President.[67]

Out of these early months also came twelve amendments to the Constitution which, subject to the ratification of the states, were intended as a bill of rights. The men at Philadelphia had omitted a bill of rights, not because they opposed the protection of civil liberties, but because they deemed the limited powers of the central government sufficiently well defined to render any explicit enumeration of these liberties superfluous. In the Convention's debate on the prohibition of *ex post facto* laws, Johnson had argued that such a safeguard was "unnecessary" and "implied an improper suspicion of the national legislature." Ellsworth had objected that "there was no lawyer, no civilian who would not say that *ex post facto* laws were void of themselves. It cannot be necessary to prohibit them." On the more general question of protecting liberty, Sherman had insisted that "The State Declarations of Rights are not repealed by this Constitution, and being in force are sufficient." Yet the omission of a bill of rights was a political miscalculation which added strength to the anti-Federalists' arguments. The Federalist-dominated first Congress acted quickly to silence the Constitution's critics. Although the amendments drafted that summer merely articulated the safeguards tacitly agreed upon by the Philadelphia framers and imposed no additional restrictions on the powers of the federal government, they promised to allay the doubts of many anti-Federalists and undermine the arguments of the rest. In June 1790, anti-Federalism would meet its final demise when Rhode Island became the thirteenth state to ratify the Constitution.[68]

Anti-Federalism posed no threat to the unity of the new government, but once the first Congress turned from erecting the machinery of government to tackling the republic's most serious problem—reestablishing its credit and securing a revenue—the singleness of purpose and spirit of comity that had held the Federalists together, even during the arduous days at the Convention, broke down. In January, Secretary of the Treasury Alexander Hamilton laid before Congress two bold proposals to restore the government's credit. His funding scheme provided that the securities of the Confederation, however depreciated in price, would be exchanged at their original value for interest-bearing certificates of the new government, and that a portion of the federal revenue would be irrevocably pledged to their liquidation. Under his assumption proposal, the federal government would assume all wartime state obligations that remained outstanding in 1790. The Constitution gave Congress the authority to tax imports, a source of revenue on which the states had previously relied. Unless the federal government assumed the debts of the states, state creditors would oppose the funding scheme and federal taxation.[69]

Hamilton's two-fold plan provoked an intense and bitter debate in Congress, with his supporters, including Johnson, pitted against Representative James Madison, Secretary of State Thomas Jefferson and men of their persuasion. Underlying the debate were two opposing views of the new nation. Hamilton envisioned a complex urban and agricultural economy with a sophisticated system of credit at the disposal of the federal government. His funding proposal was designed to establish the future credit of the United States on a firm, mutually beneficial partnership with the country's financiers. Madison's faith rested on the intrinsic value of an agrarian republic. He and his kindred spirit, Thomas Jefferson, deplored speculators and bankers as "rogues" and "vultures." Cities, they feared, made men the "tools of opulence and ambition," and "the panders of vice."[70]

Madison lost the first battle on February 22, when the House defeated his proposal for discriminating between the Confederation's original creditors and men who had purchased the obligations at depreciated prices. He then attacked assumption. State jealousies and local pride favored his cause. The southern states (except South Carolina) had already liquidated most of their debts and were loath to shoulder the burdens of their delinquent New England neighbors. The middle states were divided and undecided. In a political maneuver that allied Pennsylvania with the antiassumption forces in exchange for the temporary removal of the federal capital to Philadelphia, Madison secured a narrow majority to defeat assumption on April 12, 1790.[71]

The question then came before Johnson and his colleagues in the Senate, who had just opened debate on the location of the capital. Senator Richard H. Lee of Virginia tried Madison's successful tactic, moving that Congress establish its temporary residence at Philadelphia before the next session. The advocates of assumption called for a postponement of Lee's motion, realizing that if it succeeded it threatened a quick defeat of Hamilton's plan, but Vice-President Adams cast the tie-breaking vote in favor of considering Lee's proposal. The assumptionists hastened to round up their supporters, including Senator Johnson, whose poor health had confined him to his quarters at the college that morning. "Mr Johnson came with his night cap and wrapped in many Garments [Rufus King recalled], attended by Doctrs Bard & Romaine, and having a Cot with a [mattress] in the antechamber to repose on: by general consent [Lee's] resolution was taken up and negatived 13 to 11.[72] The entanglement between Hamiltonian finance and the location of the capital was neither coincidental nor merely strategic. Madison apprehended that the capital would set the tone for the entire nation, and, he believed, it must reside not in a city, but on the pristine Potomac.[73] To Madison the location of the capital was as important as the battle against assumption, but few southerners agreed. Rufus King was busy forging an alliance of the Senators from Connecticut, Rhode Island, Georgia, South Carolina, and North Carolina, to allow the temporary capital to remain at New York in exchange for a permanent seat at Baltimore. The Secretary of the Treasury rushed to counter King's strategy. Hamilton had private assurances from Jefferson and Madison that the location of the capital on the Potomac would bring success to assumption. On June 30 the Senate named Philadelphia as the temporary home of the Congress, and the following day approved Madison's chosen site for the permanent capital. Three weeks later the Senate passed the funding plan, including the provision for assuming state debts, and the bargain was sealed on July 26, when the House concurred.[74]

It was a political victory for Connecticut's spokesmen in Congress. Johnson had no personal financial stake in the funding-assumption plan. His only investment in public securities, $3,227 in state obligations issued after the war, would not be covered by assumption. But the plan answered the economic and political needs of the state. Connecticut's wartime debt totalled $1.6 million (face value), third highest among the states, and Connecticut citizens held continental securities amounting to $1 million (face value). Connecticut politicians such as William Williams and Joseph Hopkins—state creditors and outspoken antinationalists—had come to support the Constitution when they realized that Connecticut could not successfully levy an impost to fund its wartime obligations. These men had placed their faith in the intention of the new government to use its general taxing power to reimburse state as well as continental creditors.[75] Hamilton's scheme answered their expectations, and promised to strengthen and unify Connecticut's support for the nation's new leaders

Congress's other pressing task, to secure a national revenue, aroused even more passion than the funding-assumption plan. The legislators all agreed that tariff and tonnage duties were the proper and necessary mode of taxation, but violent disagreement emerged on a more fundamental question: Was the first duty of Congress to restore the government's finances or to uphold the republic's honor among nations? Great Britain's exclusion of American ships from the lucrative West Indian trade had long embarrassed the Confederation. The framers at Philadelphia had invested Congress with the requisite commercial powers to retaliate against British policy, and in the early weeks of the first session Madison proposed a tax on tonnage that would have discriminated against foreign nations not in commercial treaty with the United States. Madison's motion was clearly designed to favor Ameica's wartime ally, France, and injure Great Britain, but the Senate rejected it. Johnson and Hamilton had advocated retaliation against the British under the Confederation, but they, and other men of their persuasion, now realized that the federal government's financial credibility rested on import revenues, and ninety percent of American imports came from Great Britain. An Anglo-American trade war would doom Hamilton's bold financial program.[76]

Neither Johnson nor Hamilton accepted Madison's argument that the young republic could survive on trade with France. Johnson reasoned that "although Great Britain has excluded us from her American and West Indian possessions, yet [of greater importance is] that she has granted us certain advantages in her ports of Europe, that in Asia she treats us with kindness, that hers is the best market for our exports, and that, if we are intemperate, we may naturally look for an alteration in these points."[77] Johnson was quick to label the Madisonians as "Francophiles" or the "French interest."[78] But the advocates of commercial retaliation as readily condemned the Hamiltonians for bowing to America's enemy in order to benefit northern commerce. Only a defeat of British restrictions would restore national honor, at the same time benefiting the most virtuous class of citizens, the farmers, whose exports required West Indian markets. The search for a national revenue was rapidly transformed into a conflict over foreign allegiances and sectional interests, in which passion clouded reason and mutual distrust obscured the necessity for compromise.[79]

Madison's proposal in Congress prompted the British Consul-General at New York, Sir John Temple, to alert his government immediately, and in response, the British agent George Beckwith arrived in New York in the autumn of 1789.[80] Beckwith's task was twofold: to warn American statesmen that any discriminatory measure would provoke severe commercial retaliation, and to assess the strength of the so-called "British interest" in the capital. His mission was no clandestine affair.

That October, and in subsequent visits to New York the following year, he contacted several prominent national leaders,
including Johnson, Hamilton, and New York's Senator Philip
Schuyler.[81] Even President Washington knew of Beckwith's
activities.

On arriving in New York that autumn, Beckwith turned
first to William Samuel Johnson, no doubt on advice from
Temple.[82] Johnson had known Temple before the Revolution,
and afterwards they had renewed their friendship.[83] Temple
must have assured Beckwith that Johnson favored continuing
Anglo-American cooperation. Beckwith immediately warned
Johnson that had Madison's bill "passed as sent up from your
House of Representatives with those discriminating clauses,
which appeared in your public papers, we were prepared to
meet it; . . . the continuance of the indulgencies shewn to your
shipping in our ports in Europe, depends upon your conduct."[84]
Beckwith also hastened to contact Hamilton, and over the next
year the British agent met several times with both Americans.

Hamilton and Johnson seized upon Beckwith's mission as
an opportunity to counteract the damaging repercussions of
Madison's antagonistic proposal in Congress and to extend an
unofficial invitation to the British to strengthen diplomatic
and commercial ties with the United States. Time and again
they told Beckwith that American interests favored cooperation
with Great Britain, not France. "I have always preferred a con-
nexion with you, to that of any other country, *we think in
English*, and have a similarity of prejudices and of predilec-
tions," Hamilton confided. "I am free to say," he continued,
"that although France has been indulgent to us, in certain
points, yet what she can furnish, is by no means so essential
or so suited to us as your productions, nor do our raw materials
suit her as well as they do you." Johnson assured Beckwith that
the majority of the Senate "were too enlightened and too moderate to approve [Madison's] measures; they viewed the Act as
a declaration of commercial war, which it was neither just nor
wise to commence against a powerful nation."[85] In the summer
of 1790, when Great Britain temporarily felt the threat of a war
with Spain, Johnson even intimated to Beckwith that it was in
America's interest to maintain a strict neutrality. Johnson's
suggestion confounded the policy of Secretary of State Jefferson,
who hoped to win concessions from the British in return for
American neutrality, but Hamilton went even further than the

Connecticut Senator, implying to Beckwith that America would be inclined to ally with Great Britain in the event of a European war. To Hamilton, this was not a subversion, but rather his duty as a member of the cabinet. He acted on the principle that "most of the important measures of every government are connected with the Treasury."[86]

In addition to these assurances, Hamilton and Johnson repeatedly impressed upon Beckwith the importance of immediate diplomatic action, lest the spokesmen for Anglo-American cooperation lose their ascendancy in Congress. Johnson advised Beckwith that Great Britain must make the first diplomatic gesture, the appointment of an official minister to the United States. The Connecticut Senator urged that "it would be a popular measure and tend greatly to set everything in motion in a good humoured way." He added that because "we have had a Minister at your Court, [and] you did not send one in return, we should find a difficulty in taking the lead again in such a nomination."[87]

In the winter of 1790, Congress established its new temporary home in Philadelphia. The Columbia trustees allowed Johnson to leave his college duties and follow the Congress southward on the condition that he would resign his political office at the conclusion of the first Congress. He arrived in Philadelphia on December 11, reporting to his son that he enjoyed good health except for deafness, a condition that would trouble him throughout his remaining years.[88]

In February 1791, the advocates of commercial discrimination asserted their cause with new strength, proposing a bill that struck hard at the British carrying trade. The Hamiltonians managed only to postpone the measure until the next session.[89] But in June, two months after the first Congress adjourned, reliable news reached Philadelphia that the British intended to send a minister to the United States immediately. The decision, which had been announced in a report on Anglo-American trade presented by the Committee of the Privy Council on Trade in January, was a victory for the Hamiltonians. Although the report upheld the wisdom of Britain's trade policies, especially the exclusion of American ships from the West Indies and did not authorize the new minister to offer significant concessions to the Americans or conclude a commercial treaty with them, it attested to the limited success of the Hamiltonians' informal negotiations with Beckwith. The report, justifying the appointment of a minister to the United States, cited the existence in Congress, especially in the Senate, of "a party . . . already formed in favour of a Connection with Great Britain, which, by moderation on our part, may perhaps be strengthened and increased, so as to bring about, in a friendly way, all the objects we have in view."[90]

As one historian astutely concluded, "Pitt's Government had to choose between beginning diplomatic relations with a country in whose administration an influential party with an amenable leader favored more cordial relations on the one hand, or, on the other hand, prolonging a situation which could only play into the hands of the anti-British and anti-Federalist party now crystalizing under the leadership of Thomas Jefferson, the friend of France."[91] The appointment of a British minister at least temporarily sapped the strength of the anti-British forces in Congress, who had expected but failed to secure drastic reprisals against Great Britain when Congress reopened in the fall of 1791. Instead, in November Charles Pinckney was nominated Minister to the Court of St. James.[92]

Johnson had resigned from the Senate and returned to New York in March, long before the news of the British report reached Philadelphia. His departure was most timely. The exchange of ministers and the defeat of Madison's discriminatory legislation were victories for the Hamiltonians, but the Privy Council report's specific reference to a British "party" in Congress infuriated the Jefferson-Madison politicians, who quickly branded their political rivals as unpatriotic Anglophiles. It was a stigma that Hamilton and his followers would never overcome.[93] Johnson was well aware of the suspicions that the negotiations with Beckwith had aroused. In 1790 he had explained to the British agent that it was believed "you have laid a deep concerted plan to recover the Sovereignty of the States, and that your whole conduct at present leads to this point."[94] Had the former Connecticut loyalist chosen to remain in Congress for his full six-year term, he no doubt would have been a particularly vulnerable target for the accusations and suspicions voiced by the Madisonians. Even in 1788, before Anglo-American relations divided the Federalists into two hostile camps, Sir John Temple had observed that Johnson's extensive experience at Westminster made him a likely candidate for a diplomatic appointment, except that many were "fearful of his being too much attached to the interests and government of Great Britain."[95] During the next two decades, the controversy over Anglo-American relations would explode into the nation's most divisive issue, culminating in a second war against Great Britain and threatening civil war as well. Once again an attachment to Anglo-American peace would come to spell treason. But in March 1791 Johnson turned his energies from politics to education, a cause that enjoyed the undivided support of the new republic. That year the future of Columbia and its president seemed to promise almost unlimited achievements.

William Samuel Johnson, (as President of Columbia College),
by S. I. Wells, after Gilbert Stuart (1792)
Columbiana, Columbia University

Chapter Fifteen

A Young University with an Aged President

*P*resident Johnson and the trustees, like educators everywhere, faced a formidable task after the Revolution. None of the American colleges escaped the ravages of war. Yale students fled to Connecticut's inland towns in 1777, fearing a British invasion, and returned to New Haven only several months later. The dreaded raid took New Haven and the college by surprise the next year. A more chronic problem was food shortage, which forced Yale to close temporarily on more than one occasion during the war.[1] The College of Philadelphia suffered worse, occupied first as a barracks for Continental troops and then as a hospital for the British forces. Classes were suspended in 1777 and 1778.[2] The College of New Jersey, later to be renamed Princeton, endured even harsher treatment. The students fled in November 1776, as the British menace neared, and within a month the enemy had seized and pillaged Nassau Hall. In 1777 Continental troops rescued the hall for an even worse fate, ripping up the doors and floors for firewood and destroying whatever library had remained when the British evacuated. At the end of the war, old Nassau lay in ruins.[3] No other college suffered longer than King's. In April 1776, New York's Committee of Safety ordered the college authorities to disperse the students and ready the building as a medical station for American troops. The orders were hastily carried out, but to little purpose. British regulars seized the city within a few weeks and prevented the college from reopening until after the peace.[4]

When Johnson assumed his office in 1787, signs of promise appeared everywhere. The college building, which had first welcomed students in 1760, in time for President Samuel Johnson's third commencement, remained standing. Situated about 150 yards from the bank of the Hudson River, it faced southward toward Trinity Church, and commanded a view that awed the city's visitors. Its three-story frame held a central gathering hall, a library, and four staircases, each with twelve apartments for students and faculty. The east staircase was reserved for President Johnson. The building, like all colonial colleges, contained no classrooms, and students met in their teachers' apartments. War had destroyed the library and scientific apparatus and left the interior of the building in sorry disrepair, but when Johnson arrived the exterior had been restored and freshly painted. In 1787 the hall housed five of the college's thirty-nine students, the remaining number lodging in town.[5]

That Columbia had attracted thirty-nine students in just three years was also an auspicious sign. Classes had not resumed until 1784. At most times before the war, the student body had numbered less than thirty and it had never exceeded forty-five. As in colonial times, the college at New York seemed dwarfed beside its rivals. Princeton, where students had numbered more than one hundred in the last colonial decade, counted only eighteen matriculates in 1780, but by 1786 the number had swelled to ninety. Yale showed the fewest losses due to war, probably because the Connecticut legislature exempted college students from military duty. In New Haven 270 students were gathered when the conflict ended, 100 more than at Harvard, which had watched its young men march off to battle.[6]

The greatest promise of success came from the spirit of independence, and the lofty ambitions of the new republic. It was everywhere visible. Educators, political leaders, and citizens voiced an unprecedented enthusiasm and commitment to education. "The business of education has acquired a new complexion by the independence of our country," declared one speaker at the Pennsylvania Constitutional Assembly. "The form of government we have assumed has created a new class of duties to every American." Ezra Stiles agreed, concluding that "it it scarcely possible to enslave a Republic where the Body of People are civilians, well instructed in their Laws, Rights, and Liberties."[7] Military success and the establishment of a national government emboldened Americans with a heady optimism. Human improvement, Samuel Harrison Smith speculated, "seems susceptible of endless extension." If America can invent a complete constitutional government, why not also an exten-

sive system of education?[8] The American Philosophical Society
invited proposals "for the best system of liberal education,
adapted to the genius of the government of the United States."
Bold and grandiose designs were submitted. Smith and Samuel
Knox, who shared the society's prize, proposed a national university supported at public expense. So would President Washington, in his first message to Congress, and Benjamin Rush,
in his address to the Pennsylvania legislature.[9] This same
nation-wide optimism had inspired Governor Clinton and the
New York legislators to rescue the dying King's College in 1784,
and in the three ensuing years the crucial questions of leadership, finances, and educational goals were addressed. The
newly born Columbia College had set its course before its first
president took office.

Education, Clinton declared, is "the peculiar duty of a
government of a free state." Addressing the first regular session
of the state legislature in January 1784, Clinton admonished
that there was "scarce anything more worthy of your attention
than the revival and encouragement of seminaries of learning."[10] The state's lawmakers responded quickly, appointing
committees in both the Senate and the Assembly to prepare a
bill "for the establishment of Seminaries of Learning, and
Schools for the Education of Youth." The legislators' zeal
immediately attracted the notice of King's College, and in March
the college governors petitioned the Senate to revive the dying
school.[11] Despite the public enthusiasm for education, the success of the King's College request was by no means guaranteed,
for the taint of loyalism lingered heavily over that institution.
Myles Cooper, president of the college until his flight to England in 1775, had earned notoriety as a leader and polemicist
for the colony's loyalist forces.[12] Of the twenty-one governors
who most actively participated in the college's affairs on the
eve of Revolution, fifteen had joined the loyalist camp, fleeing
to the countryside or to exile in England. Three of the four
King's College faculty also had opposed the American cause.[13]
At least one-half the young men educated at King's had resisted
the Revolution, a proportion far larger than at any other colonial college.[14]

Ironically, it was a provision of King's royal charter that
enabled a group of patriots to assume leadership of the college
after 1776 and rescue it from permanent ignominy and decline.
The 1754 charter provided that the governing board include,

as ex-officio governors, the colony's chief executive officers, the judges of the Supreme Court, the Mayor of New York City, and the senior minister from each religious denomination in the city. The provision had originally been inserted to quell political opposition to the Anglican school, although some ex-officio governors did participate before the Revolution.[15] In 1784, nine patriot officials and ministers who were entitled to sit on the Board of Governors concerted with four of King's regular governors to revive the college, long neglected after the departure of Cooper and his loyalist colleagues. The thirteen governors who petitioned the New York Senate in 1784 included the state's Governor, the Treasurer, and the Attorney General. Another signer was Mayor James Duane of New York City, who had served King's as a regular governor before the war. Three postwar governors who signed the petition would never have served King's under Cooper's Tory-Anglican leadership: the "Triumvirate" spokesman John Morin Scott, whose position as Secretary of State entitled him to a seat on the college board; the Presbyterian minister, Rev. John Rodgers; and the Rev. Samuel Provoost, ardent foe of loyalist Episcopalians.[16]

Other factors, in addition to the indisputable patriotism and influential positions of King's governors, boded well for the future of the college. Duane chaired the Senate committee that would frame an educational bill for the state and consider King's petition. Robert Harpur, the only teacher at King's to support the Revolution, sat on the Assembly's educational committee.[17] Finally, despite the large number of graduates who had betrayed the American cause, King's had also educated Alexander Hamilton, John Jay, and Gouverneur Morris, men of national stature who would contribute to the renaissance of their alma mater.

On May 1, 1784, the future of the college in the new republic won official recognition and support from the New York state legislature, which adopted "An Act for granting certain Privileges to the College heretofore called King's College, for altering the Name and Charter thereof, and erecting an University within this State." The act established the University of the State of New York, an appointive body empowered to charter and govern educational institutions in the state. The act also placed King's, renamed Columbia, under the rule of the twelve university regents, two appointed by the Governor from each county, and the six ex-officio regents, including the Governor, Lieutenant Governor, President of the Senate, Speaker of the Assembly, and the Mayors of New York City and Albany. The King's governors relinquished all control of the college to the regents, who could appoint and dismiss the president and faculty, regulate the college's finances and make its statutes.[18] The new law echoed the proposals of King's bitterest enemy, William Livingston, who had campaigned thirty years earlier for a college chartered and controlled by the legislature and devoid of any sectarian affiliation. The regents promptly elected a treasurer, Brockholst Livingston, who was William Livingston's son.[19]

Dissatisfaction with the new law surfaced quickly. The governors of King's had achieved recognition for the college, but at the high cost of surrendering to statewide public control. Within months, the regents who resided in New York City, including several former King's governors and apparently led by James Duane, began a movement to subvert statewide control. By 1787, when Johnson assumed the presidency, Columbia had won its independence. In November 1784, Senator Duane persuaded the legislature to increase the number of regents from twenty-four to fifty-seven, adding twenty from new York City, thirteen from the rest of the state, and reducing the quorum to nine.[20] Duane's motive quickly became apparent. From 1784 to 1787, the regents convened in New York City to restore the finances of the college and lay plans for a faculty and curriculum. The meetings were always controlled by the New York City men, whose number guaranteed a quorum.[21] Jealousy and animosity quickened. In 1785 George Clinton, chancellor of the university, resigned in protest, and Duane thereafter customarily presided at the meetings.[22] The New York City regents' exclusive interest in Columbia, to the neglect of the educational needs of the rest of the state, evoked protest from the upstate regents and from several legislators who spoke out against financing the college.[23]

By 1787, the discord had reached intolerable proportions. In January, the regents appointed a committee, chaired by Duane, to devise a remedy. The committee's report, presented to the legislature in March, reflected the conflicting interests that divided the regents. The report lamented the neglect of lower education in the state, and announced that "erecting public schools for teaching reading, writing and arithmetic is an object of very great importance which ought not to be left to the discretion of private men, but be promoted by public

authority. Of so much knowledge no citizen ought to be destitute." The interests of the New York City regents appeared in a
proposal that "each Respective College ought to be entrusted
to a distinct Corporation with competent powers and privileges"[24] On April 13 the legislature adopted the regents' proposals in an act that removed Columbia from the immediate
supervision of the University of the State of New York and
restored the college's corporate privileges under an independent
board of trustees. The regents retained the power "to visit and
inspect" the college, "examine into the State and System of
Education and Discipline therein, and make a yearly Report
thereof to the Legislature."[25] How independent Columbia
would be was unclear, for the meaning of the regents' visitation
powers awaited practical definition, but the composition of
the new board of trustees signalled a clear victory for Duane
and the New York City faction. Twenty regents who had represented New York City took seats on the new board, but only one
of the thirty-five who had represented the counties outside New
York City joined the Columbia board.[26] The trustees, who numbered twenty-nine in all, included Mayor Duane, Secretary of
State Lewis Allaire Scott, Speaker of the Assembly Richard
Varick, who would follow Duane as the city's chief executive
and three Columbia teachers.[27] Six of the trustees had served
King's College, including Duane, who assumed the chairman-
ship of the new board.[28] Columbia, rescued from the competing
priorities and jealousies that crippled the state-wide university
system, would be ruled in future by men loyal to New York City
and its college, for the 1787 law empowered the trustees to choose
their own successors.[29]

The election of William Samuel Johnson as Columbia's
president just six months later revealed many of the aims and
aspirations of the trustees. Johnson's political prominence
promised Columbia a place of distinction in the new republic.
The city's newspapers hailed his election as "a happy proof of
the high estimate in which literature is held among us, since
characters of first importance seldom condescend to assume the
care of education." Most likely, Johnson's support for a strong
national government won for him the votes of ardent Federalist
trustees such as Richard Varick, James Duane, John Laurence,
and especially Alexander Hamilton, who was determined that
the president of Columbia must be a gentleman as well as a
scholar, and his politics must "be of the right sort."[30] It was

probably James Duane who proposed his old friend Johnson for president. As a trustee of King's, Duane had asked Johnson's legal advice on a fund-raising campaign for the college many years before.[31] The two men shared political views, church loyalties, and a long interest in King's. Johnson's discreet but dedicated churchmanship guaranteed the votes of the other Anglican trustees as well. Like Duane, they were working hard to rebuild the Episcopal church and restore it to political respectability, and they undoubtedly viewed the revival of King's College as a milestone. Also on the Columbia board were seven clergymen and several laymen from the city's other denominations, and they too had good reason to support an Episcopalian for president, especially someone of Johnson's prominence. It was the New York Anglicans who had sent their sons to King's before the war, and it was safe to expect that their continued patronage would be vital to Columbia's success. The Episcopal Church was growing rapidly in New York. In 1790, Trinity parish would celebrate the completion of its new building, and in the next decade two more Episcopal edifices would be raised to house the city's worshippers.[32]

The trustees must have also been concerned that Columbia win a following among New York's other denominations. King's failure to attract a respectable number of students had been owing in great part to its identity as an Anglican school. The city's numerous and politically important Presbyterians had withheld their support, and only on rare occasions had a Baptist, Lutheran, or Jew attended the college. Only the Dutch Reformed, who were the Anglicans' friends in church politics, had allowed their sons to go to King's, supplying about one quarter of the tiny enrollment.[33] A safeguard was needed lest Columbia, like its forbear, be regarded as a sectarian school. Johnson's distinguished career in the new national government and his conciliatory manner in matters of religion seemed to answer the needs of a college long wearied by political and religious conflicts. His demeanor contrasted starkly to the intemperate Toryism and Anglicanism of King's last president, Myles Cooper, whose aggressive campaign for an American episcopate and noisy tirades against the Continental Congress had aroused a host of enemies.[34] Johnson had won the votes of Connecticut's Congregationalists, which suggested that he could earn the support of New York's Presbyterians. But a number of the trustees must have doubted that Johnson's political popularity and quiet

churchmanship were quite sufficient. An additional safeguard
was needed, and the crux of the compromise seems to have been
the appointment of John Daniel Gros, a German Reformed
clergyman, to the professorship of moral philosophy.

The chair of moral philosophy stood above all the other
faculty positions in importance and prestige. In every colonial
college the president, always a clergyman, had reserved that
position for himself. Nowhere had this tradition been stronger
than at King's. Fourth-year students had devoted most of their
time to moral philosophy, under the watchful eye of the president. In the college's early years, seniors had studied Johnson's
own *Elementa Philosophica*, and in the last decade they had
learned Cooper's philosophical text, *Ethices Compendium*.[35]
In 1784, the Regents who set forth a plan for Columbia established a professorship of moral philosophy with a salary of
£100 per annum, but the chair remained vacant from 1784 until
1787, although Gros, professor of German and geography,
served as temporary instructor of moral philosophy for the
partial salary of £50. It seems that the regents, and their successors the trustees, awaited the election of a president. Yet soon
after Johnson assumed the presidency, the trustees appointed
Gros as professor of moral philosophy with the full salary.[36]
The fact that Johnson was not a clergyman provided a conve-
nient rationale for this unusual decision, and presented an opportunity for the trustees to reach a compromise.

The separation of these two offices was first tried at Philadelphia, and the evidence suggests that the compromise adopted
at Columbia was modeled after the Philadelphia effort. Religious conflict and revolutionary upheaval left the College of
Philadelphia, like King's, facing a perilously uncertain future.
By 1779, the College of Philadelphia had earned so many enemies that the Pennsylvania legislature disbanded the board of
trustees, dismissed Provost William Smith and the faculty, and
appointed a new governing board to rebuild the college. The
college had been chartered in 1755 as a private, nonsectarian
school, but the Anglican majority on the board and the Episcopal Rev. Smith had so completely imposed their denomina-
tional preference on the character of the college that the city's
other religious groups had refused to support it. In addition,
Smith's imprudent participation in the factional disputes that
rocked Pennsylvania politics before the war, and the blatant
loyalism of several trustees, who even withdrew to the British

lines or fled to Great Britain during the war, had cost the college many friends.[37]

In 1779, the new state-appointed board set immediately to choosing a provost (president) for the college. A number of the trustees, including the president of the board, Joseph Reed, suggested that William Samuel Johnson's talent for compromise and moderate religious views made him a suitable candidate. Johnson's supporters were eager to please both the city's Anglicans, who had handsomely supported the college in the past, and the city's Presbyterians, who had traditionally withheld their support. Johnson was to be provost and Rev. John Ewing, a Presbyterian, the vice-provost. According to one historian, animosity against the Anglicans who had governed the colonial college was too intense in 1779 to sustain the proposal, and Johnson's name was dropped. In January 1780, Ewing won the appointment as provost, and the Philadelphian David Rittenhouse, a noted scientist and statesman, became vice-provost. As provost, Ewing also assumed the professorship of moral philosophy.[38]

The failure of the state-appointed board to offer some gesture of conciliation to the city's Anglicans aroused a storm of controversy and deprived the college of much-needed support. When the demanding duties of his political career compelled Rittenhouse to resign in 1782, the board seized the opportunity to try to quiet jealousies of many Philadelphia Anglicans, if not the angry protests being raised by Smith and the disfranchised colonial trustees. The board named Rev. Samuel Magaw as the new vice-provost. Magaw was the rector of St. Paul's Church and one of Philadelphia's most prominent Episcopal divines. Three months later the board revealed its full intentions when it adopted a plan "for the better Regulation and Government" of the college. Under the new plan, Vice-Provost Magaw was appointed professor of moral philosophy, in place of Provost Ewing. The board undoubtedly hoped that this measure would dispel the appearance of Presbyterian preference at the college.[39]

New York educators must have watched the events in Philadelphia with great interest, for the two colleges faced very similar problems as the war ended. Columbia's decision to separate the offices of president and professor of moral philosophy was probably inspired by the Philadelphians' attempt at accommodation, and particularly by the suggestion of Rev. Johann

Kristoff Kunze, a Lutheran clergyman from Philadelphia, who
was named a New York regent in 1784 and a Columbia trustee
three years later. Before coming to New York, Kunze had served
on the state-appointed board and faculty in Philadelphia.[40]
When William Samuel Johnson's name was raised as a suitable
president for Columbia, and a gesture of conciliation to the
city's non-Episcopal worshippers was deemed necessary, Kunze
most likely proposed the same measure that he and his Philadelphia colleagues had devised a few years earlier.

From the very day Johnson accepted the presidency, one
could have predicted that his influence in the rebuilding of the
college would be small. The pattern of government long accepted at the colonial colleges gave little authority to the college president, and the men who became Columbia's trustees
already had shown a determination to rule alone. In colonial
times, a governing board of nonacademicians had reigned supreme over the faculty and president at every college, in matters
of finance, discipline, and even curriculum. The Massachusetts legislators had established this precedent a century and a
half earlier, when they erected Harvard College, and the founders of Yale, Princeton—in fact every colonial college—had copied it. The King's charter had expressly awarded virtually
unlimited authority to the governors over all college affairs. In
practice, President Samuel Johnson had organized and admin-
istered the school with no interference from the governors, at
least in the early years. A majority of the governors had never
attended college and knew little about higher education. But
in later years, when Samuel Johnson and the governing board
disagreed on a variety of issues, the charter had enabled the
governors to restrict Johnson's authority and eventually to
force his resignation.[41] The revival of King's under a new name
and a new charter occasioned no departure from this precedent.
Indeed, the fact that the regents ruled the college for three years
without appointing a president laid the foundation for powerful trustee government. There was no reason to expect that the
aggressive New York City regents, who first dominated the University of the State of New York, then won an independent charter and governing board for Columbia, and subsequently assumed their seats as Columbia trustees, would surrender any
leadership to the president. Unlike the King's College governors, who had initially deferred to Samuel Johnson, many of
the Columbia trustees were college graduates, and a few were

intensely interested in education. Robert Harpur had taught at King's before he embarked on a political career. In 1810, Rev. John Henry Livingston would become the president and professor of theology at Queens College. The physicians on the board of trustees were outspoken advocates of formal medical education and would soon establish a medical school at Columbia.[42]

Soon after Johnson accepted the presidency, the trustees seated him on the governing board,[43] but his presence there was by no means decisive. The trustees took command of all college affairs, and left few matters to the president, not even student discipline or the selection of books for the library.[44] At times, they excluded Johnson from important committee assignments.[45] The New York State legislature, not President Johnson, would become the trustees' essential partner in rebuilding the college. Gathering a faculty and expanding the curriculum to meet the ambitious standards of the new republic required money, and the trustees could put their plans into action only when the state's lawmakers offered adequate financial support.

The program of studies at Columbia in 1788 fell sadly short of the trustees' vision. The faculty numbered four, including President Johnson, who taught rhetoric and logic once a week to each class. Professor John Kemp instructed freshmen and sophomores in mathematics, and juniors in natural philosophy (astronomy and physics). Professor John Gros taught sophomores geography and guided seniors through the traditional course on moral philosophy. Professor William Cochran presented Latin and Greek studies to all four classes.[46] The curriculum duplicated the program at other American colleges, and the faculty was impressively large by contemporary standards.[47] Yet the men who displayed the most energy and commitment to Columbia, as regents and later as trustees, envisioned a more expansive and progressive course of study.[48] In fact, everywhere in the new republic, educators and other interested citizens were condemning mere pedantry and clamoring for the promotion of "useful knowledge," especially the modern languages and practical sciences.[49] The regents' plan, drafted in 1784, included classes in Hebrew, German, French, Low Dutch, civil history, architecture, commerce, agriculture, music, painting, and schools of medicine, law, and divinity.[50] But the money was lacking to hire teachers in any of these subjects except French, which was offered for a short time.[51] The larger vision of the regents and trustees went unrealized until 1792.

In that year, the state legislature answered Columbia's appeals and awarded £1000 for repairs, books, and scientific apparatus and an annual sum of £750 for five years to augment the faculty.[52] By 1795 the trustees' ideal of an expansive, innovative and useful arts curriculum had become a reality. Samuel Latham Mitchill, appointed to the new chair of natural history and chemistry, taught an ambitious course that included botany, mineralogy, geology, zoology, and hydrology. Monsieur Villette de Marcellin occupied the first permanent professorship of French, Rev. Johann Kunze became the first salaried teacher of Hebrew, and Professor Elijah Rattoone launched a new course in ancient history. The appointment of Rev. John Bissit as professor of rhetoric and belles lettres relieved President Johnson of his teaching duties.[53]

The new curriculum reflected both the innovative, practical spirit of the postwar years and an enduring respect for scholarship and valuable traditions. The appointment of a professor of French symbolized the era's enthusiasm for educational change. Every plan for a national university, every spokesman for the advancement of learning advocated teaching modern languages.[54] Although the conservative clergymen who ruled Yale feared that such a "Foreign influence" would corrupt religion and morals at the college, Harvard, like Columbia, responded quickly to the postwar spirit, adding French to the regular curriculum in 1787.[55] Natural philosophy also enjoyed sudden popularity in the new republic. In 1784, the College of Rhode Island appointed its first natural history professor, and Harvard followed four years later.[56] But no other American teacher in the field rivalled Samuel Latham Mitchill's creative intellect and sophisticated command of the latest chemical theories. For decades, the Scottish universities had overshadowed Oxford and Cambridge, as well as the American schools, in scientific learning. When Mitchill returned to New York in 1787, after training at the University of Edinburgh, he produced an impressive array of scientific papers and earned wide prominence, even before joining the Columbia faculty in 1792.[57] He and his Scottish-educated colleague John Kemp, who taught mathematics, astronomy, and physics at the college, elevated Columbia to scientific renown among its collegiate rivals.[58] The Columbia trustees aimed to place the modern languages and practical sciences on a par with the classics, not to eliminate the traditional learning. Benjamin Rush and Samuel Harrison Smith each proposed a national university where classical languages had no place. Rush's plan excluded all but the useful and vocational subjects, limiting even mathematical and scientific inquiry to areas with immediate practical application.[59] But few other educators agreed that mastering the abstract sciences and the ancients was useless pedantry.[60] At Columbia, as at Yale and Princeton, the curriculum continued to include heavy doses of Latin and Greek for all four classes.[61]

Columbia's rapid progress owed more to its energetic trustees and the state's lawmakers than to its aging president, but William Samuel Johnson welcomed the changes gladly. He shared the trustees' enthusiasm for a broader, more scientific curriculum. Addressing the graduates at commencement, Johnson charged, "as scholars, it is your duty, continually to cultivate your minds and improve in every branch of useful science. . . . In this seminary, you have only entered the portals of the Temple of Science. You have yet to survey and examine the august building in all its dimensions and extent." Johnson's address conveyed his ardor for both the new learning and the classical studies at which he had excelled since his own college days, and expressed the commitment shared by educators everywhere to supply the new republic with capable and earnest citizens. As recipients of a "liberal education," Johnson told the graduates, "You assume the character of scholars, of men, and of citizens, great and important characters demanding various and exalted duties. Go then, gentlemen, and exercise them with diligence, fidelity, and zeal. Fulfill . . . the demands which your country hath upon you.[62]

Johnson must also have seen in the new curriculum the fulfillment of his own father's ambitions. Political independence evoked an unprecedented nationwide discussion on the value and mode of education, but a few thoughtful teachers had recognized decades before the Revolution that education merited continued reassessment and innovation. On that very principle, Samuel Johnson had shaped King's College forty years earlier. In 1754, the elder Johnson had announced the opening of a college in New York where young men would be instructed

in the learned languages, and in the arts of reasoning exactly, of writing correctly, and speaking eloquently; and in the arts of numbering and measuring, of surveying and navigation, of geography and history, of husbandry, commerce, and government, and in the knowledge of all nature in the heavens above us, and in the air, water and earth around us, and the various kinds of meteors, stones, mines, and minerals, plants, and animals, and of everything useful for the comfort, the convenience and elegance of life, in the chief manufactures relating to any of these things; and finally to lead from the study of nature to the study of themselves, and of the God of nature and their duty to Him, themselves, and one another, and everything that contributes to their true happiness, both here and hereafter.[63]

It is not surprising that the Anglican minister had defined such a bold and expansive task for King's College. A dedication to teaching, as well as to the ministry, had shaped Samuel Johnson's life since his earliest years at Stratford, when he had tutored his own sons and boys from nearby New York for college and had catechized Yale graduates preparing for Episcopal orders. He had studied earnestly the educational proposals of John Locke, the well known Scottish reformers, and Benjamin Franklin, which assailed rigid pedantry and urged more flexible, innovative methods of schooling.[64] The theories of education that filled Samuel Johnson's own writings revealed a willingness to experiment and an inherent sensitivity to the youthful intellect.[65] He had searched for a content and method of education that would make learning more attainable without sacrificing scholarship to narrow vocational training.[66] Many of Samuel Johnson's ideas became the resounding themes of the postwar dialogue on education. But decades earlier, even before he assumed the presidency of King's, Samuel Johnson had earned recognition among the small circle of colonial teacher-scholars whose educational views ran ahead of the times. Franklin had admired Johnson's observations on education, and had undertaken to publish them in a complete text. Soon after the famous Pennsylvanian announced his own proposal for an academy at Philadelphia in 1749, he had offered the head position there to the esteemed Connecticut churchman.[67]

The early King's had failed to match Samuel Johnson's most ambitious plans, but a spirit of experiment and a zeal for modern science had nevertheless distinguished the college from its less sophisticated rivals. The faculty had never numbered more than three, including the president. Samuel Johnson had instructed the youngest class in classics and English composition, and the seniors in moral philosophy. Professor Leonard Cutting, a classicist from Cambridge, had continued the sophomores and juniors in their Latin and Greek studies. Professor Daniel Treadwell, a Harvard graduate, had taught mathematics, astronomy, and physics to all but freshmen.[68] In bare outline, the course of study may have looked much the same as the curriculum at the College of New Jersey and other schools.[69] But there were real differences. The readiness to experiment had shaped every aspect of King's. Before the 1760s, only King's and its spiritual twin, the College of Philadelphia, had abandoned the tutorial system and established specialized professorships in each subject. The tutorial system had ill suited the progressive curriculum that Franklin and Johnson envisioned.[70] Johnson had reserved an important place for science in the King's curriculum, believing that an understanding of the laws of nature would strengthen rather than undermine his young students' appreciation of the wisdom, power and goodness of the Almighty.[71] At mid-century Harvard had claimed undisputed leadership in science, but King's had acted quickly to imitate its northern neighbor. In 1757, King's had asked Harvard's renowned scientist John Winthrop to recommend a capable teacher, and Winthrop had sent one of his prize students, Daniel Treadwell.[72] In contrast, neither the College of Rhode Island nor the College of New Jersey appointed a professor of science and mathematics until the 1770s. As one historian observed, King's "marked something of a new departure in higher education, in the degree to which the useful sciences found a significant place in the curriculum and an aura of urbanity surrounded the enterprise as a whole."[73] The readiness to innovate, the commitment to science, and the broad educational goals of President Samuel Johnson had made the early King's a forerunner in spirit to the Columbia College of William Samuel Johnson's day.

Religion at Columbia, like the college's course of study, reconciled the distinctive attitudes of the new republic with colonial practices that the trustees and president wanted to perpetuate. The proper place of religion in educational institutions excited extensive debate after the war. Some believed that spiritual instruction was essential and that every student should be thoroughly schooled in the doctrines of one denomination.[74] Others insisted that church doctrine stifled free intellect, that no college should promote a particular denomination, and that clergymen should not be teachers.[75] New York's legislators took a stand in 1787, when they freed Columbia from the university and restored the college's original charter. Columbia College, they stipulated, must abandon any charter provisions requiring that the president be an Episcopalian or that college prayers conform to the Episcopal liturgy.[76] The state's ruling prohibited a narrow denominationalism at Columbia, but left the major question to the judgment of the new board of trustees: would Columbia foster a religious community or provide only a strictly secular education?

The trustees chose to perpetuate the spiritual life of the college, while carefully allowing dissent so long as it stemmed from parental convictions rather than youthful rebelliousness. The college statutes, framed in 1788, provided that President Johnson would deliver morning and evening prayers in the college hall "in such a manner and after such a form as he . . . shall think proper; and all Students shall be obliged to attend, excepting such as are prohibited in writing, by their parents or guardians."[77] Three years later, when the trustees instituted Saturday classes, they explicitly exempted from attendence those students who kept the Saturday Sabbath, probably at the suggestion of the board's one Jew, Rabbi Seixas.[78] In 1791 a committee of three trustees, appointed to assess the progress of education at the college, proposed to abolish compulsory morning and evening prayers for the convenience of students who resided far from the college. The board considered the proposal and laid it aside. As the board's decision showed, the clerical and lay trustees were of one mind on the importance of religious training. Only three of the board's nine clergymen troubled to attend the meeting at which the proposal was considered and rejected. Neither Samuel Provoost nor Abraham Beach, the two Episcopal clergymen on the board, appeared to register their opinions.[79] The laymen who made up the board's majority instituted and preserved religion at Columbia.

Religion at Columbia manifested a cosmopolitan, liberal attitude that distinguished the college from its rivals, Yale and the College of New Jersey. In addition to morning and evening prayers, Yale students attended weekly ecclesiastical lectures, Saturday evening lessons on Calvinist doctrine, and Sunday chapel services that lasted up to five or six hours. Yale's President Stiles aroused the fury of Episcopal parents when he prohibited their sons from regularly attending their own church on Sundays.[80] Both Yale and the College of New Jersey, a

Presbyterian school, maintained a narrow denominationalism after the war and continued to limit their governing boards to orthodox clergymen. This policy sparked a controversy in the New Jersey state legislature, which refused financial support to a college controlled solely by one denomination.[81] Even in Connecticut, where Congregationalism continued to enjoy the privileges of an established church, the exclusively clerical control of Yale excited opposition and deprived the college of state funds until 1791, when the college corporation acquiesced in the seating of several state officials on its board.[82]

Even at early King's, an attitude of tolerance and catholicity had prevailed, distingushing the college from its Connecticut rival. When Samuel Johnson announced the opening of the college in 1754, he had wanted it "to be understood that as to religion, there is no intention to impose on the scholars the tenets of any particular sect of Christians; but to impress on their tender minds, the great principles of Christianity and morality in which true Christians of each denomination are generally agreed. . . . Everyone is left to judge fully for himself, and to be required only to attend constantly at such places of worship on the Lord's day, as their parents or guardians shall think fit to order or permit."[83] Seniors at early King's had studied Samuel Johnson's *Elementa Philosophica*, which presented such a universal view of Christian principles that Benjamin Franklin had proposed it as a suitable text for the study of moral philosophy at the Academy of Philadelphia.[84] King's had owed its reputation for illiberal sectarianism more to the Triumvirate's noisy press campaign than to Samuel Johnson's actual policies as president, for Anglicanism had not dominated the daily life of the school.

The Columbia trustees, who jealously guarded their authority over almost all college matters, allowed William Samuel Johnson complete latitude in the form and conduct of school prayers.[85] No contemporary accounts of President Johnson as college chaplain have survived, but his views on the spiritual training of the young can be drawn from other sources. As Samuel Johnson had done a half century earlier, William Samuel Johnson offered stern parental advice to his own sons, even when they were adults and fathers themselves. "Give me leave to remind you, as I have your Brother, of your too long neglect of joining in full communion in the Church of Christ. It is a positive Command of our Lord 'Do this in remembrance of me'

& how we can neglect it without great danger I know not." [86] In 1788, Johnson and a number of other Episcopal laymen concerted to establish the Episcopal Academy in Connecticut, designed to rival Yale, where Stiles forbade Episcopal students from worshipping in their own faith. The religious regulations agreed to by Johnson and his collaborators copied the rules at old King's College. Pupils would be free to worship in the church of their parents on the Sabbath, and all students would attend the academy's morning and evening prayers, which would conform to the Episcopal liturgy.[87] At Columbia, William Samuel Johnson undoubtedly adhered to the Episcopal liturgy when he conducted daily prayers in the college hall, but his message to the students stressed broad Christian principles. Addressing the students at commencement one year, he charged: "Your first great duties, you are sensible, are those you owe to Heaven, to your Creator and Redeemer. . . . He best serves his Maker, who does most good to his country and to mankind."[88] When Samuel Johnson retired from King's in 1763, he had admonished the college governors that, in order "to give your children a truly Christian education," the president of the college "should always be not only a serious Christian, but a clergyman, a divine as well as a philosopher."[89] It was fifty years since William Samuel Johnson had renounced the ministry, but his convictions on the importance of religious discipline, the beauty of the Episcopal ceremony, and the universality of the Christian message matched in spirit his father's ideal of a college president.

The Columbia trustees' vision of a modern university included even more than an expansive, liberal arts curriculum, and in 1793, two years after the New York State legislature had relieved the college from financial stringency, the trustees appointed a professor of law, James Kent.[90] The trustee's decision reflected the temper of the times. All over the new republic, colleges were laying plans for schools of law.[91] Educators believed that instruction in America's Constitution, laws, and courts would produce good citizens and capable leaders. In his first lecture at Columbia, Kent announced that "the people of this country are under singular obligations, from the nature of their government, to place the study of law at least on a level with the pursuits of classical learning. . . . We shall by this means . . . imbibe the principles of republican government from pure foundations; and prevent any improper impressions being re-

ceived from the artificial distinctions, the oppressive establishments or the wild innovations which at present distinguish the
Trans Atlantic World."[92] The city's most accomplished lawyers, including several who sat on the Columbia Board of Trustees, applauded the undertaking because they were eager to see
formal education supplant, or at least supplement, apprenticeship training.[93]

As in most college matters, William Samuel Johnson's
part in the appointment of a law professor was small. Kent received the Columbia appointment as a political reward. As an
attorney and politician in Poughkeepsie, New York, Kent had
ardently supported the Federalist cause, and his efforts had won
the notice of powerful figures in the state, including Alexander
Hamilton, one of the Columbia trustees, and John Jay, Chief
Justice of the United States and a New York regent.[94] Despite
Johnson's small role, he must have watched the beginnings of
a law school with interest and enthusiasm. A half-century earlier, he had introduced professional standards of legal practice
in Connecticut. Later he had closely guided the legal preparation of his own two sons, who were then building promising
careers in Connecticut on their father's practice there.[95] Like the
leading New York attorneys, he was concerned that the profession suffered undeserved public resentment and distrust,[96] and
he undoubtedly hoped that educating lawyers would elevate the
profession in the public eye. Finally, Johnson agreed with
Kent that a sound understanding of the government and laws
of the new republic would produce good citizens, capable leaders, and enduring liberty. "Study carefully the fundamental
principles of civil government, especially Republican government," Johnson urged the students. "Make yourselves well acquainted with the true nature of civil liberty, which fond as we
all justly are of it, too many seem to be unacquainted with."[97]

Kent's lectures at Columbia ranged far beyond legal practice and local law, and exceeded in scope and theoretical sophistication what all but the most exceptional young men could
have obtained in apprenticeship and private study. "This is
not the proper place," he told his students when the course began, "to prescribe a system of rules for the mere mechanical
profession of our laws. The design of this institution, is undoubtedly of a more liberal kind." Kent then conducted his
pupils through "an examination of the nature and duties of
government in general, and a brief historical review of the sev-

eral forms of government which have hitherto appeared in the world." Next came a "systematic view of the Constitution and Laws of the National Government," and finally a discussion of the state constitutions and the laws of New York.[98] A spirit of excitement over the formation of the national government and the legal system pervaded Kent's lectures. In 1836, looking back on the nation's early years, he recalled, "Every thing in the law seemed, at that day, to be new. We had no domestic precedents to guide us."[99] Yet Kent's endeavors failed. In his third year at Columbia, no students appeared for his course, and in 1798 he left the college to take a seat on the New York Supreme Court. The trustees allowed the chair to remain vacant.[100] Kent's lectures were too professional to interest undergraduates who did not intend to be lawyers, and too formalized to lure apprentices from law office study. Contrary to the hopes of educators and the vision of the most learned attorneys, the legal profession was not ready to replace apprenticeship with classroom training.[101]

In 1792 the Columbia trustees engaged seven physicians to teach a complete course of medicine at the college. The new undertaking grew out of the same optimism and professional consciousness that inspired the appointment of a law professor. The city's leading medical practitioners hoped that formal training would raise the standards and reputation of their profession. The regents had committed Columbia to medical education in 1784, when they first drafted a program for the college, but the commitment had been neglected for several years.[102] In 1791 the trustees voted to begin a course of medical lectures, and appointed a committee of four, including President Johnson, to draw up a plan.[103] The real architect of the undertaking was not Johnson but another member of the committee, Dr. Samuel Bard.[104] In January, 1792 the Medical Society of the State of New York, chiefly a city organization, offered the assistance of seven of its own doctors to teach at the college, without salary, for the small fees paid by each student to his teacher.[105] The Society, which viewed itself as the chief agent for organizing and regulating the profession, was eager to see formal education supplant apprenticeship training. The Society had little difficulty persuading the college trustees to accept the offer. Dr. John Bard, the Society's president, could rely on the support of an influential trustee, his son Samuel Bard.[106]

Everywhere there were signs of promise that the medical

school would win great support. In 1791, the city's first hospital opened, a happy event for the school's founders, who believed that clinical instruction was essential.[107] The following year, the Medical Society scored a major victory when New York City established an examining board to license all new practitioners. The 1792 law set precise apprenticeship requirements for the candidates, but exempted from apprenticeship training anyone who had earned a degree at an American medical college.[108] Finally, the young republic's spirit of independence, in culture and education as well as government, boded well for the Columbia undertaking. Before the Revolution, America's most talented and ambitious doctors had sought formal medical training at several renowned universities in Europe. But during the war, the exodus to Europe had slowed to a trickle, and the constant exchange of ideas between colonial doctors and their old world mentors had subsided.[109] Dr. Benjamin Waterhouse, studying at Leyden 1780, captured the new spirit when he wrote, "I am in hopes that my countrymen will in time be convinced that it is not so necessary for a man to come to Europe to learn to cure diseases of his next door neighbor as they imagine."[110]

The postwar enthusiasm for formal medical training vanished as quickly as it had appeared. After just five years, Columbia's medical course suffered a drastic decline in enrollment.[111] Few young men saw any advantages in expensive, rigorous schooling when apprenticeship still guaranteed them the title and fees of a doctor.[112] Moreover, the failure of the regents to supply financial support for the Columbia undertaking created discontent among the medical faculty, who repeatedly complained that the pupils' fees provided an inadequate living so long as the enrollment remained so small.[113]

American everywhere had voiced an enthusiastic commitment to education after the war. As the century ended their commitment proved illusory. Educators continued to remind the public that a free, prosperous nation required a learned citizenry. But from Samuel Latham Mitchill, a Columbia trustee who sat in the state legislature, came the dismal news in 1798 that the lawmakers and public had turned a deaf ear to the college. No funds, Mitchill reported, would be provided to complete the college's building project or supply salaries for the medical department.[114] A more damaging blow came in 1799, when the state discontinued the annual subsidy that had enabled

Columbia to expand its curriculum and engage an impressive faculty. The state's action reflected no animus toward Columbia. Educational institutions of every kind in New York suffered a similar fate. Just one year later, the lawmakers, who were pressured by angry taxpayers, discontinued the state-wide subsidy to public primary schools that had been enacted in 1795.[115] New York was not unique. New Englanders hastened to restore and even improve their colonial system of publicly supported primary education, but everywhere else postwar schooling languished even below colonial standards.[116]

The withdrawal of state support left Columbia in dire circumstances. The trustees had no choice but to reduce the faculty. By March 1799, only President Johnson and two other teachers, the professor of Latin and Greek and the professor of mathematics, natural philosophy, and astronomy, remained. French and Hebrew were discontinued. The professor of Latin and Greek was deprived of his additional salary as teacher of ancient history. Science suffered drastically when the praiseworthy course on natural history and chemistry was reduced to a four-month term. Plans to revive legal instruction and replace Judge Kent were laid aside.[117] The progress of the past decade, the ambitious vision of the trustees, and the distinctive advantages of a Columbia education lay in ruins. Soon the college would lose its president too.

For William Samuel Johnson, the presidency had become increasingly arduous. In 1787, he had accepted the post as an alternative to complete retirement. Over the next thirteen years, the chronic maladies of old age had worsened. Gout crippled his legs, deafness often shrouded him in silence, and palsy so afflicted his hands that he could write only with great difficulty. Loneliness increased his trials in 1796, when his wife Ann died.[118] Yet his duties were ever increasing. After the trustees pared the faculty to accommodate the college's financial straits, the aging president resumed his lectures on belles lettres, rhetoric, and logic, and agreed to teach moral philosophy as well.[119] Since December, illness had totally disabled him, and in the spring he had retreated to Stratford, convinced that death was imminent.[120] But nineteen years of life, even a second marriage, lay ahead.

Memories of both failure and success must have filled Johnson's mind as he recalled his years at Columbia. The most ambitious undertakings—the medical department, the professorship of law, the expansive liberal arts curriculum—owed little to Johnson. The trustees had launched the college before Johnson assumed his position, and they had continued to chart its course after his arrival. Yet Johnson's political prominence and moderate religious demeanor had undoubtedly contributed to its success. The college had failed to lure adequate funds from the state legislature or to rival the soaring enrollments at Yale and Harvard, but it had succeeded in attracting nearly double the number of liberal arts students that King's had counted under the presidency of the intemperate Tory Anglican, Myles Cooper.[121] As a teacher, religious disciplinarian, and figure of leadership, Johnson had impressed his personality on the daily life of the college. Johnson realized that academic ritual would give the new college community greater solidarity and elevate it in the public eye. In his first year, he had persuaded the faculty to wear academic gowns, a custom forgotten during the war. The students had apparently applauded his action, for at about the same time they had petitioned the trustees for permission to wear academic robes too, as a "very decent and becoming badge of distinction," noting in their petition that "it is the uniform practice of all the seminaries in Europe, and also of some in the United States, for the young men in the different Classes to be distinguished in their dress from the rest of their fellow citizens by wearing Gowns."[122]

A college as small as Columbia took on the identity of its president, at least in the public's mind. Often a boy had arrived for his freshmen year with a letter of introduction from his parents, who explicitly entrusted their son's welfare and spiritual guidance to President Johnson's oversight. Senators Ralph Izard and Edward Rutledge of South Carolina, who remembered Johnson as their colleague in the national government, had sent their sons northward to study under the aged statesman's watchful eye. Rutledge had appealed to Johnson to "take under your immediate protection a youth in a strange country, and point out to him the road to happiness through the paths of virtue and wisdom." Senator Izard had implored Johnson to watch over the young Izard boy "as a part of your own Family." "My Son informs me," the worried Senator wrote, "that . . . the Students are allowed to dispose of their time as they please in the Evenings . . . placing them in a very critical situation, as the Evening Hours of a young Man, when left entirely to his own discretion, are not those which are likely to be spent to the greatest advantage."[123]

A bond of affection, it seems, had united Johnson and his charges. At most American colleges the postwar years had brought student rebellion. The presidents of Yale, Harvard, and the College of New Jersey had complained that their pupils, infected with the spirit of independence and the wild, atheistic doctrines of the French Revolution, mocked authority, spurned religious discipline, and disregarded college regulations as "slavish impositions."[124] But under Johnson's tenure, the students had shown little impatience with restraint. Harmony had prevailed also between Johnson and the trustees. The liberal, nonsectarian spirit that had characterized Johnson's overseeing of the college's religious life must have dispelled the initial doubts of some of the trustees. Their request in 1799 that Johnson teach moral philosophy had stemmed from financial necessity, but it had also symbolized their confidence in their Episcopal president. The trustees expressed their feelings in their reply to Johnson's resignation: "Though their connection with you as President of the Institution intrusted to their care will now cease, their gratitude for past services, respect for your character, and affection for your person never will."[125]

William Samuel Johnson, attributed to John Wesley Jarvis (1814)
Columbiana, Columbia University

Chapter Sixteen

The Final Years

Since Ann's death in 1796, Johnson had lived alone at the college, but in 1800 he returned to his Stratford home, where his eldest son Samuel William now resided with his wife and children. Four years earlier, Samuel William's first son had been born, and at that time the proud father had written to Johnson in New York, "We have already determined to call him Wm Samuel, and it will be our persevering study to impress him with a knowledge of the virtues and [graces] of his grandfather, and teach him unremittingly to strive to imitate the character which is set before him." The aged Johnson would hear his young grandson's lessons before school, and as the Johnson family grew, so did the affection of the grandfather for his grandchildren. "These dear Children are so near to me," he confessed, "that I cannot command my feelings."[1]

Samuel William Johnson had long worried that retirement would bring "dull moments" for his father, and in 1801 he urged him to remarry. On December 8, William Samuel Johnson set out for Kent, Connecticut, and after a full day's journey reached his destination. The next morning he "executed [a] contract of marriage to Mrs. Beach," the widow of Ann Beach Johnson's brother Abel. On the tenth, Johnson and Mary Beach began their trip home to Stratford, lodging that night at the home of Ashbel Baldwin, the Episcopal minister at Newton. The next morning, Baldwin accompanied the couple to Stratford, and at six o'clock performed the marriage ceremony at Johnson's home.[2]

Family love and marital companionship brought joy to Johnson during the perhaps difficult transition from active life to retirement. He had other reasons for gladness too. At the turn of the century, the United States was at peace with Great Britain, the Episcopal clergy enjoyed the guidance of resident bishops after nearly a century of struggle, and the Constitution was surviving even the bitter discord between Hamiltonian Federalists and Jeffersonian Republicans.

In the two years following Johnson's resignation from the Senate, the United States had made no progress toward rapprochement with Great Britain. In 1793, the violent course of the French Revolution and France's declaration of war against Great Britain divided American opinion, sharpening the cleavage between the Federalists and the followers of Jefferson and Madison. A British Order in Council of November 6, 1793, instructed naval commanders to intercept all trade with the French colonies. The capture and condemnation of American vessels by the British navy raised passions to fever pitch in Congress. On April 15, the House passed a bill to prohibit commercial intercourse with the British, but before the Senate could concur, the Hamiltonians hastened to avert a break with Great Britain. Led by Senators Cabot and Strong of Massachusetts, King of New York, and Ellsworth of Connecticut, the Senate rejected the nonintercourse bill and approved the appointment of John Jay as envoy to Great Britain. Seven months later, on November 19, 1794, Jay concluded a treaty with the British. Throughout 1795 Jay's treaty occasioned a stormy contest between the Federalists and their anti-British opponents.[3] Johnson, who deplored the horrors of the French Revolution and longed for a stable Anglo-American peace, exclaimed that August that "if so great a body of ignorance as has been produced against the Treaty should be *in constant requisition* against every other act of Government, we should soon have no Government or Liberty left. . . . those who run after the cry of 'liberty' and 'constitution,' without knowing what either means . . . [are] at the same instant on the direct train to . . . destroy both."[4]

One incident in 1795 reveals how uncomfortable the former loyalist felt during this rancorous national debate over the treaty. In November, Jeremy Belknap, the Secretary of the Massachusetts Historical Society, informed Johnson that through the generosity of Jonathan Trumbull, Jr., the Society had acquired and intended to publish the late Governor Trumbull's correspondence, including the letters Johnson had written to the Governor while serving as Connecticut's agent in London. Belknap's intentions infuriated Johnson, who replied in the harshest terms that publishing his letters would be "an extreme impropriety." To the younger Trumbull, Johnson pleaded that "I alone can distinguish word and fair purpose. . . . if they are published I shall be under the disagreeable necessity of stating the whole matter to the publick in my own defense." Belknap found Johnson's objections incomprehensible. "I have read [the letters] repeatedly with delight," the Secretary told the Governor's son, "and have gained a better Idea of the political system, than from all the Books published during that period. . . . The Publication would do him honor; as he appears in them to have been a firm friend to the Liberties of his Country, and a faithful vigilant discerning Agent; detecting the artifices, evasions & Blunders of the British Court; and giving the best information, advice & caution to his Employers." But Johnson, deeply troubled by the revival of Anglo-American tensions and no doubt fearful that the untimely disclosure of the letters would reawaken the distrust of his patriot countrymen, remained adamant that the correspondence be kept from public view.[5]

The implementation of the Jay Treaty in 1796 introduced a new era of cordial relations between America and Great Britain. On March 4, 1800, Thomas Jefferson became President of the United States, but the transition from Federalist to Republican leadership occasioned neither a violent upheaval in domestic politics nor a sudden reversal in diplomacy. The crippling effects of old age kept Johnson from recording his thoughts on the Republican accession, but he must have been gladdened by the prudent demeanor of the new President and the responsible behavior of the defeated Federalists. Johnson's former colleague in the Senate, Oliver Ellsworth, observed that Jefferson "dare not run the ship aground, nor essentially deviate from that course which has hitherto rendered her voyage so prosperous. His party *also* must support the government while he administers it; and if others are consistent and do the same, the government may even be consolidated and acquire new confidence."[6]

As the century ended and Johnson retreated to Stratford, he looked with satisfaction upon another accomplishment of the new nation, the establishment of an American episcopate. The quest for a colonial bishop had originated at Samuel Johnson's tiny Stratford mission early in the century, and after the Revolution the Connecticut missionaries once again took the lead. Despite the hardships of war, fourteen missionaries remained in 1783, eager and well prepared to resume their campaign.[7] Early that year, ten of them assembled at Woodbury for the first Connecticut convention held since the Revolution. The unresponsiveness of British church leaders and statesmen to the needs of the colonial Episcopal church had compelled the missionaries to adopt an independent spirit and cohesive organization before the war that proved vital to their cause once their ties to the SPG and the mother country were severed. At the Woodbury meeting, they elected Samuel Seabury to journey to England for consecration as the first Bishop of Connecticut.[8].

In England, Seabury encountered the same opposition that had thwarted the churchmen's appeals for decades. The North-Fox ministry, fearful of offending the new republic, refused to sanction Seabury's consecration while he lacked the official recognition of the Connecticut government.[9] The Connecticut churchmen, upon receiving word of Seabury's distress, approached the Connecticut legislature. The lawmakers informally consented to Seabury's mission but advised against any application for formal permission, apprehending that such a request might arouse jealousy and suspicion. Let the bishop-elect's authority, they counseled, rest on the recent act of the legislature, which allows all denominations the privilege of erecting churches within the state. Johnson agreed that the state's new religious laws constituted an unambiguous mandate for the Episcopal Church to organize, but the North-Fox ministry did not.[10] Seabury turned to the Episcopal Church of Scotland for assistance rather than accept defeat. On November 14, 1784 he was consecrated at Aberdeen by three Scottish bishops.[11]

Two years later William White of Philadelphia and Samuel Provoost of New York journeyed to England on a similar mission. Carrying the explicit consent of their state governments and counting the support of John Adams, minister to the Court of St. James, White and Provoost met success where Seabury had not. On February 4, 1787, at Lambeth Palace four English bishops performed the sacred rite.[12] After nearly a century of unrelenting struggle, the American churchmen now had three resident bishops—Seabury, White, and Provoost— and the clergy of New York and the states southward were laboring to establish a united ecclesiastical government for the Episcopal churches of the new republic. But on the eve of success, two obstacles imperiled the union.

Between 1784 and 1789 the churchmen outside of New England gathered annually to discuss William White's proposal for an ecclesiastical constitution. Seabury and his Connecticut colleagues refused to participate. White's design departed radically from the model of the Church of England by inviting lay participation in church government and circumscribing the traditional powers of bishops. Samuel Johnson would have regarded the plan as nothing less than heresy, and the corps of missionaries who had been trained on his principles were of the same mind. "Men for whom episcopacy and the concept of the apostolic succession had been the rationale of membership in the Church of England," Seabury's biographer explains, "were opposing men unaccustomed to giving their church's government much thought. When the crisis of the Revolution forced a consideration of such questions, this latter group had turned naturally to the principles of polity which they vigorously championed in the area of civil government. The deadlock . . . was no casual phenomenon, but rather the result of deeply rooted contrasts."[13]

Widespread opposition to Seabury exacerbated the conflict. His outspoken protests against the American Revolution had not been forgotten, and patriot churchmen were loath to recognize the former loyalist as a leader of their church. Richard Henry Lee of Virginia considered the issue "sufficient to disturb the Moderate Councils of any Whig Assembly in the world." The loudest objections were heard from the stronghold of loyalism, New York City. At the close of the war, James Duane and a number of other Anglican patriots had seized control of Trinity Church and, with the aid of the state's lawmakers, had ousted loyalist Benjamin Moore and installed Samuel Provoost as rector. Duane was as determined to erase the taint of loyalism from the Episcopal Church as from King's College. He and Provoost led the resistance against recognizing Seabury's consecration.[14]

In August 1788, Jeremiah Leaming, minister of Christ Church in Stratford, appealed to Johnson for help. Leaming hoped that a reconciliation between the three bishops would permit a loose union of the churches until the difficult question of ecclesiastical government could be resolved. Leaming proposed that the three bishops join in consecrating a fourth, the Bishop-elect of Virginia. Leaming urged Johnson to use his influence with the Virginia delegates in Congress. Johnson agreed to approach the delegates, but whatever arguments he tried proved fruitless, and in 1788 the churches remained divided.[15] One Massachusetts minister judged the situation hopeless, because "Oil & Vinegar cannot unite, Whigs & Tories cannot act cordially together, one have a democratical Constitution to act by, the other a monarchical. Connecticut preserves the Discipline of the primitive Church, New York & Philadelphia have fashioned theirs upon the principles of Republicanism."[16]

On July 29, 1789, the churchmen from south of New England assembled at Philadelphia for their third general convention. The absence of Duane and Provoost, the latter confined by illness, boded well for ecclesiastical union. Days later, the convention resolved to recognize Seabury's title, invited the Connecticut bishop and delegates from the New England churches to come to Philadelphia, and proposed that White, Provoost, and Seabury join in consecrating another American bishop. A month before the convention opened, Tench Coxe, a Philadelphia lawyer and lay delegate who longed for a conciliation, had appealed to Johnson to reason with the contending parties. In August, Coxe wrote Johnson again, asking him to assure Seabury of the good intentions of White and the convention. That autumn, the Connecticut bishop and delegates from the New England churches took their places at the Philadelphia convention, and soon the disputed points over the authority of bishops and the extent of lay participation were compromised. The union was completed three years later, when Samuel Provoost joined Seabury, White, and the Bishop of Virginia, James Madison, in the first American consecration, Thomas John Claggett as Bishop of Maryland.[17]

Johnson rejoiced at the establishment of a united American episcopate, but even more pleasing was the new "liberality and candour" that the Congregational establishment showed toward Connecticut Anglicans.[18] The Connecticut missionaries also celebrated the new harmony. Rev. John Tyler of Norwich happily reported that "we of the episcopal Church in Connecticut, are now treated by the Legislature, and by the People at large, with more Civility, Equality, and Equity than we ever were before, since the Church of England had an Existence here." Tyler explained that "Formerly the Dissenters here, were very jealous of the Missionaries and of the Professors of the Church of England; Considering us as Favorites of the British Court;

and seemed to apprehend Something to fear from us, perhaps That our Religion would be exalted, and theirs degraded by the Civil Arm. But now that Jealousy is at an end."[19] That New Englanders could finally put aside their century-old fear of crown–church conspiracy accounted for part of the change, but the spirit of religious liberty was also an outgrowth of America's campaign for civil liberty. Although the Connecticut lawmakers had not completely eliminated the privileged position of the Congregational church, they had enacted measures of relief for dissenters of every persuasion.[20] Johnson applauded the new toleration and looked forward to a time when all the states would abide by the wishes of Congress "who evidently intend that there should be no distinction or preference between any Denominations of Christians but that all should stand upon an equal footing in point of legal protection."[21]

Despite the great change, traces of mutual hostility persisted, and as always, the blame lay on both sides. The zealous Seabury, like the late Samuel Johnson, refused to respect the Congregational clergy as true ministers because they had not been ordained by a bishop. The affront enraged Ezra Stiles, who protested that Seabury's "assumed Title" as Bishop of Connecticut implied "there are no other Bps. in Connect. whereas there are 160 Bps. already in this State of the Congreg[ational] . . . Denomination." No doubt at Stiles's suggestion, the General Association of Congregational Clergy urged each of its members to assume the title "bishop of Connecticut." Nothing irritated Seabury more than the General Assembly's annual donation to Yale College, where Stiles forbade his Episcopal students to worship regularly at Trinity Church. When Johnson and a number of other Episcopal laymen concerted with Seabury to erect a rival school, the Assembly refused to grant a college charter, and the Episcopal Academy, lacking collegiate status, failed in its original purpose.[22]

In 1810, after ten quiet years at Stratford, Johnson reached his eighty-third year. No one could have been more surprised than the senior statesman himself, who had predicted imminent death when he left New York a decade earlier. He felt "some days better & others not quite so well." Although afflicted by deafness and the paralysis of his hands, he still had years of life ahead, full of happy moments and sad ones.[23]

On January 9, 1812, the Superior Court at Fairfield honored Johnson as "the brightest ornament of the Connecticut Bar."[24]

Although he—together with the other leading attorneys of his generation, Jared Ingersoll and Eliphalet Dyer—had introduced new professional standards of legal practice in Connecticut, his part in the creation of the national government deserved greater notice than his career as a lawyer. But this ceremony at the Superior Court was the only formal recognition Johnson would receive during his lifetime. The framers of the Constitution would be hailed as the nation's "founding fathers" only long after their deaths. In the early years of the new republic, political passions were too high and the framers were too divided among themselves to be revered as a group.[25] At no time was this more true than in 1812.

In that year, the United States declared war against Great Britain. The war brought disgrace to the Federalist opposition and its stronghold, New England, and probably distressed Johnson more than any other public event of his later life. The resumption of the Napoleonic Wars in 1803 led Great Britain to struggle for complete mastery of the seas, whatever the cost to the rights of neutral nations or to American lives. United States ports were blockaded, American seamen were impressed in unprecedented numbers, and American ships were seized en route to Europe and the French and Spanish colonies. President Jefferson and his successor, James Madison, tried every means of commercial suasion and diplomacy to avoid open hostilities, but Great Britain remained intransigent, and on June 18, Madison called for a declaration of war.[26] New Englanders railed against the Jeffersonians as Bonapartists, continued to trade with Great Britain, and refused to call out their militia. Federalist politicians demanded constitutional restraints on the federal government's commerce and war powers, and the extremists even talked of a New England secession. The Federalism of Johnson's day—nationalist, energetic, and creative—had turned into an ineffective opposition impelled by sectional jealousies, obstructionist rather than creative, and at war's end, tainted by treason.[27]

But there were other changes that no doubt gladdened the aged Johnson. The second decade of the century brought a fuller realization of the plan for an American Episcopal Church. A new corps of bishops, possessing the zeal and commitment that had distinguished Seabury from the other early spiritual leaders, provided the aggressive energy needed to launch the Church on an era of astonishing growth. At the same time, the religious complexion of New England was changing rapidly. The influx of Baptists, Methodists, and Unitarians—politically aggressive and determined to sever all ties between church and state—gave rise to a powerful movement for toleration. In 1818, Connecticut adopted its first written state constitution, and eliminated forever the privileged position of the Congregational Church.[28]

Nothing symbolized more vividly Johnson's place in an era than the laying aside of the Connecticut charter for a new frame of government. The major figures in Connecticut's transition from colony to state—Jonathan Trumbull, Eliphalet Dyer, Jared Ingersoll, Roger Sherman, and Oliver Ellsworth—had all died, leaving only Johnson to witness the event.[29] In old age we look backward rather than forward, and for Johnson no recollection brought greater pleasure than that of his years as Connecticut's agent in London. "In the summer of 1817," one of Johnson's friends recorded, "I visited Stratford, and never shall forget the delightful hours I passed in his company. . . . He carried me back to his residence in England, and to the company of Johnson, of Mansfield, and of Chatham. The theme made him eloquent."[30]

On Sunday, November 14, 1819, shortly after his ninety-second birthday, Johnson died quietly at his Stratford home.[31] From his earliest years as the son of a zealous Anglican missionary in a Puritan society, he had learned to respect men whose views differed from his own and even to love them. Toward the close of his life, when the Connecticut churchmen were disputing over the election of the state's next bishop, Johnson could smile and suggest that "they had better elect his friend Dr. Dwight," who was the rector of Yale College.[32] Johnson's mild temper, liberal understanding, and deep attachment to America—together with a large measure of political astuteness—had enabled him to serve his colony well, to dissent from Revolution and yet emerge from the struggle unembittered, unharmed, and ready to lead his countrymen in the quest for national unity. He was at once a devout churchman and a thorough New Englander, a loyalist and a true patriot.

Notes

Chapter 1: Fathers and Sons

[1]Samuel Johnson, *A Short Catechism for Young Children* (New York, 1765), rpt. in Herbert and Carol Schneider, eds., *Samuel Johnson*, 3:590.

[2]A brief genealogical history of the Johnson family can be found in Cutter, ed., *Genealogical and Family History of the State of Connecticut*, p. 202. Bothell presents a more extensive history in "Cloak and Gown," pp. 1-25.

[3]Ellis, *New England Mind in Transition*, pp. 1-13.

[4]Ibid., p. 1.

[5]For an excellent description of the Connecticut socio-religious order in the early eighteenth century, see Bushman, *From Puritan to Yankee*, ch. 1.

[6]Bothell, "Cloak and Gown," p. 24.

[7]Samuel Johnson, "Memoirs of the Life of the Rev. Dr. Johnson, and Several Things relating to the State Both of Religion and Learning in his Times," *Samuel Johnson*, 1:3, 10.

[8]*Ibid.*, p. 7; Morgan, *Gentle Puritan*, pp. 48-49.

[9]Samuel Johnson, "Memoirs," *Samuel Johnson*, 1:6, 7. For descriptions of the pre-Enlightenment scientific curriculum at Yale: Morgan; *Gentle Puritan*, p. 48; Tucker, *Puritan Protagonist*, pp. 81-82.

[10]Miller, *New England Mind: From Colony to Province*, pp. 438-39; Morgan, *Gentle Puritan*, pp. 53-56.

[11]An excellent description of Johnson's theological position, as it grew out of his Puritan background and his exposure to the Enlightenment thinkers can be found in Gerardi, "The American Doctor Johnson," ch. 3. Gerardi terms Johnson's philosophy "neosacramental Arminianism," denoting a combination of high-church spirituality and a rationalist challenge to orthodox Calvinism. "Sacramentalism," says Gerardi, "set Johnson apart from the neo-Calvinist revivalist tradition and the rationalism and naturalism of the Enlightenment." See also Bothell, "Cloak and Gown," pp. 126, 295; Kinlock, "Anglican Clergy," p. 205.

[12]Samuel Johnson, "Memoirs," *Samuel Johnson*, 1:13; Samuel Johnson, "Liber Dierum," *ibid.*, 1:61-63; Gerardi, "American Doctor Johnson," ch. 3; Ellis, *New England Mind in Transition*, pp. 71-73, 80; Kinlock, "The Anglican Clergy," p. 257.

[13]Samuel Johnson, "Memoirs," *Samuel Johnson*, 1:12; Samuel Johnson to Thomas Clap, February 5, 1754, *ibid.*, 1:179.

[14]The classic work on New England Puritanism in this period of disorder is Miller, *New England Mind: From Colony to Province*. See also Bushman, *From Puritan to Yankee*, chs. 10, 11; Gaustad, *Great Awakening*, ch. 1.

[15]Samuel Johnson, "Memoirs," *Samuel Johnson*, 1:10-12. Bothell, "Cloak and Gown," p. 124; Gerardi, "The American Doctor Johnson," chs. 3, 4; Ellis, *New England Mind in Transition*, p. 60.

[16]Samuel Johnson, "Memoirs," *Samuel Johnson*, 1:12.

[17]Samuel Johnson, "My Present Thoughts Concerning Episcopacy," December 20, 1719, *Samuel Johnson*, 3:3-8; Ellis, *New England Mind in Transition*, pp. 61, 75-77.

[18]*Public Records of the Colony of Connecticut*, 4:546, 5:50, 6:248, 401-2. The history of the Stratford Episcopal mission is discussed below.

[19]Dexter, *Biographical Sketches*, 1:118-20, 133-38; Shipton and Sibley, eds., *Biographical Sketches of Those Who Attended Harvard College*, 5:45-66, 191-204; Samuel Johnson, "Memoirs," *Samuel Johnson*, 1:14.

[20]Samuel Johnson, "Liber Dierum," *Samuel Johnson*, 1:62-63. Almost every history of New England contains at least a brief description of the confrontation at Yale, e.g.: Miller, *New England Mind*, p. 471; Morgan, *Gentle Puritan*, pp. 16-17.

[21]Cotton Mather to the Clergy of Connecticut, n.d., Hawks and Perry, eds., *Documentary History of the Protestant Episcopal Church*, 1:77; Joseph Moss to Cotton Mather, October 2, 1722, *ibid.*, 1:67.

[22]Warch, *School of the Prophets*, p. 114. Warch presents an extensive discussion of the confrontation and its aftermath.

[23]Samuel Johnson, "Memoirs," *Samuel Johnson*, 1:16-19; Ellis, *New England Mind in Transition*, pp. 82-88; Cross, *Anglican Episcopate*, pp. 34-35; Kinlock, "Anglican Clergy," p. 3.

[24]Samuel Johnson, "Memoirs," *Samuel Johnson*, 1:17; Ellis, *New England Mind in Transition*, p. 87.

[25]Beardsley, *Episcopal Church*, p. 50.

[26]Samuel Johnson, "Memoirs," *Samuel Johnson*, 1:47.

[27]Beardsley, *Episcopal Church*, p. 53; George Pigot to the Secretary, SPG, August 20, 1722, Hawks and Perry, eds., *Documentary History of the Protestant Episcopal Church*, 1:56.

[28]Wilcoxson, *History of Stratford*, p. 449.

[29]George Muirson to the Secretary, SPG, October 14, 1706, April 4, 1707, Hawks and Perry, eds., *Documentary History of the Protestant Episcopal Church*, 1:17, 23-24; Caleb Heathcote to the Secretary, SPG, October n.d., 1706, *ibid.*, 1:19; Beardsley, *Episcopal Church*, pp. 3-57; Orcutt, *History of the Old Town*, pp. 296-301.

[30]Heathcote told the SPG that Reed "was very inclinable to come over to the Church. . . . By reason of the good inclination he shews for the Church, he has undergone persecution by his people, who do all which is in their power to starve him." Caleb Heathcote to the Secretary, SPG, February 24, 1707, Hawks and Perry, eds., *Documentary History of the Protestant Episcopal Church*, 1:20-21. According to Orcutt, the Stratford parish was divided over the permanent settlement of Reed long before Muirson first appeared in the town. Orcutt, *History of the Old Town*, p. 296-99.

[31]Orcutt, *History of the Old Town*, pp. 296-301. Orcutt presents the basic facts. The interpretation is my own.

[32]The Churchwardens and Vestrymen of Stratford to the SPG, September 30, 1718, May 29, 1722, Hawks and Perry, eds., *Documentary History of the Protestant Episcopal Church*, 1:52-53, 55-56. For a brief biography of Pigot, see Kinlock, "Anglican Clergy," pp. 95-96. On Gold's settlement, see Orcutt, *History of the Old Town*, p. 301.

[33]Samuel Johnson to the SPG, January 18, 1722, Hawks and Perry, eds., *Documentary History of the Protestant Episcopal Church*, 1:61; George Pigot to the Secretary, SPG, January 13, 1724, *ibid.*, 1:86.

[34]The available evidence on the tax situation is confusing, but points to this interpretation. On the one hand, Orcutt maintains that "a close examination of the record of town acts between 1706 and 1730 reveals no vote in Stratford to release the

3

1. Fathers and Sons

supporters of the Episcopal church from paying taxes to the established church (*History of the Old Town*, p. 321). Wilcoxson agrees (*History of Stratford*, p. 453). On the other hand, if a compromise had been reached, the town magistrates would have been reluctant to enter it on the local records or even possibly to take an official town vote, because the agreement would have been contrary to Connecticut law. The fact that there is no record of any action taken after 1727 to comply with the new law of that year suggests that the Stratford Anglicans and Puritans had already reached an agreement. Other evidence reinforces this interpretation. From 1722 to 1727, Johnson complained to Bishop Gibson and the SPG about the taxation of his communicants, but after 1724, Johnson's complaints were against Fairfield and other nearby towns, not against Stratford. Also, in 1726, Governor Talcott wrote to the Bishop of London that "there is but one Church of England minister in this colony, and the Church with him have the same protection as the rest of our Churches and under no constraint to contribute to the support of any other minister." Richard Talcott to the Bishop of London, July 27, 1726, Hawks and Perry, eds., *Documentary History of the Protestant Episcopal Church*, 1:106. It was the Episcopalians of Fairfield, not Stratford, who approached the General Assembly in 1727 to amend the colony's tax law, although the Stratford communicants were greater in number and had long enjoyed the services of a resident missionary. Petition of the Churchwardens and Vestry of Fairfield to the Connecticut Legislature, May 15, 1727, *ibid.*, 1:124-25. If, as the evidence suggests, an accommodation was reached between the Stratford Anglicans and the town's orthodox majority, that accommodation most likely meant that the town collector demanded no taxes from the Anglicans, rather than collecting the customary amount and turning it over to Johnson. Johnson told the SPG that he had "no settled salary besides the honorable Society's bounty; only the poor people are as liberal in small amounts as can be expected of them." Samuel Johnson to the Secretary, SPG, September 20, 1727, *ibid.*, 1:118.

[35]Henry Caner to the Secretary, SPG, March 15, 1727, Hawks and Perry, eds., *Documentary History of the Protestant Episcopal Church*, 1:115. Perhaps the Anglican minorities in these towns were not large enough to create a serious discord that demanded resolution. Also, their reliance on Johnson's services did not meet traditional New England standards or the 1708 legal requirement that all worshippers be provided with a conveniently close, resident clergyman.

[36]Samuel Johnson to the Secretary, SPG, September 20, 1727, *ibid.*, 1:118; Bothell, "Cloak and Gown," pp. 156-57.

[37]Steiner, "New England Anglicanism: A Genteel Faith?" pp. 130-31. On Shelton, see Wilcoxson, *History of Stratford*, pp. 445, 449; Orcutt, *History of the Old Town*, p. 316; Beardsley, *Episcopal Church*, p. 55.

[38]Samuel Johnson, "Memoirs," *Samuel Johnson*, 1:21.

[39]Beardsley, *Episcopal Church*, p. 58; Wilcoxson, *History of Stratford*, pp. 450-52.

[40]Samuel Johnson to the Secretary, SPG, September 20, 1727, Hawks and Perry, eds., *Documentary History of the Protestant Episcopal Church*, 1:119.

[41]See notes 34 and 35 above.

[42]Samuel Johnson to the Bishop of London, June 23, 1724, November 4, 1725, Hawks and Perry, eds., *Documentary History of the Protestant Episcopal Church*, 1:95, 103-4; Samuel Johnson to the Secretary, SPG, June 11, 1724, September 20, 1727, *ibid.*, 1:101, 120.

[43]Samuel Johnson to the Secretary, SPG, January 10, 1724, *ibid.*, 1:109; Samuel Johnson to the Bishop of London, November 4, 1725, September 16, 1726, *ibid.*, 1:102, 116; Samuel Johnson to General Nicholson, May 27, 1724, *Samuel Johnson*, 3:218; Samuel Johnson to the Bishop of London, January 18, 1724, *Samuel Johnson*, 3:217-18.

[44]Sykes, From Sheldon to Secker, pp. 192, 206-8.

[45]Ibid., pp. 39-45, 67, 102; Sykes, Church and State, pp. 12, 27, 32, 45, 285, 315; Williams, The Whig Supremacy, p. 173; Bridenbaugh, Mitre and Sceptre:, pp. 35-41, 285, 287.

[46]Gerlach, "Champions of an American Episcopate," p. 393; Greene, "An Uneasy Connection," pp. 63-64.

[47]Sykes, From Sheldon to Secker, pp. 192-209.

[48]Samuel Johnson to the Bishop of London, November 4, 1725, Hawks and Perry, eds., Documentary History of the Protestant Episcopal Church, 1:104; Governor Talcott to the Bishop of London, July 27, 1726, ibid., 1: 106; Bothell, "Cloak and Gown," p. 250.

[49]George Muirson to the Secretary, SPG, October 2, 1706, April 4, 1707, Hawks and Perry, eds., Documentary History of the Protestant Episcopal Church, 1:18-19, 23-24; George Pigot to the Secretary, SPG, August 22, 1733, ibid., 1: 56-57.

[50]Samuel Johnson to the Secretary, SPG, September 20, 1727, ibid., 118; Samuel Johnson, "Memoirs," Samuel Johnson, 1:20. Evidence suggests that Johnson's marriage companion pleased his purse as well as his personality. There are no signs that Samuel Johnson's father was a man of extensive wealth, and any posthumous bequests were probably divided among Samuel and the three other Johnson children who survived to adulthood. Nor was Samuel Johnson's post at Stratford a lucrative one. The Society awarded him £200 per annum and his parishioners supplied an additional £50 per annum. Yet he was a wealthy man by Connecticut standards. In 1747, he would promise William Samuel Johnson £200 worth of land whenever his oldest son was ready to settle with a family, and the elder Johnson even suggested that the gift might be doubled in time. Samuel Johnson, "Memoirs," Samuel Johnson, 1:60; Samuel Johnson to the Secretary, SPG, June 7, 1738, ibid., 1:91; Samuel Johnson to William Samuel Johnson, July 7, 1747, ibid., 1:129.

[51]Samuel Johnson, "Memoirs," Samuel Johnson, 1:20. William Samuel Johnson was born October 7, 1727, his younger brother William ("Billy"), on March 9, 1731.

[52]Samuel Johnson, Elementa Philosophica (New York, 1752), rpt. in Samuel Johnson, 2:423-24.

[53]Kinlock, "Anglican Clergy," pp. 62-63. Caner was born to Episcopal parents.

[54]Samuel Johnson to the Bishop of London, April 2, 1728, Hawks and Perry, eds., Documentary History of the Protestant Episcopal Church, 1:145: Samuel Johnson to the Secretary, SPG, September 29, 1748, ibid., 1:145; Kinlock, "Anglican Clergy," p. 200.

[55]Kinlock, "Anglican Clergy," p. 178. Of the thirty-eight SPG missionaries who served Connecticut before the American Revolution, twenty-eight were Yale graduates, most of whom had renounced the Puritan faith of their families, and in at least ten cases, their ordinations as Congregational ministers.

[56]Samuel Johnson, "Liber Dierum," Samuel Johnson, 1:70.

[57]Groce, William Samuel Johnson, p. 11; Bothell, "Cloak and Gown," p. 240.

[58]Steiner, Samuel Seabury, p. 23. Steiner makes a similar conjecture regarding Samuel, Seabury, Sr., a New London, Connecticut missionary of the SPG.

[59]See note 56, above.

[60]Petition of the Churchwardens and Vestrymen of Fairfield to the Connecticut Legislature, May 15, 1727, Hawks and Perry, eds., Documentary History of the Protestant Episcopal Church, 1:124; Public Records, 7:107; Ellis, "Anglicans in Connecticut," p. 69.

[61]Churchwardens and Episcopal communicants of Wallingford to the Bishop of London, n.d., 1729, Hawks and Perry, eds., Documentary History of the Protestant Episcopal Church, 1:138-39; Churchwardens of Wallingford to the Secretary, SPG,

December 1, 1743, *ibid.*, 1:207; Clergy of Connecticut to the Secretary, SPG, March 28, 1744, *ibid.*, 1:205-6; Henry Caner to the Secretary, SPG, October 10, 1728, *ibid.*, 1:132-34; Minutes of the Society, read July 18, 1729, *ibid.*, 1:135; The Episcopal Clergy of Connecticut to the Secretary, SPG, November 15, 1738, *Samuel Johnson*, 1:96-97.

    [62]Unfortunately no one has studied the conventions of the Connecticut missionaries or the joint meetings of all the New England missionaries in sufficient detail. Ellis shows that Johnson organized meetings in Connecticut in 1734, 1740, 1742, and 1747. Steiner conjectures that the New England churchmen continued to meet annually after 1727, but he concedes that evidence is lacking for certain years. Ellis, "Anglicans in Connecticut," pp. 73-75; Steiner, *Samuel Seabury*, pp. 24-25, 376 n.90.

    [63]Episcopal Clergy of Connecticut to the Secretary, SPG, November 15, 1738, *Samuel Johnson*, 1:94; Samuel Johnson to the Secretary, SPG, November 3, 1738, *ibid.*, 3:224-26; Samuel Johnson to George Berkeley, May 14, 1739, *ibid.*, 1:98-99.

    [64]Samuel Johnson, *A Letter from a Minister of the Church of England to his Dissenting Parishioners . . .* (New York, 1933); *A Second Letter . . .* (Boston, 1734); *A Third Letter . . .* (Boston, 1737). The letters are reprinted in *Samuel Johnson*, *3:19-131*.

    [65]Samuel Johnson, *A Letter from a Minister of the Church of England . . .*, *Samuel Johnson*, 3:28.

    [66]*Ibid.*, 3:28, 30; Samuel Johnson,*A Second Letter . . .*, *Samuel Johnson*, 3:67-68, 73.

    [67]Bushman, *From Puritan to Yankee*, pp. 175-77.

    [68]Samuel Johnson, *A Second Letter . . . Samuel Johnson*, 3:41, 69.

    [69]Quoted in Bridenbaugh, *Mitre and Sceptre*, pp. 79-80.

    [70]Steiner, "Anglican Officeholding," pp. 370-71. Steiner argues that the accepted view of sustained hostility between a community's Anglican and orthodox churches ignores the time factor. Historians have compiled contemporary accounts of conflict and mutual suspicion in the New England towns, but, argues Steiner, these historians have neglected to locate these accounts within a geographical and temporal frame of reference. Because the introduction of the Church of England into the various towns spanned the entire century, one can easily compile an impressive picture of ongoing hostility based solely on accounts taken from towns in which the Episcopal Church was a newcomer. In contract, Steiner contends that in many towns, the initial discord gradually gave way to neighborly cooperation.

    [71]Wilcoxson, *History of Stratford*, p. 582; Orcutt, *History of the Old Town*, p. 323; Anonymous letter to the Bishop of London, October 30, 1727, Hawks and Perry, eds., *Documentary History of the Protestant Episcopal Church*, 1:121-23.

    [72]Samuel Johnson to the Secretary, SPG, June 11, 1724, September 20, 1727, November 20, 1729, Hawks and Perry, eds., *Documentary History of the Protestant Episcopal Church*, 1:101, 117, 137; Samuel Johnson to the Bishop of London, June 23, 1724, *ibid.*, 1:94; Samuel Johnson to the Secretary, SPG, November 3, 1738, *Samuel Johnson*, 3:223-24.

Chapter 2: From Pulpit to Bar

    [1]Dexter, *Biographical Sketches*, 1:756, 763.
    [2]Tucker, *Puritan Protagonist*, p. 74.
    [3]Dexter, *Biographical Sketches*, 1:756-68.
    [4]Tucker, *Puritan Protagonist*, pp. 81-82.
    [5]The best account of Thomas Clap's tenure at Yale is Tucker, *Puritan Protagonist*. On Clap's scientific attitudes, see pp. 83, 94-101.

[6]In 1742, Clap compiled *A Catalogue of the Library of Yale College in New Haven,* which was published the following year. The printed version carried an introduction by Samuel Johnson. For other evidence of the rector's friendship with the Stratford missionary, see Tucker, *Puritan Protagonist,* p. 97; William Samuel Johnson to Samuel Johnson, June 22, 1747, 1:123-24.

[7]Tucker, *Puritan Protagonist,* pp. 83-93, 101.

[8]*Ibid.,* p. 92. Under the tutelage of his fater, young William Samuel had studied Latin since age eight and Greek since age ten. Groce, *William Samuel Johnson,* p. 9.

[9]Tucker, *Puritan Protagonist,* pp. 72, 78-79, 164; Morgan, *The Gentle Puritan:,* pp. 30, 47-48.

[10]Tucker, *Puritan Protagonist,* pp. 72, 78-79, 150-66. According to Edmund Morgan, the combination of Enlightenment science and the ethics, logic and philosophy that were still based on older, theologically orientated systems,made the curriculum of the Clap era a hodgepodge of incompatible ideas. The students, writes Morgan, "were expected to assimilate Aristotelian rhetoric, Ramist theology, Berkeleyan metaphysics, and diluted Newtonian physics. They were all incompatible in varying degrees and on different levels. . . . In 1746 it would have required real genius merely to ascertain the precise points of conflict among the various parts of the Yale curriculum." Morgan, *Gentle Puritan,* pp. 55-56.

[11]Tucker, *Puritan Protagonist,* pp. 42-43, 166.

[12]*Ibid.,* p. 65; Dexter, *Biographical Sketches,* 1:756, 762, 769; Kinlock, "Anglican Clergy," p. 184.

[13]Tucker, *Puritan Protagonist,* pp. 172-73; Samuel Johnson to the Secretary, SPG, January 10, 1743, Hawks and Perry, eds., *Documentary History of the Protestant Episcopal Church,* 1:204-5.

[14]Tucker, *Puritan Protagonist,* pp. 71, 156-58; Samuel Johnson to William Samuel Johnson, July 5, 1743, *Samuel Johnson,* 1:117-18.

[15]Tucker, *Puritan Protagonist,* p. 171.

[16]*Ibid.,* pp. 167-70.

[17]*Ibid.,* 114-18; Gaustad, *Great Awakening,* pp. 25-30.

[18]Several historians have demonstrated a connection between the awakening in Connecticut and earlier pietist discontent over the Halfway Covenant, the Saybrook Platform, and the formal, conservative preaching style of the established clergy: Tucker, *Puritan Protagonist,* pp. 120-21; Bushman, *From Puritan to Yankee,* pp. 178-82, 196; Zeichner, *Connecticut's Years of Controversy,* pp. 21-22.

[19]Dexter, *Biographical Sketches,* 1:662; Tucker, *Puritan Protagonist,* pp. 122-24.

[20]Samuel Johnson to the Archbishop of Canterbury, September 29, 1741, *Samuel Johnson,* 3:228-29; Samuel Johnson to the Secretary, SPG, October 5, 1742, *ibid.,* p. 232.

[21]According to Dexter, all but three students at the college purchased Pemberton's sermon. *Biographical Sketches,* 1:662.

[22]Tucker, *Puritan Protagonist,* p. 124.

[23]*Ibid.,* pp. 123-27; Gaustad, *Great Awakening,* pp. 32-38; Morgan, *Gentle Puritan,* pp. 31-33.

[24]Bushman, *From Puritan to Yankee,* pp. 203-20; Gaustad, *Great Awakening,* pp. 102-7, 113-15.

[25]Bushman, *From Puritan to Yankee,* pp. 186, 206; Gaustad, *Great Awakening,* pp. 62-73.

[26]Morgan, *Gentle Puritan,* p. 41.

[27]Dexter, *Biographical Sketches,* 1:663, 698; Tucker, *Puritan Protagonist,* pp. 132-33.

²⁸Bushman, *From Puritan to Yankee*, p. 186; Tucker, *Puritan Protagonist*, p. 128-30.

²⁹Tucker, *Puritan Protagonist*, pp. 130-31; Bushman, *From Puritan to Yankee*, pp. 187-88, 221.

³⁰Gaustad, *Great Awakening*, pp. 75, 103; Tucker, *Puritan Protagonist*, pp. 132-35.

³¹Orcutt, *History of the Old Town*, 1:296-301; Wilcoxson, *History of Stratford*, pp. 397, 400-1; Gaustad, *Great Awakening*, p. 38.

³²Samuel Johnson to Thomas Clap, February 5, 1754, *Samuel Johnson*, 1:179. The Church of England, Johnson told Clap, was "the only stable bulwark against all heresy and infidelity which are coming in like a flood upon us, as I apprehend, by reason of the rigid Calvinism, Antinomianism, enthusiasm, and divisions, and separations, which, through the weakness and great imperfection of your constitution (if it may be called so), are so rife and rampant among us. My apprehension of this was the first occasion of my conforming to the Church. . . ."

³³Samuel Johnson to the Secretary, SPG, September 10, 1739, October 14, 1740, October 1, 1741, March 25, 1742, October 5, 1742, *Samuel Johnson*, 3:224, 227-28, 229, 230-31, 232; Wilcoxson, *History of Stratford*, p. 455; Steiner, "Anglican Officeholding," p. 396.

³⁴Hezekiah Gold to Samuel Johnson, July 14, 1741, *Samuel Johnson*, 3,135-36.

³⁵For the circumstances surrounding Gold's dismissal, see Wilcoxson, *History of Stratford*, pp. 400-1. When the movement to unseat Gold began in 1742, the Stratford congregation planned to call the Rev. Minor, the pastor of Unity Parish, to be their minister. But Minor joined the Episcopal church in 1744, probably in reaction to the revival tumult, and the Stratfordites suffered under Gold's ministry until 1752. Orcutt, *History of the Old Town*, pp. 348-49.

³⁶Tucker, *Puritan Protagonist*, p. 139; Morgan, *Gentle Puritan*, p. 42.

³⁷William Samuel Johnson to Samuel Johnson, June 22, 1747, *Samuel Johnson*, 1:123-24; Dexter, *Biographical Sketches*, 1:763.

³⁸Morgan, *Gentle Puritan*, p. 78.

³⁹Samuel Johnson to the Secretary, SPG, March 26, 1746, *Documentary History of the Protestant Episcopal Church*, 1:218-19; Groce, *William Samuel Johnson*, pp. 10-11.

⁴⁰William Samuel Johnson to William Smith, Jr., March 18, 1747, WSJ Papers.

⁴¹William Samuel Johnson to [William Samuel Fitch], April 23, 1747, WSJ Papers.

⁴²William Samuel Johnson to Agur Tomlinson, June 20, 1746, WSJ Papers.

⁴³William Smith, Jr., to William Samuel Johnson, July 12, 1746, WSJ Papers.

⁴⁴Steiner, "Anglican Officeholding," p. 396.

⁴⁵By 1769, there were many signs that the Congregationalists of Ripton had accepted the presence of the Episcopal mission. In 1765, the town fathers gave the Anglicans permission to build a new, larger church on the town green, and in 1769, they supported the Anglicans' petition to the General Assembly for tax relief.

⁴⁶Morgan, *Gentle Puritan*, pp. 80-89, 113, 114.

⁴⁷William Samuel Johnson to William Smith, Jr., July 21, 1746, WSJ Papers.

⁴⁸Farrell, "Administration of Justice," pp. 146, 151-53, 210.

⁴⁹Farrell, "Administration of Justice," p. 161. For similar developments in Massachusetts and New York, see Klein, "The Rise of the New York Bar," pp. 392-94; Berkin, *Jonathan Sewall*, pp. 11-13.

⁵⁰William Samuel Johnson to William Smith, Jr., July 21, 1746, WSJ Papers.

⁵¹Morgan, *Gentle Puritan*, pp. 113-14.

⁵²William Samuel Johnson to Thomas Bradbury Chandler, May 9, 1747, WSJ Papers; William Samuel Johnson to Samuel Johnson, July 6, 1747, WSJ Papers; William Samuel Johnson to Samuel Johnson, June 22, 1747, *Samuel Johnson*, 1:123-24.

[53]Samuel Johnson to William Samuel Johnson, June 23, 1747, *Samuel Johnson,* 1:125-26, 128.

[54]William Samuel Johnson to Nathaniel Lloyd, October 20, 1747, WSJ Papers.

[55]William Samuel Johnson to William Smith, Jr., September 1747, and undated [between September 1747 and January 1748], WSJ Papers.

[56]William Samuel Johnson to William Smith, Jr., January 1, 1748, WSJ Papers.

[57]William Samuel Johnson to the Secretary, SPG, undated [between May 30, 1748 and January 1749], WSJ Papers; William Samuel Johnson to William Smith, Jr., May 5, 1748, WSJ Papers.

[58]Samuel Johnson to the Secretary, SPG, March 26, 1746, Hawks and Perry, eds., *Documentary History of the Protestant Episcopal Church,* 1:218-19; The Churchwardens of Ripton Parish to the Secretary, SPG, September 14, 1748, *ibid.,* p. 249.

[59]William Smith, Jr. to William Samuel Johnson, March 29, 1748, September 28, 1748, and undated [between September 1747 and January 1748], WSJ Papers.

[60]William Samuel Johnson to William Smith, Jr., August 16, 1748, WSJ Papers.

[61]William Smith, Jr., to William Samuel Johnson, undated [early 1749], WSJ Papers.

[62]William Samuel Johnson to William Smith, Jr., January 1, 1748, WSJ Papers.

[63]Farrell, "Administration of Justice," pp. 152-53, 192.

[64]*Ibid.,* pp. 161, 169, 180-84, 194, 207. Farrell conferred upon Ingersoll the title "Father of the Connecticut Bar."

[65]William Samuel Johnson to William Smith, Jr., May 5, 1748, WSJ Papers.

[66]Farrell, "Administration of Justice," pp. 17, 210.

[67]*Ibid.,* p. 191.

[68]Samuel Johnson to William Samuel Johnson, July 16, 1758, *Samuel Johnson,* 1:278.

[69]Groce, *William Samuel Johnson,* p. 38.

[70]William Samuel Johnson to William Smith, Jr., undated [sometime after May 30, 1748], WSJ Papers.

[71]William Smith, Jr., to William Samuel Johnson, March 2, 1747, WSJ Papers.

[72]There is no undisputable evidence of this engagement, but the correspondence between William Samuel Johnson and his father in the summer of 1747 suggests that young Johnson pledged his hand to a Boston woman. Samuel Johnson's letters are filled with reassurances to his son, who apparently expressed doubts that he could make a woman and family happy and support them financially. Samuel Johnson to William Samuel Johnson, July 7, 1747, *Samuel Johnson,* 1:128. On May 30, 1748, William Samuel Johnson wrote to a Boston acquaintance, implying that his marriage vows would soon be broken. William Samuel Johnson to Thomas Greene, May 30, 1748, WSJ Papers.

[73]William Samuel Johnson to William Smith, Jr., August 16, 1748, WSJ Papers; William Smith, Jr., to William Samuel Johnson, undated [early 1749], WSJ Papers.

[74]The family discord is discussed below, in chapter 9.

[75]Samuel Johnson to Mrs. William Samuel [Ann] Johnson, August 20, 1761, *Samuel Johnson* 1:310; Samuel Johnson to William Samuel Johnson, February 1, 1769, *ibid.,* p. 451.

[76]Dexter, *Biographical Sketches,* 1:239-43; Steiner, "Anglican Officeholding," 95; Cross, *Anglican Episcopate,* pp. 140-44; Rev. James Wetmore, *A Vindication of the Professors of the Church of England in Connecticut, against the Invectives contained in a Sermon Preached at Stamford by Mr. Noah Hobart, December 13, 1746* (Boston, 1748); Rev. Noah Hobart, *A Serious Address to the Members of the Episcopal Separation in New England, Occasioned by Mr. Wetmore's Vindication*

of the Church of England in Connecticut (Boston, 1748); Rev. John Beach, *A Calm and Dispassionate Vindication of the Professors of the Church of England against the Abusive Misrepresentation and Fallacious Arguments of Mr. Noah Hobart . . . with a Preface by Dr. Johnson. . .* (Boston, 1749); Rov. Noah Hobart,, *A Second Address to the Members of the Episcopal Separation in New England. . . .* (Boston, 1751); Rev. John Beach, *A Continuation of the Calm and Dispassionate Vindication of the Church of England. . . .* (Boston, 1751).

Chapter 3: Ecclesiastical Warfare on Every Front

[1]Accounts of the controversy can be found in: Humphrey, *From King's College to Columbia*, chs. 1-4; Klein, ed., *Independent Reflector* pp. 32-48; Bridenbaugh, *Mitre and Sceptre*, pp. 138-68; Steiner, *Samuel Seabury*, pp. 91-92.

[2]For a detailed discussion of the origins and character of this journal, see Klein, ed., *Independent Reflector*, pp. 1-50.

[3]"Extract from the *Preface to the Independent Reflector,*" *Samuel Johnson*, 4:160, 169. This *Preface*, penned after Livingston's publisher refused to continue printing *The Independent Reflector*, appeared as a broadside dated February 29, 1754.

[4]William Livingston, in behalf of the Trustees, to Samuel Johnson, January 7, 1754, *Samuel Johnson*, 4:7; William Livingston to Chauncey Whittelsey, August 22, 1754, *ibid.*, 4:21; Samuel Johnson to the Secretary, SPG, December 3, 1754, *ibid.*, 4:28; Henry Barclay to Samuel Johnson, November 4, 1754, *ibid.*, 4:24; Steiner, *Samuel Seabury*, p. 92.

[5]Klein, ed., *Independent Reflector*, pp. 43-44. The Triumvirate's essays appeared under the title "The Watchtower," from November 1754 to November 1755, and again on January 16, 1756. The Anglicans responded in a short-lived series entitled "John Englishmen, In Defense of the English Constitution," and also printed rebuttals in the *New-York Mercury*.

[6]Klein, ed., *Independent Reflector*, p. 37; Bridenbaugh, *Mitre and Sceptre*, p. 162.

[7]Samuel Johnson to William Samuel Johnson, May 27, 1754, January 20, May 14, 1755, *Samuel Johnson*, 1:34-35, 213-14; 4:11; Samuel Johnson to William Johnson and William Samuel Johnson, November 25, 1754, *ibid.*, 4:27.

[8]William Samuel Johnson to Samuel Johnson, June 20, 1755, WSJ Papers; Samuel Johnson to William Samuel Johnson, May 14, 1755, *Samuel Johnson*, 4:34-35.

[9]Samuel Johnson to William Samuel Johnson and William Johnson, December 8, 1754, *Samuel Johnson*, 4:33; William Samuel Johnson to Samuel Johnson, December 6, 1754, *ibid.*, 4:31.

[10]Klein, ed., *Independent Reflector*, p. 276, n.1; William Samuel Johnson to Samuel Johnson, December 6, 1754, *Samuel Johnson*, 4:31.

[11]Benjamin Nicoll, *A Brief Vindication of the Proceedings of the Trustees Relating to the College. . . .* (New York, 1754), rpt. in *Samuel Johnson*, 4:191-207; Samuel Johnson to William Samuel Johnson and William Johnson, December 8, 1754, *ibid.*, 4:33.

[12]Samuel Johnson to William Samuel Johnson, June 10, 1754, *Samuel Johnson*, 4:15-16; William Samuel Johnson to Samuel Johnson, June 13, December 6, 1754, *ibid.*, 4:17, 31.

[13]Samuel Johnson to William Samuel Johnson, June 17, 1754, *ibid.*, 1:188.

[14]William Samuel Johnson to Samuel Johnson, December 6, 1754. *ibid.*, 4:31.

[15]*Public Records of the Colony of Connecticut*, 10:188, 263-64; 11:209.

[16]Steiner, "Anglican Officeholding," pp. 370-74.

[17]Klein, ed., *Independent Reflector*, pp. 30, 31, 40.

[18]Tucker, *Puritan Protagonist*, pp. 144-66, 183.

[19]Samuel Johnson to the Bishop of London, April 2, 1728, Hawks and Perry, eds., *Documentary History of the Protestant Episcopal Church*, 1:127; Samuel Johnson to the Secretary, SPG, October 25, 1730, March 28, 1749, *ibid.*, 1:145, 251-52; Samuel Johnson to George Berkeley, December 17, 1750, *Samuel Johnson*, 1:138; Samual Johnson to William Samuel Johnson, n.d. [June 1754], *ibid.*, 1:191.

[20]Tucker, *Puritan Protagonist*, pp. 173-74, 183-86; Morgan, *The Gentle Puritan*, pp. 103-6.

[21]Tucker, *Puritan Protagonist*, pp. 191-231; Bushman, *From Puritan to Yankee*, pp. 244-51.

[22]Samuel Johnson to Thomas Clap, February 5, 1754, *Samuel Johnson* 1:176; Tucker, *Puritan Protagonist*, pp. 178-81.

[23]Samuel Johnson to William Samuel Johnson and William Johnson, June 10, 1754, *Samuel Johnson*, 4:17-18.

[24]Samuel Johnson to William Samuel Johnson, n.d. [June 1754], *ibid.*, 1:192.

[25]Klein, ed., *Independent Reflector*, 44.

[26]Wilcoxson, *History of Stratford*, p. 341.

[27]Groce, *William Samuel Johnson*, pp. 41-44.

[28]Steiner, "Anglican Officeholding," pp. 372-77, 380. Steiner investigated Anglican officeholding between 1732 and 1736, and found that fifty-six adherents to the Church of England were elected deputies by twenty-five Connecticut towns. No simple ratio existed, Steiner argues, between the size of a town's Anglican population and that town's willingness to elect churchmen to high posts.

[29]In the following chart of deputies elected by the Stratford freemen to attend the General Assembly, an asterisk indicates a known affiliation with the Church of England.

June 1757	Agur Tomlinson	Robert Fairchild
October 1757	Agur Tomlinson	Theophilus Nichols*
May 1758	Agur Tomlinson	Theophilus Nichols*
November 1758	Ichabod Lewis*	Theophilus Nichols*
May 1759	Robert Walker	Samuel Adams
October 1759	Robert Walker	Ichabod Lewis*
May 1760	Robert Walker	Ichabod Lewis*
October 1760	Robert Walker	Ichabod Lewis*
May 1761	William Samuel Johnson*	Samuel Adams
October 1761	Robert Walker	Ichabod Lewis*

Johnson's opportunity to go to the Assembly was probably owing to Walker's involvement in a dispute between Stratford and Newton, which the Assembly was scheduled to arbitrate at the May 1761 session. Disinterested politics no doubt demanded that Walker not attend that session. *Public Records of the Colony of Connecticut*, 11:564-65, 569; 12:1, 73, 121, 190, 242. Johnson's second opportunity to attend the Assembly would come in May 1765, when Walker stood for election to the Governor's Council.

[30]Samuel Johnson to William Samuel Johnson, February 6, 1756, March 14, 1757, October 26, 1761, *Samuel Johnson*, 1:235, 271, 315.

[31]*Officers and Graduates of Columbia University, 1754-1900* (New York, 1900), pp. 100-3.

[32]Bishop Sherlock to Samuel Johnson, April 21, 1752, *Samuel Johnson*, 3:246.

[33]Sykes, *From Sheldon to Secker*, p. 210; Bridenbaugh, *Mitre and Sceptre*, p. 91; Cross, *Anglican Episcopate*, pp. 114-21, 256, 324-30. A most revealing statement of the British ministry's motives is a letter from Horatio Walpole, a member of the Privy Council

and brother of Sir Robert Walpole, to Bishop Sherlock. The letter, dated May 29, 1750, is reprinted in Cross, *Anglican Episcopate*, pp. 324-30.

[34]Archbishop Secker to Samuel Johnson, September 27, 1758, *Samuel Johnson*, 3:259.

[35]Samuel Johnson to William Samuel Johnson, October 12, 1755, *ibid.*, 1:224.

[36]Samuel Johnson to William Samuel Johnson, September 13, 1756, *ibid.*, 1:257.

[37]Samuel Johnson to the Secretary, SPG, December 21, 1757, *ibid.*, 4:42.

[38]Samuel Johnson to William Samuel Johnson, September 28, 1756, *ibid.*, 1:259.

[39]Samuel Johnson to William Samuel Johnson, February 19, 1756, *ibid.*, 1:240.

[40]Samuel Johnson to William Samuel Johnson, May 29, 1758, February 16, 1761, *ibid.*, 1:277-78, 306.

[41]Noah Welles, *The Real Advantages which Ministers and People may enjoy Especially in the Colonies By Conforming to the Church of England . . . In A Letter to a Young Gentleman* (n.p., 1762).

[42]Bailyn, ed. *Pamphlets*, pp. 61, 156; Bridenbaugh, *Mitre and Sceptre*, pp. 110-11.

[43]Jonathan Mayhew, *Observations on the Charter and Conduct of the Society for the Propagation of the Gospel* (London and Boston, 1763).

[44]Archbishop Secker to Samuel Johnson, December 10, 1761, *Samuel Johnson*, 4:72; Donald R. Gerlach, "Champions of an American Episcopate, p. 398; Jack Sosin, "The Proposals in the Pre-Revolutionary Decade for Establishing Anglican Bishops," pp. 76-77. Among the rebuttals were the following: Henry Caner, *A Candid Examination of Dr. Mayhew's Observations . . . With an Appendix containing a Vindication by one of its Members—Samuel Johnson* (Boston, 1763); John Beach, *A Friendly Expostulation, with All Persons Concern'd in Publishing A Late Pamphlet, Entitled the Real Advantages. . . .* (New York, 1763).

[45]Archbishop Secker to Samuel Johnson, March 30, 1763, *Samuel Johnson*, 3:269.

[46]Thomas Secker, *An Answer to Dr. Mayhew's Observations on the Charter and Conduct of the Society* (London, 1764); Cross, *Anglican Episcopate*, pp. 151-52.

[47]Jonathan Mayhew, *Remarks on an Anonymous Tract, entitled an Answer to Dr. Mayhew's Observations* (Boston, 1764; London, 1765).

[48]Sosin, "Proposals," p. 79.

[49]Archbishop Secker to Samuel Johnson, March 30, September 28, 1763, *Samuel Johnson*, 3:270-77.

[50]Mayhew, *Observations on the Charter and Conduct of the Society;* Welles, *The Real Advantages.*

[51]William Samuel Johnson to John Beach, January 4, 1763, *Samuel Johnson*, 3:264-65; Beach, *A Friendly Expostulation.*

[52]Ichabod Lewis attended the Assembly in October 1761, March, June and October 1762, May and October 1763, and October 1764. Theophilus Nichols attended in May 1764. *Public Records of the Colony of Connecticut*, 11:569; 12:1, 73, 121, 190, 242. See also note 29, above

[53]William Samuel Johnson to John Beach, January 4, 1763, *Samuel Johnson*, 3:266.

[54]Tucker, *Puritan Protagonist*, pp. 192-208.

[55]William Samuel Johnson to Jared Ingersoll, September 10, 1759, WSJ Papers; Stiles, *Extracts*, p. 582.

[56]Tucker, *Puritan Protagonist*, pp. 215-18; Bushman, *From Puritan to Yankee*, pp. 216-19, 246, 252-53.

[57]William Samuel Johnson to an unknown correspondent, November 28, 1759, WSJ Papers; William Samuel Johnson to Jared Ingersoll, September 10, 1765, *ibid.*

[58]William Samuel Johnson to Jared Ingersoll, September 10, 1765, *ibid.;* William Samuel Johnson to Samuel Johnson, May 11, 1759, *ibid.*

[59]Bushman, *From Puritan to Yankee*, pp. 267-72.
[60]Tucker, *Puritan Protagonist*, pp. 221-31.
[61]Morgan, *Gentle Puritan*, pp. 90, 107, 317; Gipson, *Jared Ingersoll*, pp. 42, 159; Morgan and Morgan, *Stamp Act Crisis*, pp. 222-27.
[62]Mayhew, *Remarks on an Anonymous Tract*.
[63]*Ibid.*

Chapter 4: Rise to Prominence

[1]Morgan and Morgan, *The Stamp Act Crisis*, pp. 21-22; Gipson, *The British Empire*, 10:200-2, 223-24, 246.
[2]Morgan and Morgan, *Stamp Act Crisis*, pp. 23-26; Gipson, *British Empire*, 10:219-20, 225, 226-31. Grenville proposed that the duty on molasses be continued but at a lower rate, which, it was reasoned, would reduce the temptation to smuggle and thereby increase the revenue collected.
[3]The American revenue program enacted that year is customarily called the Sugar Act, because colonial opposition to the new duties focused on the three-pence molasses tax. Morgan and Morgan, *Stamp Act Crisis*, p. 26.
[4]*Public Records, of the Colony of Connecticut*, 12:256; Stiles, *Extracts*, p. 202.
[5]William Samuel Johnson to Eliphalet Dyer, June 25, 1764, WSJ Papers.
[6]Jared Ingersoll to Thomas Whately, July 6, 1764, "Miscellaneous Papers of Jared Ingersoll," p. 299. Ingersoll also denouced the new import duties as "amount[ing] to a prohibition of ye trade."
[7]*Public Records of the Colony of Connecticut*, 12:229-30; [Thomas Fitch, et al.], *Reasons Why the British Colonies, in America, Should Not Be Charged with Internal Taxes . . . in Behalf of the Colony of Connecticut* (New Haven, 1764), rpt. in Bailyn, ed., *Pamphlets*, pp. 386-407. The pamphlet was almost entirely Fitch's creation.
[8]Thomas Fitch to Richard Jackson, December 7, 1764, "The Fitch Papers," p. 275; Thomas Fitch to Richard Jackson, February 23, 1765, quoted in Zeichner, *Connecticut's Years of Controversy*, p. 50.
[9]Stephen Hopkins, "A Vindication of a Late Pamphlet Entitled *The Rights of Colonies Examined,* from the Censures and Remarks Contained in A Letter from a Gentleman at Halifax . . ." *Providence Gazette*, February 23, March 2, 9, 1765, quoted in Bailyn, ed., *Pamphlets*, p. 503.
[10]James Otis, *The Rights of the British Colonies Asserted and Proved* (Boston, 1764), rpt. in Bailyn, ed., *Pamphlets*, pp. 419-82.
[11]Jared Ingersoll to Thomas Fitch, February 11, 1765, "Miscellaneous Papers of Ingersoll," pp. 312-14; Kammen, *A Rope of Sand*, pp. 114, 116-17.
[12]Jared Ingersoll to Thomas Fitch, February 11, 1765, "Miscellaneous Papers of Ingersoll," p. 306; Gipson, *British Empire*, 10:271-74.
[13]Jared Ingersoll to William Livingston, October 1, 1765, "Miscellaneous Papers of Ingersoll," pp. 349-50; Jared Ingersoll to Thomas Fitch, March 6, 1765, *ibid.*, p. 322.
[14]Jared Ingersoll to the *Connecticut Gazette*, September 13, 1765, *ibid.*, p. 332; Gipson, *Jared Ingersoll*, p. 195.
[15]William Smith to Governor Monckton, May 30, 1765, quoted in Gipson, *British Empire*, 10:286.
[16]William Samuel Johnson to Jared Ingersoll, June 3, 1765, "Miscellaneous Papers of Ingersoll," pp. 324-25. For correspondence between Ingersoll and the other volunteers, see *ibid.*, pp. 324-27.

[17]*Connecticut Courant*, April 26, 1765, quoted in Gipson, *Jared Ingersoll*, p. 160. The attack, signed "Cato," first appeared in the *Connecticut Gazette*, August 9, 1765.

[18]Morgan and Morgan, *Stamp Act Crisis*, pp. 123-25; Stiles, *Extracts*, p. 436.

[19]Nathaniel Wales to Jared Ingersoll, August 19, 1765, "Miscellaneous Papers of Ingersoll," pp. 325-26; Gipson, *Jared Ingersoll*, p. 168; Zeichner, *Connecticut's Years of Controversy*, p. 52.

[20]Gipson, *Jared Ingersoll*, pp. 168-70.

[21]Morgan and Morgan, *Stamp Act Crisis*, ch. 9.

[22]Jared Ingersoll to the General Assembly, September 18, 1765, "Miscellaneous Papers of Ingersoll," p. 340; Jared Ingersoll to the *Connecticut Gazette*, printed September 27, 1765.

[23]*Public Records of the Colony of Connecticut*, 12:409-11.

[24]Rowland is included among Ingersoll's list of volunteers. "Miscellaneous Papers of Ingersoll," p. 327.

[25]Jacobson, *John Dickinson*, p. 34. A handy documentation of the proceedings is Alden T. Vaughan, ed., *Chronicles of the American Revolution* (New York: Grosset & Dunlap, 1965), pp. 7-20.

[26]Samuel White to James Otis, Oliver Partridge, and Timothy Ruggles, n.d., Vaughan, ed., *Chronicles*, p. 9.

[27]William Samuel Johnson to Christopher Gadsden, January 10, 1766, WSJ Papers.

[28]If they "have a right to lay on us a poll tax, a land tax, a malt tax, a cider tax, a window tax, a smoke tax; and why not tax us for the light of the sun, the air we breathe, and the ground we are buried in? If they have a right to deny us the privilege of trial by juries, they have as good a right to deny us any trials at all, and to vote away our estates and lives at pleasure." Stephen Johnson, "To the Freemen of the Colony of Connecticut," *New London Gazette*, September 6, 1765, quoted in Moses Coit Tyler, *The Literary History of the American Revolution, 1763-1783*, 2nd. ed., 2 vols. (New York: Putnam, 1898) 1:99-100.

[29]Vaughan, ed., *Chronicles*, pp. 10-11.

[30]*Ibid.*, p. 10.

[31]Caesar Rodney to Thomas Rodney, October 20, 1705, quoted in Vaughan, ed., *Chronicles*, p. 21.

[32]The following discussion is based largely on Edmund and Helen Morgan's excellent interpretation, *Stamp Act Crisis*, pp. 107-13.

[33]*Ibid.*, p. 26.

[34]*Ibid.*, pp. 36-38. See also note 7, above.

[35]William Samuel Johnson, "Report of the Committee to which was refer'd the Consideration of the Rights of the British Colonies," William Samuel Johnson Papers, Library of Congress, quoted in Morgan and Morgan, *Stamp Act Crisis*, pp. 110-11.

[36]Vaughan, ed., *Chronicles*, p. 11.

[37]Robert Livingston to an unknown correspondent, November 2, 1765, Bancroft Transcripts, quoted in Morgan and Morgan, *Stamp Act Crisis*, p. 107.

[38]William Samuel Johnson to Robert Ogden, November 4, 1765, WSJ Papers; quoted in Morgan and Morgan, *Stamp Act Crisis*, p. 109.

[39]Petition to the House of Commons, Vaughan, ed., *Chronicles*, pp. 17, 19.

[40]William Samuel Johnson to Robert Ogden, November 4, 1765, WSJ Papers; William Samuel Johnson to Christopher Gadsden, January 10, 1766, *ibid.*; Eliphalet Dyer to William Samuel Johnson, December 8, 1765, *ibid.*; William Samuel Johnson to James Otis, November 4, 1765, *ibid.*, quoted in Beardsley, *William Samuel Johnson*, pp. 195-96.

[41]Petition to the King, *Chronicles*, p. 14.

[42]*Public Records*, 12:410; Morgan and Morgan, *Stamp Act Crisis*, p. 110.

[43]Gipson, *British Empire*, 10:333.

[44]*Ibid.*, p. 333.

[45]*Public Records of the Colony of Connecticut*, 12:420-21.

[46]William Samuel Johnson to Christopher Gadsden, January 10, 1766, WSJ Papers.

[47]*Public Records of the Colony of Connecticut*, 12:415. A more typical career is that of Eliphalet Dyer, who had served as a deputy to the Assembly nearly every term since 1747 before he was elevated to the Council in 1762. Willingham, "Windham, Connecticut," p. 58.

[48]William Samuel Johnson to Christopher Gadsden, January 10, June 25, 1766, WSJ Papers, James Otis to William Samuel Johnson, November 12, 1765, *ibid.*, Edmund Morgan, *The Gentle Puritan*, p. 223.

[49]Richard Jackson to Thomas Fitch, June 5, November 9, 1765, "Fitch Papers," pp. 349-51, 368-69.

[50]Colony of Connecticut to Richard Jackson (letter authorized by the Assembly at the October 1765 session), "Fitch Papers," pp. 366-67; Thomas Fitch to Richard Jackson, November 13, 1765, *ibid.*, pp. 369-72.

[51]Schlesinger, *Prelude to Independence*, p. 296.

[52]Jared Ingersoll to Thomas Whately, November 2, 1765, "Miscellaneous Papers of Ingersoll," p. 351; Jared Ingersoll to Richard Jackson, November 3, 1765, *ibid.*, p. 357.

[53]In December 1765, Fitch told the crown-appointed Governor of New York, Sir Henry Moore, that he could not accept responsibility for the stamps, and he wrote to the British Secretary of the Treasury that the stamp distributors in all the colonies had resigned and he could not enforce the Stamp Act for that reason. In October 1765, the Secretary of State, Henry Conway, had addressed a warning to Fitch that failure to submit to parliamentary authority would evoke reprisals from the mother country. Fitch did not receive Conway's warning until May, but the Governor's awareness that this attitude prevailed among British leaders no doubt persuaded him to take the oath. Thomas Fitch to Sir Henry Moore, December 20, 1765, "Fitch Papers," p. 380; Henry S. Conway to the colony of Connecticut, October 24, 1765, *ibid.*, pp. 262-63. Fitch penned a public explanation for his unpopular action: *Some Reasons that Influenced the Governor to take, and the Councillors to administer, the Oath, Required by the Act of Parliament, commonly called the Stamp Act. Humbly submitted to the Consideration of the Publick* (Hartford, 1766). For a contemporary account by a Governor's Assistant who refused to administer the oath, see Eliphalet Dyer to William Samuel Johnson, December 15, 1765, WSJ Papers.

[54]Leverett Hubbard to Ezra Stiles, November 6, 1765, *Extracts*, p. 512; Jared Ingersoll to Thomas Whately, November 2, 1765, "Miscellaneous Papers of Ingersoll," p. 352.

[55]Zeichner, *Connecticut's Years of Controversy*, pp. 62-65; Collier, *Sherman's Connecticut*, p. 52; Gipson, *Jared Ingersoll*, pp. 196-99.

[56]*Connecticut Gazette*, December 27, 1765; Gipson, *British Empire*, 10:350-52; Zeichner, *Connecticut's Years of Controversy*, p. 60; Gipson, *Jared Ingersoll*, p. 205.

[57]Collier, *Sherman's Connecticut*, pp. 54-55; Gipson, *Jared Ingersoll*, pp. 214-18; Gipson, *British Empire*, 10:350-52.

[58]William Samuel Johnson to Eliphalet Dyer, December 31, 1765, WSJ Papers; James Otis to William Samuel Johnson, November 12, 1765, *ibid.*

[59]Incidents at Fairfield, Wallingford, and Stratford were reported in the *Connecticut Gazette*, February 2, March 15, November 15, 1766. They are vividly recounted in Collier, *Sherman's Connecticut*, p. 52; Ziechner, *Connecticut's Years of Controversy*, p. 63.

[60]Jared Ingersoll to Thomas Whately, November 2, 1765, "Miscellaneous Papers of Ingersoll," p. 352.

[61]Chauncey Whittelsey to Ezra Stiles, December 24, 1765, Stiles, *Extracts,* pp. 588-89; Roger Sherman to Mathew Griswold, January 11, 1766, cited in Boardman, *Roger Sherman,* pp. 91-92.

[62]Joseph Chew to Jared Ingersoll, February 5, 1766, "Miscellaneous Papers of Ingersoll," p. 377.

[63]Jared Ingersoll to Thomas Whately, November 2, 1765, *ibid.,* p. 353; Eliphalet Dyer to William Samuel Johnson, December 8, 1765, WSJ Papers; William Samuel Johnson to Eliphalet Dyer, December 1, 19, 1765, WSJ Papers; Gipson, *Jared Ingersoll,* pp. 200-2. Ingersoll had written to Jackson, "I hope you will do Every thing in your power to obtain" for the colonists' petitions "a keen reception & hearing, however different from your Judgement they are drawn." Jared Ingersoll to Richard Jackson, November 3, 1765, "Miscellaneous Papers of Ingersoll," p. 358.

[64][Thomas Fitch], *An Explanation of Say-brook Platform. . . . By One that heartily desires the Order, Peace and Purity of those Churches* (Hartford, 1765). The most comprehensive description of the disputes that divided east and west into two hostile camps is Bushman, *From Puritan to Yankee.* On the sectional character of the clerical dispute, see pp. 190, 258.

[65]Boyd, ed., *Susquehannah Papers,* 1:xlix-lii.

[66]*Ibid.,* 1:lxi-lxxiv; For a brief discussion of the history of the company, see Julian Parks Boyd, "The Susquehannah Company, 1753-1803," *Journal of Economic and Business History,* 4 (1931), 38-69.

[67]Boyd, et., *Susquehannah Papers,* 1:lxxi, lxxxi-lxxxvii. Pennsylvania's deed, like the Susquehannah Company's document, was executed at the Albany Congress of July 1754. Several Indian delegates signed both treaties, and it is suspected that Lydius bribed some of the Indians and forced the signatures of others.

[68]*Ibid.,* 1:lix-lx.

[69]Minutes of a Meeting of the Susquehanna Company, May 1, November 20, 1754, *Susquehannah Papers,* 1:86-88, 168-80. Edith A. Bailey "Influences toward Radicalism in Connecticut, 1754-1775," *Smith College Studies in History,* 5 (July 1920), 194.

[70]Boyd, ed., *Susquehannah Papers,* 1:lxxix, lxxxvi; Letter to James Hamilton, March 13, 1754, *ibid.,* 1:63; Proclamation of Thomas Fitch Against the Susquehannah Company, *ibid.,* 2:135.

[71]Boyd, ed., *Susquehannah Papers,* 2:xxvii.

[72]Ezra Stiles to Pelatiah Webster, May 21, 1763, *Susquehannah Papers,* 2:221-23; Joseph Chew to Jared Ingersoll, June 8, 1763, *ibid.,* 2:251; James Hamilton to Jared Ingersoll, July 8, 1762, *ibid.,* 2:142-44; Thomas Penn to James Hamilton, September 9, 1762, *ibid.,* 159; Thomas Penn to Richard Peters, September 10, 1762, *ibid.,* 2: 163; Gipson, *Jared Ingersoll,* pp. 317-18.

[73]Minutes of a Meeting of the Susquehanna Company, July 27, 1762, *Susquehannah Papers,* 2:145-46.

[74]Extract from the Report of Sir William Johnson to the Board of Trade, August 1, 1762, *Susquehannah Papers,* 2:147-49; Order of the King in Council, June 15, 1763, *ibid.,* 2:255; Instructions from the Privy Council to Thomas Fitch, June 15, 1763, *ibid.,* 2:256.

[75]Boyd, ed., *Susquehannah Papers,* 2:xxxv-xxxvi.

[76]*Ibid.,* 2:xvii, xxx, xxxviii-xxxix, xl. Eliphalet Dyer to the Susquehannah and Delaware Companies, May 25, 1764, *ibid.,* 2:291-93.

[77]This is the interpretation of Zeichner, *Connecticut's Years of Controversy,* p. 71; and Morgan and Morgan, *Stamp Act Crisis,* 220-37. For a contemporary description of the colony's factional divisions by a sharp-tongued western partisan, see Benjamin Gale to Jared Ingersoll, February 8, 1766, "Miscellaneous Papers of Ingersoll," pp. 373-74.

Richard Bushman points out that deference to long-esteemed rulers had impeded the eastern politicos from ousting the conservative western lawmakers at the colony's annual elections. "Only some deeply stirring conflict could persuade the voters to evict their Old Light rulers," argues Bushman, and the stamp tax crisis provided the occasion. *From Puritan to Yankee*, p. 261.

⁷⁸John Hubbard to Ezra Stiles, January 2, 1766, Stiles, *Extracts*, pp. 509-10.

⁷⁹Benjamin Gale to Jared Ingersoll, February 8, 1766, "Miscellaneous Papers of Ingersoll," p. 373-74; *Connecticut Courant*, March 31, 1766; Gipson, *Jared Ingersoll*, pp. 218-21; Zeichner, *Connecticut's Years of Controversy*, pp. 70-75.

⁸⁰William Samuel Johnson to Eliphalet Dyer, December 19, 31, 1765, WSJ Papers.

⁸¹William Samuel Johnson to Eliphalet Dyer, December 19, 31, 1765, WSJ Papers; Eliphalet Dyer to William Samuel Johnson, December 8, 15, 1765, *ibid.*

⁸²William Samuel Johnson to Eliphalet Dyer, June 25, 1765, WSJ Papers.

⁸³See note 63, above.

⁸⁴Bushman, *From Puritan to Yankee*, p. 269; Zeichner, *Connecticut's Years of Controversy*, p. 72.

⁸⁵Benjamin Gale to Jared Ingersoll, February 8, 1766, "Miscellaneous Papers of Ingersoll," pp. 373-74.

⁸⁶John Adams, "Dissertation on the Canon and Feudal Law," printed in the *Boston Gazette* during August 1765, reprinted in Adriene Koch and William Peden, eds. *The Selected Writings of John and John Quincy Adams* (New York: Knopf, 1946), pp. 22-23.

⁸⁷John Beach to the Secretary, SPG, October 2, 1765, Hawks and Perry, eds.,*Documentary History of the Protestant Episcopal Church*, 2:83; Joseph Lamson to the Secretary, SPG, April 2, 1766, *ibid.*, 2:86; Samuel Seabury to the Secretary, SPG, April 17, 1766, quoted in Steiner, *Samuel Seabury*, p. 106.

⁸⁸Clergy of Connecticut to the Secretary, SPG, September 5, 1765, *Documentary History of the Protestant Episcopal Church*, 2:81. For a discussion of this document, see Maud O'Neil, "Samuel Andrew Peters: Connecticut Loyalist" (Ph.D. diss.: University of California at Los Angeles, 1947), p. 161.

⁸⁹O'Neil, "Samuel Andrew Peters," p. 172.

⁹⁰*Public Records of the Colony of Connecticut*, 12:453-54.

⁹¹The only prominent public figure to espouse the Tory viewpoint in 1765 was Martin Howard of Rhode Island. In his notorious pamphlet, *A Letter from a Gentleman at Halifax, to His Friend in Rhode-Island, Containing Remarks upon a Pamphlet, Entitled, The Rights of the Colonies Examined* (Newport, 1765) Howard declared that Parliament's authority was "transcendent and entire."

⁹²Nelson, *American Tory*, p. 121; Benton, *Whig-Loyalism*, pp. 177, 212. See also chapter 12, note 16, below.

⁹³Steiner, "Anglican Officeholding," pp. 378, 397.

⁹⁴Morgan, *Gentle Puritan*, pp. 215-19, 237-38; Stiles, *Extracts*, p. 64.

⁹⁵Stiles maintained a meticulous annual account of the number of Episcopalians in each Connecticut town. *Extracts*, pp. 58, 76, 77, 94, 109-10, 118-19, 172, 272, 298, 299, etc.

⁹⁶On Sherman's humble background, see Collier, *Sherman's Connecticut*, pp. 3-24. Of the six judges appointed to the county courts in 1766, only Jabez Hamlin and Hezekiah Huntington sat on the Council. David Rowland had won a place among the twenty nominees in October, but he failed in the spring election. *Public Records of the Colony of Connecticut*, 12:415, 455.

⁹⁷Of the Anglicans who were justices of the peace, most had been Congregationalists when they first won their appointments, and only later defected to Episcopacy. Before 1768, only five avowed Episcopalians received their initial appointment to that post after they had joined the Church of England: Ichabod Lewis, Theophilus Nichols, and William

Samuel Johnson, all of Stratford, and Israel Knopf and Samuel Sacket, both from Greenwich. Among all the high colonial officers, only the justice of the peace functioned exclusively within his own town, and the Assembly was careful to name Episcopal Justices only to towns with large Anglican populations. The Assembly displayed even more reserve in making other appointments. In the 1740s, two former Assistants who held field grade militia ranks abandoned the standing order for Episcopacy without losing their military posts. But not until 1758 did the Assembly elevate an avowed Anglican to a field grade rank. In 1772, when Johnson was named major of the fourth regiment, he became only the second Anglican ever appointed to a field grade position. In the entire colonial period, no Anglican sat on the bench of any probate court or county court, or served as Sheriff or King's Attorney. In 1772 Johnson became the first Anglican ever appointed to the Superior Court. Steiner, "Anglican Officeholding," pp. 374-78. Steiner overlooks Johnson's appointment to the Superior Court, and contends that no Anglican sat on that bench before the Revolution. For a verification of Johnson's appointment, see *Public Records of the Colony of Connecticut*, 14:5.

[98]*Connecticut Gazette*, May 24, 1766; Zeichner, *Connecticut's Years of Controversy*, p. 76; Collier, *Sherman's Connecticut*, p. 55.

[99]For a discussion of the origins of this phrase, see Gipson, *British Empire*, 10:387-88.

[100]*Public Records of the Colony of Connecticut*, 12:467; William Samuel Johnson to Christopher Gadsden, June 25, 1766, WSJ Papers; Morgan and Morgan, *Stamp Act Crisis*, p. 286; Gipson, *The British Empire*, 11:4-10.

[101]Gipson, *British Empire*, 10:372, 408-9; Morgan and Morgan, *Stamp Act Crisis*, p. 264.

[102]For a detailed account of the debates in Parliament on the question of repeal, see Gipson, *British Empire*, 10:388-407.

[103]*Ibid.*, p. 407.

[104]*Ibid.*, pp. 390, 400-2.

[105]William Samuel Johnson to Christopher Gadsden, June 25, 1766, WSJ Papers.

Chapter 5: A Connecticut Yankee in London

[1]William Samuel Johnson to Joseph Chew, September 12, 1767, WSJ Papers.

[2]Rudé, *Hanoverian London*, p. ix; Rudé, *Paris and London*, pp. 37-40.

[3]Bushman, *From Puritan to Yankee*, pp. 84-97.

[4]*Public Records of the Colony of Connecticut*, 12:501-2.

[5]William Samuel Johnson to Ann Johnson, December 29, 1766, January 31, 1767, WSJ Papers; William Samuel Johnson to Ebenezer Silliman, February 24, 1767, *ibid.*; William Samuel Johnson to William Pitkin, February 12, 1767, "Trumbull Papers," pp. 214-15.

[6]Diary of William Samuel Johnson, January 30-February 12, 1767, WSJ Papers; William Samuel Johnson to Samuel Johnson, February 12, 1767, *ibid.*

[7]William Samuel Johnson to Jared Ingersoll, June 9, 1767, "Miscellaneous Papers of Jared Ingersoll," p. 410; William Samuel Johnson to Eliphalet Dyer, September 12, 1767, WSJ Papers.

[8]Rudé, *Hanoverian London*, pp. 17-18; Marshall, *Dr. Johnson's London*, p. 3.

[9]Diary of William Samuel Johnson, February 9, 1767, WSJ Papers. On Jackson, see Kammen, *Rope of Sand*, pp. 22, 124, 138.

[10]Diary of William Samuel Johnson, numerous entries, e.g. February 12, 20, 21, 28, March 2, 4, 1767, WSJ Papers; Rudé, *Hanoverian London*, pp. xi, 37; Marshall, *Dr. Johnson's London*, p. 99.

¹¹Diary of William Samuel Johnson, numerous entries, 1767-1771, WSJ Papers; William Samuel Johnson to Ann Johnson, February 18, 1767, *ibid.;* Marshall, *Dr. Johnson's London,* p. 150; Sachse, *Colonial American in Britain,* pp. 202-7.

¹²William Samuel Johnson to Joseph Chew, September 12, 1767, WSJ Papers; Diary of William Samuel Johnson, almost daily entries, *ibid.;* Rudé, *Hanoverian London,* pp. 70, 77.

¹³William Samuel Johnson to Samuel Johnson, November 2, 1769, quoted in Beardsley, *William Samuel Johnson,* p. 73; William Samuel Johnson to Robert Walker, March 31, 1767, WSJ Papers; Rudé, *Paris and London,* pp. 41-42; Rudé, *Hanoverian London,* pp. 43, 83; Marshall, *Dr. Johnson's London,* p. 101.

¹⁴In contrast, Herbert Wallace Schneider depicts the elder Johnson as a lover of all things British, a scorner of everything American. *The Puritan Mind* (Ann Arbor, Mich.: University of Michigan Press, 1930), p. 165.

¹⁵Samuel Johnson to William Samuel Johnson, April 24, 1767, *Samuel Johnson,* 1:400.

¹⁶William Samuel Johnson to Samuel Johnson, August 18, 1770, WSJ Papers; Norman Sykes, *Church and State in England,* pp. 93-94; Rudé, *Hanoverian London,* pp. 100-12.

¹⁷Diary of William Samuel Johnson, November 27, 1769, WSJ Papers.

¹⁸William Samuel Johnson to Jared Ingersoll, February 18, 1767, WSJ Papers; William Samuel Johnson to Eliphalet Dyer, April 10, 1767, *ibid.;* Jared Ingersoll to William Samuel Johnson, April 17, 1759, *ibid.;* Eliphalet Dyer to Jared Ingersoll, April 14, 1764, "Miscellaneous Papers of Ingersoll," p. 288; Farrell, "Administration of Justice," pp. 154-60.

¹⁹Wickwire, *British Subminster,* pp. 3-20; Kammen, *Rope of Sand,* p. 62.

²⁰Kammen, *Rope of Sand,* p. 95.

²¹Pares, *King George III and the Politicians,* pp. 10-23, 72-75, 88-98, 112-13, 167, 195; Donoughue, *British Politics and the American Revolution,* p. 14; Guttridge, *English Whiggism and the American Revolution,* pp. 8-10, 19; Christie, *Myth and Reality,* pp. 32, 84; Ritcheson, *British Politics,* p. 67; Marshall, *Dr. Johnson's London,* p. 124; Gipson, *British Empire,* 11:193.

²²Guttridge, *English Whiggism,* p. 18.

²³Ritcheson, *British Politics,* p. 31. An excellent discussion of Grenville's American policy is Thomas C. Barrow, "Background to the Grenville Program," *William and Mary Quarterly,* 3rd. ser., 22 (January 1965): 93-114.

²⁴Kammen, *Rope of Sand,* p. 117; Pares, *King George III and the Politicians,* p. 91; Guttridge, *English Whiggism,* pp. 21-23, 65; Gipson, *British Empire,* 11:81.

²⁵Gipson, *British Empire,* 11:70-75, 81; Pares, *King George III and the Politicians,* p. 114.

²⁶Pares, *King George III and the Politicians,* pp. 89, 116; Ritcheson, *British Politics,* p. 71; Gipson, *British Empire,* 11:77-79, 88, 94-106; Guttridge, *English Whiggism,* p. 26; Sosin, *Agents and Merchants,* p. 91.

²⁷William Samuel Johnson to Jared Ingersoll, June 9, 1767, WSJ Papers.

²⁸William Samuel to William Pitkin, July 13, 1767, Bancroft Transcripts.

²⁹William Samuel Johnson to Jared Ingersoll, February 18, 1767, WSJ Papers; Kammen, *Rope of Sand,* p. 66; Donoughue, *British Politics and the American Revolution,* p. 14.

³⁰William Samuel Johnson to Jonathan Trumbull, March 14, 1767, "Trumbull Papers," pp. 484-90.

³¹William Samuel Johnson to Jedidiah Elderkin, January 23, 1768, WSJ Papers.

Chapter 6: Townshend Lays His Taxes

[1] William Samuel Johnson to Jared Ingersoll, February 18, 1767, WSJ Papers.

[2] William Samuel Johnson to William Pitkin, February 12, 1767, "Trumbull Papers," pp. 215-16.

[3] Sosin, *Whitehall and the Wilderness*, pp. 134-35; Gipson, *British Empire*, 11:80.

[4] Sosin, *Whitehall and the Wilderness*, pp. 134-35; Gipson, *British Empire*, 11:80, 89, 103; Kammen, *Rope of Sand*, p. 220.

[5] Shy, *Toward Lexington*, p. 260; Sosin, *Agents and Merchants*, pp. 67, 101.

[6] Sosin, *Agents and Merchants*, pp. 67, 101; Gipson, *British Empire*, 11:105.

[7] Gipson, *British Empire*, 11:99.

[8] Shy, *Toward Lexington*, pp. 143, 160-64; Sosin, *Agents and Merchants*, pp. 31, 39-54; Gipson, *British Empire*, 11:39-51. The New York Assembly was willing to supply the troops, but with lesser accommodations than the letter of the new law required.

[9] Sosin, *Agents and Merchants*, p. 97.

[10] *Ibid.*, p. 106; William Samuel Johnson to Agur Tomlinson, March 31, 1767, WSJ Papers; William Samuel Johnson to William Pitkin, February 12, 1767, "Trumbull Papers," p. 216.

[11] William Samuel Johnson to Jonathan Trumbull, March 14, 1767, "Trumbull Papers," p. 487.

[12] *Ibid.*, pp. 486-87; William Samuel Johnson to Agur Tomlinson, March 31, 1767, WSJ Papers.

[13] Gipson, *British Empire*, 11:10; Ritcheson, *British Politics*, p. 47.

[14] Sosin, *Agents and Merchants*, p. 99. The Massachusetts agent Dennys De Berdt had cautioned the Boston merchants against presenting a similar petition. Dennys De Berdt to the Boston Merchants, March 14, 1767, "Letters of De Berdt," pp. 451-52.

[15] William Samuel Johnson to Jared Ingersoll, February 18, 1767, WSJ Papers; Wickwire, *British Subministers* William Samuel Johnson to Ebenezer Silliman, Feb-William Samuel Johnson to Ebenezer Silliman, February 24, 1767, *ibid.*

[16] Sosin, *Agents and Merchants*, pp. 93-96; Gipson, *British Empire*, 11:55-56.

[17] William Samuel Johnson to Jonathan Trumbull, March 14, 1767, "Trumbull Papers," p. 486.

[18] Gipson, *British Empire*, 11:95, 99.

[19] Diary of William Samuel Johnson, March 13, 1767, WSJ Papers; Kammen, *Rope of Sand*, p. 128.

[20] William Samuel Johnson to Jonathan Trumbull, March 14, 1767, "Trumbull Papers," p. 490; William Samuel Johnson to Samuel Johnson, April 4, 1767, WSJ Papers; Wickwire, *British Subministers*, pp. 41, 79-82, 100-10.

[21] Thomas Whately to John Temple, May 10, 1765, "Bowdoin-Temple Papers," p. 54; Sosin, *Agents and Merchants*, p. 42.

[22] William Samuel Johnson to Jared Ingersoll, February 18, 1767, WSJ Papers; Thomas Whately to John Temple, February 25, May 2, 1767, "Bowdoin-Temple Papers," pp. 79-80, 83.

[23] Calhoon, *Loyalists in Revolutionary America*, p. 37; Gipson, *British Empire*, 11:94.

[24] Shy, *Toward Lexington*, pp. 250, 264.

[25] Thomas Gage to William Pitkin, January 8, 25, 1767, "Pitkin Papers," pp. 63, 66; William Pitkin to Thomas Gage, January 20, 31, 1767, *ibid.*, pp. 65, 67; William Pitkin to William Samuel Johnson, June 17, 1767, *ibid.*, pp. 91-92; William Samuel Johnson to Robert Walker, March 31, 1767, WSJ Papers; William Samuel Johnson to Eliphalet Dyer, April 10, 1767, WSJ Papers; William Samuel Johnson to Jonathan Trumbull, March 14,

1767, "Trumbull Papers," p. 488; Jonathan Trumbull to William Samuel Johnson, June 23, 1767, WSJ Papers.

²⁶Gipson, *British Empire*, 11:16-26.

²⁷William Samuel Johnson to William Pitkin, April 11, June 9, 1767, "Trumbull Papers," pp. 225-26, 236-38.

²⁸William Samuel Johnson to William Pitkin, April 11, 1767, "Trumbull Papers," p. 226; William Samuel Johnson to Eliphalet Dyer, April 10, 1767, WSJ Papers.

²⁹William Samuel Johnson to William Pitkin, April 11, 1767, "Trumbull Papers," pp. 224-26; Gipson, *British Empire*, 11:58.

³⁰Gipson, *British Empire*, 11:107-8.

³¹Diary of William Samuel Johnson, May 13-18, 1767, WSJ Papers; William Samuel Johnson to William Pitkin, May 16, 1767, "Trumbull Papers," pp. 228-35; Sosin, *Agents and Merchants*, pp. 103-4; Gipson, *British Empire*, 11:102.

³²Gipson, *British Empire*, 11:111; Shy, *Toward Lexington*, p. 232.

³³William Samuel Johnson to Samuel Johnson, May 18, 1767, WSJ Papers; William Samuel Johnson to William Pitkin, July 13, 1767, "Trumbull Papers," pp. 239-40.

³⁴Shy, *Toward Lexington*, p. 232.

³⁵Benjamin Franklin to Joseph Galloway, May 20, August 8, 1767, *Papers of Franklin*, 14:163-64, 230; William Samuel Johnson to Samuel Gray, June 9, 1767, WSJ Papers.

³⁶William Samuel Johnson to Samuel Gray, June 9, 1767, WSJ Papers.

³⁷Benjamin Franklin to Joseph Galloway, June 13, 1767, *Papers of Franklin*, 14:184; William Samuel Johnson to William Pitkin, June 9, 1767, "Trumbull Papers," p. 238.

³⁸William Samuel Johnson to William Pitkin, May 16, 1767, "Trumbull Papers," pp. 234-35; William Samuel Johnson to George Chapman, July 29, 1767, WSJ Papers.

³⁹Diary of William Samuel Johnson, September 17-October 24, 1767, WSJ Papers.

⁴⁰William Samuel Johnson to Jared Ingersoll, November 30, 1767, WSJ Papers; William Samuel Johnson to William Pitkin, December 26, 1767, "Trumbull Papers," pp. 246-48; Benjamin Franklin to Joseph Galloway, December 1, 1767, *Papers of Franklin*, 14:331; Marshall, *Dr. Johnson's London*, pp. 119, 136.

⁴¹Gipson, British Empire, 11:139, 142-43.

⁴²William Samuel Johnson to Ebenezer Silliman, December 8, 1767, WSJ Papers; William Samuel Johnson to Eliphalet Dyer, January 22, 1768, *ibid.*, William Samuel Johnson to Robert Walker, January 23, 1768, *ibid.*; William Samuel Johnson to William Pitkin, December 26, 1767, "Trumbull Papers," pp. 249-250; Benjamin Franklin to Joseph Galloway, August 8, 1767, *Papers of Franklin*, 14:230; Dennys De Berdt to Samuel Dexter, December 23, 1767, "Letters of De Berdt," p. 328; Dennys De Berdt to Samuel Adams, June 27, 1768, "Letters of De Berdt," pp. 333-34.

⁴³William Samuel Johnson to William Pitkin, July 13, September 15, 1767, "Trumbull Papers," pp. 241, 242-43; William Samuel Johnson to Joseph Chew, September 12, 1767, WSJ Papers; William Samuel Johnson to Ann Johnson, September 15, 1767, WSJ Papers.

⁴⁴Editors' note, *Papers of Franklin*, 15:15; Pares, *King George III and the Politicians*, p. 85; Gipson, *British Empire*, 11:223-28.

⁴⁵William Samuel Johnson to Ann Johnson, December 26, 1767, WSJ Papers; William Samuel Johnson to William Pitkin, December 26, 1767, "Trumbull Papers," pp. 251-52.

⁴⁶Introduction, *Papers of Franklin*, 15:xxv-xxviii; Gipson, *British Empire*, 11:233; Calhoon, *Loyalists in Revolutionary America*, p. 37; Kammen, *Rope of Sand*, p. 226.

⁴⁷Christie, *Wilkes, Wyvill and Reform*, p. 37; Christie, *Myth and Reality*, p. 53; Pares, *King George III and the Politicians*, p. 117.

⁴⁸William Samuel Johnson to William Pitkin, December 26, 1767, "Trumbull

Papers," pp. 247-53; Dennys De Berdt to Thomas Cushing, December 24, 1767, "Letters of De Berdt," p. 330; Shy, *Toward Lexington*, pp. 293-94.

⁴⁹Shy, *Toward Lexington*, pp. 291-94; Wickwire, *British Subminister*, p. 88.

⁵⁰Diary of William Samuel Johnson, February 2, 1767, WSJ Papers; William Samuel Johnson to William Pitkin, February 13, 1768, "Trumbull Papers," pp. 253-63. Samuel Johnson wrote to his son, "I heard so much of the fame of your letter to the Governor about your conversation with Lord Hillsborough, that I was very desirous to see it, and his Honor . . . has been so good as to send it to me." Samuel Johnson to William Samuel Johnson, March 7, 1769, *Samuel Johnson*, 1:452.

⁵¹William Samuel Johnson to William Pitkin, March 12, 1768, "Trumbull Papers," p. 266; Gipson, *British Empire*, 11:120-32.

⁵²William Samuel Johnson to William Pitkin, March 12, 1768, "Trumbull Papers," pp. 267-68, 270-72; William Samuel Johnson to Jedidiah Elderkin, January 23, 1768, WSJ Papers; Sachse, *Colonial American in Britain*, p. 207.

⁵³William Samuel Johnson to William Pitkin, March 12, 1768, "Trumbull Papers," pp. 267-68. Johnson is referring to the candidacy of Barlow Trecothick, a wealthy London merchant, alderman, and Member of Parliament. Johnson and the other agents conferred frequently with Trecothick, whose American friendships and outspoken advocacy of American rights made him suspect in England. Sachse, *Colonial American in Britain*, p. 100.

⁵⁴William Samuel Johnson to William Pitkin, July 23, 1768, "Trumbull Papers," p. 291; Gipson, *British Empire*, 11:149-51, 228.

⁵⁵Shy, *Toward Lexington*, p. 295; Gipson, *British Empire*, 11:152-56, 230.

⁵⁶William Samuel Johnson to Samuel Johnson, April 18, 1768, WSJ Papers; William Samuel Johnson to Robert Temple, April 15, 1768, *ibid.*, William Samuel Johnson to Roger Sherman, September 28, 1768, *ibid.*; William Samuel Johnson to William Pitkin, July 23, 1768, "Trumbull Papers," p. 294.

⁵⁷William Samuel Johnson to William Pitkin, July 23, 1768, "Trumbull Papers," pp. 293-95; William Samuel Johnson to Benjamin Gale, September 29, 1768, WSJ Papers. In contrast, Johnson's previous biographers have cited these admonitions to depict him as a social conservative turned loyalist, who so abhorred the disorderliness and violence of the colonial resistance that he came to repudiate the American cause. Groce, *William Samuel Johnson*, pp. 75-76; Evarts Boutell Greene; "William Samuel Johnson and the American Revolution," p. 166.

⁵⁸William Samuel Johnson to William Pitkin, July 23, 1768, "Trumbull Papers," pp. 294-95.

⁵⁹Zeichner, *Connecticut's Years of Controversy*, p. 85; Gipson, *British Empire*, 11:142-43, 181-82; Schlesinger, *Colonial Merchants*, pp. 110-19.

⁶⁰Dickinson, *Letters from a Farmer*, pp. 13-19, 38-45, 85.

⁶¹William Samuel Johnson to William Pitkin, July 23, 1768, "Trumbull Papers," p. 291; Jacobson, *John Dickinson*, p. 56.

⁶²William Samuel Johnson to William Williams, September 27, 1768, WSJ Papers; William Samuel Johnson to Roger Sherman, September 28, 1768, *ibid.*; William Samuel Johnson to Benjamin Gale, September 29, 1768, *ibid.*

⁶³*Public Records of the Colony of Connecticut*, 12:76-89.

⁶⁴William Pitkin to William Samuel Johnson, June 6, 1767, "Trumbull Papers," pp. 276-84; William Pitkin to William Samuel Johnson, June 10, 1768, "Pitkin Papers," pp. 127-29; William Pitkin to Richard Jackson, June 10, 1768, "Trumbull Papers," pp. 285-88.

⁶⁵Ebenezer Silliman to William Samuel Johnson, November 10, 1768, WSJ Papers.

⁶⁶*Public Records of the Colony of Connecticut*, 13:72-74.

⁶⁷Roger Sherman to William Samuel Johnson, June 25, 1768, WSJ Papers; William Williams, July 5, 1768, *ibid.*

⁶⁸William Samuel Johnson to William Pitkin, October 20, 1768, "Trumbull Papers," pp. 295-97; Diary of William Samuel Johnson, October 5, 1768, WSJ Papers.

⁶⁹William Samuel Johnson to Roger Sherman, September 28, 1768, WSJ Papers; William Samuel Johnson to Samuel Johnson, October 1, 1768, *ibid.;* William Samuel Johnson to William Pitkin, October 20, 1768, "Trumbull Papers," p. 297.

⁷⁰Introduction, *Franklin Papers*, 16:xiii; Appleton, "The Agents of the New England Colonies," p. 329.

⁷¹William Samuel Johnson to Jonathan Trumbull, September 29, 1768, WSJ Papers; William Samuel Johnson to Benjamin Gale, September 29, 1768, *ibid.* To De Berdt fell the difficult task of curbing the passions and rash actions of Massachusetts: Dennys De Berdt to Thomas Cushing, December 21, 24, 1767, "Letters of De Berdt," pp. 329-30; Dennys De Berdt to Samuel Adams, June 27, 1768, "Letters of De Berdt," p. 334; Dennys De Berdt to Thomas Cushing, August 26, 1768, "Letters of De Berdt," pp. 337-39.

⁷²Gipson, *British Empire*, 11:161, 164.

⁷³William Samuel Johnson to William Pitkin, November 18, 1768, "Trumbull Papers," pp. 300-1.

⁷⁴William Samuel Johnson to Jared Ingersoll, January 2, [1769], WSJ Papers.

⁷⁵William Samuel Johnson to William Pitkin, January 3, 1769, "Trumbull Papers," pp. 304-12; Van Doren, *Benjamin Franklin*, p. 381; Ritcheson, *British Politics*, p. 121; Gipson, *British Empire*, 11:232; editor's note, *Papers of Franklin*, 16:11.

⁷⁶Diary of William Samuel Johnson, December 15, 1768, January 26, February 28, 1769, WSJ Papers; William Samuel Johnson to Robert Walker, March 12, 1769, *ibid.;* William Samuel Johnson to Samuel Johnson, January 4, 1769, *ibid.;* William Samuel Johnson to William Pitkin, November 18, 1768, February 9, 1769, "Trumbull Papers," pp. 301-3, 312-18; Guttridge, *English Whiggism*, p. 66; Gipson, *British Empire*, 11:234-38; introduction, *Papers of Franklin*, 16, xxiii.

⁷⁷William Samuel Johnson to George Chapman, March 23, 1769, WSJ Papers; William Samuel Johnson to Benjamin Gale, September 29, 1768, *ibid.;* William Samuel Johnson to Robert Temple, February 4, 1769, *ibid.* Franklin was equally disgusted with the senselessness of the Hillsborough resolutions. The Pennsylvania agent wrote to Joseph Galloway, "But when they were read, I was surpriz'd to find so little in them. They seem to be mere *brutea Fulmina*, calculated chiefly to obtain Parliamentary approbation of the Steps already taken as a Minister." January 9, 1769, *Papers of Franklin*, 16:12.

⁷⁸William Samuel Johnson to Jared Ingersoll, January 2, 1769, WSJ Papers; William Samuel Johnson to Nathaniel Rogers, January 4, 1769, *ibid.;* William Samuel Johnson to William Pitkin, "Trumbull Papers," pp. 302-3.

⁷⁹William Samuel Johnson to William Pitkin, February 9, 1769, "Trumbull Papers," p. 319.

⁸⁰Zeichner, *Connecticut's Years of Controversy*, pp. 86-95, 121, 289; Shy, *Toward Lexington*, pp. 256-57; Schlesinger, *Colonial Merchants*, p. 170.

⁸¹Benjamin Gale to William Samuel Johnson, June 30, 1768, WSJ Papers; Joseph Chew to William Samuel Johnson, July 14, 1768, *ibid.;* Nathaniel Rogers to William Samuel Johnson, November 23, 1768, January 12, 1769, *ibid.*

⁸²William Samuel Johnson to Benjamin Gale, September 29, 1768, WSJ Papers; William Samuel Johnson to Robert Temple, February 4, 1769, *ibid.;* William Samuel Johnson to William Pitkin, February 9, 1769, "Trumbull Papers," pp. 318-19.

⁸³Diary of William Samuel Johnson, frequent meetings with Burke, Franklin,

De Berdt, Montague, Mauduit, Arthur and William Lee, and Jackson, September, October, and November 1768; William Samuel Johnson to William Pitkin, November 18, 1768, "Trumbull Papers," p. 303; Charles Garth to the Committee of Correspondence of the South Carolina Assembly, November 10, 1768, "Correspondence of Garth,", 30:232; Dennys De Berdt to Thomas Cushing, September 16, December 7, 1768, "Letters of De Berdt," pp. 341, 347-48.

[84]Diary of William Samuel Johnson, December 6, 1768, WSJ Papers; William Samuel Johnson to William Pitkin, January 3, 1769, "Trumbull Papers," pp. 303-6; Dennys De Berdt to Richard Crary, December, n.d., 1768, "Letters of De Berdt," pp. 348-49.

[85]Editor's note, *Papers of Franklin*, 16:54; Benjamin Franklin, draft of a Petition from the Colonial Agents to the House of Commons [between February 24 and March 7, 1769], *ibid.*, 16:54; William Samuel Johnson to William Pitkin, March 23, 1769, "Trumbull Papers," pp. 324-25; Dennys De Berdt to Thomas Cushing, March 10, 1769, "Letters of De Berdt," p. 366; Sosin, *Agents and Merchants*, p. 119; Kammen, *Rope of Sand*, pp. 172-73.

[86]William Samuel Johnson to Nathaniel Rogers, January 4, 1769, WSJ Papers; William Samuel Johnson to Robert Walker, March 12, 1769, *ibid.;* William Samuel Johnson to William Pitkin, January 3, March 23, 1769, "Trumbull Papers," pp. 309, 324-25; Kammen, *Rope of Sand*, p. 163.

[87]Kammen, *Rope of Sand*, pp. 164, 298, 315.

[88]See chapter 4, note 49, above. Also, Kammen, *Rope of Sand*, pp. 97-98, 128, 160-61, 250; Bailyn, *Ordeal of Thomas Hutchinson*, pp. 89-90; Van Doren, *Benjamin Franklin*, pp. 284-87.

[89]William Pitkin to William Samuel Johnson, "Pitkin Papers," pp. 204-5.

[90]John Nelson to John Temple, February, n.d., 1765, "Bowdoin-Temple Papers," p. 46; Thomas Whately to John Temple, February, n.d., 1765, *ibid.*, p. 49; Sosin, *Agents and Merchants*, pp. 42, 57-58.

[91]Jackson had long supported Franklin's scheme for royal government in Pennsylvania, and Franklin so trusted Jackson's political judgement that he nominated Jackson for the Pennsylvania agency. Kammen, *Rope of Sand*, pp. 23, 88-89; Van Doren, *Benjamin Franklin*, pp. 284-87.

[92]Newcomb, *Franklin and Galloway*, p. 186; Kammen, *Rope of Sand*, p. 157.

[93]Newcomb, *Franklin and Galloway*, pp. 183-85, 199; introduction, *Papers of Franklin*, 15:xxxvii; editor's note, *Franklin Papers*, 15:112.

[94]Dennys De Berdt to Samuel Adams, June 27, 1768, "Letters of De Berdt," pp. 333-34; Dennys De Berdt to Richard Crary, July 6, 1768, *ibid.*, p. 335; Kammen, *Rope of Sand*, p. 164.

[95]Charles Garth to the Committee of Correspondence of the South Carolina Assembly, n.d., "Correspondence of Charles Garth," 30: 233-35; Dennys De Berdt to the Delaware Committee of Correspondence, January 9, March 9, 1769, "Letters of De Berdt," pp. 354-55, 366.

[96]Unlike Johnson, both agents also reprimanded their constituents for bypassing Parliament to petition only the King. They reasoned astutely that it was beyond the power of the King to repeal or suspend an Act of Parliament, and that affronting Parliament only made repeal more unlikely. Dennys De Berdt to Thomas Cushing, March 18, June 27, 1768, "Letters of De Berdt," pp. 331, 332; Dennys De Berdt to Richard Crary, July 6, 1768, *ibid.*, p. 335; Dennys De Berdt to Thomas Cushing, December 7, 1768, *ibid.*, pp. 338-40; Charles Garth to the Committee of Correspondence of the South Carolina Assembly, October 14, November 10, 1768, "Correspondence of Garth," 30:229, 231-32.

De Berdt's support for the Franklin petition was dictated by another consideration as well: the sentiments of the British merchants. De Berdt was a senior partner in the trans-Atlantic trading house of De Berdt, Burkett and Sayre, and a noteworthy figure in the London mercantile community. In the early months of 1769, he labored to unite the merchants behind the colonies and to formulate a merchants' petition that could be presented in conjunction with the joint petition of the agents. The merchants wanted the duties removed, but were unimpressed with constitutional arguments. De Berdt, unable to bring the merchants completely around to the colonial position, was eager to see the agents meet the merchants halfway. Appleton, "Agents of the New England Colonies," p. 379; Sosin, *Agents and Merchants*, p. 3; Dennys De Berdt to Thomas Cushing, February 13 and 15, 1769, "Letters of De Berdt," pp. 359-61; Dennys De Berdt to the Delaware Committee, n.d. [spring 1769], "Letters of De Berdt," p. 364.

[97]William Bollan to Samuel Danforth, March 18, April 22, 1769, "Bowdoin-Temple Papers," pp. 133, 137.

[98]Sosin, *Agents and Merchants*, pp. 18-19. Bollan had cooperated in Hutchinson's defense of writs of assistance, those legal devices so odious to Massachusetts patriots.

[99]Bollan's stance on the Townshend acts contrasted embarrassingly to his earlier role as a spokesman for tight imperial control. In the early 1760s, Bollan had served as Advocate General for New England, responsible to the Board of Trade for the prosecution and preventions of illicit trade. He had complained to the Board that violations of the navigation acts were widespread and had urged new measures, such as nonjury trials, to expedite prosecution. His reports had become one basis for the new program of tough colonial regulation introduced by Townshend in 1767. Sosin, *Agents and Merchants*, pp. 38-39, 150; Bailyn, *Ordeal of Thomas Hutchinson*, p. 130; Barrow, "Background to the Grenville Program," pp. 96-97, 102-3.

[100]Charles Garth to the Committee of Correspondence of the South Carolina Assembly, March 12, 1769, "Correspondence of Charles Garth," 31:53.

[101]On Thomas Pownall's proposal in Parliament, see William Samuel Johnson to William Pitkin, April 26, 1769, "Trumbull Papers," pp. 334-41; Gipson, *British Empire*, 11:242-44; Sosin, *Agents and Merchants*, p. 120. On John Pownall: Calhoon, *Loyalists in Revolutionary America*, p. 35; Shy, *Toward Lexington*, p. 292; Wickwire, *British Subministers*, p. 69; Kammen, *Rope of Sand*, pp. 65, 259. On Pownall's cooperation with Johnson regarding a revision of the Mutiny Act: Diary of William Samuel Johnson, March 9, 10, 16, 1769, WSJ Papers; William Samuel Johnson to Jonathan Trumbull, March 28, 1770, "Trumbull Papers," p. 428. Pownall's treatises and his analysis of the Anglo-American discord are discussed in chapter 7, below.

[102]Benjamin Franklin to Noble Wimberly Jones, April 3, 1769, *Papers of Franklin*, 16:79.

[103]William Samuel Johnson to William Pitkin, March 23, 1769, "Trumbull Papers," p. 324.

Chapter 7: Conspiracy or Confusion?

[1]Robert Temple to William Samuel Johnson, February 27, 1769, WSJ Papers; Jonathan Trumbull to William Samuel Johnson, January 29, 1770, "Trumbull Papers," pp. 400-4; Charles Thomson to Benjamin Franklin, November 26, 1769, *Papers of Franklin*, 16:237-38.

[2]Charles Thomson to Benjamin Franklin, November 26, 1769, *Papers of Franklin*, 16:237-38. Bailyn, *Ideological Origins*, pp. 102-14. American fears reflected the influence of the radical political writers of the English Civil War and Commonwealth period and

their intellectual successors, the opposition politicians and publicists of the early eighteenth century. These writers had warned that Parliament was being corrupted by evil ministers who influenced elections and bribed legislators with places and pensions. Without an independent Parliament, which was the only check against tyranny by the King and his court, nothing could prevent the destruction of liberty. These writers were actually responding to the evolution of political parties in England, a change that wrought havoc in British government for the entire century. Rival factions struggled for a majority in Parliament and control of the ministry, neglecting the needs of the nation. The "real Whigs" or radical writers, disgusted with the moral temper of politics, drew the most dire predictions. Interest in eighteenth-century British theories of political corruption and the influence of these writings on America arose after the publication of Caroline Robbins, *The Eighteenth Century Commonwealthman: Studies in the Transmission, Development, and Circumstances of English Liberal Thought from the Restoration of Charles II until the War with the Thirteen Colonies* (Cambridge, Mass.: Harvard University Press, 1959). Robbins did not investigate colonial political literature, but her suggestion, that the "real Whig" doctrines found receptive ears in America, provoked new interest in the British libertarian roots of the American Revolution. For an excellent discussion of the impact of this British ideological tradition on American thought during the Anglo-American crisis, see Bailyn, *Ideological Origins.*

[3]Dickinson, *Letters from a Farmer*, pp. 13–19, 32, 38–45; Gipson, *British Empire*, 11:147.

[4]William Samuel Johnson to Ann Johnson, June 11, 1768, WSJ Papers; William Samuel Johnson to Jared Ingersoll, September 30, 1768, *ibid.*

[5]William Samuel Johnson to Robert Temple, May 13, 1769, WSJ Papers.

[6]William Samuel Johnson to William Pitkin, April 29, 1768, "Trumbull Papers," pp. 274–76; William Samuel Johnson to Samuel Johnson, May 14, 1768, WSJ Papers. On the enormous number of strikes that year, see Rudé, *Paris and London*, p. 233; Rudé, *Hanoverian London*, p. 192.

[7]William Samuel Johnson to Jedidiah Elderkin, January 23, 1768, WSJ Papers.

[8]William Samuel Johnson to Ann Johnson, June 11, 1768, WSJ Papers; William Samuel Johnson to William Williams, November 1, 1769, *ibid.*

[9]William Samuel Johnson to Robert Walker, March 12, 1769, WSJ Papers, William Samuel Johnson to Eliphalet Dyer, June 6, 1769, *ibid.;* William Samuel Johnson to Samuel Gray, June 9, 1767, *ibid.*

[10]William Samuel Johnson to William Pitkin, April 11, 1767, "Trumbull Papers," p. 226.

[11]William Samuel Johnson to William Williams, September 27, 1768, WSJ Papers.

[12]William Samuel Johnson to Joseph Trumbull, April 15, 1769, "Trumbull Papers," p. 331.

[13]Diary of William Samuel Johnson, October 25, November 21, December 30, 1768, January 20, February 3, 8, March 9, 10, 16, 21, 1769, WSJ Papers; William Samuel Johnson to Jonathan Trumbull, February 3, 1770, "Trumbull Papers," p. 407.

[14]Thomas Pownall, *The Administration of the Colonies*, 4th ed. (London, 1768), quoted in Guttridge, "Pownall's *Administration of the Colonies,*" pp. 41–42. Pownall and Johnson did not agree on everything. Pownall was willing to lay aside the question of Parliament's right to tax if repeal of the Townshend Acts could be won by more conciliatory arguments. He also suggested that because Parliament would never yield the right to tax, Americans ought to be allowed seats in Parliament. Guttridge, "Pownall's *Administration of the Colonies,*" pp. 44–46. Johnson, like most Americans, dismissed representation in Parliament as unsound. Diary of William Samuel Johnson, September 19,

1768, WSJ Papers. On October 20, 1768, Johnson told William Pitkin, "Several of the late political writers here have taken up the idea of an incorporation of the colonies with Great Britain, and urged the necessity of admitting them to a representation in Parliament, in order to put an end to the present disputes. It may perhaps even be proposed in Parliament, but if it should, it would be opposed by others as well as by all friends of the Colonies, and there is little danger of it making any progress." Bancroft Transcripts.

[15]Bernard Bailyn presents an exhaustive discussion on these letters in *Ordeal of Thomas Hutchinson*, pp. 130-31, 137, 225-30.

[16]Bailyn, *Ordeal of Thomas Hutchinson*, 231. On Hillsborough's plan, and the presentation of the Massachusetts Bay Papers in Parliament, see Gipson, *British Empire*, 11:235-41.

[17]Bailyn, *Ordeal of Thomas Hutchinson*, pp. 232-33. In Massachusetts, where factional competition split the colony into two hostile camps, Pownall and Bernard had always stood in opposite camps. *Ibid.*, p. 44. But Pownall's distress over the Bernard letters ranged beyond a partisan distrust of the Governor.

[18]Quoted in Bailyn, *Ordeal of Thomas Hutchinson*, p. 128.

[19]James Bowdoin to Thomas Pownall, May 10, 1769, "Bowdoin-Temple Papers," p. 141.

[20]Nathaniel Rogers to William Samuel Johnson, November 23, 1768, January 12, 1769, February 20, 1769, WSJ Papers; William Samuel Johnson to Nathaniel Rogers, April 22, 1769, *ibid.*

[21]Diary of William Samuel Johnson, July 27, August 23, 1768, WSJ Papers. See also entries for November 29, December 14, 1768, January 24, February 4, 1769.

[22]John Pownall had served as Secretary to the Board of Trade under countless administrations since 1753. During Grenville's ministry, Pownall and Whately had worked together on the chief minister's proposals for strict colonial regulation and an American revenue. After Grenville left the cabinet and Whately departed the Board of Trade, Pownall and Whately remained close friends. In 1768, Pownall became under-secretary to Lord Hillsborough in the new American Department. It is not surprising that when Whately received the reports from Massachusetts, he would hasten to share them with his influential friend. In addition, it was Pownall who had secured for Bernard the appointment as Governor of Massachusetts. Calhoon, *Loyalists in Revolutionary America*, p. 88; Wickwire, *British Subminister*, pp. 70-71, 97-110.

[23]William Samuel Johnson to Robert Walker, March 12, 1769, WSJ Papers.

[24]William Samuel Johnson to Eliphalet Dyer, June 6, 1769, WSJ Papers.

[25][Robert or John] Temple to William Samuel Johnson. December 1, 1768, WSJ Papers; Robert Temple to William Samuel Johnson, February 27, 1769, *ibid.*; William Samuel Johnson to Robert Temple, May 13, 1769, *ibid.* Johnson corresponded with John Temple of Massachusetts and with his brother Robert Temple, who had travelled to England in 1767 and met the Connecticut agent there. John Temple was one of the five members of the American Board of Commissioners of Customs that had been established in 1768. The appointment, for Temple, was a demotion, for he had previously filled the post of Surveyor General of Customs for the Northern District of America. He blamed the demotion on Bernard and became a vocal partisan of the anti-Bernard forces in Massachusetts. John Temple also complained to Whately that Bernard's ill-conduct was creating fear and disaffection in the colony, but Whately was unwilling to intervene against the Governor. "Bowdoin-Temple Papers," pp. xx-xvi; John Temple to Thomas Whately, September 10, 1764, August 14, 1766, November 4, 1768, *ibid.*, pp. 26, 27, 111-13.

[26]William Samuel Johnson to Robert Temple, May 13, 1769, WSJ Papers.

[27]William Samuel Johnson to Nathaniel Rogers, January 4, 1769, WSJ Papers;

William Samuel Johnson to Joseph Chew, May 5, 1769, *ibid.;* William Samuel Johnson to Robert Temple, May 13, 1769, *ibid.*

[28]William Samuel Johnson to Jonathan Trumbull, October 16, 1769, "Trumbull Papers," pp. 369-80; William Samuel Johnson to Jere Miller, May 4, 1769, WSJ Papers.

[29]William Samuel Johnson to William Pitkin, January 3, 1769, "Trumbull Papers," p. 310; William Samuel Johnson to Robert Temple, May 13, 1769, WSJ Papers.

[30]Ritcheson, *British Politics,* p. 32; Gipson, *British Empire,* 11:205-9; Christie, *Wilkes, Wyvill and Reform,* p. 27; Rudé, *Paris and London,* p. 266.

[31]William Samuel Johnson to Samuel Johnson, April 18, 1768, WSJ Papers. Historians have reached similar verdicts on Wilkes's character, e.g. Christie, *Wilkes, Wyvill and Reform,* p. 78.

[32]William Samuel Johnson to Samuel Johnson, April 18, 1768, WSJ Papers; William Samuel Johnson to William Pitkin, April 29, 1768, "Trumbull Papers," pp. 270-71, 275; Rudé, *Paris and London,* p. 255.

[33]Bailyn, *Ideological Origins,* pp. 110-11; Maier, "John Wilkes and American Disillusionment with Britain," pp. 374, 377.

[34]Bailyn, *Ideological Origins,* pp. 111-12.

[35]Gipson, *British Empire,* 11:222.

[36]William Samuel Johnson to Benjamin Gale, September 29, 1768, WSJ Papers.

[37]Gipson, *British Empire,* 11:222.

[38]*Ibid.,* 11:208-15; Rudé, *Paris and London,* pp. 230, 244; Christie, *Wilkes, Wyvill and Reform,* p. 31; Rudé, *Hanoverian London,* p. 166.

[39]Rudé, *Paris and London,* pp. 230-34.

[40]Gipson, *British Empire,* 11:192-94, 215-16. Since the beginning of the decade, London had been the seat of a large group of radical politicians who agitated against bribery at elections, pensions for Members of Parliament, and other tools of influence that could undermine the independence of Parliament. The London reformers wanted to make Parliament more representative of the nation and especially of London's great commercial interests. In 1769, the reformers' discontents crystallized around the Wilkes affair. Rudé, *Hanoverian London,* pp. 143-45; Ian Christie, *Myth and Reality,* p. 2; Christie, *Wiles, Wyvill and Reform,* p. 32.

[41]Greene, "Bridge to Revolution: The Wilkes Fund Controversy in South Carolina," pp. 19-52; Bailyn, *Ideological Crigins,* pp. 110-12, 115; Maier, "John Wilkes," p. 376.

[42]Boston Sons of Liberty to John Wilkes, November 4, 1769, quoted in Maier, "John Wilkes and American Disillusionment with Britain," p. 387.

[43]Diary of William Samuel Johnson, May 7, 10, August 13, 1768, January 16, 1769, WSJ Papers; William Samuel Johnson to Samuel Johnson, May 17, 1769, *ibid.;* William Samuel Johnson to Joseph Trumbull, April 15, 1769, "Trumbull Papers," p. 332; Christie, *Wilkes, Wyvill and Reform,* p. 227.

[44]Appleton, "Agents of the New England Colonies," p. 379; Ritcheson, *British Politics,* pp. x, 129; Shy, *Toward Lexington,* p. 300, n.104. The alliance between these parliamentary factions and the metropolitan reformers was a tenuous one, for the goals of the two groups were, at bottom, very different. For the Rockinghamites, the Wilkes campaign was a political expedient to overturn the Grafton ministry, and they had little sympathy for the reformers' war on patronage and influence. Gipson, *British Empire,* 11:202-6, 216; Christie, *Wilkes, Wyvill and Reform,* pp. 25-27; Christie, *Myth and Reality,* pp. 38-40; Ritcheson, *British Politics,* p. 138.

[45]Thomas Whately to John Temple, July 26, 1769, "Bowdoin-Temple Papers," pp. 152-53.

[46]William Samuel Johnson to William Pitkin, January 3, 1769, "Trumbull Papers,"

p. 310. On Johnson's judgement of the Rockinghamites as mere opportunists, see also William Samuel Johnson to Jonathan Trumbull, October 16, 1769, February 3, 1770, *ibid.*, pp. 376-77, 406; William Samuel Johnson to William Pitkin, September 18, 1769, *ibid.*, 363-65; William Samuel Johnson to Thomas Fitch, February 12, 1770, WSJ Papers.

⁴⁷William Samuel Johnson to William Pitkin, May 25, 1769, "Trumbull Papers," p. 354. Several historians have presented a similar portrait of the Rockingham party, stressing its commitment to parliamentary sovereignty and its opportunistic exploitation of the American issue and the Wilkes clamor to overturn the ministry. See Guttridge, *English Whiggism*, pp. 61-69, 140-42; Ritcheson, *British Politics*, p. 47; Christie, *Wilkes, Wyvill and Reform*, p. 37; Christie, *Myth and Reality*, p. 53.

⁴⁸William Samuel Johnson to William Pitkin, April 26, 1769, "Trumbull Papers," pp. 338-39.

⁴⁹William Samuel Johnson to William Pitkin, September 18, 1769, "Trumbull Papers," p. 366.

⁵⁰William Samuel Johnson to William Pitkin, April 26, 1769, "Trumbull Papers," p. 339; William Samuel Johnson to Agur Tomlinson, May 6, 1769, WSJ Papers.

⁵¹William Pitkin to William Samuel Johnson, March 11, 1768, WSJ Papers; Roger Sherman to William Samuel Johnson, June 25, 1768, *ibid.;* William Samuel Johnson to William Pitkin, July 23, 1768, "Trumbull Papers," pp. 292-93; William Samuel Johnson to Jonathan Trumbull, October 16, 1769, "Trumbull Papers," p. 374. Connecticut's conservatives were more fearful over the Superior Court's decision. See Ebenezer Silliman to William Samuel Johnson, November 10, 1768, WSJ Papers.

⁵²Johnson told Pitkin that the Boston Towns Meeting's bold disclaimers against submission to parliamentary authority were considered treasonous by the British, who were prepared to undertake a war in defense of that authority. William Samuel Johnson to William Pitkin, November 18, 1768, "Trumbull Papers," pp. 300-4.

⁵³William Samuel Johnson to Nathaniel Rogers, January 21, November 15, 1769, WSJ Papers; William Samuel Johnson to Jared Ingersoll, December 9, 1769, *ibid.*

⁵⁴Other close observers of the anti-ministry campaign corroborated Johnson's testimony. For example, Alexander Mackay to James Bowdoin, April, n.d., 1770, "Bowdoin-Temple Papers," p. 171: "Those who are your chief advisers from hence do not care a farthing for your interest," Mackay told the Boston patriot, ". . . their object is to overthrow the administration by distressing government in every quarter they can & so far from wishing an accommodation of all the differences with America, I sincerely believe, would be very sorry for it. . . ."

⁵⁵Letter of Benjamin Franklin, *Gazeteer and Daily Advertiser*, January 21, 1768, rpt. in *Papers of Franklin*, 15:19.

⁵⁶Benjamin Franklin to Lord Kames, February 25, 1767, *Papers of Franklin*, 14:70.

⁵⁷Benjamin Franklin to William Franklin, April 6, 1768, *ibid.*, 15:98.

⁵⁸Benjamin Franklin to William Franklin, October 5, 1768, *ibid.*, 15:224.

⁵⁹Maier, "John Wilkes and American Disillusionment with Britain," pp. 373-74, 391-95.

⁶⁰Jonathan Trumbull to Richard Jackson, December 15, 1769, *Susquehannah Papers*, 3:211; Jonathan Trumbull to William Samuel Johnson, December 12, 1769, "Trumbull Papers," p. 390.

⁶¹Quoted in Bridenbaugh, *Mitre and Sceptre*, p. 280.

⁶²Thomas Bradbury Chandler, *An Appeal . . .* , (New York, 1767). On the joint meetings of the clergy, see Steiner, *Samuel Seabury*, pp. 102-8; Cross, *Anglican Episcopate*, pp. 165, 215-16. Chandler began the *Appeal* in January, 1767, with Samuel Johnson as his constant reader and critic, and presented the finished piece to the joint convention held

in April 1767. Steiner, *Samuel Seabury*, p. 108. For evidence of the alarm that these meetings provoked, see Francis Alison to Ezra Stiles, August 7, 1766, quoted in Bridenbaugh, *Mitre and Sceptre*, p. 272. The clergy's impatience with their British church superiors is vividly expressed in Thomas B. Chandler to Samuel Johnson, November 12, 1765, *Samuel Johnson*, 1:355-57; Samuel Johnson to the Secretary, SPG, the Bishop of London, and the Archbishop of Canterbury, September 5, 1765, *ibid.*, 1:354-55; The Clergy of Connecticut and New York to the Bishop of London, October 8, 1766, Hawks and Perry, eds., *Documentary History of the Protestant Episcopal Church*, 2:100-2.

⁶³Charles Chauncy, *An Appeal to the Public Answered* . . . (Boston, 1768); Thomas Bradbury Chandler, *The Appeal Defended* . . . (New York, 1769); Charles Chauncy, *A Reply to Dr. Chandler's "Appeal Defended* . . . (Boston, 1770); Thomas Bradbury Chandler, *The Appeal Further Defended; in Answer to the Further Misrepresentations of Dr. Chauncy* (New York, 1771).

⁶⁴The "American Whig" appeared in the *New York Gazette or The Weekly Post Boy*. Twenty-four days after the first appearance of the "American Whig," the "Centinel" was issued in the *Pennsylvania Journal*. The major arguments of these two columns are well summarized in Cross, *Anglican Episcopate*, pp. 196, 205-6. Anglicans in both colonies hastened to rebut the arguments. Myles Cooper of King's College and Charles Inglis of Trinity Church penned a series of counterattacks entitled "A Whip of the American Whig," which covered the pages of the *New York Gazette and Weekly Mercury* from May 23, 1768 to January 29, 1770. Provost William Smith of the College of Philadelphia issued a sharp rebuttal called "The Anatomist" in the *Pennsylvania Gazette*. See Bridenbaugh, *Mitre and Sceptre*, pp. 299-301; Steiner, *Samuel Seabury*, pp. 110-23.

⁶⁵Sykes, *From Sheldon to Secker*, p. 210; Gerlach, "Champions of an American Episcopate," p. 411.

⁶⁶Samuel Johnson to the Archbishop of Canterbury, December 15, 1766, *Samuel Johnson*, 1:383-84; Samuel Johnson to William Samuel Johnson, June 8, 1767, *ibid.*, 1:403-6. See also Samuel Auchmuty to Samuel Johnson, November n.d., 1766, *ibid.*, 1:382.

⁶⁷William Samuel Johnson to Samuel Johnson, March 6, April 4, 26, 1767, Bancroft Transcripts; Diary of William Samuel Johnson, February 11, 20, 25, March 1, 9, 18, 21, 31, April 29, May 15, 19, 21, June 6, 8, 11, 1767, WSJ Papers.

⁶⁸William Samuel Johnson to Samuel Johnson, July 13, 1767, WSJ Papers. See also note 67, above.

⁶⁹William Samuel Johnson to Samuel Johnson, January 9, 1768, WSJ Papers; William Samuel Johnson to Thomas Bradbury Chandler, February 20, 1768, *ibid.*

⁷⁰Samuel Johnson to William Samuel Johnson, June 8, 1767, *Samuel Johnson*, 1:305. See also Samuel Johnson to the Archbishop of Canterbury, November 10, 1766, *ibid.*, 1:379.

⁷¹William Samuel Johnson to Samuel Johnson, July 13, 1767, August 18, 1770, WSJ Papers; William Samuel Johnson to Samuel Johnson, January 9, 1768, WSJ Papers.

⁷²Kammen, *A Rope of Sand*, p. 78; Sosin, *Agents and Merchants*, p. 78; Bailyn, *Ordeal of Thomas Hutchinson*, p. 58. For several years, the anti-Hutchinson politicians in the colony had struggled to unseat Bollan. The clamor against the Church of England in 1762 had finally enabled these politicians to rally public support for their partisan cause.

⁷³Chauncey Whittelsey to William Samuel Johnson, December 9, 1766, WSJ Papers. Johnson replied in July that the ministry contemplated no malicious design against the religious liberties of New England, but rather aimed their attack on the civil liberties of all Americans. William Samuel Johnson to Chauncey Whittelsey, July 17, 1767, *ibid.*

⁷⁴William Samuel Johnson to Samuel Johnson, April 26, 1767, Bancroft Transcripts.

[75]William Samuel Johnson to Thomas Bradbury Chandler, February 20, 1768, WSJ Papers.

[76]Jonathan Trumbull to William Samuel Johnson, December 12, 1769, "Trumbull Papers," p. 390.

[77]William Samuel Johnson to Jonathan Trumbull, February 26, 1770, "Trumbull Papers," pp. 412-13.

[78]Sosin, "Proposals in the Pre-Revolutionary Decade For Establishing Anglican Bishops," p. 82; Richard Jackson to Jonathan Trumbull, March 7, 1770, Bancroft Transcripts.

[79]Dickinson, *Letters from a Farmer*, pp. 31-32.

[80]William Pitkin to Richard Jackson, June 10, 1768, "Trumbull Papers," pp. 285-86.

[81]Jonathan Trumbull to William Samuel Johnson, January 29, 1770, "Trumbull Papers," p. 403.

[82]Nathan Whiting to William Samuel Johnson, March 10, 1770, WSJ Papers.

[83]William Samuel Johnson to Benjamin Gale, April 10, 1769, WSJ Papers.

[84]William Pitkin to William Samuel Johnson, February 15, 1769, WSJ Papers; William Pitkin to William Samuel Johnson, June 6, 1768, "Trumbull Papers," p. 283.

[85]Dickinson, *Letters from a Farmer*, p. 33: John Dickinson to William Pitt, December 21, 1765, quoted in Jacobson, *John Dickinson.*

[86]William Samuel Johnson to Benjamin Gale, April 10, 1769, WSJ Papers.

[87]William Samuel Johnson to Robert Temple, February 4, 1769, WSJ Papers.

[88]William Pitkin to William Samuel Johnson, November 1, 1768, February 15, 1769, WSJ Papers.

[89]Dickinson, *Letters from a Farmer*, p. 32.

Chapter 8: Defeat and Disillusionment

[1]Gipson, British Empire, 11:241-42, 244; Donoughue, *British Politics and the American Revolution*, p. 16.

[2]William Samuel Johnson to George Chapman, August 25, 1769, WSJ Papers; William Samuel Johnson to William Pitkin, May 25, 1769, "Trumbull Papers," pp. 246-53. One Connecticut man asked Johnson, "If it is an Evil why was it not removed immediately or was his Lordship's Letter only to Let us know that the ministry have it in their power to say what act shall pass and What shall be Repealed; this is making Very free indeed with Parliaments." Joseph Chew to William Samuel Johnson, December 9, 1769, WSJ Papers.

[3]Schlesinger, *Colonial Merchants*, p. 13.

[4]Philadelphia Merchants to Benjamin Franklin, April 18, 1769, *Papers of Franklin*, 16:115.

[5]Benjamin Franklin to the Philadelphia Merchants, July 19, 1769, *ibid.*, 16:174.

[6]Dennys De Berdt to Thomas Cushing, February 2, 1770, "Letters of Dennys De Berdt," p. 396; Massachusetts House of Representatives to Dennys De Berdt, n.d., *ibid.*, pp. 455-56. De Berdt was a partner in the commercial house of De Berdt, Burkett, and Sayre. His ties to the London merchant community made him an ardent supporter of the Wilkes crusade and a vocal opponent of the Grafton-Bedford ministry. London merchants monopolized the leadership and filled the ranks of the city's reform movement. They had long resented the underrepresentation of the nation's commercial interests in Parliament, and traditionally had formed a common front against the ministry in times of crisis. In 1769, the London merchants seized upon the Wilkes issue to make a show of

their political strength. On merchant politics, Ian Christie, *Wilkes, Wyvill and Reform,* pp. 9, 44; Rudé, *Paris and London in the Eighteenth Century,* pp. 43-44.

[7]Bailyn, *Ordeal of Thomas Hutchinson,* pp. 89-90; Gipson, *British Empire,* 11:34-40.

[8]Dennys De Berdt to Thomas Cushing, January 2, June 1, 1769, "Letters of De Berdt," pp. 350-52, 375; Dennys De Berdt to the Boston Selectmen, January 2, 1769, *ibid.,* p. 363.

[9]Diary of William Samuel Johnson, November 9, December 2, 1769, June 11, 26, July 11, November 29, 1770, January 15, 1771, WSJ Papers.

[10]William Samuel Johnson to Jonathan Trumbull, December 5, 1769, January 12, 1770, "Trumbull Papers," pp. 387-88, 392-93. Jonathan Trumbull to William Samuel Johnson, January 29, 1770, *ibid.,* pp. 402-3.

[11]Kammen, *Rope of Sand,* p. 23; Bailyn, *Ordeal of Thomas Hutchinson,* pp. 142, 146-47, 282.

[12]Sosin, *Agents and Merchants,* p. 91.

[13]"Introduction," *Papers of Franklin,* 17: xxv; Dennys De Berdt to Thomas Cushing, February 2, 1770, "Letters of De Berdt," p. 397.

[14]Diary of William Samuel Johnson, June 7-July 28, 1769, WSJ Papers.

[15]William Samuel Johnson to Samuel Johnson, November 4, 1769, WSJ Papers; Diary of William Samuel Johnson, October 18, November 3, 1769, *ibid.;* Rudé, *Hanoverian London,* p. 62; Marshall, *Dr. Johnson's London,* p. 123.

[16]William Samuel Johnson to Jonathan Trumbull, October 16, 1769, "Trumbull Papers," pp. 375-76.

[17]Gipson, *British Empire,* 11:250; Kammen, *Rope of Sand,* pp. 219, 226; Christie, *Myth and Reality,* p. 85; "Introduction," *Papers of Franklin,* 17:xxv. Whately's prediction was all too true. Thomas Whately to John Temple, July 26, 1769, "Bowdoin-Temple Papers," pp. 152-53.

[18]William Samuel Johnson to George Berkeley, February 6, 1770, Bancroft Transcripts; William Samuel Johnson to Jonathan Trumbull, February 3, 1770, "Trumbull Papers," pp. 405-11.

[19]William Samuel Johnson to Jonathan Trumbull, February 26, March 28, 1770, "Trumbull Papers," pp. 417, 426-27. On March 18, Commons passed the ministry's bill declaring that the expulsion of Wilkes was compatible with the law of the land and the custom of Parliament. Gipson, *British Empire,* 11:251-52.

[20]William Samuel Johnson to Jonathan Trumbull, March 6, 1770, "Trumbull Papers," pp. 421-26; Diary of William Samuel Johnson, March 5, 1770, WSJ Papers.

[21]William Samuel Johnson to Geroge Berkeley, March 6, 1770, Bancroft Transcripts; Gipson, *British Empire,* 11:254-56.

[22]William Samuel Johnson to Jonathan Trumbull, March 6, May 21, 1770, "Trumbull Papers," pp. 425, 437.

[23]Gipson, *British Empire,* 11:26.

[24]*Ibid.,* 11:255-56.

[25]William Samuel Johnson to Jonathan Trumbull, May 21, 1770, "Trumbull Papers," p. 435.

[26]William Samuel Johnson to Jonathan Trumbull, March 28, 1770, "Trumbull Papers," p. 428; William Samuel Johnson to Samuel Johnson, April 14, 1770, *Samuel Johnson,* 1:468.

[27]Sosin, *Agents and Merchants,* p. 127; Dennys De Berdt to [unknown correspondent] March 7, 1770, "Letters of De Berdt," p. 406.

[28]Benjamin Franklin to William Strahan, November 29, 1769, *Papers of Franklin,* 16:243-49; Benjamin Franklin to Joseph Galloway, March 21, 1770, *ibid.,* 17:115; Letter of Benjamin Franklin, *Pennsylvania Gazette,* September 6, 1770, rpt. in *ibid.,* 17:214.

[29]William Samuel Johnson to George Berkeley, May 21, 1770, Bancroft Transcripts.

[30]William Samuel Johnson to Jonathan Trumbull, March 28, 1770, "Trumbull Papers," p. 428.

[31]William Samuel Johnson to Jonathan Trumbull, November 15, 1770, "Trumbull Papers," p. 467.

[32]Thomas Pownall to the Committee of the Town of Boston, n.d., "Bowdoin-Temple Papers," pp. 189-93.

[33]Thomas Pownall to James Bowdoin, July 14, 1770, "Bowdoin-Temple Papers," pp. 196-98.

[34]Jonathan Trumbull to William Samuel Johnson, January 29, 1770, "Trumbull Papers," p. 401.

[35]Joseph Chew to William Samuel Johnson, January 29, 1770, WSJ Papers. Also, Jonathan Trumbull to William Samuel Johnson, March 3, 1770, "Trumbull Papers," p. 420. In February, merchants from nearly all the Connecticut towns held a convention at Middletown, where they swore to uphold the nonimportation agreement adopted by New York, Boston, and Philadelphia. *Connecticut Courant*, February 26, 1770.

[36]In April 1770, when Parliament adjourned without offering any terms of conciliation, Johnson had written to his father, "Happy would it have been had the other colonies imitated the firmness and integrity of New York (who it does not appear have in any respects infringed their agreements. We should I think have seen a different issue of this business even this Session." William Samuel Johnson to Samuel Johnson, April 14, 1770, *Samuel Johnson*, 1:467-68.

[37]Gipson, *British Empire*, 11:267-73; Zeichner, *Connecticut's Years of Controversy*, p. 87; Labaree, *Boston Tea Party*, pp. 46-49; Schlesinger, *Prelude to Independence*, p. 228.

[38]Schlesinger, *Colonial Merchants*, pp. 210-17.

[39]William Samuel Johnson to Jonathan Trumbull, August 20, 1770, "Trumbull Papers," p. 450. Johnson told Dyer, "We have just rec'd Intelligence that the Merch[ants] of New York have opened the Trade & that the Amer[icans] have given up the point with no little discredit to themselves & to the confusion of their advocates & to the Joy & Triumph of their Adversaries." William Samuel Johnson to Eliphalet Dyer, August 21, 1770, WSJ Papers.

[40]William Samuel Johnson to Jonathan Trumbull, August 20, 1770, "Trumbull Papers," p. 450.

Chapter 9: *The Long-awaited Passage Home*

[1]William Samuel Johnson to Ann Johnson, November 11, 1767, WSJ Papers.

[2]William Samuel Johnson to Eliphalet Dyer, January 22, 1768, WSJ Papers. See also William Samuel Johnson to William Pitkin, May 25, 1769, "Trumbull Papers," pp. 247-53.

[3]William Samuel Johnson to Jonathan Trumbull, February 5, 1771, "Trumbull Papers," p. 475. See also William Samuel Johnson to William Pitkin, July 23, 1768, *ibid.*, p. 289. Other colonial agents encountered the same problem, owing largely to the disagreeable temper of the Privy Council's chairman, Lord Northington. Kammen, *Rope of Sand*, p. 266.

[4]Roger Sherman to William Samuel Johnson, June 25, 1768, WSJ Papers; William Samuel Johnson to William Pitkin, May 25, 1769, "Trumbull Papers," p. 355: Samuel Johnson to William Samuel Johnson, November 24, 1769, *Samuel Johnson*, 1:462.

[5]Samuel Johnson to William Samuel Johnson, November 24, 1769, *Samuel Johnson*, 1:462.

[6]Samuel Johnson to Jonathan Trumbull, December 5, 1769, *Samuel Johnson*, 1:464; William Samuel Johnson to Ann Johnson, January 1, April 14, June 28, July 18, 1770, WSJ Papers.

[7]William Samuel Johnson to Samuel Johnson, August 18, 1770, WSJ Papers; William Samuel Johnson to Jonathan Trumbull, August 20, 1770, "Trumbull Papers," pp. 445-50.

[8]William Samuel Johnson to Ebenezer Kneeland, September 8, 1770, WSJ Papers.

[9]Diary of William Samuel Johnson, June 3-August 2, 1770, WSJ Papers; William Samuel Johnson to Ann Johnson, June 12, 1771, *ibid.*

[10]Thomas Life to Jonathan Trumbull, January 6, 1773, *Susquehannah Papers*, 5:65.

[11]William Samuel Johnson to Ann Johnson, July 15, 1771, WSJ Papers.

[12]Eliphalet Dyer to William Samuel Johnson, n.d. [winter], 1766, WSJ Papers, quoted in *Susquehannah Papers*, 2:337-38.

[13]See chapter 4, note 75, above.

[14]Boyd, ed., *Susquehannah Papers*, 2:xxxix-xli; Eliphalet Dyer to William Samuel Johnson, n.d. [winter] 1766, WSJ Papers.

[15]William Samuel Johnson to Eliphalet Dyer, August 5, September 12, 1767, *Susquehannah Papers*, 2:321; William Samuel Johnson to Eliphalet Dyer, April 10, 11, 1767, WSJ Papers.

[16]For evidence of Johnson's consultations with Franklin and Johnson on Susquehannah: William Samuel Johnson to Eliphalet Dyer, August 8, 1767, January 22, 1768, *Susquehannah Papers*, 2:321, 3:5-7; William Samuel Johnson to Eliphalet Dyer, September 12, 1767, WSJ Papers.

[17]Extract from the diary of Eliphalet Dyer, *Susquehannah Papers*, 2:304; Eliphalet Dyer to Jedidiah Elderkin, October 18, 1763, *ibid.*, 2:272-74; Joseph Chew to Jared Ingersoll, August 10, 1763, *ibid.*, 2:265.

[18]Wickwire, *British Subministers*, pp. 91-96; Gipson, *British Empire*, 11:431.

[19]Johnson's own encounter with Hillsborough regarding another land dispute soon confirmed the Connecticut agent's apprehensions that Hillsborough had no sympathy for land speculators. Johnson discussed Hillsborough's attitude in the following letters: William Samuel Johnson to Agur Tomlinson, March 28, 31, 1767, May 6, 1769, WSJ Papers; William Samuel Johnson to the New Hampshire Committee and Col. Ruggles, March 31, 1767, *ibid.*; William Samuel Johnson to Samuel Johnson, April 4, 1767, *ibid.* The dispute involved the present-day territory of Vermont, over which New Hampshire and New York contended at mid-century. Johnson represented the New Hampshire claimants. Crockett, *Vermont: The Green Mountain State*, pp. 176, 182, 190, 260-304.

[20]William Samuel Johnson to Eliphalet Dyer, January 22, 1768, *Susquehannah Papers*, 3:5-7.

[21]Minutes of a Meeting of the Susquehannah Company, November 11, 1767, April 7, 1768, *Susquehannah Papers*, 2:323, 3:14; Notice of a Meeting of the Susquehannah Company, January 6, 1768, *ibid.*, 3:2; Petition of Jedidiah Elderkin to the Connecticut Assembly, April 22, 1768, *ibid.*, 3:18-19; Eliphalet Dyer to William Samuel Johnson, July 12, 1768, *ibid.*, 3:19-20; William Samuel Johnson to Eliphalet Dyer, September 28, 1768, *ibid.*, 3:27.

[22]Eliphalet Dyer to William Samuel Johnson, July 12, 1768, *Susquehannah Papers*, 3:20-21; William Samuel Johnson to Eliphalet Dyer, September 28, 1768, *ibid.*, 3:28-29; *ibid.*, 3:xii-xiii.

[23]Boyd, ed., *Susquehannah Papers*, 3:xx-xxiii.

[24]William Samuel Johnson to the Committee of the Susquehannah Company, March 10, 1769, *Susquehannah Papers*, 3:89-91.

[25]*Ibid.;* Joseph Chew to William Samuel Johnson, January 14, 1769, WSJ Papers; Gipson, *British Empire*, 11:394.

[26]Boyd, ed., *Susquehannah Papers*, 3:xxvi; Eliphalet Dyer to William Samuel Johnson, August 8, 1769, *ibid.*, 3:159-61; William Samuel Johnson to Eliphalet Dyer, October 12, 1769, *ibid.*, 3:187-88.

[27]Boyd, ed., *Susquehannah Papers*, 3:xxvii-xxviii, 4:xxviii; William Samuel Johnson to Florentius Vassal, n.d., *ibid.*, 3:49; Draft of a Petition of Thomas and Richard Penn, n.d., *ibid.*, 4:23; William Samuel Johnson to Eliphalet Dyer, March 19, 1770, *ibid.*, 4:46.

[28]Boyd, ed., *Susquehannah Papers*, 4:xxxiii.

[29]*Ibid.*, 1:xvii. The Penns also counted the support of Sir William Johnson. *Ibid.*, 3:xiv.

[30]Petition of Elisha Sheldon, Eliphalet Dyer, *et al.* to the General Assembly, January n.d., 1769, *Susquehannah Papers*, 3:52-55; Petition of the Susquehannah Company to the General Assembly, January n.d., 1769, *ibid.*, 3:60-62; Actions of the Connecticut Assembly on the Petition of Eliphalet Dyer, October n.d., 1769, *ibid.*, 3:191-92; Jonathan Trumbull to William Samuel Johnson, December 12, 1769, *ibid.*, 3:209; Jonathan Trumbull to Richard Jackson, December 15, 1769, *ibid.*, 3:211.

[31]William Samuel Johnson to Jonathan Trumbull, February 26, 1770, *Susquehannah Papers*, 4:27-29. In a letter written to Dyer the following day, Johnson described his advice to the Governor. *Ibid.*, 4:35-36.

[32]William Samuel Johnson to Jonathan Trumbull, February 26, 1770, *Susquehannah Papers*, 4:27-29; Richard Jackson to Jonathan Trumbull, "Trumbull Papers," pp. 433-34.

[33]Jonathan Trumbull to William Samuel Johnson, June 30, 1770, *Susquehannah Papers*, 4:92.

[34]Diary of William Samuel Johnson, July 10, 12, 18, 1770, WSJ Papers; Representation from the Board of Trade to the Privy Council, July 13, 1770, *Susquehannah Papers*, 4:94-96; William Samuel Johnson to Jonathan Trumbull, August 20, 1770, *ibid.*, 4:112-13.

[35]William Samuel Johnson to Richard Jackson, August 31, 1770, *Susquehannah Papers*, 4:116.

[36]Eliphalet Dyer to William Samuel Johnson, August 8, December 15, 1770, *Susquehannah Papers*, 4:107, 143; *ibid.*, 4:i-xiv.

[37]Joseph Chew to William Samuel Johnson, December 9, 1769, *Susquehannah Papers*, 3:207-8. Johnson, in reply, expressed surprise and disappointment at Dyer's defeat. William Samuel Johnson to Joseph Chew, February 13, 1770, *ibid.*, 4:25.

[38][Eliphalet Dyer], *Remarks on Dr. Gale's Letter to J. W. Esq; By E. D.* (Hartford, 1769), rpt. in *Susquehannah Papers*, 3:261.

[39]Benjamin Gale, *Dr. Gale's Letter to J. W. Esquire* . . . (Hartford, 1769), rpt. in *Susquehannah Papers*, 3:224-41; Benjamin Gale, *Observations on a Pamphlet entitled Remarks on Dr. Gale's Letter to J. W. Esq; Signed E. D. of which The Hon. Eliphalet Dyer is the reputed Author* . . . (Hartford, 1770), rpt. in *ibid.*, 3:268-92; *The State of the Lands . . . West of the Province of New York Considered. By the Publick's Humble Servant* (New York, 1770), rpt. in *ibid.*, 4:345-59.

[40]Benjamin Gale to Jared Ingersoll, December 29, 1769, *Susquehannah Papers*, 3:219.

[41]*Public Records*, 13:427-28.

[42]George Chapman to William Samuel Johnson, December 11, 1770, WSJ Papers.

[43]William Samuel Johnson to Jared Ingersoll, October 28, 1771, WSJ Papers; William Samuel Johnson to Robert Walker, February 26, 1770, *ibid.* The costliness of London is an ever-recurring theme in the agents' reports. Kammen, *Rope of Sand*, pp. 59-61. On the

salaries of Hutchinson, Johnson, and Franklin, see Kammen, *Rope of Sand*, pp. 176-77; Bailyn, *Ordeal of Thomas Hutchinson*, p. 53. By mid-century, lawyers were the most prosperous group in Connecticut, but the rewards still paled beside the luxurious life of a British official. In 1764, Dyer wrote to Ingersoll from London, "I cannot bare the thought of going into that Slavish practice again on my return." Eliphalet Dyer to Jared Ingersoll, April 14, 1764, "Miscellaneous Papers of Jared Ingersoll," p. 291.

[44]Daniel Horsmanden (1694-1778) came to New York in 1732 as a lawyer with influential political connections. In 1753 he took a seat on New York's highest court, and a decade later he rose to Chief Justice. Old age and ill health kept him from active service for several years before he vacated the bench, on his death in 1778. Dumas Malone, ed., *Dictionary of American Biography* (1943), 9:237-38. When Johnson departed for England in 1766, he carried a letter of introduction from his father to the Archbishop of Canterbury. Samuel Johnson appealed to the church leader, "The Chief Justice of New York, my Lord, is a good man but almost superannuated. I should therefore be most humbly and greatly obliged to your Grace . . . for your kind influence that my son may be favoured, with the reversions, at least, of that important station. . . ." Samuel Johnson to the Archbishop of Canterbury, December 15, 1766, *Samuel Johnson*, 1:383.

[45]William Samuel Johnson to Jared Ingersoll, February 18, 1767, WSJ Papers; Richard Jackson to Jared Ingersoll, February 20, 1767, "Papers of Ingersoll," p. 290.

[46]William Samuel Johnson to Samuel Johnson, May 18, 1767, WSJ Papers; William Samuel Johnson to Nicholas Stuyvesant, July 10, 1767, *ibid.;* Diary of William Samuel Johnson, May 15, 1767, *ibid.*

[47]Samuel Johnson to the Archbishop of Canterbury, September 25, 1767, *Samuel Johnson*, 1:419-20.

[48]William Samuel Johnson to Samuel Johnson, November 23, 1767, WSJ Papers.

[49]Thomas Whately to William Samuel Johnson, November 15, 1767, WSJ Papers; William Samuel Johnson to Jared Ingersoll, November 30, 1767, September 30, 1768, *ibid.;* William Samuel Johnson to Jared Ingersoll, May 16, 1767, quoted in Gipson, *Jared Ingersoll*, pp. 291-94.

[50]Nathaniel Rogers to William Samuel Johnson, November 23, December 1, 1768, January 12, April 8, 1764, WSJ Papers; Robert Temple to William Samuel Johnson, December 1, 1768, *ibid.;* William Samuel Johnson to Nathaniel Rogers, January 4, 1769, *ibid.*

[51]George Berkeley to William Samuel Johnson, December 12, 1769, Bancroft Transcripts. Rev. Dr. George Berkeley, Prebendiary of Canterbury, had supplied Johnson with a letter of introduction to Dartmouth one year earlier. George Berkeley to William Samuel Johnson, October 20, 1768, *ibid.*

[52]Benjamin La Trobe to William Samuel Johnson, January 13, 1771, WSJ Papers.

[53]Eliphalet Dyer to William Samuel Johnson, December 15, 1770, *Susquehannah Papers*, 4:141. See also Cadwallader Colden to William Samuel Johnson, April 2, 1771, WSJ Papers.

[54]Arthur Lee to Samuel Adams, June 10, 1771, Lee, ed., *Life of Arthur Lee, LL.D.*, 1:216; *Papers of Franklin*, 17:257-58, 18:127; Kammen *Rope of Sand*, pp. 68, 133, 139-40, 191.

[55]William Samuel Johnson to Eliphalet Dyer, March 30, 1771, *Susquehannah Papers*, 4:200.

[56]William Samuel Johnson to Robert Lowth, Bishop of Oxford, July 23, 1771, WSJ Papers; Richard Terrick, Bishop of London, to William Samuel Johnson, July 23, 1771, *ibid.;* Robert Lowth, Bishop of Oxford, to William Samuel Johnson, July 23, 1771, *ibid.;* William Samuel Johnson to Alexander Wedderburn, October 25, 1771, *ibid.*

[57]Diary of William Samuel Johnson, August 2-October 4, 1771, WSJ Papers.

Chapter 10: The Illusory Peace

[1]Diary of William Samuel Johnson, September 25-October 1, 1771, WSJ Papers.

[2]William Samuel Johnson to George Livius, October 12, 1771, WSJ Papers; William Samuel Johnson to Thomas Whately, October 15, 1771, *ibid.;* William Samuel Johnson to Thomas Pownall, April 29, 1772, *ibid.*

[3]Bridenbaugh, *Mitre and Sceptre*, p. 314; Vassar, ed., "Aftermath of Revolution: Letters of the Anglican Clergymen in Connecticut," 433, 435.

[4]*Public Records of the Colony of Connecticut*, 13:427-28; Jonathan Trumbull, Address to the Connecticut Legislature, October 1771, *Susquehannah Papers*, 4:343-44. Benjamin Gale and Eliphalet Dyer were the major contenders in this pamphlet war: Benjamin Gale, *Dr. Gale's Letter to J. W. Esquire* . . . (Hartford, 1769); [Eliphalet Dyer], *Remarks on Dr. Gale's Letter to J. W. Esquire* . . . (Hartford, 1769); Benjamin Gale, *Observations on a Pamphlet entitled Remarks on Dr. Gale's Letter to J. W. Esquire; Signed E. D. of which The Hon. Eliphalet Dyer is the reputed author* . . . (Hartford, 1770). These pamphlets are reprinted in *Susquehannah Papers*, 3:224-92. See also Benjamin Gale to Jared Ingersoll, December 29, 1769, *Susquehannah Papers*, 3:219. The best secondary account of the political battle in Connecticut is Zeichner, *Connecticut's Years of Controversy*, pp. 112-27.

[5]Jonathan Trumbull to William Samuel Johnson, Jabez Hamlin, and George Wyllys, November 8, 1771, *Susquehannah Papers*, 4:283; William Samuel Johnson to Jonathan Trumbull, December 28, 1771, *ibid.*, 4:289-91. On Trumbull's authorship of the statement, see Taylor, ed., *Susquehannah Papers*, 5:229 n.1.

[6]Jonathan Trumbull to Thomas Life, January n.d., 1772, *Susquehannah Papers*, 4:301-2; Jonathan Trumbull to Richard Jackson, January, n.d., 1772, *ibid.*, 4:302.

[7]Eliphalet Dyer, Jedidiah Elderkin, and Nathaniel Wales, Jr. to the Settlers' Committee, October 20, 1772, *Susquehannah Papers*, 5:52-53.

[8]William Samuel Johnson to Robert Temple, February 10, 1772, quoted in Beardsley, *William Samuel Johnson*, pp. 200-1.

[9]Thomas Bradbury Chandler, *The Life of Samuel Johnson* (New York, 1805), pp. 124-27, 133-36; *Public Records of the Colony of Connecticut*, 14:5-6. A year earlier, on October 29, 1771, the Assembly had appointed a committee to thank their returning agent for his "faithful service" to both "the general cause of American liberty" and "the true interests of this Colony in particular." *Public Records of the Colony of Connecticut*, 13:510.

[10]William Samuel Johnson to John Sargeant, November 10, 1771, WSJ Papers.

[11]On the strength of the North ministry, see Gipson, *British Empire*, 11:251. In the autumn of 1770, Grenville died, and by 1771 most of his followers had left the opposition to support the ministry. Pares, *King George III and the Politicians*, p. 81; Ritcheson, *British Politics*, p. 140.

[12]William Samuel Johnson to Jonathan Trumbull, October 12, 1770, Bancroft Transcripts.

[13]William Samuel Johnson to Jonathan Trumbull, March 15, 1771, "Trumbull Papers," pp. 476, 479. In January 1771, the North ministry had announced that it would put aside any plans to alter the Massachusetts charter. The announcement had dispelled Johnson's last reservations toward the new chief minister. Johnson had credited North, not Hillsborough, with the decision. "Such is the moderation of *some* of his Majesty's ministers," Johnson had remarked. By 1771, Johnson had been inclined to attribute any improvement in Anglo-American relations to the good sense of Lord North, not to the prudence and fortitude of the Americans. Regarding the security of the Massachusetts

charter, he had judged, "The Massachusetts Bay by no means owe their safety as much as they ought to have done to their own conduct, or to any care they have taken of themselves or their affairs." William Samuel Johnson to Jonathan Trumbull, January 2, 1771, "Trumbull Papers," pp. 470-73; William Samuel Johnson to Robert Temple, January 5, 1771, WSJ Papers.

[14]William Samuel Johnson to Samuel Johnson (the British literary figure), June 5, 1773, WSJ Papers; William Samuel Johnson to Robert Lowth, Bishop of Oxford, June 5, 1773, *ibid.;* Laurence Reade to William Samuel Johnson, February 6, 1773, *ibid.*

[15]Ritcheson, *British Politics,* pp. 142-43.

[16]*Ibid.*

[17]William Samuel Johnson to William Bayard, September 6, 1770, WSJ Papers; Samuel Cooper to Benjamin Franklin, January 1, 1771, *Papers of Franklin,* 18:3-4.

[18]William Samuel Johnson to [John or Thomas] Pownall, April 29, 1772, WSJ Papers.

[19]Shy, *Toward Lexington,* pp. 376-77. For a narrative of the immediate circumstances leading to the clash, see *ibid.,* pp. 303-18.

[20]Quoted in Bailyn, ed., *Pamphlets,* p. 86.

[21]Committee of the Town of Boston to Benjamin Franklin, July 13, 1770, *Papers of Franklin,* 17:188; Bailyn, *Ordeal of Thomas Hutchinson,* pp. 161-62, 165-69.

[22]Gipson, *British Empire,* 12:46-55, 66-70, 105, 139. Labaree, *Boston Tea Party,* p. 85; Schlesinger, *Colonial Merchants,* p. 255.

[23]William Samuel Johnson to Richard Jackson, February 26, 1773, WSJ Papers; William Samuel Johnson to John Pownall, February 23, 1773, *ibid.;* William Samuel Johnson to Samuel Johnson (the British literary figure), June 5, 1773, *ibid.;* William Samuel Johnson to Robert Lowth, Bishop of Oxford, quoted in Beardsley, *William Samuel Johnson,* pp. 101-2.

[24]Quoted in Van Doren, *Benjamin Franklin,* pp. 449-50.

[25]Benjamin Franklin to Samuel Cooper, February 5, 1771, *Papers of Franklin,* 18:26; Benjamin Franklin to the Massachusetts House of Representatives' Committee of Correspondence, May 15, 1771, *ibid.,* 18:102.

[26]Benjamin Franklin to Thomas Cushing, June 10, 1771, *ibid.,* 18:122-23. Because of his gloomy assessment of British rule, Franklin worried over his cautious advice. "I see in this seemingly prudent course," he told Cushing, "some danger of a diminishing Attention to our Rights." It was out of just this dilemma that Johnson had extricated himself with a falsely benign view of what his countrymen might expect from the North administration.

[27]William Samuel Johnson to John Pownall, February 27, 1773, WSJ Papers.

[28]Zeichner, *Connecticut's Years of Controversy,* pp. 133-34.

[29]William Samuel Johnson to Richard Jackson, February 26, 1773, WSJ Papers; Zeichner, *Connecticut's Years of Controversy,* p. 134.

[30]Roger Sherman to William Samuel Johnson, June 25, 1768, WSJ Papers; William Samuel Johnson to William Pitkin, July 23, 1768, "Trumbull Papers," pp. 292-93; William Samuel Johnson to Jonathan Trumbull, October 16, 1769, "Trumbull Papers," p. 374. For an excellent analysis of the history of writs of assistance and colonial opposition to them, see Knollenberg, *Growth of the American Revolution,* pp. 212-16.

[31]William Samuel Johnson to George Berkeley, February 23, 1773, Bancroft Transcripts; for a discussion of the incident and the commission, see Gipson, *British Empire,* 12:24-36. Colonial outrage far exceeded the gravity of the offense. Presiding over the *Gaspee* commission was Governor Wanton of Rhode Island, a popularly elected figure who would never endanger his political following and commercial enterprises by enforcing British tyranny. At the outset, the commissioners renounced any responsibility for

arresting and transporting suspects, and shifted the burden to the Rhode Island Superior Court. The commission ended its work in June after producing no results.

[32]William Samuel Johnson to Thomas Whately, October 15, 1771, WSJ Papers; William Samuel Johnson to Richard Jackson, October 21, 1771, July 15, 1772, November 15, 1773, ibid.; William Samuel Johnson to Alexander Wedderburn, October 25, 1771, October 5, 1772, ibid., William Samuel Johnson to Lord Dartmouth, October 20, 1772, ibid.; William Samuel Johnson to John Pownall, November 3, 1772, ibid.; William Samuel Johnson to Benjamin La Trobe, May 30, 1772, ibid.; and many others.

[33]William Samuel Johnson to John Temple, April 30, 1772. "Bowdoin-Temple Papers," p. 290.

[34]Benjamin La Trobe to William Samuel Johnson, May 6, 1774, WSJ Papers.

[35]Labaree, Boston Tea Party, ch. 4, especially pp. 58-67, 70; Gipson, British Empire, pp. 12-16.

[36]Labaree, Boston Tea Party, pp. 87-103, 152-54. Historians differ on the basis of American opposition. Labaree contends that it was the issue of taxation that enraged the Americans, while Arthur Schlesinger argues that the fear of monopoly was the mainspring of the American resistance to the Tea Act. Colonial Merchants, p. 270. Johnson reported that, in Connecticut, the issue most talked about was the attempt to raise a revenue from the imported tea. William Samuel Johnson to John Sargeant, November 13, 1773, WSJ Papers.

[37]Labaree, Boston Tea Party, chs. 5, 6, 7.

[38]William Samuel Johnson to Robert Lowth, Bishop of Oxford, January 15, 1774, WSJ Papers. Johnson reported that "Those are very few indeed in any of the Colonies who were willing the tea should be landed while subject to the tea duty, yet most sober people condemn the steps taken at Boston as highly reprehensible and are apprehensive for the consequences."

[39]Benjamin Franklin to Thomas Cushing, March 22, 1774, quoted in Van Doren, Benjamin Franklin, pp. 482-83. See also Kammen, Rope of Sand, p. 289; Sosin, Agents and Merchants, p. 169; Newcomb, Franklin and Galloway, p. 242.

[40]William Samuel Johnson to Robert Lowth, Bishop of Oxford, January 15, 1774, WSJ Papers.

[41]Schlesinger, Colonial Merchants, p. 304; Zeichner, Connecticut's Years of Controversy, pp. 142, 159-61.

[42]Thomas Life to Jonathan Trumbull, July 7, 1773, Susquehannah Papers, 5:158; State of the Case, [Connecticut, 1773], rpt. in ibid., 5:243-45; Benjamin Trumbull, To the Public (New Haven, 1773), rpt. in ibid., 6:83.

[43]Boyd, ed., Susquehannah Papers, 4:xxix, xxviii; Petition of Thomas and Richard Penn to the King in Council, 1770, ibid., 4:24. Wedderburn was Solicitor General, Thurlow was Attorney General.

[44]William Samuel Johnson to Richard Jackson, October 24, 1772, April 12, 1773, Susquehannah Papers, 5:54, 119.

[45]Thomas Life to William Samuel Johnson, July 7, 1773, March 2, 1774, Susquehannah Papers, 5:158-59, 316; Thomas Life to Jonathan Trumbull, July 7, 1773, ibid., 5:158; Richard Jackson to William Samuel Johnson, April 5, 1774, WSJ Papers. Jackson added in his letter to Johnson, "though I should be unwilling what I now write to you should be read by anyone, I should not be sorry it should be understood that we all think the future decision doubtful."

[46]Richard Jackson to Jonathan Trumbull, March 25, 1772, Susquehannah Papers, 4:310-11; Jonathan Trumbull to Richard Jackson, August 3, 1772, ibid., 5:13-14.

[47]Benjamin Gale to Jared Ingersoll, December, n.d., 1769, Susquehannah Papers,

3:221; Argument by *Many* Against the Connecticut Claim, *Connecticut Courant*, February 22, 1774, rpt. in *ibid.*, 5:299; Reply to *Connecticutensis* by *A Son of Liberty, Connecticut Courant*, March 15, 1774, rpt. in *ibid.*, 5:337-38.

48Boyd, ed., *Susquehannah Papers*, 4:xvii; Minutes of a Meeting of the Susquehannah Company, June 2, 1773, *ibid.*, 5:142-43. For a discussion of Trumbull's intimate involvement in the company's affairs, see *ibid.*, 4:xiv-xvii.

49William Samuel Johnson to Thomas Life, January 23, 1773, *Susquehannah Papers*, 5:188.

50William Samuel Johnson to Richard Jackson, November 5, 1773, *ibid.*, 5:183.

51William Samuel Johnson to Thomas Life, November 23, 1773, *ibid.*, 5:188.

52*Public Records of the Colony of Connecticut*, 14:161-62; Taylor, ed., *Susquehannah Papers*, 5:xxxii. The lower house rejected William Pitkin, Joseph Trumbull, and Samuel Huntington, all company shareholders, and proposed three nonshareholders in their stead: Silas Deane, William Williams, and Jedidiah Strong.

53For a complete record of the interchange between the Pennsylvania government and the Connecticut commissioners, see the documents printed in *Susquehannah Papers*, 5:196-220.

54*Public Records of the Colony of Connecticut*, 14:217-20; William Samuel Johnson to William Smith, January 29, 1774, *Susquehannah Papers*, 5:265.

55*Susquehannah Papers*, 5:xliii.

56William Samuel Johnson to William Smith, April 25, 1774, *ibid.*, 6:227-28.

57For example, Reply to *Connecticutensis* by *A Son of Liberty, Connecticut Courant*, March 15, 1774, rpt. in *ibid.*, 5:337-38.

58*Connecticut Courant*, February 22, 1774, rpt. in *ibid.*, 5:299-301.

59Petition and Remonstrance of the Middletown Convention, March 30, 1774, *ibid.*, 6:146-50; Article by *Colonist, Connecticut Gazette*, April 22, 1774, rpt. in *ibid.*,6:218-29. Zeichner includes a description of the convention in *Connecticut's Years of Controversy*, p. 153.

60The most comprehensive defense of the company's quest came from the Governor's brother, Rev. Benjamin Trumbull, *A Plea in Vindication of the Connecticut Title to the Contested Lands Lying West of the Province of New York* (New Haven, 1774), rpt. in *Susquehannah Papers*, 6:68-114.

61[William Smith], *An Examination of the Connecticut Claims to the Lands in Pennsylvania* (Philadelphia, 1774), rpt. in *ibid.*, 6:1-58, see especially pp. 51-55; *Brutus Americanus* to Jared Ingersoll, *Connecticut Gazette*, February 25, 1774, rpt. in *ibid.*, 5:302-4; Jared Ingersoll to the *Connecticut Courant*, March 22, 1774, rpt. in *ibid.*, 5:316-20.

62*Brutus Americanus* to Jared Ingersoll, Esq., *Connecticut Gazette*, April 22, 1774, rpt. in *ibid.*, 6:223; Silas Deane, The Alarm, No. 1, *Connecticut Courant*, April 5, 1774, rpt. in *ibid.*, 6:168; Article by *Philanthropus Redivivus, Connecticut Courant*, April 5, 1774, rpt. in *ibid.*, 5:355-56.

63Minutes of a Meeting of the Inhabitants of Hartford, May 11, 1774, *Susquehannah Papers*, 6:246. See also: Article by *Verax, Connecticut Courant*, March 15, 1774, rpt. in *ibid.*, 5:345. "Many Gentlemen who are open opposers of the Western claim, to their honor, as openly oppose the present mad proceedings. . . ." Deane told Trumbull.

64Article by Roger Sherman, *Connecticut Journal*, April 8, 1774, rpt. in *ibid.*, 6:180-81; Collier, *Sherman's Connecticut*, pp. 31, 79, 81, 83.

65Dexter, *Biographical Sketches of the Graduates of Yale College*, 1:399-400.

66Benjamin Gale to Silas Deane, February 27, 1775, "Correspondence of Silas Deane," p. 202.

[67]Article by *Colonist, Connecticut Gazette,* April 22, 1774, rpt. in *Susquehannah Papers,* 6:218-20; Benj. Stevens, Isaac Laurence and Simon Tubbs to Zebulon Butler and Nathan Denison, April 1, 1774, *ibid.,* 6:155; Benjamin Trumbull, *A Plea in Vindication of the Connecticut Title . . .* , rpt. in *ibid.,* 6:104; William Samuel Johnson to William Smith, April 25, 1774, *ibid.,* 6:227-28; *Public Records,* 14:254.
[68]*Public Records of the Colony of Connecticut,* 14:262.
[69]William Samuel Johnson to Richard Jackson, August 30, 1774, WSJ Papers.

Chapter 11: The Moment of Decision

[1]Nicholas Ray to William Samuel Johnson, April 14, 1774, WSJ Papers.
[2]Knollenberg, *Growth of the American Revolution,* pp. 7-8, 103-8, 117-20.
[3]*Ibid.,* p. 174; Zeichner, *Connecticut's Years of Controversy,* pp. 163-64; Labaree, *Boston Tea Party,* p. 221; Schlesinger, *Colonial Merchants,* p. 309.
[4]Ebenizer Baldwin, *An Appendix, Stating the Heavy Grievance the Colonies Labour under from Several Late Acts of the British Parliament, and Shewing What We Have Just Reason to Fear the Consequences of These Measures Will Be* (New Haven, 1774).
[5]Knollenberg, *Growth of the American Revolution,* pp. 126-28.
[6]Silas Deane to William Samuel Johnson, July 13, 1774, WSJ Papers.
[7]William Samuel Johnson to Benjamin La Trobe, July 25, 1774, WSJ Papers; William Samuel Johnson to Richard Jackson, August 30, 1774, *ibid.;* Groce, *William Samuel Johnson,* p. 100. A document, dated July 5, 1774 (WSJ Papers), confirms Johnson's obligation to appear in Albany on August 22 to arbitrate a boundary dispute. Johnson, however, did not depart for Albany until September 26, twenty-one days after the Congress had convened. Diary of William Samuel Johnson, September 26, 1774, WSJ Papers.
[8][Thomas Jefferson], *A Summary View of the Rights of British America . . .* (Williamsburg, [1774], quoted in Bailyn, ed., *Pamphlets,* p. 74; Dickinson, *Letters to the Inhabitants of the British Colonies, No. 2* (Philadelphia, 1774), in "Writings of John Dickinson," pp. 473-74.
[9]In July, a convention of delegates from Fairfax County, Virginia, declared against Parliament's authority in these words, quoted in Knollenberg, *Growth of the American Revolution,* pp. 136-37. For other challenges to Parliament's authority, see James Wilson, *Considerations on the Nature and Extent of the Legislative Authority of the British Parliament* (Philadelphia, 1774), and the several works discussed in Davidson, *Propaganda and the American Revolution,* p. 210.
[10]*Public Records of the Colony of Connecticut,* 14: 261, 264; Gipson, *British Empire,* 12: 146, 172.
[11]Schlesinger, *Prelude to Independence,* p. 205; Knollenberg, *Growth of the American Revolution,* pp. 126-28.
[12]In April, Jackson informed him that "there was hardly an opposition" to the Coercive Acts in Parliament, which was determined upon "vigorous measures for the preservation of its authority. . . ." In May, La Trobe warned that "gov't is determined. . . ." Three months later, George Berkeley, an ardent supporter of the American cause, alerted Johnson that the ministry intended "to carry every point, in every port of North America." Richard Jackson to William Samuel Johnson, April 5, 1774, WSJ Papers; Benjamin La Trobe to William Samuel Johnson, May 6, 1774, *ibid.;* George Berkeley to William Samuel Johnson, August 11, 1774, quoted in Beardsley, *William Samuel Johnson,* pp. 106-7.
[13]Gipson, *British Empire,* 12:113-14, 117-18, 128-29, 131-32.

[14]Not all fifty-six delegates reached Philadelphia in time for the first session. Ford, ed., *Journals of Congress*, 1:13, 25, 30, 31, 42, 53, 74.

[15]*Ibid.*, 1:32–39. John Adams, one of the delegates, wrote in his diary, "this day convinced me that America will support Massachusetts or perish with her." *Ibid.*, 1:39, n.1.

[16]*Ibid.*, 1:43, 51; Knollenberg, *Growth of the American Revolution*, pp. 143–44.

[17]Burnett, *Continental Congress*, p. 37; Collier, *Sherman's Connecticut*, p. 97; Labaree, *Boston Tea Party*, p. 255; Gipson, *British Empire*, 12:244.

[18]Knollenberg, *Growth of the American Revolution*, p. 148.

[19]*Journals of Congress*, 1:63 n.1, 68; Labaree, *Boston Tea Party*, p. 254; Knollenberg, *Growth of the American Revolution*, p. 148.

[20]*Journals of Congress*, 1:90–101; Knollenberg, *Growth of the American Revolution*, pp. 153, 156–57. On another occasion, the delegates voted "That this Congress approve of the opposition by the inhabitants of Massachusetts-Bay, to the execution of the late acts of Parliament, and if the same shall be attempted to be carried into execution by force all America ought to support them in their opposition." Duane and Galloway protested the resolution, but to no avail. *Journals of Congress*, 1:58, n.1.

[21]Jacobson, *John Dickinson*, p. 82.

[22]Christopher Leffingwell to Silas Deane, August 22, 1774, "Correspondence of Silas Deane," p. 140; Gurdon Saltonstall to Silas Deane, August 29, September 5, 1774, *ibid.*, pp. 143, 151–52; Gurdon Saltonstall to the Connecticut Delegates in the Congress, September 8, 1774, *ibid.*, pp. 160–63; Thomas Mumford to Silas Deane, September 3, 1774, *ibid.*, p. 174; Zeichner, *Connecticut's Years of Controversy*, pp. 178–80.

[23]*Journals of Congress*, 1:75–81.

[24]Ebenezer Baldwin captured the spirit of the Assembly when he declared "the determination of the congress . . . may be deemed the general voice of the people. . . . The Congress we hear have come into an [agreement] that we *import* not British goods. . . . No friend of his country can hesitate a moment in such a case to deny himself the superfluities of Britain." Ebenezer Baldwin, *An Appendix, Stating the heavy Grievance the Colonies labour under.* . . . (New Haven, 1774).

[25]*Public Records*, 14:327–28, 343, 346; Baldwin, *An Appendix.* . . .

[26]*Public Records of the Colony of Connecticut*, 14:221.

[27]A draft of this letter, pencil-dated January 1774, is in the WSJ Papers. Although Johnson may have considered resigning as early as January, he did not make his final decision until after the Assembly had adjourned in May. The records for the May session include a large number of new militia assignments and replacements, but no mention is made of Johnson. The records for the October session include the following entry: "This Assembly do appoint Gold Silleck Silliman, Esq; Lieutenant-Colonel of the fourth regiment of militia in this Colony, in the room of Lieutenant-Colonel Johnson resigned." *Public Records of the Colony of Connecticut*, 14:331.

[28]William Samuel Johnson to Samuel Johnson, January 9, 1768, August 18, 1770, quoted in Beardsley, *William Samuel Johnson*, pp. 52, 78; Diary of William Samuel Johnson, numerous entries, e.g., July 14, September 7, 1767, WSJ Papers.

[29]Zeichner, *Connecticut's Years of Controversy*, p. 181; Schlesinger, *Colonial Merchants*, p. 444.

[30]For discussions of the major loyalist writings of this year, see Tyler, *Literary History of the American Revolution*, 1:293–96, chs. 16, 17; Schlesinger, *Prelude to Independence*, pp. 228–29; Nelson, *American Tory*, pp. 66–80; Steiner, *Samuel Seabury*, pp. 129–57; Benton, *Whig-Loyalism*, pp. 125–30.

[31]Steiner, *Samuel Seabury*, pp. 159–60; *Public Records of the Colony of Connecticut*, 15:192–93.

[32]Baldwin, *An Appendix* . . . ; Zeichner, *Connecticut's Years of Controversy*, pp. 181,

183–86; *Public Records of the Colony of Connecticut,* 14:392–93; Schlesinger, *Colonial Merchants,* p. 445.

[33] Wilcoxson, *History of Stratford,* p. 512.

[34] Silas Deane to William Samuel Johnson, August 1, 1774, WSJ Papers. One Connecticut man, Thomas Mumford, told Deane, "I have taken every method my prudence could suggest, in vindication of Doct. Johnson's refusing to attend the Congress as a delegate from this Colony with Col. Dyer and yourself . . . but the universal voice is, that no business or engagement whatever should be put in competition with the arduous task we now have to struggle with. Tho' I much esteem the Doctr, I must likewise declare these as my sentiments, and from the present temper of the people in this part of the Colony, I shall not be surprised if he should be dropped from the nomination of Councillors this fall, tho' I still hope otherwise. . . ." Thomas Mumford to Silas Deane, September 3, 1774, "Correspondence of Deane," p. 147.

[35] *Public Records of the Colony of Connecticut,* 14:343, 410–13; Collier, *Sherman's Connecticut,* p. 111.

[36] Benjamin La Trobe to William Samuel Johnson, March 1, 1775, WSJ Papers.

[37] Donoughue, *British Politics and the American Revolution,* pp. 216, 239, 265, 282, 284; Gipson, *British Empire,* 12:286–88, 294–300, 307; Knollenberg, *Growth of the American Revolution,* pp. 171–72, 174.

[38] Sosin, *Agents and Merchants,* pp. 177–78, 195, 220; Kammen, *Rope of Sand,* pp. 152, 219, 226; William Bollan to James Bowdoin, September 29, 1773, "Bowdoin-Temple Papers," p. 320; William Bollan to the Council of Massachusetts, February 24, May 12, 1774, "Bowdoin-Temple Papers," pp. 340, 371; Thomas Life to William Samuel Johnson, February 1, 1775, WSJ Papers.

[39] Benjamin Franklin to Joseph Galloway, n.d., 1775, quoted in Bailyn, *Ideological Origins,* p. 136; Newcomb, *Franklin and Galloway,* pp. 269, 280; Van Doren, *Benjamin Franklin,* pp. 284, 287. Since 1773, Franklin, more than any other agent, had suffered harassment and ostracism at the hands of British officials. In that year, Franklin had obtained and sent to the Speaker of the Massachusetts House of Representatives letters that Thomas Hutchinson, Andrew Oliver, Charles Paxton, and Nathaniel Rodgers had written to Thomas Whately in 1768 and 1769. Franklin's motive had been to shift the blame for British harshness and imprudence from the ministry and Parliament to the Hutchinson faction. His plan proved abortive in two respects. When the Massachusetts patriots, against Franklin's counsel, published the letters that spring, outrage against Hutchinson reached new heights but did not diminish colonial suspicions against the home government. Secondly, British officials, far from applauding Franklin's deed, exonerated Hutchinson of any misdeeds in writing the letters and accused Franklin of working to bring the Anglo-American dispute to a crisis. Franklin was immediately dismissed from his post as Deputy Postmaster General of the American colonies. The reaction in Great Britain to the exposure of the letters disillusioned Franklin deeply and pushed him far toward his ultimate conclusion that the British government had no sincere interest in healing the Anglo-American breach. Bailyn, *Ordeal of Thomas Hutchinson,* pp. 223, n.4, 224–59; Gipson, *British Empire,* 12:55–64.

[40] Stiles, *Literary Diary,* 1:530.

[41] Collier, *Sherman's Connecticut,* p. 108; Zeichner, *Connecticut's Years of Controversy,* pp. 189–90; *Public Records of the Colony of Connecticut,* 14:416; Boardman, *Roger Sherman,* p. 128. Charles Hoadly notes that the original resolve, now in the Connecticut Archives, is in the handwriting of Roger Sherman. Hoadly, ed., *Public Records of the Colony of Connecticut,* 14:416.

[42] Zeichner, *Connecticut's Years of Controversy,* p. 334, n.31.

[43] William Samuel Johnson, Memoirs, WSJ Papers.

317   *12. The War Years*

[44]John Adams to Abigail Adams, April 30, 1774, quoted in Beardsley, *William Samuel Johnson*, p. 112.

[45]*Public Records of the Colony of Connecticut*, 14:417, 419.

[46]Gurdon Saltonstall to Silas Deane, May 8, 1775, "Correspondence of Deane," p. 225; Thomas Mumford to Silas Deane, May 14, 1775, *ibid.*, p. 230; William Samuel Johnson, Memoirs, WSJ Papers.

[47]*Journals of Congress*, 2:89, 91-94, 96-97, 100-1, 109-10; Burnett, *Continental Congress*, p. 71-79.

[48]*Journals of Congress*, 2:55-56, 74, 85, 95, 109-10; *Public Records of the Colony of Connecticut*, 15:15-18, 40, 92, 96-97, 100.

[49]Quoted in Bailyn, *Ideological Origins*, p. 150; Nelson, *American Tory*, p. 122; Becker, "John Jay and Peter Van Schaack," pp. 484-92.

[50]*Journals of Congress*, 2:140-56; Burnett, *Continental Congress*, p. 86; Jacobson, *John Dickinson*, pp. 88, 95.

[51]*Journals of Congress*, 2:158-61; Jacobson, *John Dickinson*, p. 95.

[52]Quoted in Burnett, *Continental Congress*, pp. 84-85. See also Collier, *Sherman's Connecticut*, pp. 114, 119-20; Jacobson, *John Dickinson*, p. 100; Gipson, *British Empire*, 12:329; Miller *Origins of the American Revolution*, p. 460.

[53]Thomas Hutchinson to William Samuel Johnson, June 3, 1775, WSJ Papers.

[54]Quoted in Collier, *Sherman's Connecticut*, p. 120.

[55]*Public Records of the Colony of Connecticut*, 15:185, 187-93, 195-203. Johnson was appointed to a committee of four to "procure a just and well authenticated account of the hostilities committed by the ministerial troops or navy whereby any damage has been done to the property of any person or persons in this Colony. . . ." *Ibid.*, 15:202.

[56]Groce, *William Samuel Johnson*, p. 106.

Chapter 12: The War Years

[1]Smith's plan for Anglo-American reconciliation and his posture in the final crisis are discussed in Dillon, *New York Triumvirate*, pp. 127-40; Upton, *The Loyal Whig: William Smith of New York and Quebec*, pp. 31-32, 91-98; Calhoon, ed., "William Smith, Jr.'s Alternative to the American Revolution," pp. 105-18.

[2]Quoted in Burnett, *Continental Congress*, p. 117.

[3]Thomas Paine, *Common Sense . . .* (Philadelphia, 1776).

[4]Quoted in Burnett, *Continental Congress*, p. 150.

[5]Quoted in *ibid.*, p. 152.

[6]*Ibid.*, p. 150.

[7]Ford, ed., *Journals of Congress*, 4:342, 357-58; Burnett, *Continental Congress*, pp. 154-56.

[8]Benton, *Whig-Loyalism*, pp. 161-63.

[9]On June 7, Richard Henry Lee of Virginia introduced a motion for independence and confederation, but the spokesmen for delay, led by John Dickinson and James Wilson of Pennsylvania, successfully postponed the vote. They argued that political turmoil in the middle colonies made those colonies ill-prepared for political independence, and that the delegates from Pennsylvania, New York, New Jersey, and Delaware were unauthorized to vote for independence. Jacobson, *John Dickinson*, p. 111; Miller, *Origins of the American Revolution*, p. 491.

[10]Burnett, *Continental Congress*, p. 178. On June 14, the Connecticut legislature had instructed its delegates to vote for independence. *Public Records of the State of Connecticut*, 15:414-16.

[11]Burnett, *Continental Congress*, pp. 181-83, 191.

[12]*Ibid.*, pp. 188-90.

[13]Becker, "John Jay and Peter Van Schaack," pp. 285-97. In April, Stiles had noted in his diary: "At Congress is a good Majority prepared for any Question, even Independency, if necessary. . . . Messrs. Duane and Jay of the N. York Delegates are Tories at heart. . . ." Stiles, *Literary Diary*, 2:10.

[14]Jacobson, *John Dickinson*, p. 113.

[15]Dickinson, *Letters from a Farmer*, pp. 32-33. On the political turmoil in Pennsylvania in 1776 and its influence on Dickinson in the final crisis, see Benton, *Whig-Loyalism*, p. 174; Jacobson, *John Dickinson*, p. 116; Burnett, *Continental Congress* pp. 177-78. Dickinson's alienation from the American cause was short-lived. He participated sporadically in Pennsylvania's revolutionary government in the autumn of 1776, reentered Congress as a delegate from Delaware in 1778, became President of Delaware in 1781 and President of Pennsylvania the following year. Jacobson, *John Dickinson*, p. 117.

[16]Benton, *Whig-Loyalism*, pp. 177, 212; Nelson, *American Tory*, p. 121. This important distinction helps us to understand the prominence of many future loyalists in the early years of the American resistance. The nineteenth-century historian, Moses Coit Tyler, wrote: "Incomparably the strongest words then uttered, against the new proposal for Independence, were uttered, not by the American Tories but by some of the American Whigs, who, while they had been in full accord with the rough methods of opposition thus far pursued, were shocked by this project for committing them to a doctrine which from the first they had all rejected and condemned." Tyler, *Literary History of the American Revolution*, 1:481. But until very recently, most historians, unlike Tyler, neglected the distinction between Tories and Whig loyalists. The appearance of Nelson's work in 1961 encouraged a long-overdue examination of the loyalist mentality. Benton's *Whig-Loyalism* is one of many recent works that reflect Nelson's influence. Another is Wallace Brown, *The Good Americans: The Loyalists in the American Revolution* (New York: Morrow, 1969), espec. pp. 32, 66.

[17]Martin Howard, Jr., *A Letter from a Gentleman at Halifax, to His Friend in Rhode-Island, Containing Remarks upon a Pamphlet, Entitled, The Rights of the Colonies Examined* (Newport, 1765), rpt. in Bailyn, ed., *Pamphlets*, pp. 532-44. For a brief summary of Howard's pamphlet and his fate, see *ibid.*, pp. 524-30.

[18]William Samuel Johnson to Christopher Gadsden, January 10, 1766, WSJ Papers.

[19]For a complete discussion, see chapter 7 above.

[20]William Samuel Johnson to Benjamin Gale, April 10, 1769, WSJ Papers.

[21]William Samuel Johnson to Jonathan Trumbull, March 28, 1770, "Trumbull Papers," p. 427; [William Samuel Johnson] to Samuel Johnson, April 14, 1770, *Samuel Johnson*, 1:468.

[22]William Samuel Johnson to Jonathan Trumbull, August 20, 1770, "Trumbull Papers," pp. 450-51.

[23]See chapter 11, n.38, above.

[24]William Samuel Johnson to Richard Terrick, Bishop of London, January 15, 1774, "Correspondence of Samuel and Wm. S. Johnson," manuscript transcript, 2 vols., Bancroft Transcripts, 2:341.

[25]*Public Records of the Colony of Connecticut*, 14:391, 393; 15:157-59, 192-95, 203-4 Titus Hosmer to Silas Deane, May 22, 1775, "Correspondence of Silas Deane," p. 238; Zeichner, *Connecticut's Years of Controversy*, pp. 198-217; Collier, *Sherman's Connecticut*, p. 38; Gilbert, "Connecticut Loyalists," pp. 281-82; Shumway, "Early New Haven and its Leadership," p. 279.

[26]*Public Records of the Colony of Connecticut*, 15:173–74; Groce, *William Samuel Johnson*, pp. 104–6.

[27]*Public Records of the Colony of Connecticut*, 15:278.

[28]*Public Records of the State of Connecticut*, 1:4–5, 63, 100, 227, 378–79; Groce, *William Samuel Johnson*, p. 106.

[29]For varying estimates on the number of loyalists who joined the British military or actively supported the British by privateering and counterfeiting Continental currency, see Smith, *Loyalists and Redcoats*, pp. 60–64; Brown, *The Good Americans*, pp. 97, 331; Sabine, *American Loyalists*, 1:58–59.

[30]Shephard, "Tories of Connecticut," p. 150.

[31]In 1774, Episcopalians made up one-thirteenth of Connecticut's population; one-third (4,343) of all Episcopalians resided in Fairfield County. New Haven County numbered 2,551, while the eastern counties of New London, Windham, Litchfield, and Hartford had 596, 150, 655, and 1,471 respectively. Kinlock, "Anglican Clergy," pp. 43–44. On the patriotism of most Old Lights and the predominance of loyalism among the colony's Anglicans, see Daniels, "Large Town Power Structures in Eighteenth Century Connecticut," pp. 182–83, 196; Tossell, "Loyalists of Stamford, Connecticut," pp. 63–65; Shumway, "Early New Haven," pp. 279, 296. Only 7.8 percent of Tossell's loyalist sample for the western town of Stamford were Congregationalists. Almost all Stamford's loyalists worshipped in the Church of England.

[32]Benjamin Gale to Silas Deane, February 27, 1775, "Correspondence of Silas Deane," p. 202.

[33]Thomas Chandler to Samuel Johnson, September 5, 1776, *Samuel Johnson*, 1:367, Jeremiah Leaming to the Secretary, SPG, May 10, 1768. Hawks and Perry, eds., *Documentary History of the Protestant Episcopal Church*, 2:124; John Tyler to the Secretary SPG, October 9, 1771, *ibid.*, 2:170–71; Samuel Andrews to the Secretary, SPG, June 25, 1766, *ibid.*, 2:90.

[34]For sketches of all twenty-one, see Kinlock, "Anglican Clergy," pp. 52–114.

[35]William Samuel Johnson to Myles Cooper, February 12, 1766, WSJ Papers.

[36]See chapter 5, note 16, above.

[37]See note 35, above.

[38]Kinlock, "Anglican Clergy," p. 241; Vassar, "Aftermath of Revolution: Letters of the Anglican Clergymen in Connecticut," pp. 431–33, 437, 453; King, "S.P.G. in New England," p. 272; Stiles, *Literary Diary*, 2:45, 314–315; Shephard, "Tories of Connecticut," pp. 258–59; Wilcoxson, *History of Stratford*, p. 463.

[39]Brown, *Good Americans*, p. 129.

[40]Stiles, *Literary Diary*, 2:352; Collier, *Sherman's Connecticut*, pp. 161–62; Goodrich, "Invasion of New Haven by the British Troops, July 5, 1779," pp. 27–93; Beardsley, *William Samuel Johnson*, p. 112.

[41]This account is based on three documents; a copy of the interrogation conducted by Lieut. Col. Dimon, WSJ Papers; a copy of the subscription paper, dated July 12, complete with signatures, *ibid.*; William Samuel Johnson, Memoirs, *ibid.* The original plan called for Johnson, George Benjamin, Ebenezer Allen, and Philip Nichols, all of Stratford, to secretly dispatch an appeal to Tryon. Three men, Daniel Judson, George Benjamin, and George Lewis, first approached Johnson with the plan. The interrogation record shows that the plan had the support of another Stratfordite, John Brooks. Six men, therefore, collaborated with Johnson. Of the six, at least four were regarded as trustworthy patriots by their Stratford neighbors. Judson and Brooks were justices of the peace in 1779; Brooks had also been chosen town clerk at the special town meeting called in 1777 to raise taxes for the war effort. Benjamin and Lewis both bore arms for the

American cause. No data could be found on Allen and Nichols. *Public Records of the State of Connecticut*, 2:255; Wilcoxson, *History of Stratford*, pp. 512, 516, 521, 542, 544. After the incident, Brooks and Judson were reappointed justices of the peace in May 1780, and Judson won election as Stratford's deputy to the General Assembly for October 1781. *Public Records of the State of Connecticut*, 3:9, 518.

[42]Jonathan Trumbull to the People of Stratford, July 10, 1779, WSJ Papers; Hezekiah Wetmore to Jonathan Trumbull, July 9, 1779, *ibid.*; Oliver Wolcott to Jonathan Dimon, July 14, 1779, *ibid.*

[43]Record of Lieut. Col. Dimon's Inquiry, WSJ Papers; Jonathan Dimon to Oliver Wolcott, July 17, 1779, *ibid.*

[44]Oliver Wolcott to Jonathan Dimon, July 18, 1779, printed in Wilcoxson, *History of Stratford*, pp. 526-27; Stiles, *Literary Diary*, 2:352-53, 355.

[45]Oliver Wolcott to Jonathan Dimon, July 18, 1779, printed in Wilcoxson, *History of Stratford*, pp. 526-27.

[46]William Samuel Johnson, Memoirs, WSJ Papers; Jonathan Dimon to Jonathan Trumbull, July 22, 1774, *ibid.*; Wilcoxson, *History of Stratford*, pp. 526-27, 529-30.

[47]*Public Records of the State of Connecticut*, 2:251, 374-75. Only Richard Law, William Williams, and Titus Hosmer had not served on the Council with Johnson before the war.

[48]*Public Records of the State of Connecticut*, 3:375-76. Roger Sherman, William Pitkin, Abraham Davenport, and Jabez Huntington had sat with Johnson on the Council prior to 1776.

[49]William Samuel Johnson, Memoirs, WSJ Papers.

[50]Henry Wilmot to William Baker, January 16, 1776, *Susquehannah Papers*, 7:2.

[51]Resolution Proposed by the Connecticut Delegates to the Continental Congress, October 25, 1775, *Susquehannah Papers*, 6:383-84; Memorial to the Congress from the Delegates of Connecticut, December 18, 1775, *ibid.*, 6:414-16; Narrative of Roger Sherman, n.d., [early 1776], *ibid.*, 7:30-31; *Journals of Congress*, 3:283, 287-88, 295, 297, 321, 377, 439-40, 452-53, 4:283.

[52]Resolution of the Pennsylvania General Assembly, November 18, 1779, *Susquehannah Papers*, 7:54; Joseph Reed to Jonathan Trumbull, December 8, 1779, *ibid.*, 7:55; Jonathan Trumbull to Joseph Reed, March, n.d., 1780, *ibid.*, 7:57-58; *Public Records of the State of Connecticut*, 2:463.

[53]Resolution of the Pennsylvania General Assembly, March 12, 1781, *Susquehannah Papers*, 7:84; *Journals of Congress*, 21:1115-16.

[54]*Public Records of the State of Connecticut*, 4:27.

[55]In October 1773, the Connecticut Assembly had appointed a committee of four— William Samuel Johnson, Eliphalet Dyer, Roger Sherman, and Lieutenant Governor Mathew Griswold—to assist Governor Trumbull in defending Connecticut's sea-to-sea claim. In January 1782, when the legislature appointed Johnson to represent the state at Trenton, five of the nine members of the upper house in attendance had sat there in October 1773, when the first committee was appointed: Jabez Hamlin, William Pitkin, Roger Sherman, Abraham Davenport, and Joseph Spencer. In January 1782, as five years before, Governor Trumbull and Lieutenant Governor Griswold presided. *Public Records of the Colony of Connecticut*, 14:158, 161, 15:1.

[56]Jonathan Trumbull to Eliphalet Dyer, September 23, 1782, *Susquehannah Papers*, 7:123. Illness may also have detained him. See Joseph Reed to George Bryan, December 25, 1782, *ibid.*, 7:239.

[57]*Susquehannah Papers*, 7:xxi; *Journals of Congress*, 22:351-52, 389-92, 23:528-29.

[58]Extract from the Journal of William Samuel Johnson, *Susquehannah Papers*, 7:250.

[59]Editorial note, *Susquehannah Papers*, 7:144-45.

[60]Notes on the Closing Argument of William Samuel Johnson, *Susquehannah Papers*, 7:199-203; Joseph Reed's Notes on Johnson's Closing Argument, *ibid.*, 7:203-16.

[61]Joseph Reed's Notes for his Closing Argument, *Susquehannah Papers*, 7:217-38.

[62]The Trenton Trial Proceedings and Related Documents, *Susquenhannah Papers*, 7:245-46.

[63]Taylor, ed., *Susquehannah Papers*, 7:xxxii; Eliphalet Dyer to William Williams, January, n.d., 1785, *ibid.*, 7:258-60.

[64]Burnett, *Continental Congress*, pp. 217, 220, 222, 240, 250, 251, 341-42, 344-45, 495, 499-500, 536-40, 626; *Public Records of the State of Connecticut*, 3:177-78, *Journals of Congress*, 21:707, 784, 1077, 1098, 1113, 22:191, 290, 423; Collier, *Sherman's Connecticut*, pp. 141-42.

[65]Eliphalet Dyer to Jonathan Trumbull, October 19, 1782, *Susquehannah Papers*, 7:126-28.

[66]Taylor, ed., *Susquehannah Papers*, 7:xxi. The four other judges were William C. Houston and David Brearly of New Jersey, Welcome Arnold of Rhode Island, and William Whipple of New Hampshire.

[67]Eliphalet Dyer to William Williams, January, n.d., 1783, *Susquehannah Papers*, 7:259.

[68]Taylor, ed., *Susquehannah Papers*, 7:xxxv; Zebulon Butler to Elizur Talcott, May 16, 1783, *ibid.*, 7:292-93; Petition of the Susquehannah Company to the Connecticut General Assembly, May 22, 1783, *ibid.*, 7:295-96.

[69]Taylor, ed., *Susquehannah Papers*, 7:xxxiii-xxxvi.

[70]Eliphalet Dyer to William Williams, January, n.d., 1783, *Susquehannah Papers*, 7:260.

[71]Jonathan Trumbull to the President of the Continental Congress, November 15, 1783, *Susquehannah Papers*, 7:326; *Public Records of the State of Connecticut*, 5:120-21, 219-20.

[72]*Public Records of the State of Connecticut*, 5:277-78. Regarding the 1780 cession, see note 64 above.

[73]Taylor, ed., *Susquehannah Papers*, 7:xxxvi-xxxviii, 8:xvi-xxiii; First Congressional Report on the Petition of Zebulon Butler, January 21, 1784, *ibid.*, 7:345-46; *Public Records of the State of Connecticut*, 5:457.

[74]Burnett, *Continental Congress*, p. 563.

[75]*Public Records of the State of Connecticut*, 3:325, 4:102, 111-12, 256, 271-72, 337, 5:37; Jordan, "Connecticut's Politics," pp. 122, 124, 129; Zeichner, "Rehabilitation of Loyalists," p. 321.

[76]Jordan, "Connecticut's Politics," pp. 57, 100-11.

[77]In 1780 and again in 1781, Trumbull had failed to secure a majority of the votes cast for Governor. In accordance with Connecticut law, the choice had fallen to the Assembly, which in both years returned Trumbull to the Governor's seat. Jordan, "Connecticut's Politics," p. 34. In 1783, Trumbull's opponents spread a rumor that he had accepted a bribe from Smith in return for amnesty. The Assembly acquitted the Governor and reprimanded the rumor mongers. *Public Records of the State of Connecticut*, 5:29.

[78]*Public Records of the State of Connecticut*, 5:109-10, 115; Jordan, "Connecticut's Politics," pp. 132-34; Zeichner, "Rehabilitation of Loyalists," p. 319. Once again, Trumbull failed to win a clear majority and the Assembly returned him to office.

[79]Stiles, *Literary Diary*, 3:20, 118; Jordan, "Connecticut's Politics," p. 129; Zeichner, "Rehabilitation of Loyalists," p. 321; Willingham, "Windham, Connecticut: Profile of a Revolutionary Community," p. 187.

[80]In March 1784, a New Haven town meeting appointed a committee of eight to

decide the fate of their wartime enemies and named John Whiting, a well-known loyalist, to the committee. In the city election, one month earlier, three candidates vied for the mayoralty. One of the candidates, the former loyalist Thomas Darling, received 10 percent of the votes. "The City Politics," Ezra Stiles exclaimed, "are founded on an Endeavor silently to bring the Tories into an Equality & Supremacy among the Whigs. . . . Mixing all up together, the Election was come out, Mayor & two Alderman, Whigs; 2 Ald. Tories." Shumway, "Early New Haven," p. 277; Dexter, "New Haven in 1784," pp. 125, 136; Stiles, *Literary Diary*, 2:70, 111; Zeichner, "Rehabilitation of Loyalists," pp. 324-26.

[81]*Public Records of the State of Connecticut*, 5:471, 6:4.

Chapter 13: The Quest for Union

[1]*Public Records of the State of Connecticut*, 5:444; Mathew Griswold to William Samuel Johnson, November 22, 1784, WSJ Papers.

[2]Pomerantz, *New York: An American City*, pp. 461, 463, 466-68, 474-75; Alexander, *James Duane*, p. 156; Coon, *Columbia: Colossus on the Hudson* pp. 52-53; Griswold, *Republican Court*, pp. 29, 30, 87, 119.

[3]Ford, ed., *Journals of Congress*, 28:595-96, 612-14, 618, 638-41, 647, 649-50, 673; Burnett, ed., *Letters of Congress*, 8:xvi-xvii.

[4]William Samuel Johnson to Roger Sherman, April 20, 1785, *Letters of Congress*, 8:102; William Samuel Johnson to Jeremiah Wadsworth, March 26, 1785, *ibid.*, 8:74; Burnett, *Continental Congress*, p. 570.

[5]*Journals of Congress*, 28:162.

[6]Marks, *Independence on Trial*, pp. 53, 58, 65, 81, 82; Nettels, *Emergence of a National Economy*, pp. 55-56; Burnett, *Continental Congress*, p. 663; Collier, *Sherman's Connecticut*, pp. 204-5; Nathan Dane to Samuel Adams, February 11, 1786, *Letters of Congress*, 8:306.

[7]The committee was first appointed on December 6, 1784, and then renewed on January 24, 1785, with Johnson replacing John Jay. *Journals of Congress*, 28:17, 70, 148, 201-5.

[8]William Samuel Johnson to Jonathan Sturges, January 26, 1785, *Letters of Congress*, 8:13; James Monroe to Thomas Jefferson, June 16, 1785, *ibid.*, 8:143.

[9]The committee of five was appointed on April 4, 1785 to "revise and report what alterations, if any, are necessary" in the instructions supplied to John Jay as a minister plenipotentiary to the Court of St. James's. *Journals of Congress*, 28:25, 45-46, 229, 418-22. Monroe's views, which form the basis of the report, can also be found in his letter to Thomas Jefferson, April 12, 1785, *Letters of Congress*, 8:89.

[10]Richard Henry Lee to James Madison, August 11, 1785, *Letters of Congress*, 8:181; James McHenry to George Washington, August 14, 1785, *ibid.*, 8:182-83; John Habersham to Joseph Clap, June 24, 1785, *ibid.*, 8:151-52; James Monroe to Thomas Jefferson, July 15, 1785, *ibid.*, 8:166; Massachusetts Delegates to James Bowdoin, September 3, 1785, *ibid.*, 8:206; Rufus King to Nathan Dane, September 17, 1785, *ibid.*, 8:218; Rufus King to Elbridge Gerry, May 19, 1785, *ibid.*, 8:121; *Journals of Congress*, 29:533.

[11]James Monroe to Thomas Jefferson, April 12, August 15, 1785, *Letters of Congress*, 8:89, 186-87.

[12]William Samuel Johnson to Roger Sherman, April 20, 1785, *ibid.*, 8:101; New Hampshire Delegates to Mesech Ware, February 27, 1785, *ibid.*, 8:47; Samuel Hardy to William Short, April 5, 1785, *ibid.*, 8:85; President of the Congress to the States of New Jersey, Connecticut, Delaware, and Georgia, April 30, 1785, *ibid.*, 8:107; Richard Henry

Lee to George Washington, May 3, 1785, *ibid.*, 8:111; Richard Henry Lee to John Adams, August 1, 1785, *ibid.*, 8:174.

[13] *Journals of Congress*, 28:165; Burnett, *Continental Congress*, p. 622.

[14] William Samuel Johnson to Joseph Platt Cooke, May 4, 1785, *Letters to Congress*, 8:112.

[15] William Grayson to George Washington, April 15, 1785, *Letters of Congress*, 8:95–97; William Grayson to James Madison, May 28, 1785, *ibid.*, 8:129–30; William Samuel Johnson to Roger Sherman, *ibid.*, 8:101; David Howell to William Greene, April 29, 1785, *ibid.*, 8:106–7; Rufus King to Elbridge Gerry, April 26, 1785, *ibid.*, 8:104.

[16] James Monroe to Thomas Jefferson, April 12, 1785, *Letters of Congress*, 8:90; William Grayson to Timothy Pickering, April 27, 1785, *ibid.*, 8:106; William Grayson to James Monroe, May 11, 1785, *ibid.*, 8:109–10; James Monroe to James Madison, May 8, 1785, *ibid.*, 8:116; New Hampshire Delegates to Mesech Ware, May 29, 1785, *ibid.*, 8:130.

[17] William Grayson to George Washington, May 8, 1785, *Letters of Congress*, 8:118. One year later, a number of delegates moved to reexamine the Ordinance of 1785, but their attempts failed. *Journals of Congress*, 30:256–57.

[18] Connecticut Delegates to Mathew Griswold, May 27, 1785, *Letters of Congress*, 8:124.

[19] William Samuel Johnson to Roger Sherman, April 20, 1785, *Susquehannah Papers* 8:222–23; Connecticut Delegates to Mathew Griswold, February 24, 1785, *Letters of Congress*, 8:40–41; *Journals of Congress*, 28:69. The committee was renewed on April 11, May 2, 1785, and again on January 18, 1786.

[20] *Journals of Congress*, 30:44–47; James Monroe to James Madison, February 9, 1786, *Letters of Congress*, 8:299–300; Burnett, *Continental Congress*, pp. 619–21.

[21] *Journals of Congress*, 30:7–10, 31:508; Burnett, *Continental Congress*, p. 661.

[22] James Monroe to Richard Henry Lee, May 24, 1786, *Susquehannah Papers*, 8:343; William Grayson to George Washington, May 27, 1786, *Letters of Congress*, 8:371–72.

[23] *Journals of Congress*, 29:725–31, 777, 796; *Public Records of the State of Connecticut*, 6:104–5.

[24] Taylor, ed., *Susquehannah Papers*, 8:xxx–xxxi, xxxv–xxxviii; William Judd to William Samuel Johnson and Stephen Mix Mitchell, April 15, 1786, *ibid.*, 8:314; Charles Pettit to Jeremiah Wadsworth, May 14, 1786, *ibid.*, 8:323–24.

[25] Pelatiah Webster to William Samuel Johnson, March 13, 1786, *Susquehannah Papers*, 8:307–8.

[26] Taylor, ed., *Susquehannah Papers*, 8:xxx–xxxi; *Public Records of the State of Connecticut*, 5:456–57; Jordan, "Connecticut's Politics," pp. 226, 239–50.

[27] Pennsylvania Delegates to Benjamin Franklin, May 26, 1787, *Letters of Congress*, 8:386.

[28] William Grayson to George Washington, May 27, 1786, *Letters of Congress*, 8:371–72; James Monroe to Thomas Jefferson, June 16, 1786, *ibid.*, 8:391–92; Pennsylvania Delegates to Benjamin Franklin, May 7, 1786, *ibid.*, 8:357; *Journals of Congress*, 30:21–22, 158, 160.

[29] *Journals of Congress*, 30:295–96, 299–300; Connecticut Delegates to Mathew Griswold, February 24, 1785, *Susquehannah Papers*, 8:216–17.

[30] *Journals of Congress*, 30:301–2.

[31] *Ibid.*, 30:302–3.

[32] *Ibid.*, 30:304, 307–8. On the last vote of the day, the Pennsylvania delegates abandoned their unsuccessful alliance with the landless states and voted against a measure which they themselves had proposed earlier. The measure would have protected the future right of the United States to land not ceded by the states. On the twenty-fifth, Con-

necticut withdrew from the voting on a motion that would have favored the state's western reserve but left the Trenton decision unprotected. Clearly, the Pennsylvania and Connecticut delegates realized that the landed and landless factions had to be reconciled, not forced into conflict, if the cession were to succeed.

[33]*Journals of Congress*, 30:310-11; Charles Pettit to Jeremiah Wadsworth, May 27, 1786, *Susquehannah Papers*, 8:350. It is understood, Pettit told Wadsworth, "that the State of Connecticut will on her part give no farther Countenance to the Claims of the State or of her Companies with Penn[a] but on the Contrary use means to induce these Companies to relinquish their Pretension to such Claims. That Penn[a] will take the Actual Settlers on the late disputed Territory under protection & treat them with Generosity as well as Justice as to their private Rights."

[34]Stephen Mix Mitchell to William Samuel Johnson, June 18, 1786, *Letters of Congress*, 8:393.

[35]Connecticut Delegates to Mathew Griswold, April 12, 1786, *Letters of Congress*, 8:339-40; Rufus King to Elbridge Gerry, April 30, 1786, *ibid.*, 8:345-46; *Journals of Congress*, 30:57.

[36]*Journals of Congress*, 30:387; William Samuel Johnson to Richard Jackson, July 30, 1786, *Letters of Congress*, 8:408.

[37]*Journals of Congress*, 31:494-98.

[38]*Ibid.*, 29:494-96, 31:473-84; Marks, *Independence on Trial*, p. 24; Burnett, *Continental Congress*, p. 654; Henderson, "Structure of Politics in the Continental Congress," p. 187.

[39]Charles Pinckney's Speech in Answer to John Jay, August 16, 1786, *Journals of Congress*, 31:945-46; William Samuel Johnson, Notes on the Debates, August 16-August 22, 1786, *Letters of Congress*, 8:434-37; Charles Thomson, Minutes of the Proceedings, August 18, 1786, *ibid.*, 8:438-40; James Monroe to James Madison, September 3, 1786, *ibid.*, 8:460-62.

[40]Charles Thomson, Minutes of the Proceedings, August 16, 18, 21, 1786, *Letters of Congress*, 8:427-30, 438-40, 449-50; Rufus King to Elbridge Gerry, June 4, 1786, *ibid.*, 8:381-82; William Samuel Johnson, Speech before Congress, August 21, 1786, *ibid.*, 8:447-49.

[41]*Journals of Congress*, 31:595; Timothy Bloodworth to Richard Caswell, September 4, 1786, *Letters of Congress*, 8:462.

[42]*Journals of Congress*, 31:641, 882-85; Stephen Mix Mitchell to William Samuel Johnson, August 9, September 14, 1786, *Letters of Congress*, 8:418, 466; Burnett, *Continental Congress*, p. 661.

[43]Burnett, *Continental Congress*, pp. 669, 689; Ford, ed., *Journals of Congress*, 32:vii; Stephen Mix Mitchell to Jeremiah Wadsworth, *Letters of Congress*, 8:531.

[44]Stephen Mix Mitchell to William Samuel Johnson, September 14, 1786, WSJ Papers; Henry Lee to George Washington, September 8, 1786, *Letters of Congress*, 8:463.

[45]Burnett, ed., *Letters of Congress*, 8:xxxiii-xxxvii; Burnett, *Continental Congress*, pp. 665-69; Marks, *Independence on Trial*, pp. 91-95; Rossiter, *Grand Convention*, pp. 55, 154. Virginia, New Jersey, New Hampshire, Pennsylvania, North Carolina, Delaware, and Georgia had already selected delegates to the convention.

[46]Burnett, ed., *Letters of Congress*, 8:xxviii-xxxix; Massachusetts Delegates to James Bowdoin, September 3, 1785, *ibid.*, 8:209; Nathan Dane to John Choate, January 31, 1786, *ibid.*, 8:293; Edward Carrington to James Madison, December 18, 1786, *ibid.*, 8:523.

[47]For an excellent discussion of the contest between nationalists and antinationalists in Connecticut, see Jordan, "Connecticut's Politics." Jordan shows that the contest was largely unrelated to the east-west split that had shaped Connecticut politics in the prewar decades.

[48]Jordan, "Connecticut's Politics," pp. 142-220; Burnett, *Continental Congress*, p. 568; Larry Gerlach, "Connecticut and Communication, 1778-1784," *Bulletin of the Connecticut Historical Society*, 33 (April 1968), 51-52; *Public Records of the State of Connecticut*, 5:326-27; Stiles *Literary Diary*, 3:74.

[49]Jordan, "Connecticut's Politics," pp. 271-76; Collier, *Sherman's Connecticut*, pp. 223-24. Four times, between May 1785 and October 1786, the antinationalists in the Assembly had thwarted the efforts of the Governor and the Council to lay additional taxes for the purpose of meeting the federal requisition.

[50]Burnett, *Continental Congress*, p. 678; Stephen Mix Mitchell to William Samuel Johnson, September 18, 1787, *Letters of Congress*, 8:645-46; James Madison to Edmund Randolph, February 25, 1787, *ibid.*, 8:549 n.3.

[51]William Grayson to James Monroe, November 22, 1786, *Letters of Congress*, 8:510; Rufus King to Elbridge Gerry, February 11, 1787, *ibid.*, 8:539; Ernst, *Rufus King*, pp. 89-90.

[52]*Journals of Congress*, 32:73-74; William Irvine to James Wilson, March 6, 1787, *Letters of Congress*, 8:551.

[53]James Madison to Edmund Pendleton, February 24, 1787, *Letters of Congress*, 8:547; William Samuel Johnson to Hugh Williamson, March 31, 1787, *ibid.*, 8:567-68.

[54]Jordan, "Connecticut's Politics," pp. 281, 296, 298-300; Collier, *Sherman's Connecticut*, pp. 225, 228.

[55]Elkins and McKitrick, "Founding Fathers, Young Men of the Revolution," p. 391.

[56]Collier, *Sherman's Connecticut*, p. 228n.

[57]*Public Records of the State of Connecticut*, 6:282.

[58]After the delegates had been selected, Benjamin Gale told Johnson, "Your opposition to the Convention has done you Great Honour among Reublicans." Benjamin Gale to William Samuel Johnson, April 19, 1787, WSJ Papers.

[59]On May 17, Johnson set out from Stratford to the Assembly, where he remained until the twenty-eighth. Diary of William Samuel Johnson, May 17-May 28, 1787, WSJ Papers.

[60]Brown, *Oliver Ellsworth*, p. 53; Collier, *Sherman's Connecticut*, pp. 229, 231; Oliver Ellsworth to Oliver Wolcott, May 6, 1783, Flanders, ed. *Chief Justices of the Supreme Court*, 2:103. Oliver Ellsworth to Jonathan Trumbull, July 10, 1783, *ibid.*, p. 114.

[61]Collier, *Sherman's Connecticut*, p. 229.

[62]*Ibid.*, p. 189.

[63]*Ibid.*, pp. 218, 229.

Chapter 14: The Great Debate

[1]Diary of William Samuel Johnson, May 17-June 2, 1787, WSJ Papers.

[2]Rossiter, *Grand Convention*, pp. 87, 153, 239; Elkins and McKitrick, "Founding Fathers," p. 392. The four exceptions were Robert Yates and John Lansing, Jr. of New York, and Luther Martin and John F. Mercer of Maryland, all outspoken antinationalists.

[3]George Mason to George Mason, Jr., June 1, 1787, *Records of the Federal Convention*, 3:32; Benjamin Rush to Richard Price, June 2, 1787, *ibid.*, 3:33; Rossiter, *Grand Convention*, pp. 145-46.

[4]Jared Ingersoll, Jr., a member of the Pennsylvania delegation and oldest son of the notorious exstampmaster, commented on this expectation in a letter to William Samuel Johnson, April 28, 1787, *Records*, 3:18.

[5]For Pierce's sketches, see *Records of the Federal Convention*, 3:87-97.

[6]Rossiter, *Grand Convention*, pp. 122, 124, 148; Elkins and McKitrick, "Founding Fathers," p. 383.

[7]Pole, *Political Representation* p. 364; Elkins and McKitrick, "Founding Fathers," pp. 382-83.

[8]*Records of the Federal Convention*, 1:20, 23, 49, 530.

[9]*Ibid.*, 1:34-35, 46, 48.

[10]*Ibid.*, 1:46, 52, 57.

[11]*Ibid.*, 1:150, 156. Dickinson defended the proposal on very different grounds, contending that the power of the two houses should flow from different sources and act as "mutual checks on each other." *Ibid.*, 1:156-57.

[12]*Ibid.*, 1:31, 37.

[13]*Ibid.*, 1:177-79.

[14]*Ibid.*, 1:87, 192-93, 196, 202. Sherman raised his proposal before the vote on proportional representation in the lower house was taken. On the vote for proportional suffrage in the second house, Connecticut, New Jersey, Maryland and Delaware were in the minority.

[15]*Ibid.*, 1:224-32.

[16]*Ibid.*, 1:240, 242-45, 250; Rossiter, *Grand Convention*, p. 97. The New Jersey plan provided for a "federal Executive" and a "federal Judiciary," and amended the powers of Congress to include raising a revenue through import duties and a stamp tax, enforcing requisitions on the states, and regulating trade with foreign nations as well as among the states.

[17]*Records of the Federal Convention*, 1:319-320. Except for New York, which was dominated by the stalwart antinationalists Lansing and Yates, the division was between large-state nationalists and small-state nationalists. Like Patterson, most of the small-state delegates feared the power of Massachusetts, Virginia, and Pennsylvania. But the Connecticut delegation supported the one state one vote principle "not so much as a security for the small States; as for the State Govts. which could not be preserved unless they were represented & had a negative in the Genl. Government." *Ibid.*, 2:5.

[18]*Ibid.*, 1:355, 363; Diary of William Samuel Johnson, June 2, 3, 4, 1787, WSJ Papers. Johnson's diary contains numerous other references to illness in this period.

[19]*Records of the Federal Convention*, 1:461-62, 463.

[20]*Ibid.*, 1:468-69.

[21]*Ibid.*, 1:489.

[22]*Ibid.*, 1:510, 511, 524.

[23]*Ibid.*, 1:527, 2:5-6.

[24]*Ibid.*, 1:558, 563, 2:89; Rossiter, *Grand Convention*, p. 189.

[25]*Records of the Federal Convention*, 2:19-20.

[26]William Samuel Johnson to Samuel Peters, July 27, 1787, *Ibid.*, 4:72-73.

[27]*Ibid.*, 1:125, 2:38-39, 46. Similarly, on June 26, the Connecticut delegates had urged that the states assume the obligation of paying the members of the Senate. "If the Senate was meant to strengthen the Govt. it ought to have the confidence of the States," Ellsworth had said. "The States will have an interest in keeping up a representation and will make such provision for supporting the members as will ensure their attendance." But on August 14, the Connecticut delegates would reverse their stance, voting affirmatively on "the question for paying the Members of the Legislature out of the Natl Treasure." *Ibid.*, 1:427, 428, 2:290, 292.

[28]Rossiter, *Grand Convention*, p. 196.

[29]*Records of the Federal Convention*, 1:588, 593-96.

[30]*Ibid.*, 2:85, 95, 176, 183.

[31]*Ibid.*, 2:220, 221–22, 364.

[32]*Ibid.*, 2:220.

[33]Gerlach, "Toward a More Perfect Union," p. 74.

[34]*Records of the Federal Convention*, 2:364, 369–70, 374–75.

[35]*Ibid.*, 2:366, 396, 446.

[36]Rossiter, *Grand Convention*, p. 241.

[37]*Records of the Federal Convention*, 2:553, 582; Ernst, *Rufus King*, p. 112; Mintz, *Gouverneur Morris*, p. 199.

[38]*Records of the Federal Convention*, 2:631, 3:77.

[39]*Ibid.*, 2:631, 648–49.

[40]*Ibid.*, 2:649, 664–65; James Madison, "The Federalist, No. XXXVII," *Ibid.*, 3:244.

[41]Rossiter, *Grand Convention*, pp. 188, 211, 234.

[42]*Records of the Federal Convention*, 1:335–36; Kenyon, "Men of Little Faith," pp. 58–59.

[43]For a concise discussion of the instructions that the delegates carried to Philadelphia, see Rossiter, *Grand Convention*, p. 159.

[44]Stephen Mix Mitchell to William Samuel Johnson, July 26, 1787, WSJ Papers; Jordan, "Connecticut's Politics," p. 307.

[45]*Records of the Federal Convention*, 1:335, 2:88, 90–91, 93.

[46]Ernst, *Rufus King*, p. 117; Diary of William Samuel Johnson, September 18–20, 1787, WSJ Papers.

[47]Burnett, *Continental Congress*, pp. 696–98; *Journals of Congress*, 33:488, 549; Burnett, ed., *Letters of Congress*, 8:xlvi–xlviii.

[48]Jordan, "Connecticut's Politics," pp. 308–18.

[49]Collier, *Sherman's Connecticut*, p. 52; extracts from Ellsworth's public letters, signed "A Landholder," which appeared in the *Connecticut Courant* that winter, are reprinted in *Records of the Federal Convention*, 3:137, 143, 164, 165, 168, 170–72.

[50]*Public Records of the State of Connecticut*, 9:355–56.

[51]Johnson left New York on October 12 and arrived at Stratford the following day. Diary of William Samuel Johnson, WSJ Papers.

[52]Stiles, *Literary Diary*, 3:285; Diary of William Samuel Johnson, October 17–November 12, 1787, WSJ Papers; James Duane to William Samuel Johnson, May 22, 1787, Samuel Johnson Papers.

[53]Samuel William Johnson to William Samuel Johnson, June 25, October 24, 1787, WSJ Papers; William Samuel Johnson to Robert Charles Johnson, September 30, 1787, *ibid.*

[54]William Samuel Johnson to Samuel William Johnson, November 29, 1787, *ibid.;* Hugh Ledlie to William Samuel Johnson, December 3, 1787, *ibid.; Public Records of the State of Connecticut*, 6:398; Jedidiah Huntington to Andrew Huntington, May, n.d., 1787, "Huntington Papers," p. 471.

[55]Dexter, ed., *Biographical Sketches of the Graduates of Yale College*, 4:286–87; William Samuel Johnson to Samuel William Johnson, November 29, 1787, WSJ Papers.

[56]Diary of William Samuel Johnson, December 27, 1787–January 2, 1788, WSJ Papers; Jordan, "Connecticut's Politics," pp. 333–34.

[57]For Ellsworth's and Johnson's speeches at the ratifying convention, see *Public Records of the State of Connecticut*, 6:553–58. Ellsworth had followed a similar tactic in his public letters, signed "A Landholder," which appeared in the Connecticut press prior to the ratifying convention. Although the Connecticut delegates had opposed ratification by popular conventions, Ellsworth told the public in November, "It proves the

honesty and patriotism of the gentlemen who composed the general Convention, that they chose to submit their system to the people rather than the legislatures, whose decisions are often influenced by men in the higher departments of government, who have provided well for themselves and dread any change least they should be injured by its operation." Ellsworth's public letter led his readers to believe that no one at the convention, least of all the Connecticut delegates, had feared submitting the Constitution to the judgement of the populace. Extract from "A Landholder," *Records,* 3:137.

⁵⁸In June 1787, Ezra Stiles had commented that "this federal Convention embosoms some of the most sensible & great Characters in America; all of them excellent." Stiles, *Literary Diary,* 3:267.

⁵⁹Jordan, "Connecticut's Politics," pp. 350-52, 354; McDonald, *We the People,* pp. 138-40.

⁶⁰*Public Records of the State of Connecticut,* 6:569.

⁶¹Jordan, "Connecticut's Politics," pp. 347-48; McDonald, *We the People,* p. 141.

⁶²Diary of William Samuel Johnson, January 1, 1788–January 10, 1789, WSJ Papers. Johnson retired from the Continental Congress in the spring of 1788, having served the maximum number of consecutive years allowed by Connecticut law. Diary entries recording the occasional visits of Ann Johnson to New York suggest that she did not establish permanent residence at the college until after Johnson resigned from the Senate in March 1791. Johnson gave up his seat on the Council in January 1789. *Public Records of the State of Connecticut,* 6:356; Stiles, *Literary Diary,* 3:285; *Journals of Congress,* 34:208.

⁶³William Samuel Johnson to Ralph Izard, February 12, 1788, Samuel Johnson Papers; Pierre Long to William Samuel Johnson, March 14, 1789, WSJ Papers; *Public Records of the State of Connecticut,* 6:474. In November and December, when Connecticut freemen nominated their Representatives to Congress, Federalists captured all twelve nominations. Similarly, the seven presidential electors appointed by the Assembly in January were all friends to the new Constitution. Jordan, "Connecticut's Politics," pp. 371-73.

⁶⁴Diary of William Samuel Johnson, March 5, April 6, 1789, WSJ Papers; Samuel Mix Mitchel to William Samuel Johnson, March 22, 1789, WSJ Papers; Griswold, *Republican Court,* pp. 114, 119, 120.

⁶⁵Alexander, *James Duane,* p. 199; Griswold, *Republican Court,* pp. 130, 137; Diary of William Samuel Johnson, April 22, 23, 1789, WSJ Papers.

⁶⁶Griswold, *Republican Court,* p. 152; Hofstadter, *Idea of a Party System,* p. 85; Miller, *Federalist Era,* pp. 6-10; Groce, *William Samuel Johnson,* pp. 159, 161-62.

⁶⁷Miller, *Federalist Era,* pp. 5, 25-27; Rossiter, *Grand Convention,* p. 301. The Congress restricted the functioning of the executive branch only by requiring the Secretary of the Treasury to report directly to the Congress and by reserving the right of calling for information from the Secretary without the permission of the President.

⁶⁸Hofstadter, *Party System,* pp. 78-80; Rossiter, *Grand Convention,* p. 303; Miller, *Federalist Era,* pp. 24-25; *Public Records of the State of Connecticut,* 6:576, 588, 616; Morgan, *Birth of the Republic,* pp. 146, 156. The Connecticut delegation accurately expressed the views of their own state. The Connecticut legislature debated and rejected the amendments in 1790 and did not ratify the Bill of Rights until 1941. Perhaps Sherman's outspoken opposition influenced the legislature. Sherman composed a lengthy public letter against the amendments. It appeared first in the *New York Packet* in March 1789, and was reprinted throughout New England. Collier, *Sherman's Connecticut,* p. 301.

⁶⁹United States *Constitution,* art. I, sec. 8, art. VI; Ferguson, *Power of the Purse,* pp. 294-96; Miller, *Federalist Era,* pp. 39-40.

[70]Miller, *Federalist Era*, pp. 42-44, 55, 73-74, 76-78; Ferguson, *Power of the Purse*, pp. 297, 301-2; Brant, *James Madison*, pp. 294-95; Hofstadter, *American Political Tradition*, pp. 27-28, 31-32; Pole, *Political Representation*, pp. 359-61.

[71]Ferguson, *Power of the Purse*, pp. 307-19; Ernst, *Rufus King*, p. 158; Brant, *James Madison*, pp. 306, 312; Tindall, *Origin and Government of the District of Columbia*, p. 202.

[72]Rufus King, Memorandum, June 6, 1790, *Correspondence of Rufus King*, 1:383.

[73]Madison's choice also reflected his determination to secure the federal government from the crippling effects of state power. He no doubt believed that it would be far easier to erect a federal district on the rural Potomac than to divest an old and populace city of its local and state allegiances. Young, *Washington Community*, p. 14.

[74]Rufus King, Memorandum, June 30, 1790, *Correspondence of King*, 1:383-85; Ernst, *Rufus King*, pp. 159-63; Miller, *Federalist Era*, p. 48; Tindall, *District of Columbia*, pp. 71-75; Brant, *James Madison*, p. 313.

[75]McDonald, *We the People*, pp. 46, 138-43.

[76]Bemis, *Jay's Treaty*, pp. 49-50, 52-54; Combs, *The Jay Treaty* pp. 31, 39-40; Ritcheson, *Aftermath of Revolution*, pp. 92-93, 110; Lycan, *Hamilton and American Foreign Policy*, pp. 184-86; Marks, *Independence on Trial*, p. 152.

[77]The only available source material revealing Johnson's views on Anglo-American relations is his informal negotiation with an unofficial British agent in New York, Major George Beckwith, whose identity and activities are discussed later. Beckwith's reports of his conferences with Johnson and other American statesmen are collected in Douglas Brymner, ed., "Note E," *Report on Canadian Archives, 1890* (Ottawa, 1891) pp. 97-175. In 1789 and the following year, Johnson repeatedly told Beckwith that he considered commercial retaliation against Great Britian contrary to the best interests of the United States. *Canadian Archives*, pp. 136-37. For Hamilton's similar views, see *ibid.*, p. 125.

[78]*Ibid*, pp. 139, 146.

[79]Combs, *The Jay Treaty*, pp. 62-63, 83; Lycan, *Hamilton and American Foreign Policy*, pp. 186-87; Miller, *Federalist Era*, p. 19.

[80]Bemis, *Jay's Treaty*, p. 56; Ritcheson, *Aftermath of Revolution*, p. 93.

[81]Beckwith assigned numbers to his American contacts, labelling Johnson number 1, Schuyler number 2, and Hamilton number 7. Brymner, ed., *Canadian Archives*, p. xli.

[82]For this reason, no doubt, Johnson carried the number 1.

[83]Diary of William Samuel Johnson, September 30, 1787, June 25, 27, August 10, 12, September 28, 1788, January 19, August 24, 1789, WSJ Papers.

[84]*Canadian Archives*, p. 121.

[85]*Ibid.*, pp. 121, 125.

[86]*Ibid.*, p. 146; Bemis, *Jay's Treaty*, pp. 101, 103, 106-9; Miller, *Federalist Era*, p. 84. For various interpretations of Hamilton's conversations with Beckwith in the summer of 1790, regarding American policy in the event of a European war, see Brymner, ed., *Canadian Archives*, pp. xxxvii-xlix; Combs, *The Jay Treaty*, pp. 51-55; Lycan, *Hamilton and American Foreign Policy*, pp. 120-31; Boyd, *Number 7*, pp. 34-65.

[87]*Canadian Archives*, pp. 125, 136, 138, 163.

[88]"Minutes of the Trustees of Columbia College," December 4, 1790, MS typescript, Columbiana Collection; Diary of William Samuel Johnson, December 9-11, 1790, WSJ Papers; William Samuel Johnson to Samuel William Johnson, December 12, 1790, WSJ Papers.

[89]Combs, *The Jay Treaty*, p. 58; Bemis, *Jay's Treaty*, pp. 112-14.

[90]Bemis, *Jay's Treaty*, pp. 116-18; Combs, *The Jay Treaty*, pp. 87-90; Ritcheson, *Aftermath of Revolution*, pp. 31, 127-33.

[91]Bemis, *Jay's Treaty*, p. 121.

[92]*Ibid.*, pp. 119, 129.

[93]Ritcheson, *Aftermath of Revolution*, pp. 135, 137.

[94]*Canadian Archives*, p. 152.

[95]Boyd, *Number 7*, p. 21.

Chapter 15: A Young University with an Aged President

[1]Morgan, *Gentle Puritan*, pp. 329-35; Cremin, *American Education*, p. 565.

[2]Cremin, *American Education*, p. 566; Gegenheimer, *William Smith*, p. 78.

[3]Cremin, *American Education*, p. 565; Wertenbaker, *Princeton*, pp. 59-63.

[4]Moore, *An Historical Sketch of Columbia College*, p. 61; Humphrey, *King's College*, pp. 153-54.

[5]Minutes of the Trustees, November 26, 1787, "Minutes of the Trustees," p. 82; "Description of Columbia College," pp. 255-56; *Catalogue of Officers and Graduates*, pp. 5-6; Horton, *James Kent*, p. 81.

[6]Humphrey, *King's College*, pp. 117, 119-20, 251, 284; Wertenbaker, *Princeton*, pp. 46, 64; Morgan, *Gentle Puritan*, pp. 328, 359.

[7]Benjamin Rush, *A Plan for the Establishment of Public School and the Diffusion of Knowledge in Pennsylvania; To Which Are Added, Thoughts upon the Mode of Education, Proper in a Republic. Addressed to the Legislature and Citizens of the State* (Philadelphia, 1786), rpt. in Rudolph, ed., *Essays on Education*, p. 9; Morgan, *Gentle Puritan*, p. 323.

[8]Samuel Harrison Smith, *Remarks on Education: Illustrating the Close Connection Between Virtue and Wisdom. To Which Is Annexed a System of Liberal Education Which, Having Received the Premium Awarded by the American Philosophical Society, December 15th, 1797, Is Now Published by Their Order* (Philadelphia, 1798), rpt. in Rudolph, ed., *Essays on Education*, p. 175.

[9]Rudolph, ed., *Essays on Education*, p. xv; Smith, *Remarks on Education*, p. 210; Samuel Knox, *An Essay on the Best System of Liberal Education Adapted to the Genius of the Government of the United States. . . . To Which Is Prefixed, an Address to the Legislature of Maryland* (Philadelphia, 1799), rpt. in Rudolph, ed., *Essays on Education*, p. 318; George Washington to the Commissioners of the Federal District, January 28, 1795, Padover, ed., *World of the Founding Fathers*, p. 582; George Washington to Robert Brooke, March 16, 1795, Padover, ed., *World of the Founding Fathers*, p. 582; Wesley, *Proposed: The University of the United States*, pp. 4-10.

[10]Abbott, *Government Policy and Higher Education*, pp. 8-9.

[11]Pratt, ed., "Annals," pp. 98, 199.

[12]Tyler, *Literary History of the American Revolution*, 1:392-400; Vance, "Myles Cooper," pp. 275-76.

[13]Humphrey, *King's College*, p. 143. The King's faculty on the eve of Revolution included President Cooper, Samuel Clossy, John Vardill, and Robert Harpur. Only Harpur supported the patriot cause.

[14]*Ibid.*, p. 210. About 16 percent or 196 of the Harvard graduates alive in 1776 openly dissented from the Revolution. Morison, *Three Centuries of Harvard*, pp. 132, 141.

[15]"Extract from the Original Charter of King's College, October 31, 1754," *Samuel Johnson*, 4:221; Humphrey, *King's College*, pp. 69, 271.

[16]"The Petition of the Subscribers Governors of the College commonly called King's College To the honorable Legislature of the State of New York," Pratt, ed., "Annals," p. 199. The officers of state included Governor George Clinton, Treasurer Gerard Bancker,

Attorney General Egbert Benson, Secretary of State John Morin Scott, and Chief Justice
Richard Morris. The clergymen included John Henry Livingston, John Rodgers, and
Samuel Provoost. The remaining signers were Leonard Lispenard, Jonathan Livingston,
William Walton, governors of the college since 1754, and Samuel Bayard, Jr., elected to
the Board of Governors in 1781. James Duane was elected to the board in 1762, but be-
came an ex-officio member early in 1784, when he assumed the mayoralty of New York
City.

¹⁷*Ibid.*, p. 198.

¹⁸"An Act for . . . erecting an University within this State," Pratt, ed., "Annals,"
pp. 203–9.

¹⁹As Lawrence Cremin commented, "Livingston and his associates certainly set forth
many of the principles that stood at the heart of that institution; whether they were
actually instrumental in its coming to be must remain a matter of conjecture." *American
Education*, p. 431.

²⁰"An Act to amend an Act, entitled 'An Act . . . erecting an University within this
State'," Pratt, ed., "Annals," pp. 221–22.

²¹An examination of the Minutes of the Regents from May 5, 1784 to March 29, 1787
shows that only nineteen regular and ex-officio regents attended one-third or more of the
meetings. Of these nineteen men, only Clinton hailed from outside New York City. Four
of the nineteen were former governors of King's; one, Robert Harpur, had taught at
King's. Three others were newly appointed members of the Columbia faculty. Minutes of
the Regents, May 5, 1784 to March 29, 1787, Pratt, ed., "Annals," pp. 209–59. Probably the
most important committee appointed by the regents was that formed on December 9,
1784, to examine the finances of the college and establish a faculty and curriculum. On
the committee sat eight regents, all residents of New York City. Minutes of the Regents,
December 9, 1784, Pratt, ed., "Annals," p. 225.

²²Minutes of the Regents, April 4, 1785, Pratt, ed., "Annals," p. 235; Alexander,
James Duane, pp. 183, 202.

²³Discontent surfaced on February 28, 1786, when a committee was formed "to consider of Ways and Means of promoting literature throughout the State." Over two-thirds
of the committee members represented the interests of the state against the city, a stark
contrast to the customary dominance by the city regents. The committee apparently produced no immediate results. Minutes of the Regents, February 28, 1786, Pratt, ed.,
"Annals," p. 243.

Resentment among the state's lawmakers had manifested itself in November 1784,
when the legislators were debating a grant of £2552 to the college. One upstate legislator
suggested reducing the grant to £1000, while another proposed awarding the money to
frontier schools instead. Alexander, *James Duane*, p. 183.

²⁴Minutes of the Regents, January 31, February 16, 1787, Pratt, ed., "Annals," pp.
250–51, 253. The committee reported that the law of November 1784, "placing the rights
of every College in the hands of a few Individuals . . . excited jealousy and dissatisfaction
when the interest of literature require that all should be united. . . ."

²⁵"An Act to Institute An University within this State and for other Purposes therein
Mentioned," April 13, 1787, Pratt, ed., "Annals," pp. 262–70.

²⁶From Albany County came Walter Livingston; from New York City came Samuel
Provoost, John Henry Livingston, Alexander Hamilton, John Mason, John Grano,
Brockholst Livingston, Robert Harpur, John Daniel Gros, Johann Christoff Kunze,
Joseph Delaplaine, Leonard Lispenard, John Lawrence, John Rutherford, Morgan
Lewis, John Cochran, Gershom Seixas, Charles McKnight, Thomas Jones, and Nicholas
Romayne. The two trustees who had not served on the regents were Abraham Beach of
Connecticut and James Wilson of New York.

[27]The faculty members were Benjamin Kissam, Ebenezer Crosby and Samuel Bard, all former ex-officio regents.

[28]James Duane, Samuel Provoost, John Henry Livingston, Leonard Lispenard, and Thomas Jones, all governors of King's College, and Robert Harpur, a teacher at King's.

[29]"An Act to Institute An University within this State and for other Purposes therein Mentioned," Pratt, ed., "Annals," pp. 262-70.

[30]Alexander Hamilton to James Ashton Bayard, August 6, 1800, *Papers of Alexander Hamilton,* 25:56.

[31]For Duane's correspondence with Johnson in the years 1770-1772 regarding college affairs, see Groce, *William Samuel Johnson,* p. 172, n.7.

[32]Pomerantz, *New York,* pp. 373-74. During King's first decade, 60 percent of the matriculated students were Anglicans. Under Cooper, the percentage rose to 75. Humphrey, *King's College,* pp. 97-98, 136, 285.

[33]See note 32, above.

[34]Cooper's notoriety stemmed chiefly from "A Whip for the American Whig," a series of essays that he, Samuel Seabury, Charles Inglis, and Thomas Bradbury Chandler issued in 1768 and 1769 as an answer to the Triumvirate's "American Whig." Cooper also played an active role in organizing the northern missionaries, and in 1767 and 1770, the New York and New Jersey clergy chose him as president of their annual joint convocation. For detailed discussions of Cooper's leadership of the Anglican cause, see Steiner, *Samuel Seabury,* pp. 101, 105, 107-8, 110, 112, 114, 125-26, 177-78; Bridenbaugh, *Mitre and Sceptre,* pp. 246, 253, 260, 268, 298-99, 315.

[35]Cremin, *American Education,* pp. 461-65; Morgan, *Gentle Puritan,* pp. 47-48; 390; Cheyney, *University of Pennsylvania,* pp. 107, 132; Humphrey, *King's College,* pp. 108, 169, 178; Myles Cooper, *Ethics Compendium in Usum, Collegiorum* (New York, 1774); Samuel Johnson to East Apthorp, December 1, 1759, *Samuel Johnson,* 4:56; Samuel Johnson, *Elementa Philosophica: Containing Chiefly; Noetica, Or Things relating to the Mind or Understanding: And Ethica, Or Things relating to the Moral Behavior* (Philadelphia, 1752), rpt. in *Samuel Johnson,* 2:359-435.

[36]Minutes of the Regents, December 14, 30, 1784, Pratt, ed., "Annals," pp. 226, 229; "Minutes of the Trustees," November 26, December 4, 1787, pp. 81-89. No salary was attached to the professorships of German and geography under the regents.

[37]Cheyney, *University of Pennsylvania,* pp. 28-32, 117-30; Carl and Jessica Bridenbaugh, *Rebels and Gentlemen,* pp. 60-64. The legislative act of 1779 altered the name of the school from the College of Philadelphia to the University of the State of Pennsylvania.

[38]Stiles, *Literary Diary,* 2:398; 416; Cheyney, *University of Pennsylvania,* p. 132; "Minutes of the Trustees of the University of Pennsylvania," January 31, February 8, 26, 1780, pp. 45, 47, 49. Cheyney asserts that Rittenhouse assumed the duties of professor of moral philosophy, but the minutes reveal that Ewing was appointed to that chair on March 17, 1780 and that Rittenhouse agreed to lecture on geography and astronomy. "Minutes of the Trustees of the University of Pennsylvania," March 17, 1780, p. 54.

[39]Hindle, *David Rittenhouse,* pp. 221-22; Cheyney, *University of Pennsylvania,* p. 134; "Minutes of the Trustees of the University of Pennsylvania," April 18, 22, July 2, 1782, pp. 117, 119, 126.

[40]For Kunze's faculty appointment to the University of the State of Pennsylvania, see "Minutes of the Trustees of the University of Pennsylvania," January 26, 1780, p. 43. On Kunze's faculty appointment to Columbia, see Minutes of the Regents, December 30, 1784, Pratt, ed., "Annals," p. 229.

[41]Cremin, *American Education,* p. 222; Morison, *Three Centuries of Harvard,* pp. 17, 47-53, 64, 159-61; Wertenbaker, *Princeton,* p. 121; Humphrey, *King's College,* pp. 90,

135; Samuel Johnson, "A True and Just State of the Case Between the Reverend Dr. Johnson and the Governor of King's College in New York," January, 1763, *Samuel Johnson*, 4:93–96.

[42]The formation of a medical department will be discussed later in this chapter.

[43]"Minutes of the Trustees," March 29, 1788, p. 103.

[44]*Statutes of Columbia College*.

[45]"Resolved, Mr. Mason, Mr. Hamilton, Mr. Cosine, Mr. Harison, Dr. Moore & Mr. Dunscomb be a Committee to examine into the general State of the College [and] Report to this Board." "Minutes of the Trustees," April 24, 1797, p. 242. "Resolved, that Dr. Bard, Dr. Livingston, and Mr. Cosine be a Committee to confer with the newly elected Professors on the general management of their duties." "Minutes of the Trustees," May 8, 1795, p. 223.

[46]*Statutes of Columbia College*; "Minutes of the Trustees," November 26, December 3, 4, 1787, pp. 81–82, 88, 89; "Description of Columbia College," pp. 255–56. Johnson was awarded the additional salary of £50 per annum.

[47]Broderick, "Pulpit, Physics, and Politics," pp. 42–68; Morgan, *Gentle Puritan*, pp. 3, 85. In the 1780s, the Yale faculty consisted of President Stiles and four tutors. The Chair of Mathematics and Natural Philosophy and the Chair of Divinity, long occupied by Nehemiah Strong and Naphtali Daggett, respectively, lay vacant.

[48]An examination of the Minutes of the Regents between 1784 and 1787 and the Minutes of the Trustees from 1787 to 1795 shows that the regents who most actively participated in the rebuilding of the college before 1787 became the most energetic and influential trustees in the later period. For an analysis of the nineteen most active regents, see note 21, above. Thirteen Columbia trustees attended at least one-half of the meetings at which a quorum gathered between 1787 and 1795. Nine of these thirteen trustees had distinguished themselves as "most active" regents before the school was rechartered. It is reasonable to conclude that the same educational vision that had inspired the regents' plan of 1784 underlay the policies of the new governing board.

[49]For example, David Ramsay, *An Oration on the Advantages of American Independence, Spoken Before a Public Assembly of the Inhabitants of Charlestown, in South Carolina, on the Second Anniversary of that Glorious Era* (Charlestown, 1778).

[50]Minutes of the Regents, December 14, 1784, Pratt, ed., "Annals," pp. 226–27.

[51]The regents' first faculty appointment went to John Peter Tetard, professor of French, but it appears that Tetard taught only briefly. Minutes of the Regents, May 5, 1784, Pratt, ed., "Annals," p. 210; William Cochran to the Trustees of Columbia College, August 25, 1788, College Papers. The regents elected Johann Christoff Kunze as professor or Oriental languages, and John Daniel Gros as professor of German languages, but Gros and Kunze, unlike Tetard, were awarded no salary for language instruction. It was a common practice at early American colleges for teachers to provide private instruction in return for a fee from each student. Kunze and Gros may have held private classes, in keeping with this practice, but German and Hebrew were not part of the regular curriculum between 1784 and 1787. Minutes of the Regents, December 30, 1784, Pratt, ed., "Annals," p. 229.

[52]*Columbia University in the City of New York, Gifts and Endowments with the Names of the Benefactors, 1754–1898* (New York, 1898), p. 9; Petition from the Trustees of Columbia College to the Senate and State Assembly of New York, February 2, 1792, College Papers.

[53]"Minutes of the Trustees," June 25, 1792, May 6, 1794, May 8, 1795, pp. 174–78, 210, 212, 223; Report of the Regents to the Senate and State Assembly of New York, February 25, 1795, College Papers; Trustees of Columbia College to the Regents of the

University of the State of New York, March 8, 1796, College Papers; *Present State of Learning in Columbia College, Prepared by President Wm. Samuel Johnson, Mr. Brockholst Livingston, and Rev. Dr. John H. Livingston* (New York, 1794), pp. 3–9. Regarding the teaching of French, see also note 51, above.

⁵⁴Knox, *Liberal Education*, rpt. in Rudolph, ed., *Essays on Education*, p. 353; Smith, *Remarks on Education*, rpt. in *ibid.*, pp. 212–13. On Jefferson's plan to include modern languages in the curriculum of the College of William and Mary, see Butts, *The College Charts Its Course* pp. 88–89.

⁵⁵Butts, *College Charts Its Course*, p. 62; Humphrey, *King's College*, p. 181; Morgan, *Gentle Puritan*, pp. 338–39; Morison, *Harvard*, pp. 81–82. In colonial days, Harvard and King's students had studied French with private instructors, to whom the boys paid a fee directly. Harvard had excluded French from the regular curriculum for fear of offending public sensibilities.

⁵⁶Hindle, *Pursuit of Science*, pp. 81, 308.

⁵⁷*Ibid.*, pp. 86, 315. For a full-length biography of Mitchill, see Hall, *A Scientist in the Early Republic: Samuel Latham Mitchill, 1764–1831* (New York: Columbia University Press, 1934).

⁵⁸Not until Timothy Dwight became president in 1796 and named Benjamin Silliman to the chair of mathematics and natural philosophy, did Yale rival Columbia in science. Morgan, *Gentle Puritan*, p. 427; Schmidt, *Liberal Arts College*, pp. 51–52. The Scottish-educated president of the College of New Jersey, John Witherspoon, gave science an important place at that school during the Revolutionary era. Broderick, "Pulpit, Physicks, and Politics," p. 45.

⁵⁹Smith, *Remarks on Education*, rpt. in Rudolph, ed., *Essays on Education*, pp. 212–13; Rush, *A Plan for the Establishment of Public Schools*, rpt. in Rudolph, ed., *Essays on Education*, pp. 18–19.

⁶⁰Samuel Knox's prize-winning proposal and Thomas Jefferson's plan for the College of William and Mary included Latin and Greek studies. Knox, *Liberal Education*, rpt in Rudolph, ed., *Essays on Education*, pp. 282, 301, 312–15, 317, 352; Butts, *College Charts Its Course*, pp. 88–89.

⁶¹Broderick, "Pulpit, Physicks, and Politics," p. 61; Morgan, *Gentle Puritan*, pp. 385–90. In 1810, John Mason, provost of Columbia, declared, "Experience has shown that with the study or neglect of the Greek and Latin languages, sound learning flourishes or declines." Quoted in Schmidt, *Liberal Arts College*, p. 53.

⁶²Quoted in Beardsley, *William Samuel Johnson*, pp. 141–44.

⁶³Samuel Johnson, "Advertisements of the Beginning of Tuition in the College," *New-York Gazette, or Weekly Post Boy*, June 3, 1754, rpt. in *Samuel Johnson*, 4:223–24.

⁶⁴Samuel Johnson to Cadwallader Colden, June 7, 1747, *Samuel Johnson*, 2:299; Samuel Johnson to Benjamin Franklin, November, n.d., 1750, *Franklin*, 4:74–75; Humphrey, *King's College*, pp. 174–75.

⁶⁵Samuel Johnson, *Elementa Philosophica*, rpt. in *Samuel Johnson*, 2:422–26; Samuel Johnson, "Raphael or The Genius of American Rhapsody," *ibid.*, 2:561–2, 564–70.

⁶⁶Samuel Johnson, "Raphael," *ibid.*, 2:569.

⁶⁷Benjamin Franklin to Samuel Johnson, August 9, October 25, 1750, December 24, 1751, *Papers of Franklin*, 4:37–40, 71, 223, 261; Samuel Johnson to Benjamin Franklin, November, n.d., 1750, *ibid.*, 4:74–75.

⁶⁸This description is based on two documents: "Laws and Order of the College of New York, Adopted June 3, 1755," *Samuel Johnson*, 4:228; Samuel Johnson to East Apthorp, December 1, 1759, *ibid.*, pp. 55–56. Johnson taught all classes for the first year and one half, and welcomed the temporary assistance of his younger son, William John-

son, in 1755. Cutting joined the faculty in 1755 and remained until 1763, when he left King's to become an SPG missionary. Treadwell did not arrive at the college until late in 1757, and he died early in 1760. Robert Harpur, a graduate of the University of Glasgow, assumed Treadwell's chair, but not until September 1761, which left the professorship of mathematics and natural history vacant for about eighteen months. The threat of smallpox drove Johnson from the city for most of 1757, and again from October 1759 until May 1760. Thus, the faculty rarely numbered three. In 1757, Cutting taught all classes at the college for most of the year. "The Matricula or Register of Admissions and Graduations in King's College at New York," *Samuel Johnson*, 4:244–49; Humphrey, *King's College*, pp. 106–8, 118–19, 162.

⁶⁹For a description of the curriculum at the College of New Jersey, see Wertenbaker, *Princeton*, pp. 92–94; Broderick, "Pulpit, Physicks, and Politics," p. 50.

⁷⁰Initially, the distinction between the tutorial and professorial systems was more important in theory than in practice, because the faculties at the colonial colleges were so small. Although Harvard did not abandon the tutorial system completely until 1767, the college established special professorships in divinity (1721), mathematics and natural philosophy (1727), and Hebrew (1764, an elective course). Thus, the faculty at Harvard equalled in number the faculty at King's. Yale established a chair of divinity in 1753 and a chair of mathematics and natural philosophy in 1770. In 1764, the faculty of the College of New Jersey numbered only three tutors and the president. Morison, *Three Centuries of Harvard*, p. 90; Cremin, *American Education*, p. 512; Wertenbaker, *Princeton*, p. 93.

⁷¹Samuel Johnson, "Raphael," *Samuel Johnson*, 2:567; Samuel Johnson, "The Foundations of our Faith in Christ, A sermon preached Easter afternoon, at Stratford, April 18, 1731 . . ." *ibid.*, 3:390–91.

⁷²Humphrey, *King's College*, p. 106. Treadwell died prematurely in 1760. Johnson was pleased with Treadwell's successor, Robert Harpur, who shared Treadwell's Scottish training and enthusiasm for progressive education. Samuel Johnson to William Samuel Johnson, October 12, 1761, *Samuel Johnson*, 1:314.

⁷³Hindle, *Pursuit of Science*, p. 89; Cremin, *American Education*, p. 407.

⁷⁴Rush, *A Plan for the Establishment of Public Schools*, rpt. in Rudolph, *Essays on Education*, p. 12.

⁷⁵Knox, *Liberal Education*, rpt. in *ibid.*, pp. 279, 315, 365; Cremin, *American Education*, pp. 433, 442.

⁷⁶"An Act to Institute an University within this State, and for other Purposes therein Mentioned," Pratt, ed., "Annals," pp. 265–66.

⁷⁷*Statutes of Columbia College*, p. 7.

⁷⁸"Minutes of the Trustees," May 5, 1791, pp. 145–46.

⁷⁹"Minutes of the Trustees," October 11, 1790, May 5, 1791, pp. 139, 145–46; Report of a Committee on the Plan of Education, April 24, 1791, College Papers.

⁸⁰Morgan, *Gentle Puritan*, pp. 374, 392.

⁸¹Wertenbaker, *Princeton*, p. 120.

⁸²Morgan, *Gentle Puritan*, pp. 342–59; Gabriel, *Religion and Learning at Yale*, p. 44.

⁸³Samuel Johnson, "Adverstisements of the Beginning of Tuition in the College," *Samuel Johnson*, 4:223.

⁸⁴Benjamin Franklin, "Idea of the English School," in *A Sermon on Education. Wherein Some Account is given of the Academy, Established in the City of Philadelphia . . . by Richard Peters* (Philadelphia, 1751), rpt. in *Papers of Franklin*, 4:106.

⁸⁵*Statutes of Columbia College*, p. 7.

⁸⁶William Samuel Johnson to Samuel William Johnson, April 20, 1789, WSJ Papers.

⁸⁷Steiner, *Samuel Seabury*, pp. 330–31. The school opened in June 1796. It never won

recognition as an institution of higher learning, in part because the Connecticut legislature repeatedly rejected the school's applications for a college charter. *Ibid.*, p. 332.

[88]Quoted in Beardsley, *William Samuel Johnson*, pp. 142–43.

[89]Samuel Johnson, "A Paper which I Desire May be Read to the Governors of King's College at their Next Meeting after my Decease or Dismission," n.d., [September 1759], *Samuel Johnson*, 4:116.

[90]"Minutes of the Trustees," June 25, 1792, pp. 174–78; *Present State of Learning in Columbia College*, p. 10; Trustees of Columbia College to the Regents of the University of the State of New York, March 8, 1796, College Papers.

[91]For earlier developments at the College of William and Mary and the College of Philadelphia, see Warren, *American Bar*, pp. 343, 346; Goebel, *School of Law of Columbia*, p. 10.

[92]James Kent, *Introductory Lecture*.

[93]Goebel, *School of Law of Columbia*, pp. 4, 7.

[94]*Ibid.*, pp. 11–13; Horton, *James Kent*, p. 86.

[95]William Samuel Johnson to Charles Johnson, January 28, February 18, 1787, WSJ Papers; Samuel William Johnson to William Samuel Johnson, July 14, 1793, *ibid.*

[96]William Samuel Johnson to Samuel William Johnson, April 12, 1787, WSJ Papers.

[97]Quoted in Beardsley, *William Samuel Johnson*, p. 144.

[98]Kent, *Introductory Lecture*.

[99]Quoted in Warren, *American Bar*, p. 295.

[100]James Kent to the Trustees of Columbia College, May 2, 1797, College Papers; "Minutes of the Trustees," April 26, 1798, p. 256; Goebel, *School of Law of Columbia*, pp. 16–17.

[101]Horton, *James Kent*, p. 95; Warren, *American Bar*, p. 363; Goebel, *School of Law of Columbia*, p. 17. Professor James Wilson at the College of Philadelphia encountered the same difficulty and resigned in 1792, after teaching only two years. Warren, *American Bar*, p. 348. The success of Tapping Reeve's private law school at Litchfield, Connecticut pointed to the weakness of Kent's and Wilson's courses. Although Reeve's course contained a measure of legal theory and philosophy, "the students are taught the practice by being actually employed in it. A court is constituted, actions are brought and conducted through a regular process, questions are raised, and the students become advocates in form." Goebel, *School of Law of Columbia*, p. 6; Warren, *American Bar*, pp. 357–59.

[102]Minutes of the Regents, December 14, 1784, Pratt, ed., "Annals," p. 226.

[103]"Minutes of the Trustees," April 25, 1791, p. 142.

[104]Apparently Bard persuaded the trustees to institute a medical school after learning that another physician on the Columbia board, Dr. Nicholas Romayne, was working to establish his own medical college in the city. Romayne had delivered private lectures to medical students since 1787, but his school, lacking a charter from the state, had wanted authority to award degrees. In 1790 the regents still hoped to see a medical school established in the state, and Romayne petitioned them to recognize his school officially, a measure that would have endangered Columbia's educational leadership in the city. Dr. Nicholas Romayne to the Regents of the University of the State of New York, January 11, 1790, College Papers; Pomerantz, *New York*, p. 398; Toner, *Contributions to the Annals of Medical Progress*, p. 108. Bard had played a prominent role in Columbia's earlier attempt to establish a medical school in the 1780s, and he undoubtedly viewed Romayne's rival scheme with such alarm that he prevailed upon his fellow trustees to launch a medical program immediately, appoint a committee for that purpose, and appeal to Romayne to join the Columbia effort. Minutes of the Regents, December 28, 1784, Pratt, ed., "Annals," p. 226. By late spring, 1791, the trustees had persuaded Romayne to initiate a medical course at the college with the assistance of Bard. Groce, *William Samuel Johnson*, pp. 183–84; Pomerantz, *New York*, p. 398.

105 Address of the Medical Society of the State of New York to the Trustees of Columbia College, January 11, 1792, College Papers; Report of the Committee appointed by the Trustees to Confer with the Medical Society, January 23, 1792, *ibid.* The Society's offer upset the political arrangement between Romayne and the trustees. Romayne was not a member of the Society, and the Society apparently refused to entrust the city's medical instruction to an outsider. Pomerantz, New York, p. 404; Coon, *Columbia: Colossus on the Hudson,* p. 57. When the trustees accepted the Society's offer, Romayne angrily resigned from the faculty. Yet the slighted Dr. Romayne would pose serious problems in the coming years and contribute to its failure. Report of the Committees Appointed by the Trustees to Confer with the Medical Society, January 23, 1792, College Papers; Nicholas Romayne to the Trustees, February 1, 1792, *ibid.;* Pomerantz, *New York,* p. 398.

106 "Minutes of the Trustees," February 13, 27, 1792, pp. 157–58; *Present State of Learning in Columbia College,* pp. 11–16; Groce, *William Samuel Johnson,* p. 184.

107 Cremin, *American Education,* pp. 406–7; Shryock, *Medicine and Society in America, 1660–1860,* p. 22.

108 Shryock, *Medicine and Society,* p. 33.

109 Hindle, *Pursuit of Science,* pp. 281, 299.

110 Dr. Benjamin Waterhouse to Benjamin Franklin, December 10, 1780, quoted in Hindle, *Pursuit of Science,* p. 289.

111 The number of medical students dropped from fifty-nine in 1791, to twenty-nine in 1797, Groce, *William Samuel Johnson,* p. 187.

112 Shryock, *Medicine and Society,* p. 138. In addition, Romayne aroused a tempest of controversy before leaving Columbia in 1792, and on his departure he took two-thirds of the medical students with him. Nicholas Romayne to the Trustees of Columbia College, February 1, 1792, College Papers; Nicholas Romayne to William Samuel Johnson, February 28, 1792, *ibid.;* Application of the Students to have their names dropped from the College register, n.d., *ibid.;* Report of the Committee Appointed by the Trustees to consider the petition of the medical students, March 5, 1792, *ibid.;* John B. Hicks to the Trustees of Columbia College, April 24, 1793, *ibid.*

113 Address of the Faculty of Medicine to the Trustees of Columbia College, October 19, 1797, January n.d., 1801, College Papers; "Minutes of the Trustees," November 2, 1797, January 1, 1801, pp. 249, 272.

114 Samuel Latham Mitchill to the Trustees of Columbia College, February 29, 1798, College Papers.

115 Abbott, *Government Policy and Higher Education,* pp. 17–18; Pomerantz, *New York,* pp. 422–27.

116 Hindle, *Pursuit of Science,* p. 256; Frost, *Connecticut Education,* p. 17.

117 Report of the Committee on the State of the College, February 15, 1799, College Papers; "Minutes of the Trustees," Feburary 22, March 19, 1799, pp. 255–58.

118 Groce, *William Samuel Johnson,* pp. 186–88.

119 "Minutes of the Trustees," February 22, 1799, p. 255.

120 William Samuel Johnson to the Trustees of Columbia College, July 2, 1800, Samuel Johnson Papers; "Minutes of the Trustees," July 16, 1800, p. 264; Groce, *William Samuel Johnson,* pp. 187–88; Beardsley, *William Samuel Johnson,* pp. 162–64.

121 Humphrey, *King's College,* p. 284; Morgan, *Gentle Puritan,* p. 359; Wertenbaker, *Princeton,* p. 125.

122 Address of Twenty Students to the Trustees of Columbia College, August 19, 1788, College Papers; Coons, *Columbia: Colossus on the Hudson,* p. 56; Humphrey, *King's College,* pp. 202, 206.

123 Edward Rutledge to William Samuel Johnson, May 21, 1788, quoted in Beardsley, *William Samuel Johnson,* p. 153; Ralph Izard to William Samuel Johnson, December 20, 1787, Samuel Johnson Papers.

[124]Morgan, *Gentle Puritan*, p. 426; Morrison, *Harvard*, pp. 175, 184-85; Wertenbaker, *Princeton*, pp. 104, 127, 134-38.

[125]Abraham Beach, on behalf of the Trustees of Columbia College, to William Samuel Johnson, July 21, 1800, quoted in Beardsley, *William Samuel Johnson*, p. 163.

Chapter 16: The Final Years

[1]William Samuel Johnson, Memoirs, WSJ Papers; Samuel William Johnson to William Samuel Johnson, June 1, 1794, *ibid.*; Groce, *William Samuel Johnson*, p. 191.

[2]Samuel William Johnson to William Samuel Johnson June 25, 1787, WSJ Papers; Beardsley, *William Samuel Johnson*, p. 179; Groce, *William Samuel Johnson*, p. 190.

[3]Bemis, *Jay's Treaty*, pp. 253, 259, 264-72; Ernst, *Rufus King*, p. 198; Flanders, ed., *Chief Justices of the Supreme Court*, 2:170; Combs, *The Jay Treaty*, pp. 120-22, 125-27.

[4]Beardsley, *William Samuel Johnson*, p. 140.

[5]Jeremy Belknap to Willliam Samuel Johnson November 7, 1795, WSJ Papers; William Samuel Johnson to Jonathan Trumbull, Jr., December 15, 1795, *ibid.*; Jonathan Trumbull, Jr., to William Samuel Johnson, December 22, 1795, February 2, 1796, *ibid.*

[6]Hofstadter, *Idea of a Party System*, p. 142.

[7]Four emigrated to Nova Scotia in 1786, where they could once again receive the financial support of the SPG. Steiner, *Samuel Seabury*, pp. 184, 321; Kinlock "Anglican Clergy," p. 242; Stiles, *Literary Diary*, 3:235; Beardsley, *History of Episcopal Church*, p. 346.

[8]Steiner, *Samuel Seabury*, pp. 184-85, 189-90.

[9]*Ibid.*, pp. 193-94.

[10]*Ibid.*, pp. 202-6; Beardsley, *William Samuel Johnson*, p. 187; The Clergy of Connecticut to Samuel Seabury, n.d. [February 5, 1784], Hawks and Perry, eds., *Documentary History of the Protestant Episcopal Church*, 2:224-27. The act "for securing the Rights of Conscience in Matters of Religion to Christians of every Denomination in this State" allowed dissenting sects to organize, but required all dissenters to apply for a certificate exempting them from supporting the established church. The law did not free men from the obligation of worshipping regularly or remove local education from the control of the Congregational parishes.

[11]Steiner, *Samuel Seabury*, pp. 208-16.

[12]*Ibid.*, pp. 208, 264.

[13]*Ibid.*, pp. 185-88, 225-40; Addison, *Episcopal Church*, pp. 59-60, 62.

[14]Steiner, *Samuel Seabury*, pp. 249-60; Alexander, *James Duane*, pp. 176-77; Berrian, *Historical Sketch of Trinity Church*, p. 162; Abraham Jarvis to the Secretary, SPG, August 4, 1784, Stowe, ed., "Additional Letters of Reverend Abraham Beach: 1772-1791," p. 135; Addison, *Episcopal Church*, p. 52.

[15]Jeremiah Leaming to William Samuel Johnson, August 13, 1788, excerpted in Beardsley, *William Samuel Johnson*, pp. 132-33.

[16]Samuel Parker to Samuel Peters, September 29, 1787, quoted in Steiner, *Samuel Seabury*, pp. 270-71.

[17]Steiner, *Samuel Seabury*, pp. 279-87, 293, 305-6; Beardsley, *History of Episcopal Church*, pp. 406-8; Addison, *Episcopal Church*, pp. 66-69; Tench Coxe to William Samuel Johnson, June 20, August 15, 1789, WSJ Papers.

[18]William Samuel Johnson to Tench Coxe, August, n.d., 1789, WSJ Papers; WSJ to an unknown correspondent, January 8, 1790, *ibid.*

[19]John Tyler to the Secretary of the SPG, December 1, 1784, Vassar, ed., "Aftermath of Revolution," p. 458.

[20]See note 10 above. Also, Bailyn, ed., *Pamphlets*, pp. 161–62.

[21]William Samuel Johnson to an unknown correspondent, January 8, 1790, WSJ Papers.

[22]Addison, *Episcopal Church*, p. 84; Steiner, *Samuel Seabury*, pp. 326–27, 332.

[23]Groce, *William Samuel Johnson*, p. 193; Beardsley, *William Samuel Johnson*, pp. 164, 166.

[24]Committee of the Connecticut Bar to William Samuel Johnson, January 9, 1812, WSJ Papers.

[25]Rossiter, *Grand Convention*, p. 317.

[26]This too brief summary is based on Bradford Perkins, *Prologue to War*.

[27]Hofstadter, *Party System*, p. 182; Smelser *Democratic Republic*, pp. 288, 291, 296, 298; Banner, *To the Hartford Convention*, ch. 9.

[28]The developing Republican organization in Connecticut built its appeal on the issue of religious toleration. For a complete discussion of the Republican struggle, which culminated in the 1818 state constitution, see Stamps, "Political Parties in Connecticut."

[29]Ingersoll in 1781, Trumbull in 1785, Sherman in 1795, and Dyer and Ellsworth in 1807.

[30]Beardsley, *William Samuel Johnson*, p. 180.

[31]Groce, *William Samuel Johnson*, p. 193. The only extensive obituary published in the Connecticut press appeared in the *Connecticut Courant*, November 23, 1819. It tells us little about the public's view of Johnson, because, as Groce observed, it seems to have been written by Johnson's grandson, Gulian Verplanck of New York City. The *Connecticut Gazette* (New London), November 24, 1789, merely noted that William Samuel Johnson had died.

[32]Beardsley, *William Samuel Johnson*, p. 188.

Bibliography

Unpublished Primary Sources

Bancroft Transcripts. Manuscripts and Archives Division, The New York Public Library, Astor, Lenox, and Tilden Foundations (cited as Bancroft Transcripts).

College Papers. Manuscript Division, Columbia University Library, New York (cited as College Papers).

"Minutes of the Trustees of Columbia College, Vol. 2, Part 2, May 4, 1784 to February 2, 1809." Manuscript typescript, Columbiana, Columbia University, New York (cited as "Minutes of the Trustees").

"Minutes of the Trustees of the University of Pennsylvania, III: University of the State of Pennsylvania, 1779-1788." Manuscript microfilm, University of Pennsylvania Archives, Philadelphia (cited as "Minutes of the Trustees of the University of Pennsylvania").

Samuel Johnson Papers. Manuscript Division, Columbia University Library, New York (cited as Samuel Johnson Papers).

William Samuel Johnson Papers. Connecticut Historical Society, Hartford (cited as WSJ Papers).

Published Primary Sources

Backus, Isaac. *A Seasonable Plea for Liberty of Conscience against Some Late Oppressive Proceedings.* Boston, 1770.

Baldwin, Ebenezer. *An Appendix, Stating the Heavy Grievance the Colonies Labour under from Several Late Acts of the British Parliament, and Shewing What We Have Just Reason to Fear the Consequences of These Measures Will Be.* New Haven, 1774.

Beach, Abraham. "Additional Letters of the Reverend Abraham Beach: 1772-1791." Ed. Walter Herbert Stowe. *Historical Magazine of the Protestant Episcopal Church,* 5 (June 1936): 122-41.

Beach, John. *A Calm and Dispassionate Vindication of the Professors of the Church of England against the Abusive Misrepresentation and Fallacious Arguments of Mr. Noah Hobart . . . with a Preface by Dr. Johnson. . . .* Boston, 1749.

Beach, John. *A Continuation of the Calm and Dispassionate Vindication of the Church of England. . . .* Boston, 1751.

Beach, John. *A Friendly Expostulation, with All Persons Concer'd in Publishing a Late Pamphlet, Entitled the Real Advantages which Ministers and People May Enjoy Especially in the Colonies by Conforming to the Church of England.* New York, 1763.

"Bowdoin-Temple Papers." *Collections of the Massachusetts Historical Society*, 6th ser., 9(1897).

Boyd, Julian Parks, ed., *The Susquehannah Company Papers*. Vols. 1-4. Ithaca, N.Y.: Cornell University Press, 1962. Reprint of 1930 edition.

Burnett, Edmund Coty, ed. *Letters of the Members of the Continental Congress*. 8 vols. Washington, D.C.: U.S. Government Printing Office, 1921-36.

Brymner, Douglas, ed. "Note E." In *Report on Canadian Archives, 1890*. Ottawa, 1891, pp. 97-175.

Canadian Archives. *Report on Canadian Archives, 1890*. Ed. Douglas Brymner. Ottawa, 1891, pp. 97-175.

Caner, Henry. *A Candid Examination of Dr. Mayhew's Observations . . . With an Appendix containing a Vindication by one of its Members—Samuel Johnson*. Boston, 1763.

Chandler, Thomas Bradbury. *An Appeal to the Public on Behalf of the Church of England in America*. New York, 1767.

——. *The Appeal Defended. . . .* New York, 1769.

——. *The Appeal Further Defended; in Answer to the Further Misrepresentations of Dr. Chauncy*. New York, 1771.

——. *A Friendly Address to All Reasonable Ammericans. . . .*

Chauncy, Charles. *A Letter to a Friend, Containing Remarks . . . on a Sermon Preached by . . . Bishop of Llandaff. . . .* Boston, 1767.

——. *An Appeal to the Public Answered. . . .* Boston, 1768.

——. *A Reply to Dr. Chandler's "Appeal Defended." . . .* Boston, 1770.

Connecticut Courant. Hartford, 1764-1765, 1773-1774, 1819. (Entitled Connecticut Courant & *Weekly Intelligencer* after June 7, 1774.)

Connecticut Gazette. New London, 1819. (Established in 1763 as the New London Gazette, and entitled *Connecticut Gazette* from May 11, 1787.)

Connecticut Gazette. New Haven, 1765-1766. (Established in 1755, suspended April 14, 1764 to July 5, 1765, and terminated in 1768.)

Connecticut. *The Public Records of the Colony of Connecticut, 1636-1776*. 15 vols. Eds. J. H. Trumbull (vols. 1-3), C. J. Hoadly (vols. 4-15). Hartford: State of Connecticut, 1850-1890.

Connecticut. *The Public Records of the State of Connecticut, 1776-1803*. 11 vols. Eds. C. J. Hoadly, Leonard Labaree, K. Fennelley, Albert Van Deusen, and Christopher Collier. Hartford: State of Connecticut, 1894-1967.

Continental Congress. *Journals of the Continental Congress*. 34 vols. Ed. Worthington Chauncy Ford. Washington, D.C.: U.S. Government Printing Office, 1904-1936 (cited as *Journals of Congress*).

Continental Congress. *Letters of the Members of the Continental Congress*. 8 vols. Ed. Edmund Coty Burnett. Washington, D.C.: U.S. Government Printing Office, 1921-1936 (cited as *Letters of Congress*).

Deane, Silas. "Correspondence of Silas Deane, Delegate to the Congress at Philadelphia, 1774-1776." *Collections of the Connecticut Historical Society*, 2(1870).

DeBerdt, Dennys. "Letters of Dennys De Berdt." Ed. Albert Mathews. *Transactions of the Colonial Society of Massachusetts*, 13(1910-1911).

"Description of Columbia College in the City of New York." *The New York Magazine or Literary Repository*, 1, no. 5 (May 1790): 255-56 (available at Columbiana, Columbia University, New York).

Dickinson, John. *Letters from a Farmer in Pennsylvania to the Inhabitants of the British Colonies.* Philadelphia, 1768. Ed. R. T. H. Halsey. New York: Outlook, 1903.

——. "The Writings of John Dickinson, Vol. I, Political Writings, 1764–1774." Ed. Paul Leicester Ford. *Memoirs of the Historical Society of Pennsylvania,* 14(1899).

Dulany, Daniel. *Considerations on the Propriety of Imposing Taxes in the British Colonies for the Purpose of Raising a Revenue by Act of Parliament.* Annapolis, 1765.

Fitch, Thomas. *Explanation of Say-brook Platform . . . By One that heartily desires the Order, Peace and Purity of those Churches.* Hartford, 1765.

——. *Reasons Why the British Colonies in America, Should Not Be Charged with Internal Taxes . . . in Behalf of the Colony of Connecticut.* New Haven, 1764.

——. *Some Reasons that Influenced the Governor to take, and the Councillors to administer, the Oath, Required by the Act of Parliament, commonly called the Stamp Act. Humbly submitted to the Consideration of the Publick.* Hartford. 1766.

——. "The Fitch Papers: Correspondence and Documents during Thomas Fitch's Governorship of the Colony of Connecticut, 1754–1766." Ed. A. C. Bates. *Collections of the Connecticut Historical Society,* 18(1918).

Franklin, Benjamin. *The Papers of Benjamin Franklin.* 20 vols. Eds. Leonard Labaree and William B. Willcox. New Haven: Yale University Press, 1959–1976.

Gale, Benjamin. *The Present State of the Colony Considered. In a Letter From a Gentlemen in the Eastern Part of Said Colony, to his Friend in the Western Part of the Same.* n.p., 1766.

Garth, Charles. "Correspondence of Charles Garth." Ed. Joseph W. Barnwell. *The South Carolina Historical and Genealogical Magazine,* 26–30(1925–1932).

Hamilton, Alexander. *The Papers of Alexander Hamilton.* Vol. 25. Ed. Harold C. Syrett. New York: Columbia University Press, 1977.

Hawks, F. L. and W. S. Perry, eds. *Documentary History of the Protestant Episcopal Church in the United States of America, Containing Numerous Hitherto Unpublished Documents Concerning the Church in Connecticut.* 2 vols. New York, 1863.

Hobart, Noah. *A Second Address to the Members of the Episcopal Separation in New England. . . .* Boston, 1751.

——. *A Serious Address to the Members of the Episcopal Separation in New England, Occasioned by Mr. Wetmore's Vindication of the Church of England in Connecticut.* Boston, 1748.

Howard, Martin. *A Letter from a Gentleman at Halifax, to His Friend in Rhode-Island. Containing Remarks upon a Pamphlet, Entitled, The Rights of the Colonies Examined.* Newport, 1765.

Hulbert, Archer Butler, ed. *The Records of the Original Proceedings of the Ohio Company.* Marietta, Ohio, 1917.

Huntington, Joshua and Jedidiah. "Huntington Papers: Correspondence of the Brothers Joshua and Jedidiah Huntington during the Period of the American Revolution." *Collections of the Connecticut Historical Society,* 20(1923).

Ingersoll, Jared. "A Selection from the Correspondence and Miscellaneous Papers of Jared Ingersoll." Ed. Franklin Bowditch Dexter. *Papers of the New Haven Colony Historical Society.* 9(1918).

Johnson, Samuel. *Samuel Johnson, President of King's College, His Career and Writings.* 4 vols. Eds. Herbert and Carol Schneider. New York: Columbia University Press, 1929.

Johnson, William Samuel, et al. *Present State of Learning in Columbia College, Prepared by President Wm. Samuel Johnson, Mr. Brockholst Livingston, and Rev. Dr. John H. Livingston.* New York, 1794.

Kent, James. *An Introductory Lecture to a Course of Law Lectures. Delivered November 17, 1794. By James Kent Esquire, Professor of Law in Columbia College. Published at the request of the Trustees.* New York, 1794.

King, Rufus. *The Life and Correspondence of Rufus King.* 6 vols. Ed. Charles R. King. New York: Putnam, 1894-1900.

Klein, Milton M., ed. *The Independent Reflector.* . . . See following citation.

Livingston, William, et al. *The Independent Reflector/or Weekly Essays on Sundry Important Subjects More Particularly Adapted to the Province of New York by William Livingston and Others.* Ed. Milton M. Klein. Cambridge, Mass.: Harvard University Press, 1963.

Lee, Arthur. *Life of Arthur Lee, LL.D.* Ed. Richard Henry Lee. Boston: 1829.

Mayhew, Jonathan. *A Discourse Concerning Unlimited Submission and Non-Resistance to the Higher Powers.* . . Boston, 1760.

———. *Observations on the Charter and Conduct of the Society for the Propagation of the Gospel.* London, Boston, 1763.

———. *Remarks on an Anonymous Tract.* . . . Boston, 1764.

New London Gazette. New London, Ct., 1765-1766.

Otis, James, Jr. *The Rights of the British Colonies Asserted and Proved.* Boston, 1764.

Paine, Thomas. *The Writings of Thomas Paine.* Ed. Moncure Daniel Conway. New York, 1894.

Pitkin, William. "The Pitkin Papers. Correspondence and Documents during William Pitkin's Governorship of the Colony of Connecticut, 1766-1769." *Collections of the Connecticut Historical Society,* 19(1921).

Pratt, Daniel J., ed. "Annals of Public Education in the State of New York." *Proceedings of the Twelfth Anniversary of the University Convocation of the State of New York, Held July 6, 7, 8, 1875.* Albany, 1875.

Ramsay, David. *An Oration on the Advantages of American Independence, Spoken before a Public Assembly of the Inhabitants of Charlestown, in South Carolina, on the Second Anniversary of that Glorious Era.* Charlestown, 1778.

Records of the Federal Convention of 1787. 2nd ed. 4 vols. Ed. Max Farrand. New Haven: Yale University Press, 1966. Reprint of 1937 edition.

Rudolph, Frederick, ed. *Essays on Education in the Early Republic.* Cambridge, Mass.: Harvard University Press, 1965.

The Statutes of Columbia College in New-York. New York, 1788 (available at Columbiana, Columbia University, New York).

Stiles, Ezra. *Extracts from the Itineraries and other Miscellanies of Ezra Stiles, D.D., LL.D., 1755-1794 with a Selection from his Correspondence.* Ed. Franklin Bowditch Dexter. New Haven: Yale University Press, 1916.

———. *The Literary Diary of Ezra Stiles, D.D., LL.D., President of Yale College.* 3 vols. Ed. Franklin Bowditch Dexter. New York: Scribner's, 1901.

Susquehannah Company. *The Susquehannah Company Papers.* 11 vols. Eds. Julian Parks Boyd (vols. 1-4) and Robert J. Taylor. Ithaca, New York: Cornell University Press, 1962-1971. Vols. 1-4 reprint of 1930 edition.

Taylor, Robert J. ed. *The Susquehannah Company Papers.* See above citation.

Trumbull, Jonathan. "Trumbull Papers: Letters of William Samuel Johnson to the Governors of Connecticut." Ed. David Trumbull. *Collections of the Massachusetts Historical Society,* 5th ser., 9(1885).

Vassar, Rena, ed. "The Aftermath of Revolution: Letters of the Anglican Clergy in Connecticut, 1781-1785." *Historical Magazine of the Protestant Episcopal Church,* 41(December 1972): 429-61.

Vaughan, Alden T. *Chronicles of the American Revolution.* New York: Grosset & Dunlap, 1965.

Welles, Noah. *The Real Advantages Which Ministers and People May Enjoy Especially in the Colonies by Conformity to the Church of England; Faithfully Considered and Impartially Represented in a Letter to a Young Gentleman.* New York, 1762.

Wetmore, James. *A Vindication of the Professors of the Church of England in Connecticut, against the Invectives contained in a Sermon Preached at Stanford by Mr. Noah Hobart, December 13, 1746.* Boston, 1748.

Secondary Sources

Abbott, Frank C. *Government Policy and Higher Education: A Study of the Regents of the University of the State of New York, 1784-1949.* Ithaca, N.Y.: Cornell University Press, 1958.

Addison, James Thayer. *The Episcopal Church in the United States, 1789-1931.* New York: Scribner, 1951.

Alexander, Edward P. *A Revolutionary Conservative: James Duane of New York.* New York: Columbia University Press, 1938.

Appleton, Marguerite. "The Agents of the New England Colonies in the Revolutionary Period." *New England Quarterly,* 6(June 1933):371-387.

Bailey, Edith A. "Influences toward Radicalism in Connecticut, 1754-1775." *Smith College Studies in History,* 5(July 1920):179-252.

Bailyn, Bernard. *The Ideological Origins of the American Revolution.* Cambridge, Mass.: Harvard University Press, 1967; rpt. 1977.

_____. *The Ordeal of Thomas Hutchinson.* Cambridge, Mass.: Harvard University Press, 1974.

_____, ed. *Pamphlets of the American Revolution, 1750-1776.* Cambridge, Mass.: Harvard University Press, 1965. 1 vol. to date (through 1766).

Banner, James M. *To the Hartford Convention: The Federalists and the Origins of Party Politics in Massachusetts, 1789-1815.* New York: Knopf, 1970.

Barrow, Thomas C. "Background to the Grenville Program." *William and Mary Quarterly* 3rd ser., 22(January, 1965):93-104.

Beardsley, E. Edwards. *The History of the Episcopal Church in Connecticut from the Settlement of the Colony to the Death of Bishop Seabury.* New York, 1866.

_____. *Life and Times of William Samuel Johnson, LL.D.* New York, 1876.

Becker, Carl L. "John Jay and Peter Van Schaack." In *Everyman His Own Historian.* Ed. Carl L. Becker. Chicago: Quadrangle Books, 1966. Reprint of 1935 edition.

Bemis, Samuel Flagg. *Jay's Treaty: A Study in Commerce and Diplomacy.* New Haven: Yale University Press, 1962. Reprint of 1923 edition.

Benton, William A. *Whig-Loyalism: An Aspect of Political Ideology in the American Revolutionary Era.* Rutherford, N.J.: Fairleigh Dickinson University Press, 1969.

Berkin, Carol. *Jonathan Sewall: Odyssey of an American Loyalist.* New York: Columbia University Press, 1974.

Berrian, William. *An Historical Sketch of Trinity Church.* New York, 1847.

Billias, George Athan. "The First Un-Americans: The Loyalists in American Historiography." *Perspectives in Early American History.* Eds. George Billias and Alden T. Vaughan. New York, 1973, pp. 282-324.

Boardman, Roger Sherman. *Roger Sherman: Signer and Statesman.* Philadelphia: University of Pennsylvania Press, 1938.

Bothell, Larry Lee. "Cloak and Gown. A Study of Religion and Learning in the Early Career of Samuel Johnson of Connecticut." Ph.D. dissertation, Princeton University, 1967.

Boyd, Julian P. *Number 7: Alexander Hamilton's Secret Attempts to Control American Foreign Policy.* Princeton, N.J.: Princeton University Press, 1964.

Brant, Irving. *James Madison: Father of the Constitution, 1787-1800.* New York: Bobbs-Merrill, 1950.

Bridenbaugh, Carl. *Mitre and Sceptre: Transatlantic Faiths, Ideas, Personalities, and Politics, 1589-1775.* New York: Oxford University Press, 1962.

Bridenbaugh, Carl and Jessica. *Rebels and Gentlemen: Philadelphia in the Age of Franklin.* 2nd ed. New York: Oxford University Press, 1962.

Broderick, Francis L. "Pulpit, Physics, and Politics: The Curriculum of the College of New Jersey, 1746-1794." *William and Mary Quarterly.* 3rd ser., 6(January 1949):42-68.

Brown, Richard. *Revolutionary Politics in Massachusetts: The Boston Committee of Correspondence and the Towns, 1772-1774.* Cambridge, Mass.: Harvard University Press, 1970.

Brown, Wallace. *The Good Americans: The Loyalists in the American Revolution.* New York: Morrow, 1969.

Brown, William Garrott. *The Life of Oliver Ellsworth.* New York: Macmillan, 1905.

Burnett, Edmund Coty. *The Continental Congress.* New York: Norton, 1964. Reprint of 1941 edition.

Bushman, Richard. *From Puritan to Yankee: Character and Social Order in Connecticut, 1690-1765.* New York: Norton, 1970. Reprint of 1967 edition.

Butts, R. Freeman. *The College Charts Its Course.* New York: McGraw-Hill, 1939.

Calhoon, Robert M. *The Loyalists in Revolutionary America, 1760-1781.* New York: Harcourt Brace Jovanovich, 1973. Reprint of 1960 edition.

———, ed. "William Smith Jr.'s Alternative to the American Revolution." *William and Mary Quarterly.* 3rd ser., 22(January 1965):105-18.

Catalogue of Officers and Graduates of Columbia University from the Foundation of King's College in 1754. New York, 1916.

Cheyney, Edward Potts. *History of the University of Pennsylvania, 1740-1940.* Philadelphia: University of Pennsylvania Press, 1940.

Christie, Ian. *Myth and Reality in Late Eighteenth Century British Politics and Other Papers.* Berkeley: University of California Press, 1970.
_____. *Wilkes, Wyvill and Reform: The Parliamentary Reform Movement in British Politics and Other Papers.* New York: St. Martin's, 1962.
Colbourn, Trevor. "John Dickinson, Historical Revolutionary." *Pennsylvania Magazine of History and Biography,* 83(July 1959):271-93.
Collier, Christopher. *Roger Sherman's Connecticut: Yankee Politics and the American Revolution.* Middletown, Ct.: Wesleyan University Press, 1971.
Columbia University in the City of New York, Gifts and Endowments with the Names of the Benefactors, 1754-1898. New York, 1898.
Combs, Gerald. *The Jay Treaty: Political Background of the Founding Fathers.* Los Angeles: University of California Press, 1970.
Coon, Horace. *Columbia: Colossus on the Hudson.* New York: Dutton, 1947.
Cremin, Lawrence A. *American Education: The Colonial Experience, 1607-1783.* New York: Harper & Row, 1970.
Crockett, Walter Hill. *Vermont, the Green Mountain State.* New York: Century History, 1921.
Cross, Arthur Lyon. *The Anglican Episcopate and the American Colonies.* Hamden, Ct.: Archon, 1964. Reprint of 1902 edition.
Cutter, William, ed. *Genealogical and Family History of the State of Connecticut.* New York: Holt, 1911.
Daniels, Bruce. "Large Town Power Structures in Eighteenth Century Connecticut. An Analysis of Political Leadership in Hartford, Norwich, and Fairfield." Ph.D. dissertation, University of Connecticut, 1970.
Davidson, Philip. *Propaganda and the American Revolution, 1763-1783.* Chapel Hill: University of North Carolina Press, 1941.
Dexter, Franklin Bowditch. *Biographical Sketches of the Graduates of Yale College with Annals of the College History, 1701-1815.* 6 vols. New York: Holt, 1885-1912.
_____. "New Haven in 1784." *Papers of the New Haven Colony Historical Society.* 5(1888).
Dillon, Dorothy Rita. *The New York Triumvirate: A Study of the Legal and Political Careers of William Livingston, John Morin Scott, and William Smith, Jr.* Studies in History, Economics, and Public Law, Columbia University, No. 548. New York: Columbia University Press, 1949.
Donoughue, Bernard. *British Politics and the American Revolution, The Path to War, 1773-1775.* New York: St. Martin's, 1964.
Elkins, Stanley and McKitrick, Eric. "The Founding Fathers: Young Men of the Revolution." In *The Reinterpretation of the American Revolution,* ed. Jack P. Greene. New York: Harper & Row, 1968.
Ellis, Joseph J. *The New England Mind in Transition: Samuel Johnson of Connecticut, 1696-1772.* New Haven: Yale University Press, 1973.
_____. "Anglicans in Connecticut, 1725-1750: The Conversion of the Missionaries." *New England Quarterly,* 44(March 1971):65-81.
Ernst, Robert. *Rufus King: American Federalist.* Chapel Hill: University of North Carolina Press, 1968.
Farrell, John T. "The Administration of Justice in Connecticut About the Middle of the Eighteenth Century." Ph.D. dissertation, Yale University, 1937.
Ferguson, James W. *The Power of the Purse: A History of American Public*

Finance, 1776–1790. Chapel Hill: University of North Carolina Press, 1961.

Flanders, Henry F. *The Life and Times of the Chief Justice of the Supreme Court of the United States*. (In 2 vols.) vol. 2. New York: 1875.

Frost, J. William. *Connecticut Education in the Revolutionary Era*. Chester, Ct.: Pequot Press, 1974.

Gabriel, Ralph Henry. *Religion and Learning at Yale. The Church of Christ in the College and University, 1757–1957*. New Haven: Yale University Press, 1958.

Gaustad, Edwin Scott. *The Great Awakening in New England*. Chicago: Quadrangle, 1968. Reprint of 1957 edition.

Gegenheimer, Albert Frank. *William Smith, Educator and Churchman, 1727–1803*. Philadelphia: University of Pennsylvania Press, 1943.

Gerardi, Donald. "The American Doctor Johnson: Anglican Piety and the Eighteenth Century Mind." Ph.D. dissertation, Columbia University, 1973.

Gerlach, Donald R. "Champions of an American Episcopate: Thomas Secker of Canterbury and Samuel Johnson of Connecticut." *Historical Magazine of the Protestant Episcopal Church*. 41(December 1972):381–414.

Gerlach, Larry. "Connecticut and Commutation, 1778–1784." *Bulletin of the Connecticut Historical Society*, 33(April 1968):51–68.

———. "Toward a More Perfect Union: Connecticut, the Continental Congress, and the Constitutional Convention." *Bulletin of the Connecticut Historical Society*, 34(July 1969):65–78.

Gilbert, George A. "The Connecticut Loyalists." *American Historical Review*, 4(1899):273–291.

Gipson, Lawrence Henry. *The British Empire before the American Revolution*. Volume 9: *The Triumphant Empire: Thunder Clouds Gather in the West, 1763–1766*. New York: Knopf, 1961.

———. *Ibid*. Volume 10: *The Rumbling of the Coming Storm, 1766–1770*. New York: Knopf, 1965.

———. *Ibid*. Volume 11: *Britain Sails into the Storm, 1770–1776*. New York: Knopf, 1965.

———. *Jared Ingersoll: A Study of American Loyalism in Relation to British Colonial Government*. New York: Russell & Russell, 1969.

Goebel, Julius Jr. *A History of the School of Law of Columbia University*. New York: Columbia University Press, 1955.

Goodrich, Chauncey. "The Invasion of New Haven by the British Troops, July 5, 1779." *Papers of the New Haven Colony Historical Society*, 2(1877): 27–93.

Greene, Evarts Boutell. "William Samuel Johnson and the American Revolution." *Columbia University Quarterly*, 22(June 1930):152–78.

Greene, Jack P. "Bridge to Revolution: The Wilkes Fund Controversy in South Carolina." *Journal of Southern History*, 29(1963):19–52.

———. "An Uneasy Connection." In *Essays on the American Revolution*. Eds. Stephen G. Kurtz and James H. Hutson. Chapel Hill: University of North Carolina Press, 1973, pp. 32–80.

Griswold, Rufus W. *The Republican Court*. 2nd ed. New York: 1856.

Groce, George C. Jr. *William Samuel Johnson, a Maker of the Constitution*. New York: Columbia University Press, 1937.

Guttridge, George Herbert. *English Whiggism and the American Revolution.* Berkeley: University of California Press, 1942.

____. "Thomas Pownall's *Administration of the Colonies:* The Six Editions." *William and Mary Quarterly.* 3rd ser. 26(January 1969):31-46.

Hall, Courtney Robert. *A Scientist in the Early Republic: Samuel Latham Mitchill, 1764-1831.* New York: Columbia University Press, 1934.

Henderson, H. James. "The Structure of Politics in the Continental Congress." In *Essays on the American Revolution,* Eds. Stephen G. Kurtz and James Hutson. Chapel Hill: University of North Carolina Press, 1973.

Hindle, Brooke. *David Rittenhouse.* Princeton: Princeton University Press, 1964.

____. *The Pursuit of Science in Revolutionary America, 1753-1789.* Chapel Hill: University of North Carolina Press, 1956.

Hofstadter, Richard. *The American Political Tradition and the Men Who Made It.* New York: Random House, 1948.

____. *The Idea of a Party System: The Rise of Legitimate Opposition in the United States, 1786-1840.* Los Angeles: University of California Press, 1969.

Hornberger, Theodore. "Samuel Johnson at Yale." *New England Quarterly,* 8(September 1935):378-97.

Horton, John Theodore. *James Kent. A Study in Conservatism, 1763-1847.* New York: De Capo Press, 1969. Reprint of 1939 edition.

Humphrey, David C. *From King's College to Columbia, 1746-1800.* New York: Columbia University Press, 1976.

Jacobson, David L. *John Dickinson and the Revolution in Pennsylvania, 1764-1776.* University of California Publications in History, No. 78. Berkeley: University of California Press, 1965.

Jordan, Philip, Jr. "Connecticut's Politics During the Revolution and Confederation, 1776-1789." Ph.D. dissertation, Yale University, 1962.

Kammen, Michael. *A Rope of Sand: Colonial Agents, British Politics, and the American Revolution.* Ithaca, N.Y.: Cornell University Press, 1968.

Kenyon, Cecelia. "Men of Little Faith: The Anti-Federalists on the Nature of Representative Government." In *The Confederation and the Constitution: The Critical Period.* Ed. Gordon S. Wood. Boston: Little, Brown, 1973, pp. 56-86.

King, Irving Henry. "The S.P.G. in New England, 1701-1784." Ph.D. dissertation, University of Maine, 1968.

Kinlock, Hector Gilchrist. "The Anglican Clergy in Connecticut, 1701-1785." Ph.D. dissertation, Yale University, 1959.

Klein, Milton. "The Rise of the New York Bar: The Legal Career of William Livingston." In *Essays in the History of Early American Law,* ed. David Flaherty. Chapel Hill: University of North Carolina Press, 1967, pp. 392-417.

Knollenberg, Bernard. *Growth of the American Revolution, 1766-1775.* New York: Free Press, 1975.

Labaree, Benjamin Woods. *The Boston Tea Party.* New York: Oxford University Press, 1964.

Lycan, Gilbert L. *Alexander Hamilton and American Foreign Policy.* Norman, Okla.: University of Oklahoma Press, 1970.

McDonald, Forest M. *We the People: The Economic Origins of the Constitu-*

tion. 2nd ed. Chicago: University of Chicago Press, 1965. Reprint of 1963 edition.

Maier, Pauline. "John Wilkes and American Disillusionment with Britian." *William and Mary Quarterly*. 3rd ser., 20(July 1963):373–95.

Marks, Frederick W. *Independence on Trial: Foreign Affairs and the Making of the Constitution*. Baton Rouge: Louisiana State University Press, 1973.

Marshall, Dorothy. *Dr. Johnson's London*. New York: Wiley, 1968.

———. *Eighteenth Century England*. New York: McKay, 1962.

Miller, John Chester. *The Federalist Era, 1789–1801*. 2nd ed. New York: Harper & Row, 1963.

———. *The Origins of the American Revolution*. Boston: Little Brown, 1943.

Miller, Perry. *The New England Mind: From Colony to Province*. Boston: Beacon Press, 1966. Reprint of 1953 edition.

Mintz, Max. *Gouverneur Morris and the American Revolution*. Norman, Okla.: University of Oklahoma Press, 1970.

Moore, N. F. *An Historical Sketch of Columbia College in the City of New York*. New York, 1846.

Morgan, Edmund S. *The Birth of the Republic, 1763–1789*. Chicago: University of Chicago Press, 1966. Reprint of 1956 edition.

———. *The Gentle Puritan: A Life of Ezra Stiles, 1727–1795*. New Haven: Yale University Press, 1962.

Morgan, Edmund S. and Helen M. Morgan. *The Stamp Act Crisis: Prologue to Revolution*. Chapel Hill: University of North Carolina Press, 1953.

Morison, Samuel Eliot. *Three Centuries of Harvard, 1636–1936*. Cambridge, Mass.: Harvard University Press, 1936.

Nelson, William H. *The American Tory*. Oxford, England: Clarendon, 1961.

Nettels, Curtis P. *The Emergence of a National Economy, 1775–1815*. New York: Holt, Rinehart & Winston, 1962.

Newcomb, Benjamin. *Franklin and Galloway: A Political Partnership*. New Haven: Yale University Press, 1972.

Onuf, Peter. "State Sovereignty in the New Nation. Virginia's Western Policy, 1776–1792." Typed manuscript, Department of History, Columbia University.

Orcutt, Samuel. *A History of the Old Town of Stratford and the City of Bridgeport, Connecticut*. New Haven, 1886.

Padover, Saul K., ed. *The World of the Founding Fathers*. New York: Yoseloff, 1960.

Pares, Richard. *King George III and the Politicians*. Oxford, England: Clarendon, 1963. Reprint of 1953 edition.

Perkins, Bradford. *Prologue to War: England and the United States, 1805–1812*. Berkeley: University of California Press, 1961.

Pole, J. R. *Political Representation in England and the Origins of the American Republic*. Los Angeles: University of California Press, 1971. Reprint of 1966 editions.

Pomerantz, Sidney. *New York: An American City, 1783–1803*. Port Washington, N.Y.: Empire State Historical Publications, 1965. Reprint of 1938 edition.

Purcell, Richard. "Connecticut in Transition, 1775–1818." Ph.D. dissertation, Yale University, 1916.

Ritcheson, Charles R. *Aftermath of Revolution: British Policy toward the United States, 1783-1795*. Dallas: Southern Methodist University Press, 1970.

_____. *British Politics and the American Revolution*. Norman, Okla.: University of Oklahoma Press, 1954.

Robinson, Rowland. *Vermont, a Study of Independence*. New York, 1894.

Rossiter, Clinton, *1787: The Grand Convention*. New York: Macmillan, 1966.

Rudé, George. *Hanoverian London, 1714-1808*. Berkeley: University of California Press, 1971.

_____. *Paris and London in the Eighteenth Century*. New York: Viking, 1971.

Sabine, Lorenzo. *The American Loyalists or Biographical Sketches of Loyalists of the American Revolution with an Historical Essay*. 2 vols. Boston, 1864.

Sachse, William L. *The Colonial American in Great Britain*. Madison, Wisc.: University of Wisconsin Press, 1956.

Schlesinger, Arthur Meier. *The Colonial Merchants and the American Revolution, 1763-1776*. New York: Ungar, 1957. Reprint of 1918 edition.

_____. *Prelude to Independence: The Newspaper War on Britain, 1764-1776*. New York: Knopf, 1958.

Schmidt, George P. *The Liberal Arts College. A Chapter in American Cultural History*. New Brunswick, N.J.: Rutgers University Press, 1957.

Shephard, James. "The Tories of Connecticut." *Connecticut Quarterly*. 4(January, July 1898):146-51, 257-63.

Shipton, Clifford K. and John L. Sibley, eds. *Biographical Sketches of Those Who Attended Harvard College*. 14 vols. Cambridge, Mass.: W. C. Sever and Harvard University Press, 1873-1968.

Shryock, Richard Harrison. *Medicine and Society in America, 1660-1860*. Ithaca, N.Y.: Cornell University Press, 1972. Reprint of 1960 edition.

Shumway, Floyd Mallory. "Early New Haven and its Leadership." Ph.D. dissertation, Columbia University, 1968.

Shy, John. *Toward Lexington: The Role of the British Army in the Coming of the American Revolution*. Princeton, N.J.: Princeton University Press, 1965.

Smelser, Marshall. *The Democratic Republic, 1801-1815*. New York: Harper & Row, 1968.

Smith, Paul H. *Loyalists and Redcoats: A Study in British Revolutionary Policy*. Chapel Hill: University of North Carolina Press, 1964.

Sosin, Jack M. *Agents and Merchants: British Colonial Policy and the Origins of the American Revolution, 1763-1775*. Lincoln, Neb.: University of Nebraska Press, 1965.

_____. "The Proposals in the Pre-Revolutionary Decade for Establishing Anglican Bishops." *Journal of Ecclesiastical History*, 15(April 1962).

_____. *Whitehall and the Wilderness: The Middle West in British Colonial Policy, 1760-1775*. Lincoln, Neb.: University of Nebraska Press, 1961.

Stamps, Norman Levaun. "Political Parties in Connecticut, 1789-1819." Ph.D. dissertation, Yale University, 1950.

Steiner, Bruce E. "Anglican Officeholding in Pre-Revolutionary Connecticut: The Parameters of New England Community." *William and Mary Quarterly*, 3rd ser., 31(July 1974):369-406.

_____. "New England Anglicanism: A Genteel Faith?" *William and Mary Quarterly*. 3rd ser., 27(January 1970):122-25.

——. *Samuel Seabury, 1729-1796: A Study in the High Church Tradition.* Oberlin, Ohio: Ohio University Press, 1971.

Sykes, Norman. *Church and State in England in the Eighteenth Century.* Cambridge, England: Cambridge University Press, 1934.

——. *From Sheldon to Secker: Aspects of English Church History, 1660-1768.* Cambridge, England: Cambridge University Press, 1959.

Tindall, William. *Origin and Government of the District of Columbia.* Washington, D.C.: U.S. Government Printing Office, 1908.

Toner, Joseph M. *Contributions to the Annals of Medical Progress in the United States Before and During the War for Independence.* Washington, D.C., 1874.

Tossell, Julia W. "The Loyalists of Stamford, Connecticut, 1754-1785." Master's Essay, Columbia University, 1970.

Tucker, Louis Leonard. *Puritan Protagonist: President Thomas Clap of Yale College.* Chapel Hill: University of North Carolina Press, 1962.

Tyler, Moses Coit. *The Literary History of the American Revolution,* see p. 509.

Upton, Leslie Francis Stokes. *The Loyal Whig: William Smith of New York and Quebec.* Toronto: University of Toronto Press, 1969.

Vance, Clarence Hayden. "Myles Cooper, M.A., D.C.L., LL.D., Second President of King's College, Now Columbia University, New York City." *Columbia University Quarterly,* 22(September 1930):261-88.

Van Doren, Carl. *Benjamin Franklin.* New York; Viking, 1938.

Warch, Richard. *School of the Prophets: Yale College, 1701-1741.* New Haven Yale University Press, 1973.

Warren, Charles. *A History of the American Bar.* Boston: Little, Brown, 1911.

Wertenbaker, Thomas Jefferson. *Princeton, 1746-1896.* Princeton: Princeton University Press, 1946.

Wesley, Edgar Bruce. *Proposed: The University of the United States.* Minneapolis: University of Minnesota Press, 1936.

Wickwire, Franklin B. *British Subministers and Colonial America, 1763-1783.* Princeton, N.J.: Princeton University Press, 1966.

Wilcoxson, William Howard. *History of Stratford, Connecticut, 1639-1939.* Stratford, Conn.: Stratford Tercentary Commission, 1939.

Williams, Basil. *The Whig Supremacy, 1714-1760.* Oxford, England: Clarendon, 1939.

Willingham, William Floyd. "Windham, Connecticut. Profile of a Revolutionary Community, 1755-1818." Ph.D. dissertation, Northwestern University, 1972.

Young, James Sterling. *The Washington Community, 1800-1828.* New York: Columbia University Press, 1966.

Zeichner, Oscar. *Connecticut's Years of Controversy, 1750-1776.* Chapel Hill: University of North Carolina Press, 1949.

——. "The Rehabilitation of Loyalists in Connecticut." *New England Quarterly,* 11(June 1938):308-30.

Index

Adams, John, 231, 268; thwarts mission to Gage, 173-74; impatient for independence, 176, 179
Adams, Samuel, 180
Admiralty courts, 49, 54-55, 57-58, 92, 105, 122, 145
Agents, colonial: meet with Hillsborough, 99-100; disagree on strategy, 99-104, 297 n.96, 298 n.99; and American distrust of Anglicans, 120-21, 303 n.64; insist on total repeal, 126-28; salaries of, 144, 308 n.43; on Boston tea party, 155-56; ineffectiveness of, 171, 316 n.39; disagree on authority of Parliament, 100-103, 171-72, 297 n.96
"American Whig," 119, 303 n.64
Anglicans: at Yale, 5-6, 12, 19-20, 38-39, 254-55, 256, 271; in Connecticut politics, 37, 40, 44-45, 68-69, 284 n.28, n.29, 290 n.97; and loyalism in Connecticut, 184-86, 319 n.31; wartime sufferings of, 186; at King's College, 245. See also Church of England; Episcopal Church, American
Arminianism, 3
Army, British, in America, 93, 96-97, 105, 114, 122, 163, 171, 184, 186-87; quartering of, 49, 70, 82; and Boston massacre, 152

Bard, Dr. John, 258
Bard, Dr. Samuel, 258, 336 n.104
Beach, John, 33-34, 43, 185, 186
Beckwith, George, 233-36
Bedford, John Russell, 4th Duke of, 78-80, 85, 90, 91
Bedford Whigs, 90, 91, 93, 97, 125, 129. See also Grafton-Bedford ministry
Belknap, Jeremy, 266-67
Berkeley, Rev. Dr. George, 146, 314 n.12

Bernard, Francis, 300 n.25; corresponds with Hillsborough, 108-10; campaigns against Massachusetts charter, 126; complains against Connecticut law, 131-32
Bishop of London. See Gibson, Edmund, Bishop of London, and Sherlock, Thomas, Bishop of London
Bishops, American. See Episcopate, American
Bollan William: on strategy to repeal Townshend Acts, 102-03, 298 n.99; steals Bernard letters, 110; distrusted because of Anglicanism, 120, 308 n.72; presents Declaration of Rights and Grievances, 172
Boston massacre, 152
Boston tea party, 155-56, 163, 312 n.38
British government, structure of colonial administration, 76-80
Browne, Daniel, 5, 6, 7, 17
Bute, Earl of, 78, 112
Butler, Pierce, 219-20

"Centinel," 119, 303 n.64
Chandler, Thomas Bradbury: campaigns for American bishops, 118-20; An Appeal. . . , 119-20, 312 n.62; loyalism of, 168-69
Chatham ministry: formation, 79; divisions and weaknesses in, 79-80, 81-82, 84, 90, 107; sponsors Townshend Acts, 88; reorganized by Duke of Grafton, 90-91; opposes American episcopate, 119
Chatham, William Pitt, 1st Earl of, 112; as Lord Privy Seal, 79-80, 81; Anglo-American policy of, 79, 82, 83, 88, 115-16, 117, 130, 302 n.54; resigns from ministry, 97; followers of support Wilkes, 114
Chauncy, Charles, 119
Chew, Joseph, 61-62, 133, 139, 304 n.2

353